332.02₄

D0312190

NORTHEAST COLORADO BOOKMOBILE SERVICES
325 WEST 7th STREET
WRAY, COLORADO 80758

Praise for *Go Green, Live Rich*

"Great news: there is no green premium! By demonstrating how going green can fit any budget, David Bach shows that good environmental and financial decisions go hand-in-hand. *Go Green, Live Rich* gives great tips, useful to everyone, about how to save money and the planet at once."　　　　　　—Robert F. Kennedy Jr.

"*Go Green, Live Rich* is as much about saving money as it is about preserving our world of natural wonders for future generations. This is the rich-green-book of a promising tomorrow."　　　　　　—Matthew Modine, Founder: Bicycle for a Day

Praise for *The Automatic Millionaire Homeowner*

"[Bach's] cheery, can-do message . . . cuts through the intimidating challenge of buying a house for the first-timer . . . for a newcomer, it's fundamental reading."
　　　　　　—*USA Today*

"If you read only one real estate book this year, it should be *The Automatic Millionaire Homeowner* . . . This is one of the few real estate books that cannot be recommended too highly for both beginners and experienced homeowners."
　　　　　　—Robert J. Bruss, *Miami Herald*

Praise for *Start Late, Finish Rich*

"Financial wizard David Bach's new book, *Start Late, Finish Rich*, offers solid advice for getting our finances in order, no matter how old we are."　　　　　　—AARP

"With feel-good sensibilities, David Bach delivers levelheaded strategies for reaching financial goals. . . . Bach's clever approach will make readers feel as if they're having a one-on-one conversation with a friendly personal financial counselor. . . . Powerful, poignant and pleasing, *Start Late, Finish Rich* can't be read fast enough."　　—*Bookpage*

Praise for *The Automatic Millionaire*

"*The Automatic Millionaire* is an automatic winner. David Bach really cares about you: on every page you can hear him cheering you on to financial fitness. No matter who you are or what your income is, you can benefit from this easy-to-apply program. Do it now. You and your loved ones deserve big bucks!"
　　　　　　—Ken Blanchard, coauthor of *The One Minute Manager*®

"*The Automatic Millionaire* gives you, step by step, everything you need to secure your financial future. When you do it David Bach's way, failure is not an option."
　　　　　　—Jean Chatzky, Financial Editor, NBC's *Today*

"*The Automatic Millionaire* proves that you don't have to make a lot of money or have a complicated financial plan to get started—you can literally start toward your financial dreams today, in a matter of hours, with just one life-changing secret: Pay yourself first and make it automatic! Equally important, this book shows you how to simplify and automate your entire financial life."

—Harry S. Dent, Jr., investment strategist and
author of *The Roaring 2000s*

Praise for *Smart Couples Finish Rich*

"*Smart Couples Finish Rich* teaches women and men to work together as a team when it comes to money. Bach's nine steps are powerful, yet easy to understand and fun to implement. The entire family can benefit from this great book."

—Robert T. Kiyosaki, author of
Rich Dad, Poor Dad

"I know how hard it is to make a personal-finance book user-friendly. Bach has done it. *Smart Couples Finish Rich* picks up where *Smart Women Finish Rich* left off. . . . This is an easy, lively read filled with tips that made me smile and at least once made me laugh."
—*USA Weekend*

"David Bach offers a prescription both to avoid money conflicts and to plan a harmonious future together. . . . The bottom line is action, and Bach's chatty writing style helps motivate you to that end."
—*BusinessWeek*

Praise for *Smart Women Finish Rich*

"Inspires women to start planning today for a secure financial future. Every woman can benefit from this book. . . . Bach is an excellent money coach."

—John Gray, bestselling author of
Men Are from Mars, Women Are from Venus

"David Bach is the one expert to listen to when you're intimidated by your finances. His easy-to-understand program will show you how to afford your dreams."

—Anthony Robbins, author of
Awaken the Giant Within and *Unlimited Power*

"[David] Bach gets across some complicated stuff: how to organize a portfolio, keep the taxman at bay, invest in yourself, and earn more, all of which makes this book one of the best overall."
—*Working Woman*

FIGHT

FOR YOUR

MONEY

Also by David Bach

Smart Women Finish Rich

Smart Couples Finish Rich

The Finish Rich Workbook

The Finish Rich Dictionary

The Automatic Millionaire

The Automatic Millionaire Workbook

Start Late, Finish Rich

The Automatic Millionaire Homeowner

Go Green, Live Rich

FIGHT
FOR YOUR
MONEY

HOW TO STOP GETTING RIPPED OFF AND
SAVE A FORTUNE

3NECBS0074449X

DAVID BACH

NORTHEAST COLORADO BOOKMOBILE SERVICES
325 WEST 7th STREET
WRAY, COLORADO 80758

BROADWAY BOOKS
New York

PUBLISHED BY BROADWAY BOOKS

Copyright © 2009 by David Bach. All Rights Reserved

No part of this book may be reproduced or transmitted in any form or by any means, electronic or mechanical, including photocopying, recording, or by any information storage and retrieval system, without written permission from the publisher. For information, address Broadway Books, a division of Random House, Inc.

The Automatic Millionaire Homeowner, The Automatic Millionaire, The Latte Factor, Smart Women Finish Rich, Smart Couples Finish Rich are registered trademarks of FinishRich, Inc.

Published in the United States by Broadway Books, an imprint of The Doubleday Broadway Publishing Group, a division of Random House, Inc., New York.

www.broadwaybooks.com

BROADWAY BOOKS and its logo, a letter B bisected on the diagonal, are trademarks of Random House, Inc.

This book is designed to provide accurate and authoritative information on the subject of personal finances. While all of the stories and anecdotes described in the book are based on true experiences, most of the names are pseudonyms, and some situations have been changed slightly for educational purposes and to protect each individual's privacy. It is sold with the understanding that neither the Author nor the Publisher is engaged in rendering legal, accounting, or other professional services by publishing this book. As each individual situation is unique, questions relevant to personal finances and specific to the individual should be addressed to an appropriate professional to ensure that the situation has been evaluated carefully and appropriately. The Author and Publisher specifically disclaim any liability, loss, or risk which is incurred as a consequence, directly or indirectly, of the use and application of any of the contents of this work.

Book design by Ralph Fowler / rlf design

Library of Congress Cataloging-in-Publication Data
Bach, David.
Fight for your money : how to stop getting ripped off and save a fortune / David Bach.—
1st ed.
p. cm.
Includes index.
1. Finance, Personal. I. Title.

HG179.B2343 2009
332.024—dc22

2008045401

ISBN 978-0-7679-2984-4

PRINTED IN THE UNITED STATES OF AMERICA

10 9 8 7 6 5 4 3 2 1

First Edition

To my son, Jack Bach—

you are the best thing that ever happened in my life.

I love you more than the "whole world"!

CONTENTS

FIGHT FOR YOUR MONEY A–Z

. . . or scammed every time you open your wallet, pay a bill, read your email, or take a trip? You're not alone!

What if I told you that there are simple things you can do RIGHT NOW to get a better deal on almost everything you pay for—and if you devoted just a few hours to a handful of them, you might be able to cut your overall expenses by 10 to 20 percent this year?

What if I told you that by using this book and spending just a few hours of your time learning how the major corporations take advantage of you (legally), you could put hundreds, if not thousands of dollars back in your pocket?

What if I told you that you don't have to be the victim of a bad deal, rip-off or scam ever again?

Would I have your attention?

Spend a few hours with me and use the tools inside this book as your guide. Let me share with you the secrets that big businesses don't want you to know. Then see for yourself how quickly you can start keeping more of your hard earned paycheck for yourself once you learn to FIGHT FOR YOUR MONEY.

Are you ready? Then turn the page. Let's get started.

—David Bach

Introduction

Why Fight for Your Money?

You hold in your hands a book that could change the way you think about and deal with money from this day forward for the rest of your life.

That's a pretty major statement, because virtually everything you do every day of your life has something to do with money. Think about it. What are the odds that you will go the next 24 hours without spending any money? What are the odds that you will go another five minutes?

And don't think, just because you're not taking out your wallet and forking over a few dollars for something, that you're not spending. Are the lights on as you read this? Is there a cell phone in your pocket? Do you own or rent a place to live? Are you covered by insurance of any kind?

I thought so. Just sitting there, you're spending money. And the unpleasant truth is that though you may not realize it, you are spending too much.

Everything You Do Every Day That Involves Money Is a Battle

The great truth about money is that in order to keep it and grow it, you have to fight for it. For years, I have said that it doesn't matter what you earn, it is what you keep that determines whether you will be financially free. Yet each year our money has become harder and harder to keep. That's because, at every turn, the companies we deal with every day in every aspect of our lives are working as hard as they can to take as much money from us as they can.

Whether you realize it or not, we are all engaged in a never-ending battle with giant corporations and economic institutions whose only goal is to separate us from our hard-earned dollars.

This is a battle we consumers have been losing because they are better equipped to take our money than we are to keep it.

Lose the Battle and You Lose the War

Think about it. We live in a world now where even once-respectable institutions like banks and brokerage houses, insurance companies and hospitals, no longer seem to have any scruples about how they accomplish the task of separating us from our money. And whether you let them do that will ultimately make a huge difference in the way you live.

When you pay just 10% or 20% too much for the products and services you use every day, you will have to work 10 to 20 extra years before you can retire. Or, to put it another way, if you *let yourself* be overcharged by 10% to 20% percent for the things you buy, you are in effect spending one or two months a year working without pay for the companies that rip you off. *And trust me—until you fight for your money, you will overpay for almost everything you buy.*

My hope is that this book will change your life by giving you the tools to FIGHT FOR YOUR MONEY and WIN.

The World Has Changed Financially

I have no idea when you will actually read this book, but as I sit here writing it in October of 2008, the world is going through tremendous financial turmoil. In a single week this month, the U.S. stock market plunged more than 18%—the worst one-week drop in history—while at the same time real estate prices in many cities across America were down 20% or more from their peak in 2005 and 2006. As our government struggles to figure out the details of a trillion-dollar banking bailout—and coordinate its efforts with other governments around the world to break the worst credit logjam since the 1930s—ordinary people can't help but worry about what new crisis tomorrow might bring.

The fact is, this turmoil has already hit you and me in our homes, in our pocketbooks, and in our bank accounts. Most likely, you have less money today than you did a few years ago. If you're a homeowner, you probably have less equity in your home than you did a few years ago. There's also a real possibility that you not only owe more than you used to but that you have fewer options for paying off that debt than ever before in your life.

It is also possible that your income from your job or business is less secure than it has been in years, maybe in decades.

No wonder the Conference Board reported in October 2008 that consumer confidence had fallen to its lowest level since they first started measuring it in 1967.

The point of all this is not to depress you, but simply to be real about what is happening. And whether we like it or not, it is happening.

A War for Your Money Is Raging

With easy money no longer so easy, companies are struggling to remain profitable and continue to grow. The challenges they face are immense. At a time when everyone is stressed financially and has zero confidence, they can't just raise prices. Instead, they've got to be creative—they've got to figure out how to get more money out of you and me without our realizing it.

In an effort to solve this problem, companies have spent billions and billions of dollars developing ways to "sneak" money from us. The techniques they've come up with include hidden fees, obscure rules, misleading come-ons, and occasionally outright fraud. Some people call this unfair. Others call it infuriating. I call it a war.

Who Am I to Help You Fight Back?

For the better part of two decades now, I have devoted myself to helping people live better by being smarter about their money. This book is the tenth one I've published in the last 10 years. The previous nine were all focused on how to live and finish rich. You may have read one or more of them. There are currently upward of 7 million of my "FinishRich" books in print *worldwide*.

Most people know me for my "take action" advice about money. Because I tell it like it is—and make it simple and "doable"—millions of people have used my books to change their lives completely. If you are one of those whom I've helped, thank you for giving me the opportunity to inspire you again. If this is our first time together, then let me say, "Welcome, and thank you for inviting me to be your financial coach."

My life is completely dedicated to the mission of helping people live a great life. A life of meaning and hope. I have spent so much time and energy teaching millions of people how to be smarter with their money for one simple reason: I believe with all my heart that acting positively to get your financial life together is the best and fastest way to achieve the great life you want and deserve. Fix your money problems, and it will be so much easier to live your life more powerfully and purposefully.

Financial Knowledge Is Power

For us as consumers, this age of global economic uncertainty is especially challenging. In order to survive in these tough times, the companies that sell us goods and services have launched a new war for our wealth. The battle to separate us from our hard-earned money has been going on for a long time, but now it's been kicked up to an entirely new level, with companies becoming trickier and more ruthless than ever, not just nickel-and-diming but nickel-and-*dollaring* us to death.

What this means is that you have to be smarter with your money and take your finances more seriously than ever before. Financial ignorance is now a luxury none of us can afford. And I'm not just talking about getting a better handle on the stock market or the housing market. I'm talking about being smarter about how you spend money every single day on every single product and service you use.

Companies Need Your Money—But You Need It More

Never before have corporations been so successful at taking us financially without our really realizing it.

Here's what I mean:

You take your credit card company up on its invitation to skip a payment without penalty—not realizing they will still hit you with a finance charge for the unpaid balance.

You sign up for basic local phone service at $13 a month—not realizing that a laundry list of fees (for things they never told you about or bothered to explain) will inflate your actual monthly bill to nearly twice what they promised.

You buy an extended warranty for a new appliance—not realizing there's virtually no chance you'll ever use it enough to justify the cost.

You agree to pay an extra $12 a day for insurance on your rental car—not realizing that you're already covered by your credit card company.

You say "Sure!" to the nice salesclerk at the department store who urges you to "save 10% right now" on the clothing you're buying by signing up for a store credit card—not realizing that they charge 29% interest and won't even discuss lowering the rate.

You trustingly sign on the dotted line when the tax-preparation firm offers to give you an immediate "convenient" advance on your refund—not realizing the interest and service fees they're charging you may equal 500% or more in annual interest.

You buy a new car and thank the dealer for getting you financing even though he said your credit rating was poor—not realizing that he lied to you about your credit score and that you could have easily gotten a bank loan for thousands of dollars less.

They Are Taking Us for Billions— And We Are Now Working for Them

In the past, when times were good, it was easier to shrug off this sort of thing. To tell ourselves that's the way the world is and there isn't anything we can do about it. We were busy and flush with cash and so we let much of this go. But times have changed. *And in truth, being ripped off is never okay.*

If we don't fight the fight and protect ourselves from the companies that rip us off with sneaky fees and absurd systems, we end up working for them. What happens when you're forced to spend more than you should on everything you pay for? Well, not only do you wind up getting less for your money—you also end up working longer and harder to simply get by.

Here are a few facts to consider while you're thinking about how hard you have to work to keep your head above water these days.

- By encouraging debit card transactions and allowing over-the-limit ATM withdrawals, the banking industry picks our pockets to the tune of nearly $10 billion a year in overdraft fees, according to the Center for Responsible Lending.

- In 2008, while nearly 25% of the population (some 72 million people in all) either delayed or did without needed medical care because they couldn't afford the bills, the 20 biggest health insurers recorded total profits in excess of $17 billion. (The year before, the CEO of CIGNA Corp., the nation's fifth-largest health insurer, *personally* earned more than $24 million.)

- By playing games with payment deadlines and bamboozling customers into inadvertently breaking the rules, the credit card industry is able to shake us down for tens of billions of dollars in penalty fees— more than $23 billion in 2007 alone.

- In 2008, the major airlines hit up travelers for well over $1 billion in unprecedented new charges for checked baggage, in-flight meals, and a variety of other services they used to provide for free.

- Payday lenders (those places with the neon signs that say "Cash Checks Here") claim to be helping strapped wage-earners, but they actually gouge them out of $4.2 billion a year in predatory fees— charging what amount to annual interest rates of *400%* and more.

- Between the end of 2001 and the summer of 2008, as gasoline prices soared from just over $1 to nearly $5 a gallon, oil industry profits totaled upward of half a *trillion* dollars. In 2007, ExxonMobil earned $40.6 billion—"the highest profits ever recorded by any company," according to the *New York Times*—and its 2008 profits were expected to be even higher.

- Manufacturers tempt consumers into buying their products by offering some $8 billion worth of rebates each year, but they make the process of collecting the rebates so difficult that 80% of them are never redeemed.

- A typical appendectomy, including two days in a semiprivate room, costs the hospital about $5,000, yet they will charge Blue Cross $10,000—and if you're uninsured, they'll send you a bill for $35,000.

And It's Not Just the Corporations Taking You— It's the Swindlers!

What may be most outrageous about these sorts of rip-offs is that they are all perfectly legal. Factor in the criminal con men who bombard us with enticing come-ons over the phone, via email, or even in the form of a car parked by the side of the road with a "For Sale" sign stuck in the windshield, and your head begins to swim.

According to the Federal Trade Commission, which tries to keep track of such things, nearly one out of every seven adult Americans—more than 30 million of us—is the victim of a scam or swindle every year. What this means is that unless you are *extremely* careful, it's a virtual certainty that you will be scammed at least once over the next decade.

The cost of all this is phenomenal. Telemarketing scams alone cost us an estimated $40 billion a year, and they are just a small fraction of the total problem.

Fight for Your Money—Shop for Your Money

The fact that you are reading this book right now tells me that you are truly hopeful and that you believe you can do better financially. My mission with this book is to give you the knowledge, the tools, and the action steps you need to make you an advocate for your own financial rights. The FIGHT FOR YOUR MONEY goal is for you to be smart and in charge of your money so others can't separate you from what you have worked so hard to earn.

The first step in this process is recognizing that while there is a problem, there is also a solution—that you have the power to do something about it. The challenge of keeping yourself from being ripped off is not hopeless. It is, in fact, HOPEFUL.

You deserve to be in control of your money.

Why give up control to some powerful corporation that doesn't care about you personally? You know you are smart. All you need are the right tools.

As you read this book, you may notice there are some general rules that apply to almost every single financial or consumer issue we cover—from buying a used car on eBay to paying for your groceries with a debit card. Most are plain old common sense. The trick is not just to know them but to live them. If you can, you'll never have to worry about being ripped off again.

The "Fight for Your Money" Rules

- THERE IS NO SUCH THING AS A FREE LUNCH. If a deal sounds too good to be true, it probably is.

- FIGURE OUT THE TOTAL COST. The price they advertise isn't necessarily what something really costs. Make sure you know what the advertised price covers, what it doesn't cover—and how much you'll have to pay for the stuff you're going to need that isn't included.

- DON'T TAKE ANYBODY'S WORD FOR ANYTHING. Guarantees and promises don't mean anything unless they are in writing.

- DO YOUR HOMEWORK. Comparison-shop, educate yourself about the product, and unless you know whom you're dealing with, check them out before you send them a money order or sign a contract.

- BE CAREFUL WHAT YOU SIGN. Read *all* the paperwork, including the small print, and make sure you understand it.

- RESIST EFFORTS TO PRESSURE OR INTIMIDATE YOU. Not every salesman who employs the hard sell is a crook. But honest ones rarely do. When they badger you to "Act now!" that's a sure sign you shouldn't. When they urge you not to tell anyone else about this "very special opportunity," you definitely should—preferably someone who carries a badge.

- IF YOU THINK YOU'VE BEEN SCAMMED, REPORT IT TO THE APPROPRIATE AUTHORITIES. As an official for the National Consumers League put it in an interview with consumer reporter Bob Sullivan, "Complaining is to being a good consumer what voting is to being a good citizen. If there are no complaints, there's no impetus for legislative change and the enforcement officers don't know what's going on. If you only complain to friends but don't report something . . . then nobody who can do something about it knows what happened to you."

- THERE IS NO SUCH THING AS A SET PRICE. With most services and many consumer goods (cars, cable TV, gym membership), not everyone pays the same price. How much often depends on when you signed up, what incentives you were offered, and how well you negotiated. As a consumer, you have more power than you think.

- PACKAGE DEALS ARE OFTEN NOT GOOD DEALS. They may sound great, but they typically require you to buy something you don't really want or need.

- MONEY GIVES YOU CONTROL, SO HOLD ON TO IT AS LONG AS YOU CAN. It's easier to reverse an unfair charge than to try to get a refund once you've paid out cash. So don't agree to automatic debits—use a credit card instead. Similarly, parcel out payments to repairmen and contractors, and avoid years-long service contracts.

- PROTECT YOUR IDENTITY. Personal information, such as credit card and bank account numbers, should be shared only with salespeople and companies you know and trust—and never by email.

Rich or Poor—The Odds Are Against You Until You Fight Back

You might think this book was timed to coincide with the current economic crisis. It actually wasn't. I had been thinking about writing it since January of 2004, when I appeared on *The Oprah Winfrey Show* to launch my fifth book, *The Automatic Millionaire*. That show inspired millions, as Oprah's shows always do, and *The Automatic Millionaire* went on to become the top-selling business book of the year. The experience I had while taping the *Oprah* show that day changed my life. It opened my eyes even more to all the financial challenges tens of millions of Americans face on a daily basis.

Appearing along with me on the show were several couples with serious financial issues. My job was to diagnose the nature of their problems and create a plan to solve them—to do what we called a money makeover. Over the next few years, I would do a half-dozen shows like this with Oprah and ultimately dozens more money makeovers on other TV shows.

Doing these money makeovers inserted me into a world that was both eye-opening and heartbreaking. When I was a financial planner and senior vice president at Morgan Stanley, which is what I did before I began writing books, I never had clients who owed $50,000 to $125,000 in credit card debt. I never worked with people who'd taken out payday loans that were costing them 900% annually. I didn't even know such rip-off products existed.

I had never known anyone who paid 35% too much for a car, then got it financed at 15%, then was talked into buying an insurance policy to pay off the debt, and then took out another loan, also at 15%, to pay for the insurance policy.

I had never known anyone who had gone to what was supposed to be a nonprofit credit-repair agency—only to have their money stolen and their credit destroyed completely. I had never known anyone who bought a home with no money down and an adjustable mortgage with a rate north of 10% that changed every month—plus a 10% early-payment penalty, meaning it would cost them tens of thousands of dollars to get out of that terrible deal and into a better one.

To put it simply, until I appeared on *Oprah* that day and met a bunch of "real" people leading real lives of daily financial desperation, I hadn't been exposed on a daily basis to what so many of us are really up against when it comes to our money—how many tens of millions of Americans are being taken to the cleaners EVERY SINGLE DAY by companies, banks, and brokers all operating PERFECTLY LEGALLY.

Doing those makeovers opened my eyes to the enormous odds that the average person has to battle every day simply to survive financially. And it left me determined to try to do something to help.

You Don't Deserve to Be Taken

I believe you should have a fighting chance to avoid being ripped off, even if those "rip-offs" are legal. Whether you are rich or living paycheck to paycheck, you don't deserve to be taken financially—EVER!

But to be able to protect yourself effectively, you must have the mind-set, the attitude, and the action plan of a FIGHTER. How do you acquire all that? This book will be your guide.

How to Use This Book

The heart and soul (and most of the pages) of *Fight for Your Money* consists of a guide to protecting yourself from financial rip-offs. This guide is divided into 6 sections, each of which concerns a basic area of financial life (Automobiles, Banking, Credit, and so on). Within these sections, you will find a number of entries devoted to specific consumer issues, such as car buying or travel packages, that tell you how to find a good deal, what to watch out for, and where you can go for help if things go wrong. At the end of the book, we have included a concise toolkit filled with sample letters—the specific tools you will need to become your own consumer advocate.

We chose the topics we did because we felt that they represent the most critical areas for most people. In fact, some of them may not seem particularly relevant to you *right now*. Maybe you are single and the topic of divorce holds no interest for you. If this is the case, simply skip that section. (Then again, if you know someone going through a divorce, maybe you should give it a look—you could wind up saving your friend some unneeded heartache, not to mention a lot of money.)

Unlike my previous books, which were written to be read straight through, this one can be read cover-to-cover or it can be dipped into where and when it serves your particular needs. So scan the list of topics and go straight to what matters to you most right now. Taking action based on one idea in just one chapter could easily save you ten to twenty times the cost of this book. For example:

- Skip car-loan insurance that only helps the dealer and save $7,500.

- Don't rent a car at the airport (take a cab to a nearby location), and save $300 in a week.

- Use a credit card, not a debit card, and fraudulent charges will cost you $0 instead of $500.

- Raise your credit score (you can do it yourself) and save $95,040 in interest on a 30-year mortgage.

- Book your airline tickets one at a time and save as much as $275 per ticket.

- Cut your life insurance premiums *in half* by making one call.

And, what's more, you'll avoid huge rip-offs like:

- medical credit cards that help the hospital and financially take advantage of you with high interest rates you can't renegotiate

- sneaky renewals of your cell-phone plan

- 401(k) debit cards that make it too easy to drain your wealth

- bank-issued gift cards whose fees and expiration dates erode their value

- refund-anticipation loans, whose fees and finance charges add up to an outrageous interest rate of 150%

In short, this book is yours to use in any way you need to use it. I hope it will become a guide that you come back to time and time again, as the need arises.

Join Our Movement of Smart, Empowered Consumers

My goal with this book is to create a movement of smart, empowered consumers who FIGHT FOR THEIR MONEY. Over the years, I have received thousands upon thousands of letters and emails from readers like you who have used my books to change their lives. These messages have inspired me—and, more important, countless readers like you—to continue to fight to live and finish rich.

I hope this book will inspire you to take action. I want to hear what has happened to you and how you have fought back. This is the first edition of a book that we plan to continue updating in the future—so if we overlooked a crucial FIGHT FOR YOUR MONEY topic that you would like to see covered, let us know. We want your suggestions and input.

Please email me at success@finishrich.com and visit our web site at www.finishrich.com. We are transforming the FinishRich site into an active community where savvy consumers like you can share what they have done to fight for their money. We will have stories from you and others that you can review to get more ideas as well as specific resources of what has worked (or hasn't).

Together, we will be a team that FIGHTS—and ultimately WINS!

Your friend and coach,
David Bach

Take Your Fight to the Next Level!

Here's a special offer for all my readers.

Visit my web site at **www.finishrich.com/ffymdownload** to access our 7-day trial for the all new Fight for Your Money Power Pack. Log on today to test drive this 13-step battle plan for living a debt-free lifestyle.

Enjoy!

Buying a New Car

High gas prices and an economic slowdown have decimated auto sales, but Americans still buy roughly 14 million new cars, minivans, SUVs, and pickup trucks each year. And on virtually every one of those transactions, we get taken. The National Automobile Dealers Association says their members actually lose $30 or so on every new car they sell, but that doesn't mean we are getting anything close to a fair bargain. That's because what the dealers lose on the cars, they more than make up for by sticking us with outrageous finance charges and overpriced add-ons like extended warranties, rustproofing, and paint sealants. The extended warranties alone bring in upward of $5 billion a year—*three-quarters of which is pure profit.*

The fact is, even without the tricks and scams, buying a new car is almost always a bad investment. If you're hooked on newness and the latest technology, it makes much more sense from a financial point of view to go for a one- or two-year-old low-mileage used vehicle. That's because new cars take their biggest depreciation hit in the first year after they roll off the dealer's lot, typically losing 25% to 30% of their value. Really savvy consumers let someone else absorb that loss and buy *nearly* new cars—which are generally still under manufacturer's warranty, are equipped with most of the latest bells and whistles, and have suffered relatively little wear and tear—for less than 70 cents on the dollar.

Then again, economic common sense has never been much of a match for new-car lust. Maybe we shouldn't buy them, but we do. And if we're going to do it, we might as well do it right.

How to Fight for Your Money

There are roughly 21,000 new-car dealers in the United States. They comprise the exclusive channel through which new cars are distributed, so if you buy a new car, it will probably be through one of them.

As a group, car dealers have a pretty crummy reputation. This may not be totally fair, but it is understandable. It wasn't all that long ago that practices like "rolling a stiff"—urging prospective customers to take a car home overnight, only to threaten them the next morning with arrest for grand-theft auto if they didn't pay for the car immediately—were practiced more widely than anyone would like to admit.

These sorts of outrageous scams have pretty much been eliminated, but we still think of car salesmen as scary, and for good reason. Most of them work on commission, and many subscribe to the belief that once a customer walks into the showroom, it's their job to do whatever it takes to make sure he or she does not leave without signing a sales contract.

So if you've decided to buy a new car, understand what you're getting yourself into—the typical dealership is not a friendly oasis but rather a vicious battleground.

Here are a few key DOs and DON'Ts.

Focus on the Price

In an effort to maximize profits, car dealers try to manipulate every variable involved in the car-buying process, from the cost of the financing to the price of the floor mats. In this cutthroat environment, the best way to protect your money is to focus on one number and one number only—the purchase price of the car.

This may seem obvious, but the one thing most car dealers don't really want to talk about is the price. That's because once they commit to a price, it's much harder for them to bamboozle you into taking their money-making add-ons (like dealer financing) without the extra cost being obvious. So instead of giving you a straight answer when you ask how much a particular car costs, the dealer will ask you what kind of monthly payment you're looking for. Tell him you're not looking for a monthly payment; you're looking for a car. If he still won't name a price, take your business elsewhere.

Know the Real Price—Not the Fake "MSRP"

To get the best possible deal, you need to educate yourself in advance about what the dealer actually paid for the car you're interested in, the cost of all of the options you want, what kind of incentives and rebates the manufacturer is offering dealers, and how much of a markup local market conditions currently allow. It is these figures—and not the manufacturers' suggested retail price (the "MSRP" you'll find on the window sticker)—that should serve as the basis for your negotiations. Such information is available online from sources like Cars.com, Consumer Reports (www.consumerreports.org), Edmunds.com, and Kelley Blue Book (www.kbb.com).

Keep in mind that the invoice price of a car is not the dealer's true cost, since it generally includes what's called a holdback—a fee (usually 2% to 4% of the MSRP) that most car manufacturers pay their dealers each time they sell a car. On top of this, there are often factory-to-dealer incentives—particularly near the end of a model year—that can lower the dealer's cost still further.

This is what makes it possible for dealers to make what they hope you will regard as an offer you can't refuse. If they sense you're not a pushover, they will sometimes take you aside, compliment you on your negotiating skills, and offer to let you have the car for "just one dollar over invoice." To demonstrate their sincerity, they may even show you a copy of the invoice.

All well and good, but this is definitely an offer you can and should refuse, since the invoice price is actually an artificial construct. What you want is a deal pegged to the dealer's *actual* cost—which, as a result of all those kickbacks and rebates, may be hundreds of dollars less than the invoice price.

WHAT A 2009 VW JETTA REALLY COSTS

MSRP:	$19,090
Invoice Price:	$18,445
Dealer's Actual Cost:	$18,063

Hundreds of dollars might seem like a reasonable profit for a dealer to make, but even on a $20,000 car it's actually a very narrow margin—no more than a few percentage points. This is why, as we will see, most dealers try to squeeze as much profit as they can out of service, financing, options, and extended warranties. It's because they can't make a decent profit on the sale of the car itself.

Remember, you can get all this information online. Chances are that the dealer will talk turkey once you let him know that *you* know how much he's getting back in manufacturer incentives.

Ask to See the Dealer's Paperwork

An easy way to gauge a dealer's trustworthiness is by assessing his financial transparency. Responsible dealers will let you see the paperwork showing the actual cost to them of the car you want, and they will tell you about any rebates, holdbacks, and manufacturer's incentives that may apply. Since you can get all this information online, checking their figures against yours is a great way to make sure you're dealing with a straight shooter. If the sales staff gives you any doubletalk about why your numbers aren't applicable—or if they refuse to disclose their numbers—don't bother arguing with them. Just leave.

Borrow from a Bank—Not from a Car Dealer

More than a quarter of car dealers' profits come from what they call F&I—finance and insurance. Indeed, this part of the business is so lucrative that many dealerships depend on it to make back the profits they surrender when they are forced to give customers a good deal on the purchase price.

On the finance side, what car dealers often do to boost their margins is tell customers with perfectly good credit that they don't qualify for low-interest financing and thus will have to accept more expensive loan terms. The technical term for this is lying.

This is precisely what happened to Tom Costibile of Union Grove, Wisconsin. After agreeing to a reasonable price for the car Tom wanted, the salesman went off to confer with his manager about the financing. "Eventually, he came back and told my wife and me that our credit scores were very, very low, but they could get us a loan—with a 25% interest rate."

Tom and his wife wisely fled the dealership and went home to do what they should have done before they started car shopping—check their credit rating. "I went on the Internet and ordered up my credit report," he says. "The dealership had lowballed our score by 120 points."

Here's a hard-and-fast rule: If you're not planning to pay cash for a new car, you should get your auto loan from a bank or credit union—not a car dealer. Take it as a given that any interest rate a car dealer quotes you is bound to be higher—often much higher—than you should be able to get from a reputable financial institution.

It's true that dealers often advertise super-low-rate auto loans (sometimes even with 0% interest) as part of a sales incentive from the manufacturer. The catch is that these loans are typically granted only to customers with the highest credit scores, and then only for extremely limited terms.

Start Paying Now

A similarly misleading come-on is the "zero down/zero payments for one year" scam. Steer clear of this. All it does is defer your paying for the car for a year. This might sound appealing, but two things happen during that year. Interest accrues on your loan and the car depreciates. As a result, by the time you start repaying the loan, the amount you owe will have increased by hundreds or thousands of dollars—and your car will probably have lost somewhere between 20% and 30% of its value.

In fact, you could easily wind up owing considerably more on your car than the vehicle is actually worth. In finance circles, this is known as being "upside down" on a loan. This can be both uncomfortable and quite dangerous. That's because your auto insurance will only cover the actual value of the vehicle—so if your car is stolen or totaled in a crash, your insurance payout won't be big enough to pay off your loan. And you will have to continue making payments on a car you no longer have.

And Don't Buy Insurance from Them, Either

If you let them handle the financing, dealerships will also sometimes try to sell you insurance "to pay off the car loan if you die." This is another deal that's great for them, terrible for you. I once did a money makeover on *The Oprah Winfrey Show* with a couple that agreed to pay $7,500 for a policy to cover their $50,000 auto loan. To make matters worse, they didn't have the $7,500, so they let the dealership finance it for them! Talk about a rip-off! Even if you're a smoker, you can get $50,000 worth of 10-year term life insurance for not much more than $100 a year.

THE CAR-LOAN INSURANCE RIP-OFF

What you might pay:	$7,500
What you *should* pay:	$0
You save:	**$7,500**

Bottom line is this: You can't be forced by a car dealer to have insurance that pays off the car if you die. And if they try and force you to buy it, then leave the car dealership and go to an ethical dealership that won't pull something like this.

Don't Trade in Your Old Car

It's certainly more convenient to let the dealer take your old car as a trade-in than to sell it separately. But that convenience comes at a huge price.

Make no mistake—the trade-in allowance is yet another variable that the dealership can and will manipulate to pad their profits and rip you off. To put it bluntly, they will lowball your trade-in to make up for the good price they gave you on your purchase. They get away with this because, with the end of the transaction in sight, most car buyers don't object.

This is why dealers often insist on taking your old car around back to be appraised. Taking away your ride home not only makes it harder for you to leave the dealership, it also puts the issue of your old car's value on the table, which takes the focus off the price of the car you are buying.

So don't trade in your old car. Sell it privately or to another dealer. Chances are, a separate sale will bring you a lot more for your car than the dealer will give you in a trade-in allowance.

What to Watch Out For

Buying into the Fantasy

The automakers spend literally billions of dollars each year on advertising designed to convince us that by changing cars, we can change who we are. This is true up to a point. Buying an expensive gas-guzzler can transform a rich person into a poor one pretty quickly. But that's about it. Driving an overmuscled SUV to soccer practice won't make you more of a hipster—or any less a soccer mom (or dad)—than driving a minivan. Nor will jumping into a 4 × 4 for a late-night diaper run remove the spit-up from your shirt.

So don't buy into the fantasy that purchasing a particular vehicle will change who you are or even how you are perceived. Choose the kind of car you're going to buy based on what you need it for and how much it will cost you to operate—which means figuring in not just the purchase price but also fuel economy, maintenance and insurance costs, depreciation, resale value, and finance charges, if any. All the other stuff is just an excuse to spend more than you need to. Edmunds.com has a terrific "Total Cost to Own" calculator that weighs all of the key factors and tells you how much any particular model is likely to *really* cost you over your first five years of ownership.

OWNING A 2009 JETTA*

Monthly car payment:	$394
Total ownership cost per month:	$698

*Based on a 60-month car loan for a 2009 Volkswagen Jetta Sedan and Edmunds.com's "Total Cost to Own" calculation over five years.

Dealers Who Haggle

According to most surveys, the thing people hate the most about buying a car is haggling over the price. That's probably because most of us are not very good at haggling, while most car dealers are pros.

It used to be that you had no choice. The only way to buy a car sensibly was to walk into the dealership armed with plenty of data about invoice prices, manufacturers' holdbacks, and residual values (how much the car will be worth after a few years), not to mention a strong stomach and a major attitude.

Happily, this is no longer the case. An increasing number of new-car dealers follow a no-haggle, posted-price policy. Saturn made this approach the cornerstone of its brand, so that is how all of its cars are sold. The same is true of CarMax. It is best known as a late-model used-car superstore, but it also sells some new cars, all under no-haggle pricing policy. Other dealership chains, such as Fitzgerald's Auto Mall, apply this policy to all the brands they represent.

In large part, we can thank the Internet for this. Web sites like Autos.com, Cars.com, CarsDirect (www.carsdirect.com), InvoiceDealers (www.invoice dealers.com), Edmunds.com, MyRide.com, and Yahoo!Autos (http://autos. yahoo.com/) make it possible to comparison-shop and choose the least expensive dealer without having to drive anywhere or argue with anyone.

And if you think doing online research is too much of a hassle, you can outsource the process. Many credit unions and nonprofit consumer groups offer services that will do all the researching and shopping around for you. Some, like the American Automobile Association's Car Buying Service (www. aaa.com), are free to members; others, like Consumer Checkbook's CarBargains (www.checkbook.org), charge a fee. All you have to do is specify the make, model, color, and options you want. They do the rest, either hooking you up with a recommended dealer willing to offer a prenegotiated price (usually well below the MSRP) or getting a number of dealers to bid against one another and provide firm offers you can choose from.

The point is that you no longer need to haggle to get a good price on a new car. So why bother? Let the professionals duke it out for you. And avoid dealerships where they try to force you to do it yourself.

Options You Didn't Ask for and Don't Need

With their margins stretched razor thin, car dealers look for profits wherever they can find them. One big source is optional equipment. The markup on extras ranging from floor mats to theft-detection systems is phenomenal. There's only one problem, as far as the dealers are concerned. It's that options are optional. There's no guarantee car buyers will order them on their own.

To eliminate this uncertainty—and maximize their bottom line—many dealers install options in virtually every car on the lot and then insist that you accept and pay for them, regardless of whether you actually want or need them. The theory is that given a choice between a car with a bunch of un-wanted options and no car at all, most customers will take the car with the options.

Dealers will also attempt to gouge you by pushing such unnecessary add-ons as paint protection and undercoating. Rustproofing is a typical scam. Even though most new cars come with six-year/100,000-mile rust warran-ties, many dealers will try to sell you on an $800 rustproofing treatment that costs them all of $40. The same is true for things like paint sealant and fabric protector. (What the dealer will do to your upholstery for $300, you can do for yourself with a $10 can of Scotchgard™.)

IS THIS OPTION NECESSARY?

Cost of dealer's "Fabric Protection Package":	$300
Cost of a can of Scotchgard™:	$10
You save:	**$290**

Fortunately, there is a simple way of dealing with this sort of thing. To quote the old antidrug slogan, "Just say no!"

Extended Warranties

One of the most unnecessary add-ons that a dealership will try to sell you is the extended warranty. Earlier, I shared how "extended warranties" are huge sources of business for car dealerships (over $5 billion in revenue annually). Car salesmen like to say that such warranties provide "peace of mind." This is true only if getting ripped off makes you feel peaceful rather than angry.

The fact is that cars are built better and last longer than they used to—and, reflecting this, they come with increasingly generous factory warranties. Nonetheless, more new-car buyers than ever before—more than a third these days, compared to only one out of five in the late 1990s—get suckered into purchasing extended service agreements. Suckered is the right word, since the price tags on these plans average around $1,000, while the total repair costs they actually wind up absorbing are typically just $250 or so.

> The price tags on extended service agreements average around $1,000, while the total repair costs they actually wind up absorbing are typically just $250 or so.

The typical extended warranty isn't actually a warranty. It's a private insurance policy. Essentially, you are betting that your shiny new car will suffer a catastrophically expensive failure within a specific period of time—usually, in the two or three years after the factory warranty expires. If you think your car is unreliable enough to make this a good bet, you shouldn't be buying it in the first place.

What to Do if Something Goes Wrong

If you've bought a car from an authorized dealership and are dissatisfied with some aspect of the transaction, the best course of action is to discuss the matter with the dealer's general manager. A short, clear, cordial letter outlining your concerns will generally get results. (You'll find a sample letter you can use as a model on page 391 of the FFYM Toolkit.) Avoid making threats or calling people names. This might make you feel better for the moment, but it NEVER helps your case. If anything, it will turn people off and make them less likely to want to help you.

Generally speaking, the first few weeks or months after you buy a new car are the best times to air a complaint with a dealership. Dealers do not want to be dinged on the car companies' customer-satisfaction surveys, so they tend to be extremely responsive to complaints.

If your letter to the general manager doesn't provoke a satisfactory response, write a similar letter to the owner of the dealership, pointing out that you were not able to resolve things at a lower level. You can find out who and where the owner is by looking on the dealership's web site or by calling the showroom and asking the receptionist. If the owner is a company, contact its

CEO. Corporate dealers such as AutoNation and CarMax have dedicated customer-service contacts at their headquarters, though they say that the vast majority of problems are resolved by the general manager at the dealer location in question.

If the owner isn't sympathetic and you are convinced your gripe is legitimate, you should inform the car company through the customer-service telephone number or email address you will find on its web site.

At this point, if you still haven't gotten satisfaction, then it may be time to involve the government and/or lawyers. If the problem involves fraud or deceptive practices by the dealer or the automaker, you should complain to the Federal Trade Commission (www.ftc.gov) as well as the state attorney general's office. (Most have a consumer-protection division.)

You can also contact the local chapter of the Better Business Bureau (www.bbb.org) and possibly even a news-media outlet, such as the consumer reporter at your local television station. (His or her contact information will be on the station's web site.) Car dealers hate it when a news crew rolls into their showroom wanting to know why they are cheating customers.

If your complaint is that your new car is a lemon—meaning that it has some kind of recurring, unfixable mechanical problem—your state's lemon law may be applicable.

Know the Lemon Law—It Can Save You a Fortune!

When I got out of school in 1990 and started working in commercial real estate, I needed a nice car to drive clients around. So even though I could barely afford it, I went to a reputable local dealer and bought a brand-new Volkswagen Passat. Unfortunately, the car turned out to be a lemon. Within a year, it had been to the service department half a dozen times—and many of the repairs made were not covered by the warranty. Then someone told me about California's "Lemon Law"—legislation that protects new-car buyers if their vehicle turns out to have some unfixable problem that numerous trips to the garage fail to correct. The law defines this kind of car as a "lemon" and requires the manufacturer to either fix it (at their own expense) or replace it.

Armed with this knowledge, I wrote a detailed letter to the owner of the dealership where I'd bought my Passat, telling him in no uncertain terms that I was no longer willing to accept my car's problems and that I expected him to either get my car fixed once and for all or give me a new one. A few days later, the head of the dealership's service department called me personally to give me his commitment that they would get my car fixed at no charge to me—and that until it was completely repaired, they would provide me with a loaner car (a brand-new dealership car), also at no charge.

In the end, it took them SIX WEEKS to fix my car. The total cost was more than $11,000—a huge sum, considering the car cost only $17,000—but of course they paid it, not me.

WHY WE HAVE LEMON LAWS

Cost to fix my brand-new car:	$11,000
Cost to me:	$0

This is why we have lemon laws—and why you should know about them. Although the details vary from state to state, every state has one. Like California's, they all require manufacturers to "do the right thing" in the event a new car they've sold you turns out to be a lemon. There's a helpful web site called Lemon Law America (www.lemonlawamerica.com) that lists each state's statutes as well as local lawyers specializing in lemon law cases. Refer to page 391 in our Toolkit for a sample new-car "lemon law" complaint letter.

Fight for Your Money Action Steps

- ☐ If you're not paying cash for a car, know your credit score before you apply for credit. Visit www.annualcreditreport.com.

- ☐ Go online and check out the many invaluable resources for car buyers. Use them for comparison shopping, to determine dealer costs, and also to figure out how much your trade-in is really worth.

- ☐ Focus on the total cost of ownership, not just your monthly payment.

- ☐ Avoid trading in your old car. Sell it separately to another dealer.

- ☐ Just say no to extended warranties!

Buying a Used Car

There's no question that if you need a set of wheels, it makes a lot more sense to buy a well-maintained, late-model car than a new one. Why? Because if it's less than three years old, a good used car is bound to have nearly all the latest bells and whistles, not to mention the manufacturer's original warranty. And thanks to the massive depreciation that virtually all new cars suffer the minute their new owners drive them out of the showroom, you can generally get a good used one at anywhere from 20% to 50% off the new-car price.

The problem is that dealing with used-car salesmen (and women) can be a nightmare. They're not all crooks, but they *are* all out to take you for as much as they can. If that means selling you a car you don't really like for more than you can afford, that's just what they'll try to do.

They're pretty good at it, too. Americans bought 41.4 million used cars in 2007, two-thirds of them from dealers (as opposed to private individuals). And unlike new-car dealers, used-car salesmen make money on the cars they sell—an average profit of roughly $300 per vehicle, which works out to more than $8.3 billion in all. (Most new-car dealers make their money on service, financing, options, and extended warranties—they actually lose a little money on the sale of the car itself.)

There's nothing wrong with a little profit, of course—as long as you make sure it doesn't come at your expense.

How to Fight for Your Money

Back in the bad old days when the big carmakers believed in planned obsolescence, automobile odometers only went up to 99,999 miles—and for good reason. Until well into the 1980s, most cars really weren't built to last. They began showing their age around 50,000 miles and were ready for the scrap heap long before they hit 100,000 miles.

These days, odometers go up to 999,999 miles. That may be a little optimistic, but the fact is that most modern cars will easily give you 200,000 miles or more. Indeed, according to industry analysis group R. L. Polk, in 2007 the average passenger vehicle on the road in 2007 was 9.2 years old. What this means is that a three-year-old used car with 36,000 miles on it has expended less than a third of its useful life—maybe much less.

Here's what makes this statistic important to you. Even though that used car still has at least 70% of its life ahead of it, its price is bound to be a lot less than 70% of what it cost when it was new. Most likely, you can buy a car like that for just 60%—and sometimes as little as 50%—of its original price.

Older cars can be even bigger bargains. A five-year-old car with 60,000 miles on it probably has at least another 100,000 miles of good driving left in it—yet will cost you maybe a quarter of what it did when it was new.

This is why I say used cars are generally a much better buy than new cars.

Here's how to maximize your chances of getting a great deal.

Remember—They Are Called "Salespeople" for a Reason

It's no accident that used-car salesmen have such a sleazy reputation. "You know what our motto is?" one of them once asked me. *"If you ain't cheating, you ain't trying."* He later said he was just kidding, but I'm not so sure. Of course, for all the "old school" salespeople like this one, there are many others who consider themselves to be "transportation specialists" or "consultants." But whatever you call the person selling you the car, what is for sure is that he or she has been trained to sell you that car. In particular, they know all kinds of psychological tricks to keep you off balance, make you feel guilty about not trusting them, and distract you from the issues you should be focusing on.

For example, the last thing they want you to know is how much the car they're pushing you to buy really costs. So they never talk about actual price, just what the monthly payments will be. ("It's just $200 a month. You can afford that, can't you?" *Well, not if it's for 200 months.*) And they'll never admit they don't have the kind of car you're looking for. (As one salesman once told me: "If I tell the customer we have a certain vehicle even when we don't, I still have a 50% chance of making a sale. If I tell him that we don't have it, I've got zero chance.") Or if you say you need to discuss a potential deal with a spouse, parent, or friend (which is a smart thing to do anytime you're making a major purchase), they'll roll their eyes, implying you must be some sort of a wuss. They may even pretend to have lost your car keys to keep you from leaving their lot.

They also like to brag that they sell more cars in a week than most people buy in their entire lives—and they use this fact to try to intimidate you into playing their game. But you know what? You don't have to fall for their bull. Do some research before you start shopping so you have at least a general idea of what you're looking for and what it's likely to cost. Talk to friends and coworkers; check out the major auto-sales web sites like Edmunds.com and Kelley Blue Book (www.kbb.com); and see what reputable consumer advocates like Consumer Reports (www.consumerreports.org) and the American Automobile Association (www.aaa.com) have to say. And don't take any abuse. Remember, used-car dealers need you a lot more than you need them. If you don't like the way you're being treated at a particular lot, just thank them for their time and take your business elsewhere.

Check the History—Get the VIN Number and Have It Verified

How can you tell if a used-car salesman is lying?

His lips are moving.

Seriously, though, when you're shopping for a used car, there's no reason to take anything a dealer tells you on faith. Instead of wondering whether that cute Toyota that caught your eye really did have only one previous owner who never had a single accident, you can order up a vehicle history report that will tell you for sure.

One great thing about cars is that we keep records on them—billions and billions of records. Every time you bring your car in for a smog check, have an accident, register an insurance claim, or transfer the title, a record goes into a file somewhere.

For a long time, this fact did ordinary consumers like you and me no good, because those records were scattered all over the place—in insurance company offices, auto service centers, and the DMV offices in 50 different states. But these days, outfits like Carfax (www.carfax.com) and Experian AutoCheck (www.autocheck.com) maintain vast databases containing literally billions of automobile records from thousands of government and private sources. For a fee of $20 to $25, they will take any VIN number you give them and email you a report telling you everything you need to know about that particular car's past, including all the owners it's ever had, whether it's ever been wrecked or stolen, how it did on smog tests, whether its odometer has been rolled back, and when the dealer took delivery (a piece of information that could give you some negotiating leverage if it turns out the car has been sitting on his lot for months).

Twenty-five bucks may seem like a lot, but trust me—given how good used-car dealers are on taking a salvaged wreck and making it look "good as new," it's more than worth it. Buying a used car without checking the history is just asking for trouble. The price of this verification is less than one tank of gas. Make the investment—you'll be glad you did.

Look for "CPO" Certification

While a vehicle history report can reveal a lot about a car's past, it doesn't say anything about the car's likely future. That's why you should never buy a used car without a warranty. And the very best warranties are the ones that come with cars that have been inspected and personally guaranteed by a reputable dealership. In most cases, it's the manufacturer who bestows the coveted label of Certified Pre-Owned on a well-maintained, low-mileage car, but some national used-car chains like CarMax also operate impressive certification programs. (This is one reason why it's generally not a good idea to buy a car from a private individual. You might get a good price, but you definitely won't get a warranty.)

Most Certified Pre-Owned cars tend to be upscale brands, like Mercedes, Lexus, and BMW, whose long-term reliability is reflected in the fact that their original factory warranties are generally longer than the standard three years or 36,000 miles. But there are an increasing number of more affordable mainstream brands, like Chevy and Ford, that certify their used cars.

Certified Pre-Owned cars can cost as much as $2,500 more than less-desirable, uncertified used cars. But they're often worth the extra cost, since they tend to be the cleanest, best-maintained, most like-new used cars you can find.

Consider Mainstream Brands and Clone Cars

It may sound strange, but sometimes a car can be too reliable. If you check the Kelley Blue Book (www.kbb.com), which is one of the standard references for used-car prices, you'll see that the brands with the highest resale values—BMW, Honda, Scion, Mini, and Volkswagen—are among the most reliable. That shouldn't be surprising. Reliability is one of the most important factors to consider in buying a car, so you would expect the most reliable ones to be the most in demand—and hence the most expensive.

If money were no object, you should certainly buy one of these cars. But of course money *is* an object, which means you need to think about whether the extra money you have to pay for that extra reliability is really worth it. In fact, it may not be.

Why? Because there are cars just a little less reliable that sell for a *lot* less money—which is to say that, even though they may be slightly less reliable than a BMW or a Mini, they are a much better value. Mainstream brands like Chevrolet, Ford, Nissan, and Mazda—all of which manufacture reasonably reliable vehicles—may actually be the most sensible choices for used-car buyers because their cars depreciate faster than their more reliable counterparts and therefore sell for lower prices on the used-car lot.

The same is true for some luxury American brands like Cadillac, Buick, and Lincoln. You don't want to buy them new, because their value drops like a rock the minute you drive off the dealer's lot. But for precisely the same reason, they tend to be great buys when used. Not only do they come with long factory warranties, good reliability ratings, and a nationwide network of customer-friendly dealers, but because of that awful depreciation, the price of used models tends to be quite reasonable.

And don't overlook clone cars. Clone cars are essentially identical cars built on the same assembly line but sold under different names by different manufacturers. For example, the Pontiac Vibe is a clone of the Toyota Matrix. It may be identical to the Matrix in all but name, but the name is what counts when it comes to depreciation. And since Pontiacs depreciate faster than Toyotas, a used Vibe is a better value than a used Matrix. Similarly, a used Chrysler Crossfire, which was built from the same hardware in the same factory as the old Mercedes SLK, may be a much better value used than a used SLK.

SEND IN THE CLONES

Cost of a 3-year-old Toyota Matrix:	$15,015
Cost of a 3-year-old Pontiac Vibe:	$14,230
You save:	**$785**

Based on Kelley Blue Book suggested retail value of 2006 Toyota Matrix Sport Wagon and Pontiac Vibe Sport Wagon, each with 45,000 miles.

Go Online for Bargains

While the best used cars may be the Certified Pre-Owned ones you find at a big dealership, serious bargain hunters like to buy their cars directly from the previous owner. In large part, that's because you no longer have to pore over the Sunday classifieds in your hometown newspaper to find who's selling what. These days, you simply boot up your computer and surf the web.

Given the enormous popularity of online classified ad sites like Craigslist (www.craigslist.org) and online auction sites like giant eBay Motors (www.ebaymotors.com), it's no wonder that the Internet now figures in more than a quarter of all used-car sales. Craigslist carries ads for upward of 3 million used cars each month. For its part, eBay welcomes 11 million visitors each month and sells upward of about $18 billion worth of cars and related products each year.

There are all sorts of reasons for the popularity of these sites, but the main ones are price and selection. All things being equal, owner-sold used cars tend to be cheaper than those sold by dealerships. And the nature of the Internet means that you're not restricted to looking at ads for only the used cars that happen to be available in your town. You can see ads for cars anywhere in the country (Craigslist has separate listings for 450 cities)—which means that it's up to you to decide how far you are willing to travel to retrieve a car or how much you are willing to pay to have it shipped to you.

This is a huge advantage. A Toyota Prius might be hard to come by in Dallas or Houston, but might be more available in not-too-distant Austin. So the ability to consider cars from other markets can make it easier to locate the car you want.

Keep in mind that when you buy from private individuals, you're not likely to get a warranty. That said, eBay Motors does have an online Certified Pre-Owned "showroom" that offers thousands of CPO vehicles.

Of course, dealerships advertise on the Internet too, and there are also plenty of good referral web sites—like Autos.com, AutoNation (www.autonation.com), AutoTrader.com, Cars.com, CarsDirect (www.carsdirect.com), Edmunds.com, InvoiceDealers (www.invoicedealers.com), MyRide.com, and Yahoo!Autos (http://autos.yahoo.com)—that can hook you up with a local used-car dealer who has the kind of car you're looking for. But they're not likely to get you the kind of bargains you can find on Craigslist and eBay.

You Can Also Get Good Deals from Specialists

For the most part, you should avoid independent used-car dealers—the kind of guys who have small lots filled with a jumble of old cars. The best cars tend to be snapped up by franchised dealers, who get first crack at trade-ins, leaving these guys with mainly junk. But there is one exception to this rule: independent used-car dealers who specialize in a particular kind of car, usually an upscale foreign brand.

I'm talking about the stand-alone independent dealers who sell and service nothing but BMWs, or Mercedeses or Saabs, or other similar cars. These guys generally know their cars inside and out, offer a good variety of their brand, and frequently provide a warranty. Most important, they are enthusiasts first and car dealers second—meaning they're much more fun to deal with. They also tend to buy their inventory from fanatical repeat customers who take great care of their cars, so the vehicles they sell rival those sold by franchised dealers—except that they are usually less expensive.

My friend Allan, for example, bought an old Mercedes convertible from a big Mercedes dealer in Southern California for around $28,000 several years ago. Then, a few months later, he saw the same year and model Mercedes at a small specialty lot for just $22,500. And the cheaper car was actually in slightly better condition!

Don't Overlook the Rental Companies

Rental-car companies like to get rid of cars before the mileage gets too high—usually before the odometer hits 20,000 miles. This can happen quickly in a rental car, so rental companies regularly sell vehicles that are not much more than a year old—sometimes not even that.

Virtually all the major companies have sales arms that offer their used cars to the public, and they all have web sites that provide detailed descriptions of what's available. The most popular include:

- Avis (www.avisnj.com/sales.htm)

- Budget (www.budgetcarsales.com)

- Dollar (www. dollarcarsales.com)

- Enterprise (www.enterprisecarsales.com)

- Hertz (www.hertzcarsales.com)

- Thrifty (www.thriftycarsales.com)

You might think it's a bad idea to buy a used car that's mainly been driven by people who didn't own it. In fact, rental cars are among the best-maintained vehicles on the road today. They are checked over by professionals every time they are turned in, and they are serviced religiously.

As a result, rental companies generally offer solid warranties on the used vehicles they sell. And that's on top of the original factory warranties, which, given how new these cars tend to be, are usually still several years and tens of thousands of miles away from expiring.

Rental companies sometimes charge a little more for their cars than most used-car dealers, but given the excellent maintenance they get, their vehicles are generally worth it. In addition, most of the companies have a no-haggle sales policy, which can make the purchase process pretty painless. And some of the deals are pretty darn good. For instance, as I write this, Enterprise is offering a 2007 VW Jetta Sedan with 32,000 miles on it for $15,499—$316 *less* than the Kelley Blue Book price.

What to Watch Out For

There are countless used-car scams, ranging from bait-and-switch advertising (where you're lured in by an ad promising the proverbial "cream puff," only to be told when you arrive that it's just been sold) to selling stolen vehicles. Most of them aren't hard to spot—if you know what to look for. Here are the top red flags to avoid.

Cars with Suspiciously Low Mileage

Odometer fraud used to be one of the biggest perils facing used-car buyers.

It still is.

Carmakers thought that by making digital odometers standard equipment, dishonest dealers would no longer be able to make an old warhorse seem young and fresh by rolling back the mileage. They were wrong. Digital odometers have turned out to be just as susceptible to tampering as the old mechanical ones—and unscrupulous used-car dealers have no compunctions about taking advantage of this fact.

The statistics are astounding. Roughly one out of every ten used cars sold these days has had its odometer rolled back. According to U.S. government figures, this illegal practice costs car buyers more than *$1 billion* each year in inflated prices

To make sure you're not one of the victims, be skeptical when you come across a "cream puff" with unusually low mileage. Keep in mind that the average car racks up around 12,000 miles a year. So if you're looking at a three-year-old convertible and its odometer reads just 18,000 miles, be skeptical. Was it *really* owned by a little old lady from Pasadena who drove it only on

Sundays? Check the tires. If the odometer shows fewer than 20,000 miles, the car should still have its original set. (If all four tires don't match or they're not a major brand, you'll know something is wrong.) And take a look at the gas and brake pedals. There shouldn't be much wear and tear if the car really is a "low-mileage special."

Mismatched or Missing VIN Numbers

Since the early 1980s, every motor vehicle manufactured in or imported to the United States has been required to have a 17-digit Vehicle Identification Number stamped onto a small metal plate that is attached to various spots in the car, including the dashboard by the windshield, the driver's-side door post, the firewall, the engine, and the frame.

The VIN number is a unique identifier as important to your car as your Social Security number is to you. If a car's VIN number is missing or seems to have been altered in any way, that's a sure sign there's something fishy about the vehicle—most likely that it's either a stolen car or a salvaged wreck. Whatever the case, you want no part of it.

So before you buy a used car, make sure that all the VIN numbers are where they are supposed to be, that all match exactly, and that none of them have been filed down or otherwise tampered with.

Cars That Are Sold "As Is"

Under federal law, used-car dealers must affix what's called a "Buyer's Guide" sticker to the window of every car they sell. This sticker has check boxes that indicate whether the car is being sold with a warranty or "as is" (meaning the buyer is willing to accept the vehicle in whatever condition it happens to be). No matter how great the car looks, if the "as is" box is checked, walk away. You don't want to buy it.

As a rule, you should never buy a used car that doesn't come with at least a 30- to 90-day warranty that will protect you against any non-obvious mechanical problems the car may have. Remember Murphy's Law: "If anything can go wrong, it will." It wasn't written with used cars in mind, but it might as well have been.

And don't be swayed by a salesman who tells you not to worry about the "as is" box being checked—that the dealership will take care of you if any problems arise.

No matter what the salesman may promise, "as is" means you're on your own. When you buy "as is"—and before they give you the keys, they will require you to sign a paper specifically acknowledging that this is what you've done—you are disclaiming all warranties, verbal or otherwise. In other words, you are taking on sole responsibility for fixing anything that may be wrong with the car—and you should not expect anyone to come to your aid if the car turns out to be a lemon.

"Katrina Cars"—They Are All "Wet"

As many as 10% of all the cars and trucks in Louisiana and Mississippi—some 571,000 vehicles in all—were ruined by Hurricane Katrina in August 2005. A month later, Hurricane Rita wrecked tens of thousands more. Many of these so-called "Katrina Cars" were scrapped—but many were not. Instead, they were cleaned up and offered for sale, in some cases by unscrupulous dealers who hid their past.

The same thing happens every year after hurricane season. The only variable is the scale of the problem. In any given year, there are tens of thousands of flood-damaged cars being offered to unsuspecting buyers all over the country. They may look okay and seem to run just fine, but they are literally just problems waiting to happen. As one auto safety expert told the *Washington Post,* "All the electronic components are hopelessly compromised. They will inevitably corrode. Anti-lock brakes will fail, engines will intermittently die in traffic, and air bags may not inflate in a crash."

Fortunately, these Katrina Cars have telltale signs. Your antennae should go up if a used car you're considering has any underbody rust or a moldy smell—or there is any evidence (like Louisiana or Mississippi plates) that it may have been in an affected area during a hurricane. Look under the carpeting in both the trunk and the passenger compartment for any sign of contained moisture or mold. Also check under the hood to see if there's a ring around the engine compartment. A water line marked by rust, mud, or silt is a sure indication that the engine was submerged in water at some point.

The Car in the Wal-Mart Lot with the "For Sale" Sign in the Window

You see them all the time: cars parked by the side of the road or in a shopping-mall parking lot with those red and white "For Sale" signs taped to the side or rear window. The sellers usually say that it's their personal car and they just want to make a quick cash deal, guy to guy (or gal), without any middlemen or paperwork. Sometimes they are completely legitimate, but many of these sellers are what's called "curbstoners"—illegal, unlicensed used-car dealers who operate from the curb, rather than a legitimate lot. Most of the cars curbstoners sell are either salvage vehicles or have failed inspections. More than a few are stolen. So beware of street sales—however attractive the price may seem to be.

What to Do if Things Go Wrong

Many of the scams that dishonest used-car dealers try to pull are not simply unfair; they are also against the law. Swindles like bait-and-switch advertising, odometer tampering, and title-washing (where a badly damaged car is registered in another state and given a new title that doesn't reflect its true condition) are all crimes. So if you think you've been victimized by this sort of thing, take heart—the law is on your side.

But before you call the cops, there are a few less drastic actions you should try if you think there's something fishy about the used car you just bought.

In most cases, the first thing you should do is confront the seller and attempt to resolve the problem directly. If it's a big chain like AutoNation and CarMax or a franchised dealer connected to one of the big carmakers, chances are they'll have a customer-service department that will do its best to resolve the issue. If it's an independent dealer, you should go to the salesman or his supervisor.

The important thing is to keep your cool and put your complaint—along with what you would like them to do about it—in writing.

Obviously, you shouldn't expect them to be happy to see you. In fact, most used-car salesmen will run the other way when they spot an unhappy former customer stomping onto their lot. This can be incredibly frustrating. In fact, I can't think of anything more infuriating than getting the brush-off from the same guy who pretended to be your best buddy when he was trying to sell you a vehicle just a few days or weeks earlier. But even though it might make you feel better, the way to get results isn't to call him every name in the book and threaten to have him arrested. What you want to do is send a clear, concise letter to his boss or the owner of the dealership outlining your gripe, suggesting a proposed solution and politely expressing your hope that it won't be necessary for you to resort to legal action.

Chances are this will produce results. If it doesn't, it's time to go to the authorities and/or hire a lawyer. In addition to contacting the consumer-protection division in the office of your state's attorney general, you should also complain to the Better Business Bureau (www.bbb.org). And think about calling the consumer affairs reporter at your local TV station or newspaper. Consumer reporters love exposing used-car scams. (On the other hand, they are totally uninterested in "he said/she said" disputes between buyers and sellers, so if your problem isn't really a dealer who makes a practice of scamming his customers, don't bother.)

If you have issues with a used car that you bought in a private transaction (whether you found it through a newspaper ad or on Craigslist), you have fewer options. If the seller refuses to do anything about your complaint—or even respond to your letter—there's not a lot you can do short of hiring a lawyer and suing him or her. This is one benefit of doing business with a dealership.

However, there is one kind of private used-car transaction where used-car buyers do enjoy protection: vehicles sold through eBay. Under its Vehicle Purchase Protection policy, eBay will reimburse its customers up to $50,000 if a car they bought through the site turns out to have been stolen or damaged or has otherwise failed to live up to how it was advertised.

Fight for Your Money Action Steps

- ☐ Start by using sites like Edmunds.com and Kelley Blue Book (www.kbb.com) to research car values, prices, makes, and models. Know before you go!

- ☐ Before you buy any used car, check its history at www.carfax.com or www.autocheck.com.

- ☐ Always have an independent mechanic do a thorough diagnostic test before purchasing.

- ☐ Look for CPO certification when buying from a dealership.

- ☐ Shop online for bargains at sites like www.craigslist.com and www.ebaymotors.com.

- ☐ Don't forget the rental-car company used-car sales! Visit their individual sites to shop their inventory.

Car Leasing

You want to make a car dealer happy? Walk into his showroom and tell him you're interested in a lease. Car dealers just love customers who lease.

There's a good reason for this. Leasing can be so complicated and confusing that fooling customers is a breeze. Indeed, it's so easy to play games with the numbers that car dealers average twice as much profit on a lease as they do on a conventional purchase.

Given that roughly 25% of all new cars (and more than 85% of some luxury models) are leased rather than bought, we're talking about a lot of money—as much as $10 billion a year in excess profits, according to some estimates. This doesn't mean that leasing is always a rip-off. There are situations where it makes good sense to lease rather than buy. In fact, I have leased successfully myself. The trick is recognizing when you're in the right situation—and when you're not.

Leaser Beware!

Car dealers average twice as much profit on a lease
as they do on a conventional purchase.

How to Fight for Your Money

Car leasing can sound simpler than it really is. When you lease, what you're doing is getting the use of a car for a set period of time (usually between two and five years), during which you agree to cover the cost of the car's depreciation. Let's say you lease a $25,000 Honda for three years. Since a Honda typically depreciates by 40% over three years, the car will be worth just $15,000 or so when your lease ends. So for the right to use the Honda over those three years, you have to compensate the leasing company for the $10,000 drop in its value.*

Theoretically, you could put up $10,000 in cash at the beginning of the lease and be done with it. Some people actually do this, even though it defeats one of the main purposes of most car leases, which is to minimize your up-front costs. But the vast majority of people who lease cars put little or nothing down up front to cover the depreciation. Instead, they pay off the depreciation charge in monthly installments—plus interest.

This is why lease payments are generally so much smaller than car-loan payments. With a car loan, you're paying off the purchase price of the car—its full value. With a lease, you're paying off only part of its value—often less than half. Of course, once you've paid off an auto loan, you own the car free and clear. When you finish a lease, you own nothing. It's true that you can usually buy a car at the end of a lease by paying the depreciated price—known in leasing jargon as the residual value. But unless the leasing company has miscalculated—which they sometimes do—it's generally a lot cheaper simply to take out a car loan and buy the vehicle new than to lease a car for several years and then buy it—that's because the interest rates on auto loans are often lower than those for leases.

So which is a better deal—paying a lot less every month but having to give up the car at the end of the lease, or paying more but getting to keep the car? In fact, there is no single answer for everyone. It depends on a wide variety of factors—how you drive, where you drive, how much the car depreciates, what kind of interest you have to pay, and on and on.

Car dealers will always tell you what a great deal leasing is. They will emphasize the lower monthly payments and the lower up-front costs, the "convenience" of being able to walk away from the car at the end of the lease, and

---

*Even though you negotiate the lease with a car dealer, you actually lease the car from a leasing company. What happens is that once you and the dealer agree on the terms, the dealer sells the car to a leasing company, which then leases it to you.

most of all the ability to put yourself behind the wheel of a fancier car than you could otherwise afford.

They will talk a good game, and a lot of what they say may even be true. But keep your guard up. There's an awful lot they don't tell you—and for good reason.

When Leasing Makes Sense . . . and When It Doesn't

Leasing appeals to people because it can seem to be a lot less expensive than buying a new car. As we'll see shortly, this can be misleading. Still, there's no question that leasing can put you behind the wheel (at least for a while) of a much nicer car than you could probably afford to buy. But you shouldn't really consider it unless you fit into most if not all of the following categories.

1. YOU NEED TO HAVE A NEW CAR EVERY TWO OR THREE YEARS.
    Leasing doesn't make a lot of sense if you don't really care about having a new car. The fact is, when you're leasing, you're continually paying new-car prices without ever actually getting to own it—so if you'd just as well be driving a decent used car, why bother?

2. YOU GENERALLY DRIVE LESS THAN 15,000 MILES A YEAR.
    Since the value of a used car is directly related to how much it's been driven, most leases limit how many miles you can put on the car. You can choose the limit—generally, 10,000, 12,000, or 15,000 miles per year—and the higher the limit, the more expensive the lease. If you go over whatever limit you've chosen, you have to pay a stiff penalty, usually somewhere between 15 and 25 cents a mile. According to a study by CNW Marketing Research, more than a third of people who lease cars exceed their annual limit—typically by around 2,500 miles a year. This may not sound like much, but over the course of a three-year lease, the overage could easily cost you nearly $2,000 in penalty fees. And if you wildly overshoot the limit, it could end up costing you so much that you would be better off simply buying the car out of the lease for the residual value and reselling it.

3. YOU'RE GOOD ABOUT KEEPING YOUR CAR WELL MAINTAINED.
    You should think twice about leasing if you like to modify or customize your car—or, conversely, if you're not good about taking care of it. You're expected to return your car in *near showroom condition* when your lease is up. Scratch a wheel rim on a curb and that will cost you hundreds of dollars—maybe thousands—depending on what kind of wheels you have. Suffer any dings, dents, windshield

cracks or nicks, worn-out floor mats—
you name it and you will be charged for
"excessive" wear and tear. And trust me,
they charge you full value. Often the "nick
fees" are simply absurd. According to
CNW, wear-and-tear assessments averaged $1,700 in 2006.

> Wear-and-tear assessments averaged $1,700 in 2006.

With this in mind, before you give back a leased car, you should photograph it from head to toe to prove it was returned in good shape. The dealer won't do this when you bring the car in. They assess the charges later on and then send you a bill or deduct them from your deposit if there was one.

4. YOU'RE A BUSINESS OWNER OR SELF-EMPLOYED AND YOU USE YOUR CAR IN YOUR WORK.

If you're a business owner or a self-employed person who leases a car for your work, the entire cost of the lease may be tax-deductible. For someone in the 35% bracket, this can reduce the real cost of the lease by more than a third—making it hands down a better deal than buying. Regular wage-earners can sometimes deduct automobile expenses (basically, 58.5 cents for every business-related mile they drive), but they generally can't simply write off the cost of a car lease.

5. YOUR JOB IS SECURE AND YOU DON'T ANTICIPATE ANY LIFESTYLE CHANGES THAT MIGHT AFFECT THE KIND OF CAR YOU NEED.

A car lease is a contract, and the leasing companies can be brutal about enforcing them. The fact that your circumstances may have changed—that you've lost your job, or had triplets, or been called up by the National Guard—doesn't matter to them. Most leasing companies will not let you turn in a car early without paying huge penalties—often the equivalent of all the remaining lease payments. Indeed, once you've signed a car lease, it's virtually impossible to get out of it, short of declaring bankruptcy. So don't even think of leasing a car unless you are very sure that it will continue to be the right vehicle for you for the entire term of the lease and that you will be able to make all your payments.

How to Get a Good Deal—Focus on the Total Cost

So you've considered all these factors and you think leasing might make sense for you. Now the real work starts. There's no question that compared to financing a purchase with a car loan, leasing generally offers lower monthly payments and lower up-front costs. And as I said, the car dealer will keep making that point over and over again. The thing is, it's not the whole story. And to make sure you get a good deal, you need to know the whole story.

It's definitely nice to have low monthly payments and low up-front costs. But what really matters is the total cost of the lease—how many of those low monthly payments there will be, what other fees you are likely to incur, and what it will all add up to.

There are several basic variables that affect the total cost of a lease. They can sound complicated, but if you don't let the jargon throw you, they are actually fairly easy to understand.

First of all, there's the actual price of the car, which is called the "capitalized cost." Then there's the term of the lease (how many years it will run), the mileage limit, and the residual value, which is how much the lease company says the car will be worth when the lease ends. The difference between the capitalized cost and the residual value is the depreciation—which is the basic cost you as the lessee will have to pay. There are also up-front costs, which generally include the first month's payment, a refundable security deposit, taxes, registration fees, and other charges. Finally, there is something called the "money factor," which determines how much interest you must pay on top of the depreciation.

Obviously, the smaller the depreciation, the less expensive your lease is going to be. What makes things complicated is that there are any number of different ways you can reduce the depreciation figure. One way is to lower the capitalized cost, which you can do either by haggling with the dealer or agreeing to make a down payment (known in leasing circles as a "capitalized cost reduction"). Typically, when you're negotiating a lease, a salesman will urge you to put a few thousand dollars down—dangling the prospect of a lower monthly payment. Don't fall for this. Sure, your monthly payment will be lower, but you'll be out a big chunk of money—and if you happen to total the car in the first few months of your lease, you won't get it back.

A better way to reduce your depreciation is to increase the residual value, which you can do by negotiating with the dealer, agreeing to a lower mileage limit, or picking a car known for retaining its value (a Lexus or Honda, say, as opposed to a Cadillac or Kia). You could also reduce the term of the lease, since the shorter the lease, the younger the car will be at its end and the less it will have depreciated.

You can also reduce the cost of a lease by trying to get the lowest possible money factor. This can be difficult, since dealers are not required to disclose this number. But if you tell him that you will not sign a lease without knowing what the money factor is, most will tell you. If yours refuses, take your business elsewhere.

A Simple System to Beat the Old Shell Game

Because there are so many moving parts, many car dealers turn lease negotiations into a kind of shell game, in which they keep trying to distract you with talk of low monthly payments, while they hike the capitalized cost, shave a few hundred miles off the annual limit, and add a few extra months onto the term—and then at the very end surprise you with a bunch of non-negotiable one-time administrative fees and add-ons.

It's not impossible to beat the dealer at his own game, but it takes real discipline and focus. Fortunately, there's a much simpler way to make sure you get a good deal on a car lease. All you need to do is decide four things in advance: what model car you'd like, how much of a down payment you're willing to make (if any), how long you'd like your lease to run, and how big or small a mileage limitation you feel you can live with.

With these four variables set in your mind, you no longer need to worry about all the other complicated factors that go into calculating the total lease cost. Good places to research what's reasonable to pay include:

- Automotive.com

- CarsDirect.com

- Edmunds.com

- InvoiceDealers.com

- LeaseCompare.com

- Yahoo!Autos (http://autos.yahoo.com/)

Then you simply go online or get on the phone and start calling local dealerships.

Tell the car dealers you contact your four specifications ("I'm looking for a three-year lease on a Honda Accord LX, no more than $2,500 down, and 12,000 miles a year"). Then ask them what's the best monthly payment they can give you.

When you approach the leasing process this way, it doesn't matter what the other numbers are or how the dealer arrived at them. Since you've already specified how much cash you will be paying up front and exactly how many monthly payments you will be making, there's only one thing you need to find out in order to be able to calculate the total cost of the lease: the size of the monthly payment.

Once you know the monthly payment, you just multiply it by the number of months in your lease and then add your down payment. Bingo—you've got your total cost!

This system also makes it easy to figure out which dealer is offering you the best deal. When you're juggling all those different factors, every deal you're offered is bound to be structured differently, and you often wind up comparing apples and oranges. With this simplified approach, it's always apples and apples, since the only variable you're comparing is the monthly price.

If all this seems too complicated or time-consuming, there are services that will handle all the calculating and bargaining for you. Some, like 1Click AutoBrokers.com, charge a fee; others, like Auto Leasing Direct (http://www. autoleasingdirect.info) and LeaseByNet.com, build their compensation into the deal they put together for you. They all claim they can get you such good deals that, even figuring in their fees, you still come out ahead. The catch is that these services tend to specialize in luxury cars, so if you're looking for a Chevy or a Volkswagen, they may not be of much use.

Protect Yourself with Gap Insurance

When you lease a car, you're responsible for returning it to the leasing company in good condition at the end of your lease. So what happens if the car gets totaled or stolen? Under most standard leasing agreements, you will still have to pay the leasing company all the remaining monthly payments plus the car's residual value. You may think your auto insurance will take care of this, but most policies will pay only the car's current value—and that may be a lot less than what you owe the leasing company. (Keep in mind that the minute you drove your leased car off the lot, its value dropped as much as 20% or 30%.) On a $25,000 car stolen or totaled early in its lease, the gap between what your insurance will pay and what you might owe the leasing company could easily run as much as $7,000. And, believe me, they will expect you to pay it.

To protect yourself from this possibility, you can get what's called gap insurance, which pays off the difference between what you owe and what your regular auto insurance will actually pay out. Some lease contracts automatically include it. If yours doesn't, ask your insurance company for gap coverage. The premiums shouldn't run more than $100 a year. (Warning: Don't buy it from the dealer. He'll try to charge you several times that.)

What to Watch Out For

Claims That It's Always Cheaper to Lease

A salesman who tells you that it's always cheaper to lease is not a salesman you can or should trust. When it comes to leasing, there is no "always." If you're likely to trade in a car before the loan is paid off, leasing is probably a better deal for you than buying. But if you generally keep driving a car long after you make the final payment (or if you paid cash for it in the first place), buying is probably cheaper. As a recent study by *Consumer Reports* showed, in the first year or two, leasing usually costs you less, but around the third year the balance begins to shift in favor of buying.

In the first year or two, leasing usually costs you less, but around the third year the balance begins to shift in favor of buying.

Promises That You Can Swap Your Old Lease for a New One

Salesmen eager to close a deal will sometimes tell you that if you get tired of your car before your lease is over, they will be happy to get you out of the original lease and into a new one. Don't believe them. They certainly will be happy to take care of you, but that's only because you're giving them a chance to extract even more money from you. In fact, there is no such thing as trading in an old lease for a new one. What actually happens is that the dealer will turn in your car early and roll the cost of all the early-termination fees, penalties, and unpaid depreciation into your new lease. The dealer may also pocket your security deposit in the process.

Interest-Rate Confusion

Car dealers love to confuse customers by talking about the money factor as if it were an interest rate. "We're giving you a 4.6 rate on this lease," a dealer will tell you. "Try getting an auto loan for that." In fact, the 4.6 figure the salesman is throwing around isn't a 4.6% annual interest rate. It's shorthand for the money factor, which in this case is .0046. To convert the money factor to an annual interest rate, you multiply it by 2,400. So multiplying a .0046 money factor by 2,400 gives you an interest rate of 11.04%—which is not such a great rate at all.

Fiddling with the Figures

After spending hours going back and forth with the salesmen, you've finally agreed on the terms of your lease. At this point, he disappears into a back room to write up the lease. You then spend 20 minutes twiddling your thumbs and wondering what's going on. When he finally reappears, he presents you with the lease. You glance at it and notice that the monthly payment is $30 higher than it was supposed to be. "When you and I were figuring things, we must have made a small error in our calculations," he tells you. "No biggie." Don't believe him. For one thing, on a 36-month lease, this "small error" will cost you more than $1,000. For another, it probably wasn't an error at all, but rather the result of him fiddling with the figures—for instance, trying to squeeze out some extra profit by writing down a capitalized cost $1,000 higher than what you agreed to.

Even though car-lease contracts are long, complicated forms filled with tiny print and literally dozens of different numbers written in, check every figure before you sign. Make sure the administrative fees, down payment, capitalized cost, mileage limit, residual cost, monthly payment, and term are all exactly what you agreed to. Some dealers will get everything right but then write up what was supposed to be a 36-month lease as a 39-month lease—hoping you won't notice until it's too late that you've been stuck with three extra payments. Some will try to cut the mileage limit.

Assume the worst and go over your lease agreement carefully. And if you're unsure about anything, DON'T SIGN IT! Once they've got your signature, you're on the hook and there's no going back.

Unnecessary Add-Ons

Car dealers are car dealers, and whether they are selling or leasing a new vehicle, they will try to bamboozle you into paying for overpriced unnecessary add-ons like extended warranties, rustproofing, paint sealers, and the like. Some will even suggest that the leasing companies require you to buy some or all of these "protections." Don't fall for this. If a salesman uses this line, go to another dealer.

In fact, as unnecessary as these things are for a car you buy, they are even more unnecessary for one that's leased. Remember, the car you are leasing is brand new and, since you should never lease a car for a period longer than the manufacturer's warranty is in effect, you'll be protected for the entire lease period. So an extended warranty is a total waste of money. So are all the other add-ons.

I once had a salesperson look me in the eye and suggest rustproofing for a car I leased in California. I said, "You have to be kidding, right? A convertible in California—you really think I need rustproofing?" He replied, "I have to ask."

What to Do if Things Go Wrong

A variety of federal and state laws require dealerships and leasing companies to disclose key terms and conditions of car leases, including the capitalized cost, the residual value, the finance charge (that is, the dollar amount of interest you will be paying—NOT the money factor or interest rate used to calculate that amount), as well as things like wear-and-tear charges and early-termination penalties. If you've been the victim of deceptive or unfair practices, you can fight back by contacting your state's consumer-protection agency or attorney general's office. You can also complain to the Federal Trade Commission (www.ftc.gov) and the Federal Reserve Board, whose job it is to enforce the Consumer Leasing Act, which governs most consumer leases.

You can call the FTC's Consumer Response Center toll-free at (877) FTC-HELP (877-382-4357) or write to them at:

Federal Trade Commission
Consumer Response Center—240
600 Pennsylvania Ave., NW
Washington, DC 20580

You can call the Federal Reserve's Consumer Help line toll-free at (888) 851-1920 or file a complaint online at www.federalreserveconsumerhelp.gov. You can also write to the Fed at:

Federal Reserve Consumer Help
P.O. Box 1200
Minneapolis, MN 55480

If you have problems with the car itself (and not the leasing process), you have the same lemon-law protections as someone who bought a new vehicle. For details, see the section BUYING A NEW CAR.

A Safe, Legal Way to Get Out of a Car Lease

As I said before, once you sign a lease agreement, you're on the hook. If you try to give back the car early, they will hit you with big penalties. And if you default on the payments, they will ruin your credit. So what do you do if you lose your job or have kids or otherwise go through some change in your life that makes you desperate to get out of your car lease? The answer may be to transfer your lease to somebody else.

Taking over a lease can be a good deal, since all the up-front costs are already paid, along with a chunk of the depreciation.

For a fee that usually totals several hundred dollars, web sites like Swapalease.com and Lease Trader.com put people trying to get out of a lease together with folks looking to get in. Taking over a lease can be a good deal, since all the up-front costs are already paid, along with a chunk of the depreciation.

Once a match has been made, the site verifies the buyer's credit and handles the paperwork transferring the car to the new lessee. At this point, you're off the hook. And even though you sometimes have to offer big financial concessions to entice a buyer into taking over your lease, it's still almost always a *lot* cheaper than paying those early-termination penalties.

Fight for Your Money Action Steps

☐ Be sure leasing a car is the right decision for you. (It usually isn't.)

☐ Focus on the four factors that make up the total cost to get yourself the best deal financially.

☐ Do your homework before attempting to negotiate a new-car lease. Make use of sites like CarBuyingTips.com and Edmunds.com that offer lots of great information and research tools.

☐ Take over someone else's lease for the best deal.

Car Rentals

The problem with renting a car isn't that the rates are high. In fact, they're often pretty reasonable, depending on the state and city you rent in. But car-rental companies have the same attitude toward maximizing profits that the airlines do. With intense competition making it difficult for them to raise their basic prices, they try to pick your pocket by hitting you up for all sorts of fees and special charges—many of them for things you probably don't need. This brings them billions of dollars in additional revenue—and raises the price you wind up actually paying by anywhere from 20% to 60% over their basic advertised rates.

The trick to renting a car, then, is making sure you get only what you want and need—as opposed to what the car-rental company will try to sell you.

How to Fight for Your Money

The car-rental business is a big one. There are half a dozen major companies operating eight national brands—Alamo, Avis, Budget, Dollar, Enterprise, Hertz, National, and Thrifty. Altogether, they take in more than $20 billion a year.

You probably have a horror story about how you were mistreated by one or another of them. I know I've got a bunch. But according to a 2007 survey by the Consumer Reports National Research Center, they all offer pretty much the same level of service. So there's no need to drive yourself crazy trying to decide which company to rent from. Just go with the one that offers you the best rates.

Here's how to make sure you get a good deal.

Shop Around and Negotiate!

Thanks to the Internet, it's easy to get price quotes from every major company and a host of minor ones. Comparison sites like www.kayak.com, www.hotwire.com, and www.sidestep.com, along with travel sites like Expedia (www.expedia.com), Orbitz (www.orbitz.com), and Travelocity (www.travelocity.com), can get you competing rates for any model car, on any date, at any location. Once you've got these in hand, you can contact the rental companies themselves, either through their web sites or by phone, and see if they can do better. Often, they can—and will.

> Basically, when it comes to renting a car there simply is not a "fixed price." What you are quoted is not what you have to accept.

Also—and this is really important—when you call the rental company directly, I recommend you have their web site open and in front of you, because it's very possible that there will be a lower price on the web site than they quote you. This has happened to me half a dozen times. And with that said, here's why you also need to be ready to negotiate. Sometimes, the price online can be beat by who you are speaking with on the phone at the same company. And now to make it even crazier—when you physically arrive at the rental counter, simply ask, "How can I get a better price" to see if you can negotiate them down a bit further. Basically, when it comes to renting a car there simply is not a "fixed price." What you are quoted is not what you have to accept.

And don't restrict your search to the major brands. There are a number of smaller car-rental companies (such as ACE, Advantage, Fox, Triangle, and even U-Haul) that may not be nationally known but still rent the same kind of late-model, low-mileage cars as the majors. You can get rate information and make reservations through web sites like Car-rental Express (www.carrentalexpress.com) or CarRentals.com (www.carrentals.com).

Lastly, book early for the best values, because you can always cancel without penalty since you're usually not required to hold a reservation with a credit card.

Rent on the Weekend—If You Have the Flexibility

You can save plenty when you rent on a weekend. Weekends are usually pretty slow for the car-rental companies, since most of their demand comes from business people who do most of their traveling during the week. So, in an effort to generate traffic, they cut prices sharply on Saturdays and Sundays. And I do mean sharply. At Enterprise recently, the same compact that will cost you $78.59 a day during the week goes for just $29.89 a day on a Saturday or Sunday. So if you have any flexibility, save your rentals for the weekend.

Read Your Contract

The time you initially pick the car up is probably the most likely time something could go wrong. You absolutely must take a few minutes to read the contract before you sign. With many rental agencies now offering "gold clubs" that allow you to just get in your car and drive off, it's all too easy to miss something important. The contract may have insurance checked off because that's what's in your profile, when in fact you don't need it. Or worse—the car you drive off in could have damages, scratches, or dings that you might get charged for. So before you rush off, check the car out and make sure it's in the same shape as indicated on your contract. Any damages need to be noted on the contract. Also make sure the mileage noted matches the odometer and that the gas tank is full.

Make Sure You Know What You'll Really Be Paying

The basic daily or weekly rate you'll be charged for a rental car is only part of the price you'll wind up paying. There are all sorts of extra costs that get tacked on. Some are mandatory, like:

- airport-concession fees
- special municipal surcharges
- excise and sales taxes

Others are optional, like:

- insurance premiums
- refueling charges
- special equipment like GPS devices, baby seats, and satellite radios

When you add them all up, these extra charges can easily wind up doubling the cost of your rental. So ask about them in advance—and make sure that all applicable extra charges are included in your price quote. Also don't be afraid to ask nicely, "Can you throw in a GPS, or the car seat, etc."—often the manager at the rental-car lot can do just that. I regularly get "free" extras by just asking nicely. Just last week I got an upgrade and a car seat "thrown in"—saving me $75 during my rental.

RIP-OFF OPTIONAL

If you rent a Ford Taurus at Chicago O'Hare Airport:	
Your approximate total cost per day without options:	$120.94
Your cost per day with GPS, satellite radio, and a car seat:	$153.68
Skip the extras and, over the course of a week, you save:	**$230**

Don't Be Shy About Asking for Discounts

Do you belong to the American Automobile Association? AARP? Costco or Sam's Club? If so, you probably can get a discount of anywhere from 5% to 25% off the price of your rental. Most of the major car-rental companies offer discounts to members of certain organizations, employees of certain companies, customers of certain merchants—even people who attend certain conventions and trade shows. I once belonged to a gym that gave clients a Hertz discount card. There are so many of these deals available that you should always make a point of asking if any of your professional or personal affiliations qualify you for one.

In addition to these group discounts, rental companies also often offer discount coupons on travel web sites, in travel magazines, and at the checkout areas of big-box retailers like Costco. So keep your eyes peeled. You can also visit consumer discount sites like www.rentalcarmomma.com and www.rentalcodes.com for some decent savings. Lastly, ALWAYS ask at the counter, "Are you having any specials? Is there anything I can do to get a better price or better deal today?"

Members Only

- Save 25% with your Costco card at National, Alamo, and Avis; or 20% at Hertz and Budget.
- Save 20% with your AAA membership card on Premium car classes at Hertz or 15% on Economy through Full Size.

Renting at the Airport Can Cost You 25% More!

According to a 2005 study by Travelocity, renting at the average major airport adds more than 25% to your total bill. There's no question that it's more convenient when you're flying, but it's almost always a lot more expensive to pick up a rental car at the airport than at a neighborhood location. That's because most airports and the local governments that oversee them impose a variety of special taxes and fees on car rentals—the idea being that the customers getting screwed aren't usually local residents, so who cares if they don't like it? Houston's George Bush Intercontinental Airport had the most outrageous charges—its taxes increased the cost of renting by more than 66%.

So if you're renting for more than a day or two, it's probably worth your while to bypass the big airport car-rental center and instead arrange to pick up your car at a neighborhood office near where you're staying. In recent years, the major rental companies have opened thousands of new non-airport branches, so finding one isn't usually too difficult.

TWENTY MINUTES TO SAVINGS

Renting a Chevy Impala from Avis at Minneapolis/St. Paul Airport location:	$132.36 per day
Renting a Chevy Impala from Avis at Maplewood, MN, location (a 20-minute cab ride away):	$70.13 per day
Including cab fare, which will cost you approximately $50 each way if you're renting the car for a week, you save:	**$300!**

Review Your Insurance Coverage Before You Get a Rental Car

The biggest and most profitable part of the car-rental business is rental insurance. Roughly a third of all rental-car customers sign up for it—paying as much as $40 a day for coverage most of them don't need. This is great for the car-rental companies, since most of the charges they collect are pure profit, but it's generally an expensive rip-off for you (if you already have the coverage).

Let's go through the basics of the complicated insurance coverage policies and then see if you really need them. The basic policies offered by car-rental agencies include the Collision Damage Waiver (CDW), the Loss Damage Waiver (LDW), the Supplemental Liability Protection, Personal Accident

Insurance (PAI), and Personal Effects Coverage (PEC). In theory, this is all perfectly reasonable. In practice, it's largely unnecessary.

COLLISION DAMAGE WAIVER (CDW)

This is actually not even an insurance policy. Rather, it's a legal agreement that relieves you of responsibility for any collision damage the car may suffer while you're renting it. This is nice protection to have—but if you happen to own a car, chances are you already have it. That's because most auto insurance policies cover not only accidents you have while driving your own car, but also those while you're driving other vehicles. And that includes rented ones.

LOSS DAMAGE WAIVER (LDW)

The only protection you should consider is the loss damage waiver (LDW), which protects you from having to reimburse the rental company for the income it's losing while the car is in the shop. There are only eight states in which regular auto insurance policies cover this loss damage, so if you don't happen to live in Alaska, Connecticut, Louisiana, Minnesota, New York, North Dakota, Rhode Island, or Texas, you might want to think about taking the LDW.

SUPPLEMENTAL LIABILITY PROTECTION

Supplemental liability coverage provides additional liability protection if someone makes a claim against you while you're driving a rental car—for example, if you have an accident and the other driver files a claim against you for injuries and vehicle damage that exceed your regular policy limits. Again, there's a strong possibility that you already have this coverage on your own personal auto insurance policy.

PERSONAL ACCIDENT INSURANCE (PAI)

Personal Accident Insurance will cover you or your passengers for injuries sustained while driving a rental. If you already have health insurance or sufficient medical coverage under your auto policy, you probably don't need this.

PERSONAL EFFECTS COVERAGE (PEC)

Personal Effects Coverage protects items and property you own if they're damaged. If you have homeowner's or renter's insurance, you may already have this coverage.

Don't Duplicate Efforts

Skip unnecessary car-rental insurance and you save up to $40 per day.

Don't Own a Car? You May Still Be Covered!

If you don't own a car—and so don't have any auto insurance—you still may be covered . . . by your credit card. Many credit card companies automatically provide rental-car insurance to customers who use their cards when renting. BUT don't assume this. Call your credit card company first to make sure you qualify, before you decline coverage through the rental agency. Be advised that most credit card companies only offer insurance for 30 days—so if you rent long term you would need to return the car on the thirtieth day, then rent a new one in order to ensure continuous coverage. Some credit cards have certain cars they won't insure at all, so again you need to know the specifics of what your credit card really covers. Make the phone call.

There is one exception to all of this—if you're renting a car abroad. Most U.S. auto insurance policies do not necessarily cover accidents that occur outside the country.

So before you rent a car, check your existing insurance policies—and check with your credit card company—to see if there's any reason for you to buy additional coverage from the car-rental firm. Most likely, there won't be. (And once you've said no, double-check your contract. Many rental clerks will automatically check the "Yes" box for insurance, even after you've told them you don't want it.)

Fill 'Er Up!

The most important advice I can give you now with gas prices skyrocketing is to make sure your car has the amount of gas in it that the car-rental company says it does. If they say the car is full and it's actually a quarter tank less than full, that's a quick financial hit of over $10 to $20, depending on the tank of the car. Go back to the counter and let them know right away—don't just drive away and assume you can fix this when you return. Also, as you know, most car-rental companies require you to return the car with a full tank of gas. If you don't, they'll fill it up themselves—and charge you through the nose for it. In fact, the rental-car companies now promote this "service" as a perk! But you'll end up paying from $7 to $14 over and above what you'd pay if you pumped the gas yourself. And with prices nearing almost $4 a gallon as I write this, aren't we paying enough for gas as it is? The refueling fee is almost always posted in the reception area, because it is such a profit center for the rental-car companies and also such a sore issue with customers. So as you're driving away from the rental-car lot, make a point of noticing where the nearest gas station is—and then, on your way back, top up the tank before you turn in the car. If you've got an early-morning flight and you're afraid you won't have time for a refueling stop, then do it the night before.

DO IT YOURSELF SAVINGS

What you'll pay to let Budget fill the tank of your Toyota Camry:	$82
What you'll pay to refuel yourself:	$68
You save:	**$14**

Returning the Car

Here's another likely place where something can go wrong—when you're returning the car. That's where you're usually rushing off—maybe to catch your flight—and you're quickly handed your bill. Now is the time to catch any final mistakes on your bill, so take a moment to fully review it. Make sure they credit you properly for gas and for mileage.

Recently, I brought in my car and the woman looked at the mileage and noted that I drove 12,000 miles! I started laughing, because that just wasn't possible—I hadn't even driven 500 miles. The contract was wrong—and even she recognized instantly it couldn't be possible. Fortunately for me, I didn't have to argue the point.

What to Watch Out For

Unwanted Upgrades

It's funny how times change. It used to be that savvy rental customers would always reserve a car a little smaller than they really wanted. The idea was that since most rental agencies have a lot more intermediate and full-size cars than compacts and subcompacts, they'd probably wind up getting a free upgrade to a larger model. But now, with gasoline prices sky-high, the situation is reversed. Most rental customers want economy cars, not big sedans and SUVs. Since there aren't enough to go around, it's become increasingly common for customers to be pushed into larger cars against their will.

That's exactly what happened to me recently in New York. Having just recently written a book on the environment called *Go Green, Live Rich*, it's important to me to drive a hybrid car—it's better for the environment and it saves me money on gas. I don't want to drive a gas-guzzling SUV. So recently I rented a Toyota Prius from Hertz. Because they are so in demand in New York, a Prius is very difficult to get, so I reserved mine nearly two weeks in advance. When I showed up to get my car, they let me know that they were going to do me a wonderful favor and upgrade me at no extra charge to a luxury SUV. Normally, the SUV rental was nearly $50 a day more—and I should be thrilled. But I wasn't thrilled—in fact, I was very upset. I had reserved the Hybrid two weeks early and I wanted that specific car, not an SUV. I insisted they find a Prius somewhere else and get it delivered to the rental location I was at. After about 15 minutes of searching, they found a car and had it sent over to the car location I was at. It would have cost me twice as much to drive the SUV just in gas costs alone.

> At Hertz you'll pay $7 a day more to rent a Toyota Prius over a Ford Explorer. But you'll get more than double the gas mileage!

Given how heavily their fleets are weighted toward big cars and SUVs, it will probably take the car-rental companies several years to shift the balance noticeably toward "greener" vehicles. In the meantime, don't be surprised if a company tries to "upgrade" you into a less fuel-efficient car than you reserved. But stand your ground. If you insist, they'll accommodate you, if they can. On the other hand, you might want to take advantage of the fact that some companies now charge less for some larger gas-guzzlers than for some smaller, more efficient cars. This may be where you have leverage to get a great deal; just remember these gas guzzlers are not good for the planet.

The Disappearing Grace Period

The car-rental companies didn't used to be sticklers about the rules. If your car was due back at noon on Tuesday and you didn't show up until 1:30 P.M., they'd usually turn a blind eye and not charge you extra. Nowadays, if you roll in more than 30 minutes past the scheduled return time, you shouldn't be surprised if you're charged for a full extra day.

Even more annoying, the companies have started enforcing fine-print rules about pick-up times. Since some discounted rates are based on what time you're picking up the car, if your flight is delayed, the rental company is technically entitled to cancel your discount and charge you more. They rarely used to do this, but with everyone in the industry now trying to squeeze out as much revenue as they can, if you give them an excuse to take back a discount, chances are that they will.

So before you rent, find out whether you will be subject to any penalty if your flight is late or if you have to cancel the reservation entirely. If you don't like the answer you get, switch to another company.

Unnecessary Options

Next to insurance, the car-rental companies' main source of additional profit are heavily promoted—and expensive—options like prepaid fuel, GPS devices, and satellite radios. While GPS devices, E-ZPass transmitters, satellite radios, and seat-back entertainment units are fun to play, they can add as much as 20% to the cost of renting a car.

Alamo, one of the smaller of the big eight rental companies, earned an extra $30 million from GPS devices alone in 2007—and that was when the trend was just getting started. As I shared earlier, I often get these extras for free just by asking nicely—so try asking. It can't hurt.

The prepaid-fuel option is probably the trickiest of their tricks. The rental companies used to charge two or three times the going rate for gas. But with pump prices as high as they are, they can't get away with that sort of thing anymore. So they've come up with a new scam. What most of them do now is offer to sell you a full tank of gas at the beginning of the rental for a price just below what it would cost you at a gas station. The trick is that once you've bought the gas, it's yours—whether or not you use it all. There are no refunds, even if you bring the car back with a nearly full tank. So unless you know you're going to drive more than the 300 to 400 miles it takes to empty a modern gas tank, don't take the prepaid-fuel option.

And if you're traveling with a small child, think about bringing along your own safety seat. Most airlines will not charge a fee to check a car seat—although be sure to double-check beforehand. The rental companies charge as much as $12 a day extra to provide them.

GO DIRECTLY TO SAVINGS

Cost of GPS per weekly rental:	$59.75
Cost of buying a map:	$2.95
You save:	**$56.80**

What to Do if Something Goes Wrong

In the event of a problem with a rental-car company, the best course of action is to deal with the manager at the car-rental place you are renting from. She or he has the most power to fix your problem the fastest (while you are there). In my experience, these managers are overworked and stressed and most people are furious when they interact with them, so if you try a little kindness you have a better chance to get further faster. If you can't make progress with your problem or get it fixed on site, then contact the company directly with an explanation of the problem. All of the major companies have customer-service departments. You can find the necessary contact information on the company's web site.

If that doesn't help and you used a travel agency or some booking service, contact them to ask them to intervene on your behalf. And don't hesitate to complain to both the Better Business Bureau (www.bbb.org) and the Federal Trade Commission (www.ftc.gov).

Also, if you are a member of AAA or AARP, those organizations will act to help you if you aren't able to resolve any problems through other means.

Fight for Your Money Action Steps

☐ Shop around online. My favorite sites include:

www.kayak.com www.hotwire.com
www.sidestep.com www.expedia
www.orbitz.com www.travelocity
www.carrentals.com www.carrentalexpress.com

☐ Get your discounts! AARP, AAA, Costco, or Sam's Club member? Take advantage of the benefits! And check out consumer discount sites like: www.rentalcodes.com or www.rentalcarmomma.com.

☐ Don't rent at an airport if at all possible.

☐ Know what you're already insured for so you don't buy coverage you don't need.

☐ Read your contract and inspect the condition of the car *before* you drive off the lot.

☐ Fill up the tank before you return if you didn't prepay.

Car Repairs

I n the chapter on new-car buying, I shared the story about the time I bought a new car with such terrible mechanical problems that I had to threaten the dealer with California's "Lemon Law." If you purchased a new car recently and are having problems with it, flip to page 22 and read that section now.

Car repairs can be a financial disaster. Time and again, in doing money makeovers for people, I find out that it was car problems that first put them in debt. Often the story starts with someone taking their car in for what they think is a small problem only to be told it's actually a much, much bigger problem that will cost them thousands of dollars. The challenge is that most of us know little or nothing about how to fix an automobile, so it's really difficult to know if the advice we are being given is honest.

Just about everybody has a story about how a dishonest auto mechanic tried to rip them off. I remember my friend Allan telling me about how he brought his car into the service department at a big California dealership a few years ago and was told that unless he spent $3,300 on a new exhaust system, he would definitely fail its smog test and probably ruin his engine. He almost fell for these scare tactics, but at the last minute he decided to have another garage take a look at the car. Sure enough, all it needed was a minor adjustment that cost him less than $75. He passed the smog test and drove the car problem-free for another five years.

I had a similar situation involving brake pads on my car. Every single time I brought the car in for service, I was told I needed new brake pads and an alignment—at a cost of $1,500 or more. Finally, I checked the owner's manual and discovered that there was no way the brake pads should need to be changed this often. I took the car to another mechanic, who told me that the pads my dealer had described as being shot and dangerous were actually fine.

It's rip-offs like these that can make car repairs cost us a fortune if we don't watch our mechanics—and fight for our money.

Not all auto mechanics are dishonest, but as a group they do not have a great reputation. Car-repair shops consistently rank among the Better Business Bureau's Top 10 most complained-about industries, and some experts claim that as many as *a third* of all auto repairs are fraudulent, which would put the annual cost to consumers at somewhere around $30 billion.

Finding a good mechanic has always been a challenge, but these days it's both tougher and more important than ever. Cars have gotten so technologically sophisticated that it practically takes a degree in computer science to understand what's going on under the hood. Forget about trying to figure out what's causing that strange rattle. You need a repair shop you can trust. Fortunately, there *are* some out there—and finding one isn't as hard as you might think.

How to Fight for Your Money

Do Your Homework

There are basically two ways to find a good mechanic: trial and error or old-fashioned research. The first can be expensive and painful, while all the second requires is a little time and effort.

So let's focus on research. Word of mouth is usually the best place to start. This means soliciting suggestions from friends, relatives, and coworkers. And thanks to the Internet, you don't have to stop there. Online services like Angie's List (www.angieslist.com) and Consumers' Checkbook (www.consumerscheckbook.org) rate all sorts of service businesses, including auto-repair shops, based on reports submitted by thousands of consumers around the country. These services aren't free (fees range between $25 and $50 a year), but the guidance they provide is certainly worth it.

Once you've gotten a few leads on good garages, you need to verify that they really are as good as they're cracked up to be. One of the best ways to do this is by checking out whether the people who work at a place you're considering meet the standards of the National Institute for Automotive Service Excellence (ASE), a nonprofit organization that tests and certifies auto mechanics in specialties ranging from engine repair to heating and air-conditioning.

Garages that employ at least one ASE-certified mechanic generally display an ASE sticker in their window. Of course, all this means is that there's at least one mechanic on the floor who has passed at least one ASE test. It doesn't mean he's going to be working on your car. What you want is a garage where *most* of the mechanics are ASE-certified—and where at least a few hold ASE Master Technician certificates, meaning they have passed the exams in all eight automotive specialties. The ASE awards what it calls its "Blue Seal of Excellence" to garages where at least 75% of their service personnel are ASE-certified. (To find a Blue Seal garage near you, use the ASE's Blue Seal locator online at http://locator.ase.com/blue/.)

It's also a good idea to make sure a repair shop you're considering is endorsed by the American Automobile Association. Garages that pass a strict AAA inspection, have at least one ASE Master Technician on the payroll, and earn a customer-satisfaction rating of 90% or better are allowed to display the AAA's blue-and-red "Approved Auto Repair" sign.

Don't Wait Until the Last Minute

There's nothing like driving around town with black smoke pouring out of your exhaust frantically searching for a decent-looking service center that's (1) open, and (2) capable of figuring out and fixing what's wrong. You want to establish a relationship with a good repair shop *before* you're in desperate need of their services. So start looking for one now, while your car is still problem-free.

Pick the Right Shop for the Right Job

At bottom, there are three different kinds of auto-service facilities to choose from—there are dealerships, there are national chains like Sears or Midas or Jiffy Lube, and there are independent garages. Which is best? Well, in fact, they all are . . . for different things.

It used to be that having your car serviced or repaired at a dealership was almost always a rip-off, since dealers' prices were generally much higher than those of independent shops. But that's not true anymore. With new-car sales no longer producing much if anything in the way of profits, the service business has become incredibly important to most dealerships. As a result, dealers have become more competitive with their shop rates, often offering special prices on oil changes, brake jobs, and the like.

Still, that doesn't mean you should bring your car **to the dealer** every time it needs servicing or repair work. For sure, you should always have any work covered by the manufacturer's warranty done by the dealer. If money is no object—and when the work is covered by the warranty, it's not—you don't need to worry about whether parts and labor might be cheaper somewhere else. The only thing that matters is the fact that dealers tend to have the most up-to-date equipment for your particular car and their mechanics are likely to have had the latest training in how to fix it.

For most routine work, however—things like changing a muffler, replacing a battery, or flushing a cooling system—you don't necessarily need an ASE-certified master technician. Depending on the nature of the job, one of the **big national chains** can probably do it much more cheaply than a dealership and, as long it's nothing out of the ordinary, every bit as well. Just don't get talked into having them do more than a basic job—and definitely not something outside their main specialty.

A good **independent mechanic** can be worth his weight in gold. He may charge more than the chains, but it's worth paying a little extra to have someone you trust handle the routine maintenance. Keep in mind that federal law gives you the right to service your vehicle wherever you like without affecting your warranty. The only drawback is that as cars have grown more sophisticated, it's become more difficult for independent garages to keep up with the latest technology and equipment. So the most complicated repairs are probably best left to a dealer—especially when they involve systems that are unique to your brand of car.

Follow the Manufacturer's Advice—Not the Garage's

Lots of mechanics, including those at dealerships, will tell you to ignore the owner's manual and instead take their advice on how often to change the oil and perform other routine maintenance. Amazingly enough, their advice almost always involves bringing in the car more often than the manual says or scheduling procedures like engine or transmission flushes that the manual doesn't call for (like having the brake pads changed every 15,000 miles!). This is almost always a rip-off. Remember, your owner's manual was written by the same company that built your car and backs your warranty. So trust what it says.

Always Get a Detailed Estimate— And Get It in Writing

Whether you're bringing your car in for a big repair job or a routine servicing, a good mechanic should be able to tell you in advance what it's going to cost. And he should be willing to put it in writing. As the saying goes, verbal estimates aren't worth the paper they're not printed on.

Never let anyone work on your car without first getting a written estimate that specifies exactly what all the parts and labor for your job are likely to cost. The estimate should also make it clear that the garage is not authorized to do any additional work without your approval. (This is why we have telephones—so the garage can call you if they discover some unanticipated problem once they've begun work on your vehicle.) Any garage that doesn't automatically give you a repair authorization form to sign before you leave your car with them is not a garage you can trust.

Get a Second Opinion

If your mechanic says your car needs major surgery, do the same thing you'd do if you got a similarly serious diagnosis from your doctor—get a second opinion. It's not simply that your mechanic may have a vested interest in persuading you that major work is necessary. It's also that everyone makes mistakes, even good mechanics.

If your mechanic really is honest, he won't mind your taking the car to a diagnostic center for a backup check. Just tell the people at the second garage that you're interested only in a diagnosis—if they conclude that your car happens to need work, it will be done elsewhere. As long as you make this clear, they'll have no reason to recommend unnecessary repairs.

What to Watch Out For

The Old Bait-and-Switch

Local newspapers and pennysavers are constantly filled with ads from garages offering all sorts of bargains—oil changes for $19.99, free brake inspections, $95 tune-up specials. The idea, of course, is to get you in the door—and your car up on their lift. Once there, a dishonest mechanic will miraculously find all sorts of problems you need to take care of right away. And before you know it, your $95 tune-up will have turned into an $800 valve job.

Don't let them stampede you. If a garage tries too hard to sell you on anything beyond the deal that attracted you in the first place, tell them you appreciate their advice but you'd prefer to have the extra work done by your regular mechanic (even if you don't have one). Then get the heck out of there.

And be wary of those "free" brake inspections. No one I know has ever had a free inspection that didn't end with the mechanic saying they needed new pads, rotors, and calipers.

Mechanics Who Make Everything Sound Like an Emergency

Dishonest mechanics prey on ignorance and anxiety. They know that most of us don't really understand how our cars work, and they take advantage of that, painting all sorts of dire pictures about what might happen if we don't have the transmission flushed or the timing belt replaced RIGHT AWAY!

The worst of the scam artists actually try to *cause* problems—or at least the appearance of a problem. It's not unknown for gas station attendants to drip some oil under a car in an effort to convince the owner he's got a leak. Even worse, some may puncture water hoses or nick fan belts—which is why you should never let a mechanic you don't know look under your hood without you looking over his shoulder.

And don't think these sorts of things happen only at fly-by-night independent garages. It was just this sort of "overselling" that eventually forced Sears to pay a $46 million settlement after it was sued for conning customers into unnecessary auto repairs and service in the 1990s.

Nonexistent Replacement Parts

Another way dishonest repair shops take advantage of us is to insist we need to replace some supposedly broken part—say, a water pump—that's actually working just fine. They then do nothing—except charge us for the nonexistent new water pump and the nonexistent labor to install it, assuming we'll never be the wiser.

There's one way to prevent being ripped off in this way. Anytime you agree to have a part replaced, tell the mechanic you'll expect him to give you the old, damaged part when he's done. (In fact, some states have laws that require repair shops to do this.) Needless to say, an honest mechanic should not have any problem with this request.

Prices That Seem Unusually High

These days all repair prices seem high, but if what the garage is quoting you seems really astronomical, take the time to call a number of other garages and see what they would charge for the same job. A really good repair shop may well be more expensive than the average garage, but if your mechanic's prices are more than 20% or 30% higher than everybody else's, something may be wrong. Ask your guy why his prices are so out of line. If the answer is not convincing, find yourself a new mechanic.

A "Mistake" That Can Cost You

Tax you should pay on labor: 0%

Tax Confusion

Lazy or unscrupulous shops (which are often the same thing) may try to charge you sales tax on the total amount of your repair bill. In fact, you're supposed to pay tax only on the parts you purchased for the repair and not on the cost of the labor that was performed. So check your bill carefully. A 5% sales tax misapplied to a big job that included $1,000 of labor takes an unearned $50 out of your pocket and puts it into the garage owner's.

What to Do if Something Goes Wrong

If you think you've been a victim of an auto-repair scam, there's a lot you can—and should—do.

If the work was done at a new-car dealership, you should begin by working your way up the chain of command, first bringing your complaint to the attention of the service manager, then to the dealership's general manager and owner, and then finally to the car company whose franchise they hold.

The process is similar if your problem is with a chain repair shop like Midas or Sears. If the local shop doesn't address your concerns, contact the customer-service department at their national headquarters. You can find the necessary telephone numbers and email addresses on the chain's web site.

If none of this does any good—or if your problem is with an independent garage—report the shop to your state attorney general's office and local consumer-protection agency. Some states have departments that specialize in combating auto-repair fraud. For example, California has a Bureau of Automotive Repair (www.bar.ca.gov) that investigates complaints and tries to mediate solutions. To check if your state has a similar agency, contact your state highway department.

You should also file a complaint with the Better Business Bureau (www.bbb.org) and, if you're a member, with your local branch of the AAA. Even if you're not a member, you should contact the AAA if the garage displays one of its "AAA Approved Auto Repair" signs. If your complaint is serious enough, the garage could lose its seal of approval.

Fight for Your Money Action Steps

☐ Find an ace mechanic you can trust before your car breaks down. Get a recommendation from a friend or neighbor, or subscribe to a service like www.angieslist.com or www.consumerscheckbook.org. Look for ASE certification and AAA approval.

☐ Have all repairs covered by your warranty done by the dealership where you purchased your car.

☐ Always get a detailed estimate in writing before any work is done.

☐ For major repairs, get that second opinion!

☐ Make sure you're not taxed on labor.

Bank Accounts

The first thing you need to know about dealing with banks is that banking is a business—a *big* business. There are more bank branches in the United States than there are movie theaters or shopping malls—upward of 91,000 by the most recent count. In all, there are more than 8,400 different banks with more than $10 trillion in assets and more than $1 trillion in capital.

By any measure, the banking industry is a crucial component of our economy. And as we are learning in the banking crisis of 2008, which is going on as I write, we need our banks to be safe and strong. That said, it's not your job to personally make your bank rich. Unfortunately, if you handle your checking and savings accounts like most people, chances are you are unwittingly making your bank richer at your expense.

In the old days, banks were a place simply to park your savings and borrow money. In fact, for most of the twentieth century that was pretty much all commercial banks were good for. That's because the Depression-era Glass-Steagall Act specifically barred them from getting into the investment or insurance businesses. But in 1999, Congress repealed that law—and today, banks are truly full-service financial firms, offering everything from checking and savings accounts to credit cards and mortgage lending to brokerage services, financial planning, and investment banking.

While banks used to make most of their money making mortgages and other loans, these days an increasing proportion of their profits come from getting customers to use as many of their products and services as possible. This one-stop financial shopping certainly can be incredibly convenient. But if you're not careful, it can also be very expensive.

Is Free Checking Really Free? Probably Not!

Between 2000 and 2006, the total amount of fees U.S. banks collected from checking and savings customers climbed from $24 billion to $36 billion—a whopping 50% increase in just six years. And the numbers have been rising steadily ever since. As a result, banks now earn well over a quarter of all their profits from what the professionals call non-interest income—that is, mainly from fees. There are service fees, maintenance fees, ATM fees, check-cashing fees, overdraft fees, overdraft-protection fees, stop-payment fees, dormant-account fees—you name it, banks charge a fee for it. Some banks even charge you to talk to a teller.

Penalty and service fees typically cost you in excess of $300 a year.

You know the old saying, "There's no such thing as a free lunch"? Well, when it comes to banking, there's no such thing as free checking. You may not be charged for each individual check you write, but whatever that "giveaway" costs the bank, you can be sure they are more than making up for it in penalty and service fees that typically run well in excess of $300 a year, according to Bankrate.com.

So when you're deciding where to do your banking, you need to consider not only what kind of interest rates they are offering to pay on your deposits, but also what sort of fees they are going to try to ding you with.

Of course, getting information about fees isn't always easy. In 2008, at the request of New York congresswoman Carolyn Maloney, the federal Government Accountability Office sent staff members to 185 different banks to pose as customers and see what they could find out about account terms and how much they might be charged for overdrafts, returned checks, stop-payment orders, and the like. Even though federal law requires banks to fully inform customers about all this stuff, the GAO investigators couldn't get complete answers at more than 20% of the branches they visited.

As Representative Maloney put it: "You don't have to buy a car before you find out how many miles per gallon it gets, and you don't have to buy a house before you find out what your taxes will be. Why should consumers be forced to walk blindly into the terms and conditions of a bank account?"

How to Fight for Your Money

The good news about dealing with banks is that the vast majority of them follow the rules. The bad news is that it's often hard to find out just what the rules are. So the most important thing to know about handling your bank accounts is that you have to be ready, willing, and able to ask a lot of questions. And if you don't get clear answers, you shouldn't hesitate to take your business elsewhere.

You'll never get the best out of a bank if it's not the right bank for you. So whether you are looking to open your first account or have been banking at the same place for years, consider *all* your options: online institutions, credit unions, savings-and-loan associations (also known as thrifts), small local banks, large national associations.

Take a hard look at what you need, what your bank offers, and what it costs. Review your monthly statements. How much are you keeping in your accounts? What are you earning?

Who offers the best interest rates is only the first point of comparison. Just because an account pays a competitive rate doesn't mean it's a good deal. Does the account come with a free debit card, charge for checks, or require a minimum balance? Can you verify balances, transfer funds, pay bills, and otherwise manage the account online or over the phone? What kind of fees do they charge for bounced checks, overdrafts, or using another bank's ATM—and how often are you likely to get hit?

Shop around. Compare a wide variety of checking, savings, and money market accounts using web sites like www.Bankrate.com and Yahoo Finance. Only then will you have any idea if you're being well taken care of—or just taken.

Here are a few basic tips to keep in mind when selecting and using a bank.

Choosing a Bank—National vs. Local

Of the 8,400 different banks in America, only about 20 actually failed in 2007 and 2008. Nonetheless, there is concern that another 100 or so could collapse by the end of 2009. Indeed, as I write this, the Federal Deposit Insurance Corp., which insures depositors against bank failures, is said to have a "watch list" of 117 institutions it regards as particularly risky. But because it won't disclose any of their names (for fear of panicking depositors), it's really anyone's guess which bank will be the next to fold or be bought out by a larger competitor.

So how do you choose a bank? My personal recommendation is that you go with one of the larger national banks—institutions like Bank of America, Citibank, HSBC, JPMorgan Chase, or Wells Fargo. In uncertain economic times, I think it makes more sense to be with one of the largest banks in the country than to be with a local bank.

Go Online for Higher Yields and Lower Fees

Online banking has come of age. According to Forrester Research, 41 million households now bank online—a number that is expected to nearly double by 2011—and for good reason.

According to a 2007 study conducted by Bankrate.com, the average service fee charged by an Internet bank is roughly a quarter of what a traditional bank charges—just $2.91, compared to $11.72 for brick-and-mortar banks. At the same time, they pay interest rates that are more than eight times higher than what you get from brick-and-mortar banks—an average yield of 2.7% online, versus just 0.32% in the real world. Most of the top-rated online banks offer their services exclusively on the Internet. Among the best are E*Trade Bank (https://us.etrade.com/e/t/banking), EverBank (www.everbank.com), and ING Direct (http://home.ingdirect.com).

That said, you can also bank online with most of the top national banks. Their rates may not be quite as high as those offered by the Internet banks, but they are close—and along with good rates, you get the convenience and stability of a major brick-and-mortar institution. Bank of America (www.bankofamerica.com), Citibank (www.citibank.com), and HSBC (www.hsbc direct.com) are winning praise for their online extensions—mainly because they offer more services (such as extensive ATM networks and financial-planning tools) than their online-only counterparts.

Make Sure Your Deposits Are Insured

As I noted earlier, despite the recent economic crisis, bank failures are still relatively rare occurrences. But as we saw with IndyMac and Washington Mutual in the summer of 2008, they do happen. Fortunately, the government provides depositors with a safety net. It's called the Federal Deposit Insurance Corporation and it insures about $4.2 trillion worth of deposits at 8,451 banks and savings associations. Make sure yours is one of them. You can do this by calling the FDIC toll-free at (877) 275-3342, or by going online to the FDIC's "EDIE the Estimator" web site at www.fdic.gov/edie/. EDIE, which stands for Electronic Deposit Insurance Estimator, can help you figure which of your bank accounts are covered by FDIC insurance and for how much.

As part of the $700 billion bailout package it passed in October 2008, Congress increased the amount of coverage the FDIC provides. At least through the end of 2009 (and longer, if Congress acts to extend the increase), FDIC insurance will cover all deposits at insured banks, including checking and savings accounts, money market accounts, and certificates of deposit (CDs), up to a maximum of $250,000 per depositor at each bank. The same is true of certain retirement accounts, such as IRAs.

This is almost definitely *not* the last time the rules will change. You can keep abreast of future changes by visiting the FDIC web site at www.myFDIC insurance.gov.

Keep in mind that the FDIC does NOT insure the money invested in stocks, bonds, mutual funds, life insurance policies, annuities, or municipal securities—even if you purchased these products from an insured bank.

Keep in mind, too, that as of August 2008, the FDIC had only about $45 billion in its Deposit Insurance Fund—just a bit more than 1% of those $4.2 trillion in deposits it is supposed to be protecting. It is estimated that the FDIC will need another $150 billion to be able to bail out the additional bank failures experts see coming.

Two Simple Tricks to Prevent Overdrafts

The first is to link your checking account to a savings or credit card account you have with the same bank. That way, if you ever accidentally overdraw your checking account, the bank can automatically draw on the other accounts to cover the shortfall. You may incur a transfer fee that could run anywhere from $5 (which is what Chase charges) to well over $29 (which, according to Bankrate.com, is the industry average), but it will still likely be cheaper than an overdraft fee, which can run $35 or more. And in any case, you will be spared the embarrassment—and damage to your credit history— of a bounced check.

If you don't have any other accounts to which you can link your checking account, use this old bookkeeping trick: Record a $1,000 check to yourself, but never actually write it or cash it. Just like setting your watch ahead to keep you from being late to appointments, this will make it seem as if you have $1,000 less in your account than you really have—and make it all the more unlikely that you will ever incur an overdraft.

What to Watch Out For

There are lots of things banking customers should watch out for, but the biggest scams involve fees, bank policies on deposits, and old-fashioned con men looking to rob you. Here are six of the most outrageous.

Unexpected Overdraft Fees

Probably the biggest trap your bank sets for you is the overdraft penalty they hit you with when you don't have enough money in your account to cover a check you've written or an electronic debit you've authorized. And, boy, does it pay off for them. In 2007 alone, U.S. banks earned an estimated $17.5 billion from overdraft fees, according to the Center for Responsible Lending, a consumer advocacy group.

For one thing, these overdraft fees are expensive, ranging from an average of $22 at credit unions to upward of $35 at some large banks and thrifts. For another, in an effort to generate as much of this sort of revenue as possible, the banks deliberately try to fool you into overspending your balance.

In the old days, banks wouldn't let you make an ATM withdrawal or a debit purchase if you didn't have enough in your account to cover it. But these days, banks routinely approve such transactions, often without alerting you that you've spent more than you have—and that as a result you are going to be charged an overdraft fee.

How unfair is that? See why we need to fight for our money?

Many banks run a similar scam with old-fashioned paper checks. They enroll checking customers in "courtesy" overdraft-protection programs without their knowledge, so that checks that once would have bounced now are honored—again with a penalty fee added on. As if that's not sneaky enough, in addition to the initial overdraft penalty, some banks also charge a daily fee for every day that your account remains overdrawn.

The banks claim they do this sort of thing to save customers hassles and embarrassment. Great, I'm all for the service, but let's be real—this is also about profits. Really big profits. The banks make huge amounts of money tricking customers into overdrawing their accounts and then charging them for it.

There is one surefire way to avoid getting socked with an overdraft fee: Keep a close and constant eye on how much money you've got in the bank, and NEVER write a check or authorize a debit you can't cover. If you do overdraw your account, deposit enough money back into it as soon as possible to cover the shortfall plus any fees and daily charges your bank may have assessed. This won't undo the initial damage, but it will help you avoid additional overdrafts and fees.

Check-Processing Policies That Push You into Overdrawing

Not only do banks try to trick you into overdrawing your account without realizing it, but they also have check-processing policies that seem deliberately designed to maximize the number of bad checks they can charge you for. Again, they claim what they're doing is meant to "protect" customers, but as the Consumer Federation of America and other watchdog groups point out, what really happens in the end is that the bank winds up with more of our money.

Here's how this rip-off works.

When several of your checks arrive at the bank on the same day, the bank does not process them in the order in which you wrote them or even the order in which they arrived. What most of the nation's biggest banks do is process them in the order of size, starting with the largest dollar amount and working down to the smallest.

Say you have $100 in your checking account and you write two checks, one for $30 and one for $40. Then, the next day, you have an emergency and you write a check for $75, figuring you can cover it with a deposit you're expecting to make. Worst case, you think, you may bounce the $75 check, but your other checks should be fine. Wrong.

If all three checks hit the bank on the same day, the bank would clear the $75 one first, leaving you with a balance of just $25—not enough to cover either of your other checks. So even though you wrote those checks first, the bank would bounce both of them—entitling it to charge you for two bounced checks (at as much as $35 each), instead of just one.

The banks claim they do this to give priority to their customers' largest checks, which tend to be for really important transactions like mortgage payments. As a spokesman for the American Bankers Association told *USA Today*: "Their mortgage payment is the last check they want to bounce. There are severe penalties and embarrassment."

Maybe—but I don't think it's just coincidental that this policy allows them to charge more fees.

So it's really important to monitor your account balances. Most banks let you do this both online and over the phone as well as through ATMs. (If yours doesn't, switch to one that does.) Some banks also allow consumers to sign up for alerts by email or text messages on their mobile phones to let them know if their account balance drops below a certain level.

Sign up for alerts by e-mail or text message if your account balance drops below a certain level.

But don't depend entirely on your computer. Record all checking and electronic transactions when you make them, and as boring as it may be, reconcile your checkbook with your monthly statements. Review those statements carefully, and notify your bank immediately if you see a transaction you did not authorize.

The Disappearing "Float"

It used to take as long as a week for a check to clear. Not anymore. These days the bank grabs your money out of your account within 24 to 48 hours. That's because of a 2003 law called the Check Clearing for the 21st Century Act, which allows banks and merchants to process checks electronically instead of having to send them physically around the country.

That's great for the banks, but it can be murder for cash-strapped consumers who used to be able to count on having four or five "float days" to give them a little breathing room when paying bills.

Don't assume that you'll have a day or two to make a deposit to cover a check you wrote yesterday.

To avoid being caught out—and getting hit with one of those outsized overdraft penalties—keep a close watch on your account balance. And don't assume that you'll have a day or two to make a deposit to cover a check you wrote yesterday.

As you'll see in a moment, deposits aren't credited nearly as fast as checks are debited. So don't write any checks unless you know for sure that you already have enough money in your account to cover them.

Unnecessary ATM Fees (That Earn the Banks Nearly $5 Billion in Profits)

Virtually every bank that has automatic teller machines charges a fee (ranging from $1.50 to $3) to users who are customers of some other bank. And some large banks, like Bank of America, get you coming and going, by charging customers for withdrawing their own money through another bank's ATM. (If you bank with BofA but make a withdrawal through, say, a Chase ATM, the transaction could cost you $5: $3 from Chase for using one of their machines—and $2 from BofA for *not* using one of theirs.)

In all, U.S. banks raked in $4.4 billion in ATM fees in 2007. That's a lot to pay for a little convenience.

The banks claim they actually lose money on many of their ATMs because most of their users are their own customers, who don't pay anything for the privilege. And it's true that not only are ATM machines expensive (they cost $9,000 to $15,000 each), but the banks also have to pay an interchange fee for each noncustomer transaction they send through the ATM network.

The good news is that these fees are easy to avoid, or at least reduce. Look on the back of your ATM card for the logo that indicates which ATM network your bank belongs to. Then, the next time you can't find one of your own bank's ATMs, look for a machine bearing the same network logo. If you use an in-network ATM, you may not have to pay any fee at all—and if you do, at least your own bank won't charge you the out-of-network fee.

You might also think about taking your business to a local bank or credit union that participates in a network that doesn't impose fees of any kind when you use another bank's ATM. Among such surcharge-free networks are Allpoint, Co-op Financial, Credit Union 24, and Star, each of which boasts tens of thousands of ATMs nationwide. Or you could open an account at one of the increasing number of banks, both online and off, that reimburse customers for at least a portion of any ATM fees they may incur when using other banks' machines. I do this myself, and I estimate it saves me at least $300 a year.

Deposit Holds—Know Your Rights!

When you deposit a check, the bank is supposed to give you access to the funds within two business days. In fact, most let you have the money even more quickly than that. But they don't have to. Under some circumstances, federal law allows banks to take a week or more to credit a deposit to your account. If you deposit an out-of-state check or a check for more than $5,000, the bank must make $100 available to you immediately, but it can make you wait five to 10 business days before it frees up the remainder. Banks can also hold checks for a "reasonable period of time" if your account has been repeatedly overdrawn, if you're a new customer, or if the bank has reason to believe the check won't clear.

If the bank plans to hold your deposit for more than the usual two days, the law requires it to tell you how long it intends to hang on to it and why. So if it's been three business days since you deposited a check, and the amount still hasn't been added to your balance, don't be afraid to ask your banker what's going on. Speak directly with a branch manager at your bank and tell him that if the "hold" on your check isn't taken off, you'll take your business elsewhere. The fact is, if you are a good customer—especially if you've got money in the bank—there is absolutely no reason for them to put a hold on any deposit you make. The only reason they do it is that it's profitable for them.

Requests for Your Account Information

Here's a scary thought: Anyone who knows your checking account number and bank routing number can rob you blind. That's because this information is all that's needed to create a phony check or what's called a "demand draft," which a bank will honor even though it does not bear the account holder's signature.

What makes this especially scary is that every check you write contains this information. It's those long strings of computerized digits printed at the bottom. This is one big reason why old-fashioned paper checks are probably more risky to use than electronic transfers. As a senior official at the Federal Reserve puts it: "Paper inherently goes through a lot of hands. And every person who handles a check has the ability to commit check fraud."

This doesn't mean you should give up writing checks. But be careful whom you write them to. And be *very* careful about giving out your account information to anyone.

One of the most popular bank-related swindles involves being conned into doing just that. Here's how it works. A guy calls you up and tells you that you've won a free prize or are eligible for a major credit card. At the end of the sales pitch, he adds that in order to qualify for whatever it is he's offering you, he needs to know the numbers that appear at the bottom of your checks. If you are foolish enough to let him have this information, he and his confederates will use it to send your bank a demand draft, ostensibly from you, ordering a transfer of funds—usually a *lot* of funds—to an account of theirs. You may not know any of this has occurred until you receive your next bank statement. At that point, it's usually way too late for any of the money to be recovered.

What to Do if Things Go Wrong

Banks are one of the most heavily regulated institutions around. So if you have a problem with one—and complaining directly to the bank's customer-service department hasn't brought any relief—chances are there's a federal or state government agency that would love to hear about it. A list of the appropriate agencies is below. But before you call or write any of them directly, visit its web site to make sure it is the right one for your particular bank. Also make sure that the problem you think you have really *is* a problem—as opposed to your misunderstanding what the bank's obligations to you are.

The biggest potential problem banking customers face is getting hit with an erroneous or fraudulent charge. If you discover that any bank account of yours has been debited with any unauthorized payments, electronic transfers, or other charges (including unexplained penalty or service fees), you should notify the bank immediately. Were you charged the wrong amount on a debit transaction? Was there an error in a direct deposit? Do you see an ATM withdrawal or bank transfer that you did not authorize?

Depending on the nature of the problem, you have anywhere between 30 days and a year to report it. If your bank made an error processing a check (say, paying the wrong amount), you have 30 days from the date you discovered the error to notify them. If you discover an unauthorized electronic transaction, you generally have 60 days. If the problem is a fraudulent endorsement of a check, state laws typically give you up to one year to complain.

Most likely, since it's your hard-earned money that's been taken, you won't wait nearly that long to file a complaint. Your instinct will probably be to pick up the phone or send an email immediately. That's fine, but keep in mind that you have to be able to prove that you acted before the applicable deadline. So in addition to calling or emailing, always write a letter outlining your complaint and send it to the bank via certified mail. (You should be able to find the right mailing address by looking at your bank statement or on the bank's web site under "Customer Service.")

Depending on the nature of your complaint, the bank must initiate and complete an investigation within a specified period of time. If you are unhappy with the speed or nature of its response—or have any other issue with your bank—take your complaint to the appropriate government agency.

For problems involving national banks (banks with "national" in their name or the initials "N.A." after it), you should contact the Comptroller of the Currency (www.occ.treas.gov).

Office of the Comptroller of the Currency
Customer Assistance Group
1301 McKinney Street, Suite 3450
Houston, TX 77010
(800) 613-6743
customer.assistance@occ.treas.gov

For problems involving state-chartered banks that are members of the Federal Reserve System, you should contact the Federal Reserve's Consumer Help department (www.FederalReserveConsumerHelp.gov).

Federal Reserve Consumer Help
P.O. Box 1200
Minneapolis, MN 55480
(888) 851-1920
ConsumerHelp@FederalReserve.gov

For problems involving state-chartered banks that are not members of the Federal Reserve System, you should contact the FDIC (www.fdic.gov). Most complaints are best filed using their Electronic Customer Assistance Form, available online at www4.fdic.gov/STARSMAIL/index.asp.

Federal Deposit Insurance Corporation
Consumer Response Center
2345 Grand Boulevard, Suite 100
Kansas City, MO 64108
(877) 275-3342
consumeralerts@fdic.gov

For problems involving federally chartered credit unions (those with "federal" in their name), you should contact the National Credit Union Administration (www.ncua.gov).

National Credit Union Administration
Consumer Assistance Center
1775 Duke Street
Alexandria, VA 22314-3428
(800) 755-1030
consumerassistance@ncua.gov

For problems involving state-chartered credit unions, you should contact your state's regulatory agency. A complete list is available at the National Credit Union Administration's web site at www.ncua.gov. (Click on "Resources for Consumers," then on "Consumer Complaint Center," and then on "My complaint concerns a state-chartered credit union.")

For problems involving **federal and some state savings associations**, you should contact the federal Office of Thrift Supervision (www.ots.treas.gov).

Office of Thrift Supervision
Consumer Inquiries
1700 G Street NW, 6th Floor
Washington, DC 20552
(800) 842-6929
consumer.complaint@ots.treas.gov

For problems involving the electronic processing of a check (also known as electronic check conversion), you should contact the Federal Trade Commission, either by telephoning its Consumer Response Center toll-free at (877) 382-4357 or through its online complaint form at www.ftccomplaint assistant.gov, or by writing to them at:

Federal Trade Commission
Consumer Response Center
600 Pennsylvania Ave., NW
Washington, DC 20580

For complaints about possible check fraud or scam attempts of any sort, contact local law enforcement as well as the office of your state's attorney general and the local office of the FBI. You should also file a complaint with the National Consumer League's National Fraud Information Center. You can contact them online at www.fraud.org or telephone them toll-free at (800) 876-7060.

Fight for Your Money Action Steps

☐ Shop around and switch banks if necessary. Compare a wide variety of checking, savings, and money market accounts—be sure to compare fees as well. A great web site for this is www.Bankrate.com.

☐ Read the fine print before selecting an account.

☐ Go with a national bank—one that offers online savings accounts for the highest yields and lowest fees.

☐ Make sure your deposits are insured. Visit www.fdic.gov/edie.

Debit Cards

As much as we Americans love our credit cards, we seem to love debit cards even more. In 2006, we used debit cards—which draw on an existing source of funds such as a checking account—nearly 20% more often than credit cards, roughly 26 billion times in all. And the numbers have been growing steadily. Debit card purchases now total well over $1 trillion a year, accounting for two-thirds of all Visa transactions and half of Visa's dollar volume.

Debit cards are particularly popular among young people between the ages of 18 and 25 who use them instead of cash, even for small purchases. (Around 60% of debit card transactions involve less than $25.) It's easy to see why. Debit cards are simple to use, extremely convenient, and they can keep us from running up credit card balances.

But for all that, debit cards are not nearly as good a deal as most people seem to think. For one thing, they don't offer nearly the same amount of protection against fraud and bad service as credit cards. And for another, if you're not careful with them, they can wind up costing you big-time.

Banks make a lot of money from debit cards. The overdraft fees alone that they generate bring in close to $9 billion a year.

We may think of debit cards as "free" compared to credit cards, which charge interest and late fees, but consider this shocking statistic. According to calculations by *Consumer Reports,* a typical overdraft fee on a debit card purchase translates to an annual interest rate in excess of *1,000%*!

According to the Center for Responsible Lending, on average the typical debit card transaction that spurs a $34 overdraft fee is for a $20 purchase! Imagine you've now paid $54 for a $20 item. With overdraft fees like this, a debit card can quickly turn into an extremely high-cost credit card if you're not careful.

What really makes debit cards so popular is the fact that the banks promote them aggressively—offering all sorts of rewards programs and incentives to encourage you to use them, as Wachovia Bank suggested in a direct-mail promotion, "for ALL of your everyday purchases." The reason the banks do this is simple: They make a lot of money from debit cards. The overdraft fees alone that they generate bring in close to $9 billion a year.

How to Fight for Your Money

There are two basic ways to use a debit card. You can punch in a PIN number, as you do with an ATM card, or you can do what is called an "offline" transaction that involves signing a credit slip. Either way, the transaction is treated the same—as a cash withdrawal from your checking account.

The most obvious difference to you is that when you go the PIN route, the money is deducted from your account almost immediately, while offline transactions generally take a day or so to hit your account. This may not matter much to you, but whether you punch in a PIN or sign a slip makes a huge difference to the folks on the other side of the counter—by which I mean both the merchant you are dealing with and the bank whose debit card you're using. That's because the processing fees that banks charge merchants are as much as seven times higher for offline purchases as they are for PIN-based transactions.

Know Your Debit Card's Liability Policy

Many banks advertise that they offer "zero-liability" debit cards. This means that if an unauthorized charge is made on your card and the transaction is signed for, you are not liable for the fraudulent purchase—much like if you were to use a credit card. However, it's really important to understand that in most cases, this zero-liability policy applies only to signature-based transactions when you're using a debit card with the Visa or MasterCard logo.

In contrast to credit cards, the zero-liability policy for debit cards is just that—a policy, not a federal law.

This means that if an unauthorized purchase is made using your debit card with your personal identification number (PIN), in most cases the zero-liability policy won't apply. What's more, the zero-liability policy for debit cards is just that—a policy, not a federal law.

Ultimately, then, liability for fraudulent transactions is subject to review by the bank that issued the card. It can take months for your fraud complaint to be confirmed and your money returned. As the U.S. Public Interest Research Group points out, "When a credit card is fraudulently used, you are only disputing whether you owe the bank money." By contrast, when you file a report of debit card fraud, you are trying to get the bank to return money that has already been stolen from you.

Lose Your PIN, Lose Your Money

Because PIN-based debit card transactions (processed via electronic fund transfer) generally don't carry the same protection as signature-based debit card transactions (processed through the Visa/MasterCard network), you want to do everything possible to safeguard that PIN. If your debit card information is stolen along with your PIN and you don't notify your bank right away, your entire bank account could potentially be wiped out.

Unlike credit card transactions, which are regulated by the Truth in Lending Act (Regulation Z), debit card transactions are regulated by the Electronic Funds Transfer Act (Regulation E). According to Regulation E, in order to limit your liability you must report suspicious debit card use for PIN-based transactions to your bank within two business days—which will only put you on the hook for $50. Losses reported after two days will increase your liability to $500.

That's not all. If you report unauthorized use of your debit card after 60 days from the time you received your statement, the bank doesn't have to reimburse you at all. In fact, you might even be liable for the maximum overdraft line of credit they extended to you. It's possible that your bank could have a greater protection policy than what the law requires; check to make sure you know what yours is.

DON'T BE LEFT HOLDING THE BAG

Cost to you for a fraudulent debit charge:	up to $500
Cost to you for a fraudulent credit charge:	$0

Bottom line: Use your credit card instead of a debit card for big purchases and you're protected.

It's Easier Than You Think to Have Your Debit Card Information Stolen

Your physical debit card doesn't need to be stolen out of your wallet or lost in the mall parking lot in order for your information to be compromised.

Last year, the *Wall Street Journal* ran an article on an increasingly common debit card scam.

In this scam, criminals attach "skimmers" to the card-swiping devices at grocery stores, gas stations, and even banks. Undetected by consumers, these skimmers copy debit card numbers—including PINs—that are entered. Once the skimmer is retrieved by the criminal, the information is sold or used to create fake debit cards. (Actually, this scam applies to both credit and debit cards. However, thieves prefer to steal debit card information, since credit cards are monitored more closely by banks.)

So be on the lookout for physical tampering at your ATM or checkout line, which could indicate that a skimming device is present. Don't use unbranded ATMs, either—the kind you find in convenience stores or gas stations.

Also be aware of people lurking too closely at ATMs, or even for hidden cameras when you're entering your PIN. Use your hand to shield the numbers you're entering on the keypad.

Check Your Bank Statements Online Every Day

Does that sound extreme? Trust me, it's not. While you're online checking email every day, take two minutes to log on to your bank's web site (from a secure computer, of course) and pull up your current statement.

Glance over your recent transactions and make sure they're all legitimate. If you see anything suspicious, call your bank immediately. Don't wait for your paper statement in the mail. By then it might be too late.

Don't Let Your Debit Card Out of Your Sight

Make sure all your debit transactions are handled without the card being taken out of your line of sight. Once you take your eye off the card, anyone who handles it has the opportunity to steal the card information.

Check Your Credit Report Regularly

If you suspect that your debit card information has been compromised, report it to the credit bureaus right away. Order a copy of your credit report and monitor it regularly.

As I mention in the credit score section of this book, go to AnnualCredit Report.com, where you can get a free credit report once every 12 months from each of the three nationwide consumer credit reporting companies, in accordance with the Fair and Accurate Credit Transactions Act.

Be Careful of Blocking

When you use a debit card for any transaction that may not be completed for a while—like, say, renting a car or booking a hotel room—the merchant is likely to estimate what he thinks it's going to cost and then have your bank put a temporary hold on your account for that amount. This is known as blocking, and what it does is deny you access to your money until the transaction clears or the block is lifted. Merchants do the same thing with credit card transactions, but with credit cards, all a hold does is tie up part of your available credit. A debit card hold ties up actual cash—which can lead you to overdraw your account without meaning to.

A debit card hold can lead you to overdraw your account without meaning to.

This can even happen when you're buying gas. When you swipe a debit card into the pump, the gas station will typically create two transactions—the first to get approval from your bank for an estimated amount (say, $50), which is then blocked, and the second for the actual charges when you're done. Unfortunately, the initial $50 block isn't always lifted right away. In some cases, it may be several days before they get around to lifting it. In the meantime, you effectively have $50 less in your account than you think. The same thing can happen at a hotel when they ask you for a card for "incidentals." Find out how much they are going to put your card on hold for (it could be hundreds of dollars).

The way to avoid this problem is to make a point of using debit cards only for small, immediate transactions. As one expert put it to *Consumer Reports*: "Debit cards may be fine for buying a cup of coffee but not so good to use for rental cars or hotel bills, where blocking can tie up hundreds of dollars."

What to Watch Out For

Accidental Overdrafts—and the Huge Fees They Generate

It used to be that if you didn't have enough money in your account to cover an ATM withdrawal or debit card purchase, standard bank practice was to deny the transaction. But these days the opposite is true. Banks now routinely approve such transactions, often without alerting you that you've spent more than you have—and that as a result you are going to be charged an overdraft fee that could be as high as $40.

Given how things like "blocking" can lead unwary debit card users to overestimate how much available cash they've got at any given moment, it's no surprise that these unanticipated, unnoticed overdrafts happen all the time. Indeed, it's partly why debit cards are so profitable for the banks. According to the Center for Responsible Lending, roughly half of the $17.5 billion in overdraft fees the banks collected in 2007 were the result of ATM and debit card overdrafts.

These overdraft fees are not only unfair, they are also extremely expensive. That's because what they really are is a finance charge on a short-term loan to cover your overdraft. And on that basis, they may be one of the most outrageous rip-offs around. As I mentioned in the introduction to this chapter, according to calculations by *Consumer Reports,* a typical overdraft fee translates to an annual interest rate in excess of *1,000%!*

A Debit Card You Didn't Ask For

When your ATM card expires, most banks will replace it with a debit card—without even asking you if you want one. Given all the risks associated with debit cards, you shouldn't be shy about sending it back. The banks will give you a plain ATM card, if that's what you prefer.

What to Do if Things Go Wrong

Contact your bank immediately if your debit card is lost or stolen, or if you spot a fraud. And then monitor the situation closely.

Get It in Writing on Your Record—and Follow Up

Again, as you have learned in previous sections, start by calling the bank directly and then immediately follow up with a complaint in writing to the bank. When you place your call, be sure you request that a note be made in your file and also let them know you want to follow up by sending a letter directly to the bank in order to establish a paper trail of the complaint. Get the name of the bank manager during this call and address your letter directly to him or her. And don't forget to note the name or employee number of the person who takes your phone call. (Many of these customer-service lines are now recorded also—so your asking for this information will potentially go on record.) Check back the next day to confirm that the note is in your file. If it isn't, ask for your complaint to be recorded again, then call

She Fought for Her Money!

Here's a cautionary tale I heard from a 53-year-old woman named Jill from Tacoma, Washington.

Right after Christmas a few years ago, Jill discovered that someone was using her debit card to make purchases online. First, it was a $9.75 charge for some cosmetics, then a $269 wire payment to Western Union. Jill immediately informed the bank that she hadn't authorized those charges and asked that her card be canceled.

A few days later, she noticed another $150 in unauthorized charges—and when she called her bank's fraud department to report them, she learned that her debit card had not been canceled as promised. Even worse, the bank told her they would not stop payment on these new charges. Rather, she would have to wait for the results of an investigation before she could get a credit. After countless phone calls, she finally got through to a supervisor who was willing to refund a portion of her money, but Jill was still out about $360. It took her another 10 days to get a credit for the full amount.

"My best advice is to take this very seriously and be persistent," Jill says. "The only reason I got my money back was because I wouldn't give up. I wouldn't let them toss me aside simply because they had more claims than employees. Lenders place the burden of proof on the customer and they have no guilt about freezing disputed funds. I was lucky. Unlike many people, I still had enough cash so this wasn't a real problem. But I can imagine how someone less secure could be placed in a real financial hardship by something like this."

Jill is right. By law, even if you report debit fraud in a timely way, banks can wait two weeks or even longer to restore the funds to your account. So be prepared to be a squeaky wheel.

back to confirm that the account has been closed, is being protected or credited back, et cetera (whatever your situation requires).

If you think a bank or other financial institution has failed to fulfill its responsibilities to you, file a complaint with the federal agency that has enforcement jurisdiction over it. You'll find a full list covering all types of banks on page 77, in the section BANK ACCOUNTS. You should also file a complaint with the Federal Trade Commission either through its web site at www.FTCComplaintAssistant.gov, by calling toll-free 877-FTC-HELP (877-382-4357), or by writing to them at:

Federal Trade Commission
Consumer Response Center
600 Pennsylvania Ave., NW
Washington, DC 20580

Fight for Your Money Action Steps

☐ Call your bank today to find out what their specific liability policy is for debit cards.

☐ Know your balance before using your debit card to avoid excessive overdraft fees.

☐ Safeguard your PIN at all times.

☐ Never use your debit card at a machine with signs of physical tampering—or at an unbranded ATM.

☐ Check your bank statement online every day.

☐ *Use your debit card only for small, immediate transactions.*

Credit Cards

few years ago, I appeared on Oprah Winfrey's "Debt Diet"—a series of TV shows on which we coached America on how to get out of debt. The shows featured three couples battling to turn their finances around. The couple I coached, Dan and Sally Eggleston, had gone from a pleasant middle-class existence to a financial nightmare in just two years—mainly the result of overusing their credit cards when Dan quit his teaching job to go back to school. By the time I met them, they had maxed out a dozen credit card accounts and owed more than $72,000 in credit card debt. Struggling under the burden of interest rates as high as 29%, they found themselves getting dinged for $500 a month just in late fees and over-the-limit penalties.

Basically, they were drowning.

The sad fact is that there are millions of people just like the Egglestons. As I write this in the summer of 2008, roughly 53 million American households are carrying nearly *$1 trillion* in credit card debt. This averages out to nearly $18,000 per household, but the debt isn't actually spread evenly over everyone. According to a survey by CardTrak.com, while the median household debt is just $6,700, nearly 7 million families owe more than $25,000 each—and, not surprisingly, the number of cardholders unable to make even their minimum payments is at record levels.

Fortunately for Dan and Sally, I was able to help them put together a plan to get them back on track. But it wasn't easy and it wasn't fast. Getting out of debt rarely is easy or fast. It can take decades—unless you have a smart plan and know how to FIGHT FOR YOUR MONEY.

Unfortunately for most of us, the credit card companies are experts at encouraging us to go into debt—and keeping us there as long as possible. In fact, keeping you in debt for as long as possible is how they make money.

And they make LOTS of money—most of it from the high interest rates we pay on our unpaid balances and the unfair penalty fees they trick us into incurring. In 2007 alone, those interest charges totaled $116 billion, while fees added another $23 billion to the industry's coffers.

How to Fight for Your Money

The fact is that when they're used responsibly, credit cards are a good deal. They free you from having to pay for everything in cash, which can be a huge convenience. They also allow you to borrow money interest-free—*if* you pay your bill before the grace period ends. But let's be honest. Most people don't do this.

To be smart with your credit cards, here is what you need to know—and do.

Pick the Right Card for You

There are literally thousands of different credit cards to choose from these days: low-interest cards, rewards cards, balance-transfer cards, airline cards, student cards, prepaid cards, business cards, cash-back cards—the list goes on and on. Are you an Oakland Raiders fan? You can have an Oakland Raiders credit card. Do you love country music? You can get a Reba McEntire or Alan Jackson card. You can even get one from World Championship Wrestling with Hulk Hogan's picture on it.

But is that the right card for you? How much is the annual fee? What's the interest rate? Who issued the credit card? What happens if you are late paying? How much is the penalty? Does the contract include the dreaded Universal Default Clause? (More about this later.)

These are the types of questions you need to answer BEFORE you sign up for any credit card.

Some cards provide cardholders with elaborate concierge services, but they charge annual membership fees in the hundreds—and sometimes thousands—of dollars. Are these services worth that much to you? Other cards have no annual fee if you pay your balance in full every month. Are you going to carry a balance? If so, then you need a card with the lowest possible interest rate.

There are two easy ways to get a good sense of what's out there for you to choose from. First, simply hang on to all the junk mail you get this month. I promise you—there will be a dozen credit card offers in the pile, maybe more. Simply spread them out on your kitchen table, side by side, and compare them.

The other way is to go online. Web sites like Bankrate.com, cardratings.com, creditcards.com, lowcards.com, and lowermybills.com all offer excellent comparisons of interest rates and card features. Also, the Federal Reserve Board surveys credit card plans every six months and publishes an interactive report that makes it easy to make comparisons. You can find it online at www.federalreserve.gov/Pubs/shop/survey.htm.

Read the Fine Print

I did a public television special a few years ago where I blew up a credit card agreement and pointed out all the legal tricks the credit card companies like to play. I had to blow it up because the fine print was so small. But these agreements are not simply hard to read. They are also hard to understand. All the same, you need to read them and do your best to understand what they say. At the very least, study the disclosure box that spells out the agreement's basic terms. These include:

- The annual percentage rates (APRs) you'll be charged if you carry over a balance, transfer a balance, or get a cash advance.

- The minimum payment required and how long you can take to pay your bill in full before you get hit with a finance charge (known as the grace period).

- The method used to calculate your outstanding balance if you don't pay in full.

- Your credit limit and whether they can change it without notifying you.

- What the penalty fee is if you exceed your credit limit.

- The annual fee, if any.

- When your payment is due—and when it is considered late.

- What the penalty fee is for late payments, and whether paying late will trigger an increase in your interest rate.

- Whether the agreement includes a universal default clause (which allows the credit card company to penalize you with fees or an interest-rate hike if you are late paying some other company's bill).

Using a credit card without knowing the terms of your account is simply dangerous. It can cost you hundreds if not thousands of dollars a year. To make sure you're not ripped off, you have to pay attention—you have to FIGHT.

Ask for a Lower Rate

Just because a credit card company sticks you with a high interest rate doesn't mean you have to accept it. This is especially true if you have decent credit, a record of paying on time, and haven't maxed out your card.

Here's what you do. First make sure you know the rate you're currently paying and the kind of rates other banks are offering. (You can do this by checking your latest credit card statement and then going online to a site like Bankrate.com that posts comprehensive lists of what kind of interest virtually every credit card company in the country is charging.) Then find the "Customer Service" phone number on your statement, call your credit card company, and ask to speak with a supervisor. Don't try to negotiate a lower rate with the first person who answers the phone. The people who answer the phones generally don't have the authority to approve changes, so you'd just be wasting your time.

When you are connected to the supervisor, tell him or her that a competing bank is offering you a much lower interest rate than the one you're currently paying—and that unless he can match or beat the competitor's rate, you intend to transfer your balance to that competitor. Don't be vague: Tell the supervisor the name of the competing bank and the actual interest rate it is offering. Chances are that the supervisor will agree to lower your rate on the spot. This is particularly likely if your interest rate is, say, 25% and the average on cards at the time of your call is 12%. According to the *Wall Street Journal,* more than 75% of the people who call their credit card companies to ask for a lower rate are successful on the first call. If you are not that fortunate, don't give up. Just call back and speak to someone else.

> More than 75% of the people who call their credit card companies to ask for a lower rate are successful on the first call.

Be aware that there are often many levels of supervisors. The departments that handle these calls have on average two to five levels of management. So if the supervisor you get the first time around doesn't give you what you want, ask to speak to that supervisor's manager. And if you don't like what he or she tells you, ask to speak to his or her superior.

One other thing: Make sure you write down the names of everyone you talk to. If you're told company policy forbids giving out last names, ask for an identification number. Not only will this enable you to keep track of all the different supervisors and managers you're bound to wind up dealing with, it will also make the customer-service people wary of offending you. Generally speaking, as long as you are polite and reasonable, they will probably try their best to satisfy your request because ultimately they want to keep your business.

If They Won't Negotiate, Ask to Have the Account Closed

If they won't work with you, tell them you want to close your account. Often this will lead the person who took your call to transfer you to a new department—one whose job is to talk customers like you out of canceling their cards. They will likely ask you why are you closing your account—at which point you can explain that it's because of the high interest rate you're being charged: Their refusal to lower it gives you no choice but to transfer your balance to a competitor.

Time and time again, this "close my account" approach gets cardholders a lower interest rate. (If it doesn't work, then you should transfer your balance to a competitor with better rates.)

Once your interest rate has been lowered, keep in mind that there's nothing preventing you from calling back and asking them to lower it AGAIN. In fact, I recommend you put a reminder in your calendar to call the credit card company 90 days after you get your rate lowered to see if they will lower it again. Often, they will—especially if you have paid your bills on time.

And don't give up. I have been in situations where it took as many as nine calls to get a rate lowered. Believe me—it's worth the effort. In total, those nine calls took a total of maybe two hours spread over a few weeks—and they resulted in thousands of dollars in lower interest payments in the first year alone.

Don't Mix Purchases, Balance Transfers, and Cash Advances

If you carry over balances and use your card for a variety of different kinds of transactions—that is, purchases *and* cash advances *and* balance transfers—chances are you will be charged a variety of different interest rates. Usually, the rate for balance transfers is the lowest, with the purchase rate in the middle and the cash-advance rate up in the stratosphere somewhere. Common sense will tell you that you should try first to pay off the portion of the balance with the highest interest rate. Common sense is correct, but as we've seen, the banks don't like it when consumers act sensibly. So they make it difficult if not impossible to do this.

Say you're carrying a total balance on your card of $5,000. Of that, $1,500 is for purchases, for which the interest rate is 11.9%; $1,000 is for cash advances, which have a painful 19.99% rate; and the remaining $2,500 is the result of a balance transfer, which you made because they offered you a special promotional rate of just 4.99%. Now, if you could afford to send the company only $1,000, you would probably want it to be applied to that high-interest cash advance.

Unfortunately, that's not what the bank will do. Generally speaking, when you make a partial payment on a balance with several different interest rates, the bank will first apply your payment not to the portion with the highest rate but to the portion with the *lowest* rate—in this case, the $2,500 you owe for the balance transfer. Once that's been paid off, they'll start applying payments to the balance with next-highest interest rate—your purchase balance. And only then, after that's been paid off, will they start letting you get rid of the high-interest cash-advance balance. This is very good for them and very bad for you.

The Federal Reserve has proposed a rule that would bar this practice, and by the time you read this, it may have been adopted. If it hasn't been, there are only two things you can do to protect your money. Either pay off your balance in full or, if this is impossible, adopt a policy of using separate credit cards for purchases, cash advances, and balance transfers. That way you—and not the bank—can decide how your monthly payment should be allocated.

Opt Out of Preapproved Solicitations

Credit card companies send out about 6 billion such solicitations a year. The most dangerous of these are the preapproved or prescreened offers, where card issuers have checked out your credit history in advance. Not only do they pose a dangerous temptation, but if they fall into the wrong hands, they can expose you to the risk of identity theft. Fortunately, there is an easy way to stop the credit card companies from sending you these sorts of offers. The major credit-reporting companies have a service called OptOutPrescreen, which allows you to opt out of receiving offers of credit or insurance that you didn't ask for. You can do so permanently or just for five years. For details, call them toll-free at 888-5-OPTOUT (888-567-8688) or visit them online at www.optoutprescreen.com.

What to Watch Out For

The Minimum-Payment Trap

The dirty secret of the modern credit card industry is that the banks don't want you to pay off your balance. Their profits go up if you only make "minimum payments." And they're smart enough to know that if they ratchet the minimum payment down low enough (usually between 2% and 4% of your total balance), you'll keep spending money and they can make a fortune on you.

Not surprisingly, they don't want you to understand this. They don't want you to know that if you carry a $10,000 balance at an interest rate of 18% (which is typical of credit card users who don't pay off their bills in full each month) and make only a $200 minimum payment each month, it will take you *nearly 32 years* to get out of debt—and before you do, you will have forked over nearly $15,000 in interest charges. And that's assuming you never charge another dime on the card, never get hit with a late charge, are never billed for an annual service fee, and your interest rate never goes up.

WHAT HAPPENS WHEN YOU MAKE THE MINIMUM PAYMENT
ON A $10,000 BALANCE

Interest Rate	How Long to Pay Off in Full	Total Interest Charges
8%	18 years, 5 months	$3,558
10%	20 years, 1 month	$4,888
12%	22 years, 1 month	$6,513
18%	31 years, 10 months	$14,615
20%	37 years, 8 months	$19,466
30%	50 years, 1 month	$150,250

The Old Switcheroo

Credit card issuers can change the terms of your account, hiking your interest rate, lowering your credit limit, and shortening your payment deadlines, anytime they want for no particular reason. Generally speaking, the bank must notify you of any changes at least 15 days in advance and give you the chance to opt out if you don't like the new rules. (If you choose to opt out, they can close your account but you get to pay off your balance at the old terms.)

But don't expect the notification to be all that noticeable. The banks deliberately design these notices to look like junk mail so most people will throw them away without opening them.

> The banks deliberately design change notifications to look like junk mail so most people will throw them away without opening them.

The problem is that throwing out or otherwise ignoring the notice means you've accepted the new terms. You have to take action to opt out, either calling or writing to the bank.

There is one situation where the credit card company doesn't have to notify you of a change: when an increase in your interest rate is triggered by what's considered a *default* on your part—in other words, when you exceed your credit limit or make a late payment. Most credit card agreements entitle the issuer to jack you up to a much higher penalty rate for violating any of the rules. And those penalty rates can be brutal. Some run as high as 35%.

Since the banks are entitled to impose this kind of increase without warning, you should always scrutinize your statements, even if you don't think you've done anything wrong. An interest-rate hike may not necessarily be announced on a separate piece of paper. It may be buried somewhere on your bill.

Double-Cycle Billing

If you pay part of your bill before the due date and carry over part of your balance, don't assume that you'll be charged interest only on the part of your balance that you don't pay off. When you carry a balance, the bank cancels the grace period you normally get to pay off a charge without incurring interest. Instead, the bank calculates your interest charge based on your average daily balance for the entire month.

That's bad enough, but more than a third of the credit-issuing banks in the United States do something even worse. They practice what's called double-cycle billing, in which interest charges are based on your average daily balance for the past *two* billing cycles. If you always carry a balance that doesn't vary much from month to month, this may not be a big deal. But if you usually pay your bill in full and carry over a balance only occasionally, double-cycle billing can be a huge rip-off, since it can result in your being charged interest for balances you've already paid off on time.

Here's how it works. Say you put $5,000 worth of purchases on your card in January and, when the bill arrives in February, you immediately pay it in full. Assuming you didn't owe anything from any previous bills, your interest charge would be zero, since you paid off all your January charges before the grace period expired. Then, in February, you put another $1,000 worth of purchases on your card. But when the bill for these purchases arrives in March, you pay off only part of the balance. In figuring how much interest you will have to pay on your February charges, a bank that practices double-cycle billing will base its calculations not just on your average daily balance in February but on your average daily balance for both February *and* January. And since your average daily balance in January was much higher than it was in February, your interest charge will be higher—even though you paid off your January balance on time.

Not surprisingly, Congress is considering legislation to outlaw this practice. In the meantime, check the fine print of your credit card agreement. Look in the disclosure box for the entry under "Method of Computing the Balance for Purchases." If it says, "Two-cycle Average Daily Balance (including new purchases)," you're being screwed and you should switch to another credit card.

Be Wary of Balance Transfers

Credit card companies love to send you special checks you can use to pay off other credit card bills by transferring the balance to their card—usually at a lower-than-normal rate (occasionally even at zero interest). Sometimes this can be a good deal for you, but most of the time it's not.

The interest rate may be low, but hidden in the fine print you'll often find a balance-transfer fee that is usually around 3% of the total amount. This may not sound like much, but that 3% fee is really the equivalent of an additional 6% to 9% in annual interest, since most of these special balance-transfer offers—and the low interest rates that go along with them—last for only four to six months. When you figure this in, those attractive special offers lose a lot of their appeal.

So before you take advantage of any special balance-transfer offer, be sure to read the fine print and check out the terms. How long will the promotional interest rate last? How much is the balance-transfer fee? And keep in mind that if you miss the due date by even one day for just one payment, the special offer will likely be canceled and your low promotional percentage will be replaced by a stratospheric penalty rate that might be retroactively applied to the entire amount you transferred—even if most of it has already been paid off!

Universal Default—The Ultimate "Gotcha" Clause

Buried deep in most credit card agreements is a provision that gives the card company the right to jack up your interest rate if you're more than 30 days late paying *any* bill you owe to anyone—even a telephone or utility bill that has nothing to do with your credit card. This is known as universal default. Following congressional hearings in 2007, Citibank and Chase, the nation's two largest credit card issuers, announced they would end this practice. But according to Bankrate.com, nearly 40% of all credit card issuers still apply the provision to customers, even if they had no late payments on their own card.

Of all the games the credit card companies play, this one may be the most unfair. Generally, a universal default clause states that a creditor reserves the right to penalize you with an increased interest rate if you're late paying any other creditor. They justify this practice because, in theory, if you've fallen behind on any of your other debts, you pose a greater credit risk to them.

According to a study by the nonprofit advocacy and education group Consumer Action, the top three default triggers are a decline in credit score, paying your mortgage late, and paying your car loan late. How will your credit card company know? You may not realize it, but your creditors have the right to routinely monitor your credit file. So a credit card company with a universal default clause will be watching—and waiting.

> Under the universal default clause, your interest rates can be increased for exceeding your credit limit, bouncing a check, having too much debt, having too much credit, getting a new credit card, applying for a car loan, and applying for a mortgage loan.

Let's say your Visa card has a universal default clause. Any late payment—whether it's on your utility bill, home equity loan, or Macy's charge account—acts as a "default trigger" allowing the bank that issued the Visa card to double or even triple your interest rate overnight. Your all-important credit score will be hurt as well.

And that's not the half of it. Under the universal default clause, your interest rates can also be increased for exceeding your credit limit, bouncing a check, having too much debt, having too much credit, getting a new credit card, applying for a car loan, and applying for a mortgage loan.

There are basically only two ways you can protect yourself from universal default: Don't use cards that have them—or, if you have no choice, make sure to pay all your bills on time (which these days really means paying them all a few days early).

To make sure you're not caught by surprise, check your current credit card agreements to see if any of them contain a universal default clause. If you're confused by the fine print (welcome to the club!), call your credit card company and ask them what specific circumstances can affect your interest rate. If it turns out that your cards do have the clause, you should consider transferring your balance to a card that doesn't. But don't rush to cancel the account altogether, because that could have a negative effect on your credit score.

Confusing Deadlines

The quickest way to make your interest rate skyrocket is to pay your credit card bill late. Needless to say, the banks love it when you do this because it adds to their profits. As a result, they do everything they can to make it difficult for you to pay on time.

When you're paying your taxes, all the IRS asks is that you get your payment in the mail by the deadline date. Visa and MasterCard are not so easygoing. If you mail in your payment, it needs to *arrive* at the bank by the due date; it's not enough for it to be postmarked by the due date. To make matters worse, many card issuers have a daily cutoff—often 3 P.M. Eastern Standard Time—after which they will no longer credit your payment that day. And many won't process payments made on a holiday or a weekend until the following business day.

So read your credit card agreement carefully and make sure you know what the cutoff deadline is. Ideally, you should pay your bill the same day you receive it, or at the very least four or five days before the due date.

> Ideally, you should pay your bill the same day you receive it, or at the very least four or five days before the due date.

If you have trouble making your due date because it's out of sync with when you get paid, call your credit card company and ask them whether they can change your due date so it coincides with your payroll schedule. And to eliminate the risk of forgetting, consider arranging an automatic-payment program for your credit card bills. You can also sign up for free email or phone alerts to help you remember to pay your bill on time.

What to Do if Things Go Wrong

Thanks to the Fair Credit Billing Act, which was enacted by Congress back in 1986, credit card users have plenty of protection when it comes to fraudulent purchases, poor-quality or damaged merchandise, or merchandise that was never delivered. Here's how it works.

Unauthorized Charges

Everyone knows that you should report a lost or stolen card immediately. That's because if you report the loss before the card is used, you can't be held responsible for any unauthorized charges. But even if you don't and a thief goes on a spending spree with it, the law limits your liability to a maximum of $50. What's more, most of the major companies (including American Express, MasterCard, and Visa) have zero-liability policies that free you of any responsibility for the unauthorized use of a lost or stolen card regardless of when you report it.

Most issuers maintain a 24-hour toll-free "lost or stolen card" number for you to call when your card goes missing. You'll find it on your statement. It's a good idea to follow up your telephone report with a letter. Include your account number, the date you noticed your card missing, and the date you reported the loss.

Billing Errors

If your credit card statement includes a bill from a merchant who over-charged you, charged you for a product you never received, or sent you defective goods, you can and should dispute it. Provided you register your complaint in writing within 60 days, credit card companies are obliged to look into the problem and cancel any improper charges.

To dispute an improper or erroneous charge, write to your credit card company at the address listed on your statement for "billing inquiries"—not the same address where you send payments. Send the letter by certified mail and request a return receipt. This is your proof that you responded during the required 60-day period. Include your name, address, account number, and a description of the billing error, including the amount and date of the error. (You'll find a sample letter you can use as a model on page 392 of the FFYM Toolkit.) Even if an identity thief changed the address on your account and you did not receive the bill, you still must dispute the charge within 60 days. So try to keep track of your billing statements and contact your card company if your bill doesn't arrive on time.

While you're disputing an error, you don't have to pay the disputed amount or any finance charges on it and your credit card company cannot report the nonpayment to a credit bureau as a delinquency. (Of course, a dispute doesn't get you off the hook from paying the rest of your credit card bill.) The credit card company must acknowledge your complaint in writing within 30 days of getting your letter and it must resolve the dispute within two billing cycles and in no case more than 90 days. When all is said and done, they must either issue you a permanent credit against the disputed charge or explain to you in writing why your complaint was rejected.

Bad Products or Services

One of the advantages of using a credit card is that if you are not satisfied with the quality of the product or service you purchased with it, you can withhold payment. Before you do so, you must make a good-faith effort to resolve the issue with the merchant. And you can only invoke this right if what you bought with your card cost more than $50 and was purchased within 100 miles of your mailing address. These limitations don't apply if your credit card issuer was also the merchant who sold you the disputed goods (for example, if you bought something at a department store using the store's own card) or if you made the purchase in response to an advertisement sent to you by the seller.

If you and the merchant are unable to work things out relatively quickly, you should write to your credit card company and inform them you wish to withhold payment. But do this *only* if you have a valid complaint against the merchant. Simply changing your mind about a purchase you made isn't good enough. As with a disputed charge, once you inform the credit card company that you want to withhold payment, they can't report the amount as delinquent until the dispute is settled or a court judgment is issued against you.

Poor Treatment by the Credit Card Issuer

If your credit card company itself is the problem, you should obviously first try to work things out through its customer-service department. But if they are unable or unwilling to help, there are a number of outside agencies you can turn to, including the Better Business Bureau (www.bbb.org) and, if you are a senior, AARP (www.aarp.org). You should also contact the appropriate government agency from the list below. And if the case is particularly egregious, you might also want to complain to your local congressman. (You can find his or her contact information by going online to www.congress.org/congressorg/home and entering your ZIP code.)

For problems involving credit cards issued by national banks (banks with "national" in their name or the initials "N.A." after it), you should contact the Comptroller of the Currency (www.occ.treas.gov).

Office of the Comptroller of the Currency
Customer Assistance Group
1301 McKinney Street, Suite 3450
Houston, TX 77010
(800) 613-6743
customer.assistance@occ.treas.gov

For problems involving credit cards issued by state-chartered banks that are members of the Federal Reserve System, you should contact the Federal Reserve's Consumer Help department (www.FederalReserveConsumer Help.gov).

Federal Reserve Consumer Help
P.O. Box 1200
Minneapolis, MN 55480
(888) 851-1920
ConsumerHelp@FederalReserve.gov

For problems involving credit cards issued by state-chartered banks that are not members of the Federal Reserve System, you should contact the FDIC (www.fdic.gov). Most complaints are best filed using their Electronic Customer Assistance Form, available online at www4.fdic.gov/STARSMAIL/index.asp.

Federal Deposit Insurance Corporation
Consumer Response Center
2345 Grand Boulevard, Suite 100
Kansas City, MO 64108
(877) 275-3342
consumeralerts@fdic.gov

For problems involving credit cards issued by federally chartered credit unions (those with "federal" in their name), you should contact the National Credit Union Administration (www.ncua.gov).

National Credit Union Administration
Consumer Assistance Center
1775 Duke Street
Alexandria, VA 22314-3428
(800) 755-1030
consumerassistance@ncua.gov

For problems involving credit cards issued by federal savings-and-loan associations and federal savings banks, you should contact the federal Office of Thrift Supervision (www.ots.treas.gov).

Office of Thrift Supervision
Consumer Inquiries
1700 G Street NW, 6th Floor
Washington, DC 20552
(800) 842-6929
consumer.complaint@ots.treas.gov

For problems involving credit cards issued by finance companies or stores, you should contact the Federal Trade Commission (www.ftc.gov):

Federal Trade Commission
Consumer Response Center
600 Pennsylvania Ave., NW
Washington, DC 20580
(877) FTC-HELP (877-382-4357)

Fight for Your Money Action Steps

☐ Go online to research credit cards with the best rates.

☐ Know your payment due dates. Set up an automatic-payment program to avoid being late and incurring fees.

☐ Never pay only the minimum.

☐ Scrutinize your statements for sneaky interest-rate hikes and unexpected fees.

☐ Renegotiate your interest rates.

☐ Don't accept a credit card with a universal default clause or two-cycle billing.

Free! My Gift to You

In *The Finish Rich Workbook*, I wrote a detailed chapter on credit card debt. If you feel you need help, visit my web site at **www.finishrich.com** to download this chapter for free.

Credit Scores

P eople get measured and tested in all sorts of ways these days, but of all the scores that are applied to you, probably none—not your IQ score, your SAT score, or your cholesterol score—has more immediate impact on how you live than your credit score. This three-digit figure pretty much determines whether you'll be able to get a credit card, a car loan, or a mortgage—and how much interest you'll have to pay if you do. In many states, it may even affect your insurance rates and your ability to get a job or rent an apartment. And in the aftermath of the 2008 mortgage meltdown, with the credit markets tighter and lenders more conservative, your credit score is more important today than ever.

So you need to know your credit score now. And if it's not so good, you need to know what you can do to improve it. The good news here is that no matter how irresponsible or unlucky you have been, you can fight your way back. The bad news is that there are no quick fixes or magic solutions. Unfortunately, this doesn't stop tens of thousands of desperate people from paying millions of dollars each year to phony "credit repair" outfits that claim they can boost anyone's credit score, regardless of how bad their credit history might be.

How to Fight for Your Money

The most important thing you can do to help your credit score is understand what it is. To begin with, you should know that you don't have just one credit score—you have a bunch of them. That's because lenders, creditors, and the three national credit-reporting agencies (Equifax, Experian, and TransUnion) all have their own particular methods and formulas for calculating what kind of a credit risk you are. They may also have different information about you.

The most widely used credit-scoring system was developed back in 1989 by a company called Fair Isaac Corp. The idea was to give lenders a quick and easy way to judge an individual's creditworthiness. What Fair Isaac does is take your credit history and run it through a complicated series of calculations. The result is a number somewhere between 300 and 850. This is your FICO score. Anything over 700 is considered good. Score 750 or higher and most lenders will give you their best deals. On the other hand, a score below 500 means you will have trouble getting a loan no matter how high an interest rate you're willing to pay. As of 2008, the median FICO score in the United States was 723—meaning that half of all Americans scored higher than that and half scored lower.

The table below is similar to one you'll find on the FICO web site (www.myfico.com) that shows how differing FICO scores will affect the mortgage rates banks are willing to offer you.

HOW FICO SCORES AFFECT YOUR MORTGAGE

Score	Interest Rate	Monthly Payment
760–850	6.26%	$1,849
700–759	6.48%	$1,893
680–699	6.77%	$1,949
620–659	7.58%	$2,113
580–619	9.45%	$2,512
500–579	10.31%	$2,702

(based on a $300,000, 30-year, fixed-rate mortgage, as of 7/22/08)

As you can see, a difference of just a few dozen points in your credit score can make a difference of hundreds of dollars in interest payments each month—and tens, if not hundreds, of thousands of dollars over the life of a mortgage. The same is true for auto loans and credit card rates.

WHAT YOU WILL PAY OVER 30 YEARS ON A $300,000 MORTGAGE

With a 760 FICO Score:	$665,640
With a 650 FICO Score:	$760,680
Improve your credit score and you save:	**$95,040**

While FICO is the oldest and most popular credit-scoring system, it's not the only one. Since 2006, Experian, Equifax, and TransUnion have been pushing their own rating system, which they call VantageScore. Its gimmick is that its three-digit scores, which run from 501 to 990, translate into letter grades just like you got in elementary school. A score of 901 to 990 earns you an A, a score of 801 to 900 is worth a B—and so on, right down to a score of 501 to 600, which gets you an F.

Whether you're talking about FICO or VantageScore or some other system, the main factors that go into determining your credit score are all related to how you handle money in general and debt in particular. They include:

- Your payment history (whether you pay your bills on time, how often you're late, and for how long)

- Your utilization rate—how much of your total available credit you are using. (The lower the better.)

- How much you currently owe. (Less is better.)

- Whether you've gotten any new credit lately. (This could lower your score.)

- How far back your credit history goes. (The longer your credit history, the better your score.)

By changing these factors—say, by paying off a big chunk of what you owe—you can change your credit score.

Here are some basic tips for managing your credit score effectively.

Find Out How You Rate

The first thing you need to do is find out how you rate. By law, the three big credit bureaus must provide every consumer who asks with a free copy of their credit report once a year. You can get yours by going online to a web site the three companies jointly sponsor at www.annualcreditreport.com. You can also mail in a request to Annual Credit Report Request Service at P.O. Box 105281, Atlanta, GA 30348-5281, or call them toll-free at (877) 322-8228.

As I indicated above, each credit bureau has its own records and issues its own reports, so you need to get a copy of what each of them is saying about you. But don't get all three reports at once. Instead, stagger your requests— for example, ordering your Equifax report first, then your Experian report four months later, and finally your TransUnion report four months after that. And then, in another four months, a full year will have passed since you ordered your Equifax reports and you can start all over again. In this way, you can monitor your credit activity throughout the year for free.

> Through www. annualcreditreport. com, you can monitor your credit activity throughout the year for free.

Keep in mind that your credit report is not your credit score. Your score is *based* on your reports— and, unfortunately, while the law gives you free access to your credit report, you have to pay extra to get the score. You can buy your FICO score from Fair Isaac through its web site at www.MyFico.com. The cost is $38.28 for your scores from all three credit bureaus, or $15.95 each. You can get your VantageScore, for about the same price, from Equifax (www.equifax.com), Experian (www.experian.com) or TransUnion (www.transunion.com), or through www.annualcreditreport.com.

Look for Errors—and Correct Them!

One of the most important reasons to get copies of your credit reports is so you can check them for accuracy. Having coached thousands of people on the process of both pulling and fixing their credit scores, I can tell you from personal experience that you will probably find they contain some incorrect information about you or your credit history. In fact, according to a 2004 study by the U.S. Public Interest Research Group, no fewer than one of every four credit reports contains at least one major mistake serious enough to keep you from getting a loan, a credit card, and in some cases a job.

Given what's at stake, it's vitally important that you check out your credit reports and get any errors corrected as quickly as possible. Fortunately, it's not very difficult to do this. Under the Fair Credit Reporting Act, both the credit-reporting agencies and the banks and merchants that provide them with data are required to correct inaccurate or incomplete information in your report when it's pointed out to them.

So if you find any inaccuracies, point them out! You can do this by sending the credit agency a letter by certified mail that explains what information was inaccurate, including copies of documents (such as bank records or mortgage statements) that verify what you're saying, along with a copy of your credit report with the disputed information circled in red. Unless your complaint is clearly frivolous, the company is generally required to investigate it within 30 days.

In the FFYM Toolkit on page 393, there's a sample letter you can use as a model. Here's contact information for the three national companies.

Equifax Information Services, LLC
P.O. Box 740256
Atlanta, GA 30374-0256
(800) 685-1111
www.equifax.com

Experian
888-EXPERIAN (888-397-3742)
www.experian.com

Experian requires consumers who have found inaccuracies in their credit reports to file their disputes online. For details, go to www.experian.com/disputes/index.html.

TransUnion Consumer Solutions
P.O. Box 2000
Chester, PA 19022-2000
(800) 916-8800
www.transunion.com

You can download a dispute form at www.transunion.com/corporate/personal/creditDisputes/mail.page.

Raise Your Score by Paying Down High Balances

There are lots of myths about things you can do to improve your credit score. In fact, there really isn't any mystery about it. On its web site, Fair Isaac spells out how it weighs the various factors that go into calculating your score: payment history counts for 35%, amount owed (which includes both the dollar amount and your utilization rate) is 30%, length of credit history is 15%, how many new accounts you've opened is 10%, and types of credit used is 10%. If you want to raise your score, the question is: Which of these factors can you affect? And how long will it take?

Obviously, there's not a lot you can do about the most important factor, your payment history. It is what it is. If you have a habit of making late payments, you should certainly try to do better. But even if you never miss a payment deadline again, it will take several years for this to be reflected in your credit score. As the Federal Trade Commission points out on its web site: "When negative information in your report is accurate, only the passage of time can assure its removal. A consumer reporting company can report most accurate negative information for seven years and bankruptcy information for 10 years."

On the other hand, the second most important factor, amounts owed, *is* something you can change. Indeed, there is nothing you can do that will have a positive impact on your credit score more quickly than reducing the amount you owe.

She Fought for Her Money!

What if your credit is terrible? The fact is, you can turn an awful credit score into a great one. It just takes time and discipline. I know a woman from Houston, a realtor and mother of two named Susan, who managed to raise her credit score by 186 points—from 582 to 768—in three years. She did it by setting a goal and sticking to it.

The first step was to get her whole family to make a commitment to becoming debt-free. "It's important to involve the whole family or it won't work right," Susan says. "Don't make it like a fad diet that makes you feel like you are neglecting yourself or that life is all of a sudden plain and boring, because if you do that, you'll wind up going back to old habits."

Once her family was on board, Susan cut up her credit cards and started paying off the balances, one by one. The family lived frugally, on a strict budget that eliminated all unnecessary spending. They canceled premium cable and Netflix, and cut back on family vacations.

Susan first paid off the credit cards with the lowest balances, so she could enjoy some small successes. She kept track of her debts on a computer spreadsheet, and each time she zeroed one out, it gave her additional motivation to keep going.

Thirty days after she paid off each credit card, Susan would check her credit report and credit score to make sure her accomplishment had been accurately reported to the credit-reporting agencies. At the same time, she was careful not to add on any new debt, never to miss a payment deadline, and to refrain from opening any new accounts.

Today, her credit is excellent. But that doesn't mean she's easing up. Her goal now is to see her score crack 800.

Closing Old Acccounts Doesn't Help—It Hurts

One of the myths about credit scores is that you can improve your numbers by closing down old credit card accounts that you no longer use. In fact, the opposite is true. Closing down old accounts generally hurts your credit score.

Closing down old accounts generally hurts your credit score.

Not only does it shorten your credit history, which accounts for 15% of your FICO score, but it also can increase your credit utilization rate, which is an even more important factor.

Here's how that works. Let's say you have two credit cards, a Visa and a MasterCard, each with a $5,000 credit limit, but you use only the Visa card. If you are carrying a $2,500 balance on your Visa account, your credit-utilization rate would be 25%, since your total available credit from both cards is $10,000. However, if you closed the MasterCard account, your total available credit would drop to $5,000, which would raise your credit-utilization rate to 50%—and that would hurt your credit score.

That's not to say you shouldn't close some accounts if you think doing so will help you manage credit more wisely and prevent you from racking up too much debt. But don't do it because you think it might help your credit score.

Watch Those Inquiries

Too many credit inquiries can hurt your credit score. You may think there's no harm in having an auto dealership or mortgage broker run your credit, but to the credit-rating companies, a sudden surge in inquiries is a sign that you may be in danger of overextending yourself. That may sound silly, but according to Fair Isaac, people with six or more inquiries on their credit report are up to eight times more likely to declare bankruptcy than people with none. So don't let merchants or financial institutions run your credit unless it's absolutely necessary. (This isn't the case when you check your own credit score.)

What to Watch Out For

Credit-Repair Firms That Promise to "Clean Up" Your Credit Report

"Increase your credit score by 61 points in 30 days!"
   "We can erase your bad credit—100% guaranteed!"

"We can remove bankruptcies, judgments, liens, and bad loans from your credit file forever!"

The come-ons can be hard to resist, especially if you've got real credit problems.

Too bad it's all bunk. The fact is that when it comes to credit repair there are no magic bullets. Certainly, there is no legal way to rid a credit report of negative information that is accurate and timely. Nor is it really possible, as some of these outfits claim, to take advantage of the 30-day investigation deadline by swamping the credit bureaus with baseless error disputes. As for the folks who say you can create a new, unblemished credit identity for yourself by applying for an Employer Identification Number and using that instead of your Social Security number—well, there's a word for that sort of thing (actually two words): criminal fraud.

The bottom line is that there isn't anything a credit-repair company can do for you legally that you can't do for yourself—and probably for free.

> There isn't anything that a credit-repair company can do for you legally that you can't do for yourself—and probably for free.

As Steve Baker, an FTC official who spearheaded a government crackdown on credit-repair scams in 2007, told the *Los Angeles Times*: "I remember the head of our consumer protection bureau saying a few years ago [that] she had never seen a legitimate credit repair company. And I don't think we have yet."

There are three big tip-offs that a credit-repair offer is not to be trusted.

- THEY GUARANTEE AMAZING RESULTS UP FRONT. Legitimate credit counselors don't give guarantees—and certainly not before they know your situation.

- THEY ASK FOR PAYMENT IN ADVANCE. This is actually illegal. Under both federal and some states' laws, credit-repair services are not allowed to accept payment until they have actually performed the services they promised.

- THEY ADVISE YOU NOT TO CONTACT A CREDIT BUREAU DIRECTLY. Usually, this is so they can get you to pay them to file a dispute that you could easily file yourself for free.

Credit-repair outfits are sometimes confused with credit-counseling services, which are usually nonprofit entities that help people figure out how to pay off their debts. If your situation is so bad that you're tempted to try a credit-repair service, try a credit counselor instead. Sadly, some credit-counseling services have earned a bad reputation for charging high fees. So before signing up with one, be sure to check them out with the Better Business Bureau.

One of the better bets is a local Consumer Credit Counseling Service affiliated with the National Foundation for Credit Counseling. The NFCC can refer you to an office in your area. You can contact them by calling toll-free (800) 388-2227 or by visiting their web site at www.nfcc.org.

Make Sure Your "Free" Credit Report Really Is Free and Not a Membership

If you watch television, you are bound to see commercials offering a "free credit report." These ads will push you to web sites that promote the importance of getting your free credit report and having your credit regularly monitored. But before you sign up for anything, READ THE FINE PRINT! A lot of these offers really aren't free. For example, Experian sponsors a web site called FreeCreditReport.com through which you can order a supposedly "free" credit report. But as the site points out (in hard-to-read type), there's a catch: "When you order your free report here, you will begin your free trial membership in Triple Advantage^{SM} Credit Monitoring. If you don't cancel your membership within the 7-day trial period, you will be billed $14.95 for each month that you continue your membership." As I mentioned earlier, the way to get a really free credit report is through www.annualcreditreport.com.

Outdated Information on Your Credit Report

There is one foolproof way to get accurate negative information removed from your credit report, and that's to be patient. Most bad marks are supposed to stay in your file for only seven years; the main exceptions are bankruptcies (which stick around for ten years) and criminal convictions (which never come off).

That said, don't expect the credit bureau to automatically clean up your report without your requesting it. So when you're going over your credit report, keep an eye out not only for errors but also for negative information that should have already dropped off but hasn't. If you find any, file a dispute report.

What to Do if Things Go Wrong

The dispute-resolution process with the credit-rating companies is strictly regulated, and while it's not foolproof, it is chock-full of protections for the consumer.

Specifically, you have the right to dispute any information in your credit report that you regard as incomplete or inaccurate—and unless your dispute is frivolous, the credit agency must investigate it. Moreover, if it turns out you're right, the credit agency must correct or delete the bad information within 30 days (though they can continue to report information they have verified as being accurate). And even if your complaint is rejected by the credit agency, you have the right to insist that a statement of the dispute be included in your file and in all future reports. You can even make the company send your dispute statement to anyone who received a copy of your report in the recent past (though you may have to pay a fee for this).

Still, no process is perfect, and if you have a complaint with any of the credit-rating agencies—or with a credit-repair outfit—you should report it to the Federal Trade Commission (www.ftc.gov), which enforces the Federal Fair Credit Reporting Act. You can use the FTC online complaint form at www.ftccomplaintassistant.gov or you can contact the FTC Consumer Response Center in Washington, D.C. The toll-free telephone number is 877-FTC-HELP (877-382-4357) and the mailing address is:

Federal Trade Commission
Consumer Response Center
600 Pennsylvania Ave., NW
Washington, DC 20580

Fight for Your Money Action Steps

☐ Find out your credit score today by visiting www.myfico.com.

☐ Get a free copy of your credit report from www.annualcreditreport.com.

☐ Review your credit report for mistakes. Report any inaccuracies right away, and follow up to be sure they've been corrected.

☐ Work on paying off your balances in order to raise your credit score.

☐ Have patience *and* persistence. Set a goal and stick to it—and watch your credit score improve.

Payday Loans

Not too long ago, I got a letter from a reader in Raleigh, North Carolina, that told me everything I needed to know about payday loans. Alicia was a 64-year-old retail clerk with a problem. Christmas was approaching and she didn't have enough money in her checking account to be able to buy her grandchildren gifts *and* pay her utility bills. So she did what 19 million or so other Americans do every year. She went to one of those stores with a sign in the window saying "Get Cash Now! Bad Credit OK!" and took out a payday loan.

The result was a financial nightmare. Alicia originally borrowed $400 for what was supposed to be two weeks, but when the due date came around, she didn't have the $460 she now owed (for the principal plus a $60 loan fee). Because the lender wouldn't take a partial payment, she had no choice but to take out a new loan with a higher fee to pay back the old one. Before she knew it, she was caught in a vicious cycle. Every other Friday, she would get up early in the morning, use her paycheck to pay off one loan, and immediately turn around and take out another one. "It was like a merry-go-round," Alicia wrote me. "I was a wreck."

By the time she managed to get off the treadmill, she had forked out $1,780 to repay a $400 loan.

Payday lending is a booming business. With upward of 25,000 outlets across the country—more than Starbucks and McDonald's combined—payday lenders claim they are helping out cash-strapped wage earners by providing some $40 billion a year in short-term loans. In fact, they make their money by charging INSANELY HIGH FEES that end up trapping people in a never-ending cycle of two-week cash advances that they are unable to pay off. Because the lenders don't accept installment payments, payday borrowers who can't come up with the entire amount they owe have to keep "flipping" their loans—and each time they do, a new, higher loan fee is added to the total.

Of course, what the lenders call fees are really exorbitant interest charges, typically with APRs as high as 400%—and sometimes more than 1,000%. As a result, according to figures compiled by the Center for Responsible Lending in 2006, even though the average payday loan customer borrows only $325, he winds up paying back $793.

While payday borrowers struggle to make ends meet, the lenders make out like bandits. In that same 2006 report, the CRL estimated that payday lenders were raking in more than $4.2 billion a year in predatory fees. The numbers today are probably much worse.

The bottom line about payday loans is: YOU MUST KNOW THE FACTS AND THE COSTS. It is truly in your financial self-interest to do just about anything else you can before you turn to this as a solution.

How to Fight for Your Money

There's no question that payday loans can be tempting if you're short of cash. It doesn't matter how bad your credit is. As long as you have a checking account and can produce a payroll stub showing that you receive a regular paycheck, a payday lender will be happy to take care of you.

What they do is have you write them a postdated check for the amount you want to borrow plus fees. The lender holds your check until your next payday, at which point he either deposits your check or you come in with the cash and take back your check.

If you don't have the money to cover your check, the lender will be happy to roll over your loan—that is, make you a new loan to pay off the old one. Of course, the new loan will be bigger than what you initially borrowed, since you now owe not only the original principal but also the fee they charged you. And that means the fee for the new loan will be larger too.

Do You Really Want to Pay 1,564% Interest?

Typically, payday lenders charge around $17.50 for every $100 you borrow. On a two-week loan, this is the equivalent of an annual interest rate of 426.25%! And if you think that's high, consider that some of these guys charge as much as $30 for a $100 loan—which works out to an APR of 1,564%!

ANYTHING IS BETTER THAN THIS

Average interest rate on a credit card:	12%
Average interest rate on a payday loan:	426%

Say you're borrowing $100. To begin with, you write the lender a post-dated check for $117.50. If you can't cover that check when the loan comes due, the only way to get him to rip it up is for you to take out a new loan covering the $100 you borrowed and the $17.50 you were charged. But the amount of the new loan won't be $117.50. It will be $138.06—the $117.50 you failed to pay plus a *new* fee of $20.56 for this new loan. So now you write the lender a postdated check for $138.06. If you can't cover this when it comes due, your third loan will be even bigger—the $138.06 you already owe plus another new fee of $24.16, for a grand total of $162.22. By the time you get to your third flip, you will owe more than $191—or nearly twice what you borrowed in the first place. And on and on it goes.

Anything Is Better Than This

Those numbers add up to a royal rip-off. That's why, according to the Consumer Federation of America, as of 2008 payday lending was banned outright or otherwise prevented by legislation in a dozen states, Puerto Rico, the Virgin Islands, and the District of Columbia. And it's why Congress responded to complaints that payday lenders were targeting young soldiers by passing a law in 2006 barring anyone from making loans to military personnel with APRs higher than 36%. Unfortunately, the practice is still legal everywhere else.

As Alicia, the grandmother from Raleigh, wrote me: "These gifts that I bought, they were long gone and half of them were destroyed, and I was still paying for them. At the time, you think there's no other way, and you're desperate, and they make it so easy. You think, 'Well, I could do this and I can pay it back.' If you're desperate, go to your family or a close friend, or try to deal with your problem. Talk to your creditors and try to set up some kind of arrangement. Or go to your church to ask for help."

A Sign That Something Is Amiss?

Number of states where payday loans are banned outright: 12
Anything is better than a payday loan.

Alicia is right. No matter how desperate you are, there are plenty of alternatives to borrowing from a payday lender. To begin with, ask your boss if you can get an advance on your paycheck. If you're a reliable worker, he may well say yes—and not even charge you any interest.

If that's not an option, check with your credit union, bank, or local community-based organization to see if they offer short-term loans at more reasonable rates. And contact your creditors to ask for more time to pay your bills or negotiate a payment plan.

Take it from Alicia—anything is better than a payday loan. "You feel like it's a quick fix," she said. "You think you're going to be paying back just what you borrow. But it's just an endless merry-go-round. You feel like you're never going to get off. People can justify it all that they want. I've got the scars."

What to Do if Things Go Wrong

If you're trapped in the revolving door of payday loans, there are many nonprofit credit-counseling services that will give you good advice for little or no cost. Some may even provide emergency assistance, including help with paying essential bills. You can find a nationally accredited agency in your area by calling the National Foundation for Credit Counseling toll-free at 800-388-2227 or visiting its web site at www.debtadvice.org.

If you believe you've been treated unfairly or victimized by deceptive practices (which is practically a given with many payday lenders), contact your local consumer-protection agency and your state's banking department. You should also complain to the Federal Trade Commission either through its web site at www.ftc.gov, by calling toll-free 877-FTC-HELP (877-382-4357), or by writing to them at:

Federal Trade Commission
Consumer Response Center
600 Pennsylvania Ave., NW
Washington, DC 20580

You might also contact the Community Financial Services Association of America (www.cfsa.net), the trade association for the payday-loan industry. (It represents more than 150 companies, representing roughly half of the nation's 25,000 payday loan outlets.) The CFSA has spent millions promoting responsible use of payday loans and "best practices" among payday lenders. Of course, its mission is to promote more business for its members, but the CFSA does understand the value of good PR, and if you've got a problem with a payday lender, it could be helpful in working it out. You can reach them by calling 703-684-1029 or by writing to:

Community Financial Services Association of America
515 King Street
Suite 300
Alexandria, VA 22314

Fight for Your Money Action Steps

☐ Avoid taking out a payday loan at all costs.

☐ Explore all alternatives—talk to your employer, your church, your credit union, bank, or local nonprofit community organization that might be able to offer a short-term loan at a reasonable rate.

☐ Contact your creditors to negotiate a payment plan on outstanding bills.

☐ Never roll over a payday loan.

☐ To get help if you are in debt, contact a nationally accredited consumer counseling agency in your area by visiting www.debtadvice.org.

Identity Theft

I n 2007, identity theft was the Federal Trade Commission's number one consumer complaint—*for the eighth year in a row*. It's an epidemic that affects roughly 10 million Americans who have their identities stolen each year, at a cost of nearly $50 billion. The good news is that you don't have to be one of them.

Identity theft is an absolute nightmare for its victims. Your personal data—Social Security number, credit card numbers, and bank account numbers—can all be stolen by a thief posing as you who uses this information to spend thousands of dollars or more. And you may not even have a clue that anything is wrong until your application for a mortgage is rejected or you are contacted by a collection agency over a debt you never heard of.

The damage goes way beyond money, too. Identity theft can have a devastating impact on your entire life—destroying your credit score and taking you months or even years to recover from the damage. Identity theft is truly the epitome of needing to learn to "fight for your money."

How to Fight for Your Money

Each year, Javelin Strategy & Research publishes their Identity Fraud Survey Report—said to be the largest, most up-to-date study of ID fraud in the United States. As the 2008 report reveals—contrary to popular belief, in cases where victims knew how their data was stolen, online identity-theft methods (like phishing, hacking, and spyware) only represented 12% of fraud cases. The report goes on to say that a huge 79% of known identity-theft cases occur through traditional methods when a criminal makes direct contact with the consumer's personal identification—including stolen or lost wallets, checkbooks, or credit cards, "shoulder surfing" (when someone looks over your shoulder at the ATM or cash register), and stolen mail from unlocked mailboxes. And still another 17% report "friendly theft"—when friends, family, or in-home employees steal your personal data.

Here's how to protect yourself.

Safeguard Your Personal Information

Sounds obvious enough, right? But you would be surprised how easily people are tricked into providing their private information to complete strangers.

You're probably already familiar with online "phishing" scams, where a fraudulent email asking you to resolve an account problem will redirect you to a bogus web site. Well, a scam dubbed "vishing" is even less sophisticated and low-tech yet has increased from 3% of identity theft in 2006 to 40% in 2007. Here's how it works, as described by the Javelin study mentioned above. In one version, you get an email that appears to be from your bank, like a traditional phishing scam. Instead of being directed to a fake web site, you are given a number to call where you'll then be asked or prompted for your personal information. In the second variation, you are contacted over the phone, either by a real person or a recorded message requesting that you solve a problem with your account.

Vishers often use VOIP (Voice Over Internet Protocol) to autodial credit card or bank customers with a security warning about possible fraudulent activity on your accounts. Customers are asked to call "the bank" back, and when you do, you're told to input your account numbers and other private information.

Here's the bottom line: Never provide personal information over the phone unless you have initiated the call to a verified phone number. Do not click on a web site when responding to emails or text messages. Do not respond to automated phone messages or emails prompting you to call a number to resolve a bank account issue. Instead, use only contact addresses, sites, or phone numbers that you have verified are legitimate.

Also, make it a habit not to leave things lying around at home or in the office—specifically, your wallet, checkbook, or anything else containing private or financial information.

Buy a Shredder—and Use It

You might not think you have any top-secret documents worth shredding, but bank and credit card statements, utility bills, canceled checks, and the like all contain exactly the kind of personal information that ID thieves need. So before you throw out these sorts of documents, shred them. ID thieves have no compunctions about Dumpster diving—and they count on the fact that most people think shredding documents is silly or paranoid. This isn't new advice, but I'd be remiss not to mention it.

Clean Out Your Mailbox

You probably regard those credit card offers that come in the mail all the time as a nuisance, but ID thieves love them. That's because they're easy to steal and they often contain useful personal information. So tell the banks to stop sending them to you. Equifax, Experian, and TransUnion (which provide your credit history to the card issuers) have created a service called OptOutPrescreen that allows you to opt out of receiving offers of credit or insurance that you didn't ask for. You can do so permanently or just for five years. For details, call them toll-free at 888-5-OPTOUT (888-567-8688) or visit them online at www.optoutprescreen.com.

The point is that you want to do as much as you can to keep sensitive information *out* of your mailbox. So in addition to opting out of unsolicited credit offers, you should take advantage of any invitations you get from your bank, credit card companies, and utilities to start receiving your statements and bills online instead of through the mail. (This is not only more secure; it's also better for the environment.) By the same token, when ordering new checks, don't have them mailed to your home. Instead, arrange to pick them up at the bank.

When Asked for Your Social Security Number— Just Say "No"

Your Social Security number is the key to everything. So guard it carefully. Don't carry your Social Security card in your wallet and don't give out your number to businesses that have no need for it, such as a local gym or retail store. It's entirely proper for a new employer or a bank or credit card company with whom you're opening an account to ask for your Social Security number. The same is true of businesses that need to run a credit check on you, such as a cell phone provider. But keep in mind that the Privacy Act requires any federal, state, or local government agency that asks you for your SSN to tell you the statutory authority for requesting it, whether disclosure is mandatory or voluntary, what they'll use the information for, and the consequences, if any, if you refuse to give it up.

Everyone seems to want your Social Security number, from the video store to the health club to the dentist.

Why do so many businesses and organizations request this private data? Simple—because "it's on the form." But just because you're asked for the information doesn't mean you have to give it.

Who does have the right to it? Your employer, the DMV, welfare and tax departments, and institutions that handle transactions involving your taxes, like your bank. If you're unsure, the Social Security Administration recommends that you ask the following questions of anyone asking for your Social Security number:

- Why is my number needed?
- How will my number be used?
- What happens if I refuse to give my number?
- What law requires me to give the number?

For example, when my dentist's office asked for my Social Security number and I said "no," they still cleaned my teeth and took my credit card for payment.

How Accessible Is Your Social Security Number?

Right now anyone who knows your name can log on to various web sites and access your Social Security number in a matter of seconds. Don't believe me? Check out the NetDetective.com web site. For $29, an identity thief can use it to pull up not only your Social Security number and date of birth, but also your employer name, salary, and the name of your spouse! Chilling.

Check Your Statements Weekly

One of the great things about online banking is that you can log on and check your account at any time. Make a point of checking your bank statement weekly to be sure there aren't any red flags.

> You may want to consider opting for online statements. You're more likely to have personal information stolen from your mail than from the Internet.

The same goes for your credit card statements. In fact, as I mentioned previously, you may want to consider canceling your paper statements altogether and opting for online statements. After all, you're more likely to have personal information stolen from your mail than from the Internet.

That said, be sure to always use a secure computer. Using a public computer, like one at your local library, is risky due to tracking software that thieves can use to steal your passwords.

Beware of Wireless Computer Connections

Even though a relatively small percentage of identity theft occurs online, you should still take necessary precautions.

In addition to being careful about surfing the Web on public computers, you should also be aware of the risks involved when using a wireless connection. Wi-Fi and Bluetooth are becoming increasingly popular, and as a result there's bound to be an increase in wireless hacking.

Wireless connectivity is the perfect platform for thieves to get your personal data. If you have a wireless network at home or work, make sure you're incorporating password protection and encryption. When accessing public hotspots, use a personal firewall.

Also, keep your computer safe by updating your antivirus and antispyware programs regularly. Use passwords so that others can't log on to your computer, laptop, or even your PDA, and be sure to change your passwords often.

Make Sure Deleted Data Is Really Deleted!

The *Washington Post* recently ran an article on mobile phones—specifically, "smartphones" like the Palm Treo and BlackBerry—that was quite an eye-opener.

According to the story, resetting your phone to wipe out personal data doesn't exactly delete information. It turns out that your phone's operating system never actually deletes data, only the pointers to where the data is located. Anyone with the right software can recover information that was stored on your phone once you sell or discard it.

What you need to do is contact the device manufacturer for complete instructions on what to do to wipe your data clean. You can also visit www.WirelessRecycling.com for instructions. Click on "Online Tools/Cell Phone Data Eraser." And think twice about what information you store on your device in case it's ever lost or stolen.

Opt Out Wherever and Whenever Possible

The fine print—it'll get you every time. Whether you're completing an application for a new bank account, credit card, or sweepstakes, you need to read the fine print carefully to find out how to opt out, which means your personal information won't be shared.

It may seem perfectly harmless to provide your personal information without getting a guarantee that it won't be sold or shared. But when this happens, your information enters the public domain and becomes part of the ever-expanding information industry. You just have no way of knowing what's in these information files, which soon become permanent.

So try this. Log on to your bank's web site. Chances are that if you scroll all the way to the bottom you'll see a "Privacy" or "Privacy Statement" link. Click it and read what your bank's privacy policy is. It should provide instructions on how to choose not to have your personal information shared—that is, to opt out. If so, protect your privacy and opt out today.

Monitor Your Credit Report for Unusual Activity

Once ID thieves have your Social Security number, date of birth, and other crucial information, they typically use the data to open bank and credit accounts in your name but with a different home address. As a result, you never get any bills and statements from these accounts—and you never have any idea that they exist. Until, of course, it's too late.

Fortunately, there is an easy way to make sure no one is using your identity to open any bogus accounts. The credit reports generated by the three big credit-reporting bureaus—Equifax, Experian, and TransUnion—list every bank and credit account that exists in your name. So as long as you keep checking your credit reports regularly—through each one of the three credit bureaus—you should be able to spot any fraudulent accounts. Go to page 106 to learn how to monitor your credit report throughout the year for free.

Identity-Theft Protection and Monitoring Services— Do They Really Work?

It may sound like a no-brainer to monitor your credit report automatically by subscribing to a credit-monitoring service. However, *Consumer Reports* ran an article last year that says these services "are often overrated, oversold, and overpriced."

Many credit-monitoring services pull only from one credit bureau, not all three.

There are over 24 million customers who subscribe to credit monitoring through services like those offered by Equifax, Experian, or TransUnion—paying between $60 and $180 a year for the peace of mind they may offer. The problem is that many credit-monitoring services pull only from one credit bureau, not all three.

If you're going to purchase one of these services, make sure it monitors all three credit bureaus and be sure you understand what kind of credit-report activity will trigger an alert and how quickly you will be notified. As *Consumer Reports* points out, some products don't alert you to sudden activity in dormant accounts, unexpected increases in balance levels, changes in existing accounts, or the appearance of a negative public record.

The Next Generation of Credit-Monitoring Services

You've probably seen the ads for LifeLock (www.lifelock.com), a company that professes to provide *proactive* identity-theft protection (unlike monitoring services, which are more *reactive*) by placing fraud alerts with the three major credit bureaus in addition to reducing junk mail and credit card offers—all with a $1 million service guarantee.

The CEO, Todd Davis, runs full-page ads with his Social Security number as well as posting it on the web site, to prove just how ironclad his company is in preventing identity theft.

As a customer, you'll end up paying $110 a year for LifeLock's service. But as the Federal Trade Commission warns, before you pay for an identity-theft prevention product or service, make sure you understand *exactly* what you're paying for. As stated on the FTC's web site (www.FTC.gov):

> *Many people find value and convenience in paying an outside party to help them exercise their rights and protect their information. At the same time, some rights and protections you have under federal or state laws can help you protect your identity and recover from identity theft at no cost. Knowing and understanding your rights can help you determine whether— or which—commercial products or services may be appropriate for you.*

So the bottom line here is get a service like LifeLock if you want to pay for the convenience. But remember that you can also provide the same protection—all on your very own—for free by placing a fraud alert on your credit file. To do this, you'll need to contact the three major credit bureaus (Experian, TransUnion and Equifax) directly. Also (and this is important) you will need to remember to renew the fraud alert every three months. And as far as reducing credit card offers and junk mail goes (which is the other part of the LifeLock service), that can easily be done on your own as I mentioned previously by simply calling 888-5OPTOUT or by visiting www.optoutprescreen.com.

Consider "Freezing" Your Credit File

One way to control how much personal information of yours is available to outsiders is to ask the three credit-reporting bureaus to have a "security freeze" put on your credit file. This prohibits anyone from accessing your credit history unless you give permission.

It's not necessarily the most convenient solution to protect yourself from fraud. Anytime you need to have your credit checked—for instance, if you're buying a car or cell phone or even interviewing for a job—you'll need to lift the block ("thaw" your record), which may take up to three days.

Some states will only grant a credit freeze if you're already a victim of identity theft. Find out if your state has a credit-freeze law, including what it costs, by visiting FinancialPrivacyNow.org.

Depending on which state you live in, putting a freeze on your file may cost you between $5 and $10. For victims of identity theft, however, it's free.

What to Do if Things Go Wrong

The moment you suspect you may be the victim of identity theft, ask the credit agencies to place a fraud alert on your credit file. A fraud alert requires creditors to verify your identity before issuing any credit in your name. This can make it difficult for thieves who are trying to use your name to obtain new credit, but it won't affect your existing accounts.

To request a fraud alert, contact one of the three credit agencies listed below. Whichever one you contact will inform the other two.

Equifax
P.O. Box 740241
Atlanta, GA 30374-0241
(800) 525-6285
www.equifax.com

Experian
P.O. Box 9532
Allen, TX 75013
888-EXPERIAN (888-397-3742)
www.experian.com

TransUnion
Fraud Victim Assistance Division
P.O. Box 6790
Fullerton, CA 92834-6790
(800) 680-7289
www.transunion.com

Among other things, placing a fraud alert entitles you to a free copy of your credit report. When you receive it, look for references to companies you never contacted, accounts you didn't open, and debts you can't explain. If you find any inaccurate information, contact the credit agency to correct the errors. (For details on how to do this, see page 107 in the section CREDIT SCORES.)

As soon as you know that someone has opened a fraudulent account in your name or otherwise appropriated your identity, call the police either where you live or where you believe the theft took place. Get a copy of the identity-theft report that results from your complaint and make multiple copies. You want the actual report, not just a case number. You will need it in order to prove that you were the victim of a crime and are not a scam artist yourself.

Another reason you want a police report confirming that you've been a victim of identity theft is that providing one to a credit-reporting agency entitles you to an extended fraud alert, which lasts for seven years. As part of an extended alert, you get two free credit reports within 12 months from each of the three credit bureaus and they will automatically opt you out of receiving any prescreened credit offers for five years (unless you specifically ask them to put your name back on the list).

You should also file an identity-theft report with the Federal Trade Commission, either online through the FTC's Complaint Assistant at www.FTCComplaintAssistant.gov, by calling the FTC Identity Theft Hotline at 877-ID-THEFT (877-438-4338), or by writing to:

Identity Theft Clearinghouse
Federal Trade Commission
600 Pennsylvania Ave., NW
Washington, DC 20580

If you use the FTC's online complaint form, make sure you print a copy for your records. The information may help the police with their report and it will give you another document to help clear your name.

Close Any Unauthorized Accounts Immediately

If you discover that any bank, credit, or other business accounts have been opened or accessed without your permission, contact the appropriate company's fraud department and ask to have the accounts closed immediately. Follow up in writing. Be sure to keep copies and send all letters by certified mail, return receipt requested.

You should also inform the credit-reporting agencies of any fraudulent accounts you've discovered and request that they remove all information regarding these accounts from your credit report. This will help protect your credit score and prevent a company from hiring a debt collector to go after you.

In addition, if you suspect that an identity thief has submitted a change-of-address form with the Post Office to redirect your mail, or has used the mail to commit frauds involving your identity, file a complaint with the U.S. Postal Inspection Service at http://postalinspectors.uspis.gov/forms/idtheft.aspx.

Know Your Rights

If you are the victim of identity theft, there are certain rights that you are entitled to:

- rights to document and report the theft
- rights involving dealing with the credit-reporting companies
- rights when it comes to dealing with creditors, debt collectors, and merchants
- rights around limiting your losses
- other federal *and* state rights

The FTC web site is truly an amazing source for this information, and I strongly encourage you to explore it. Get full details on the specifics of victim rights as well as tools for victims, including:

- sample letters to credit-reporting companies
- sample letters to a company to dispute charges
- sample letters to law enforcement

Visit www.ftc.gov and enter "Identity Theft Tools for Victims" in the search box.

Fight for Your Money Action Steps

☐ Visit www.annualcreditreport.com today and start requesting your credit report on a regular basis.

☐ Shred your documents and mail instead of just tossing them in the trash.

☐ Opt out of unsolicited credit card offers by visiting www.optout prescreen.com.

- ☐ Check your bank and credit card statements weekly at the very least.

- ☐ Use password protection and encryption if you have wireless Internet access.

- ☐ Stop giving out your Social Security number unless the law requires it.

- ☐ Visit www.financialprivacynow.org to find out about your state's credit-freeze law.

- ☐ Visit www.ftc.gov and explore the identity-theft resources there.

Divorce

Nothing causes more trouble in marriage than arguments over money. And what's true for marriage tends to be true for divorce. Next to child custody, money is generally *the* major issue during the divorce process.

The fact is, whatever else it does to you, a divorce will put your finances through the wringer. Think about these statistics. The average woman experiences a 45% decrease in her standard of living after going through a divorce. And while the average man experiences a 15% improvement in his standard of living, that boost is just temporary. Over the long term, U.S. government data show that a divorce reduces the average man's ability to earn a living as much as 40% below his married counterpart's.

The point is that divorce can be a financial nightmare in which no one comes out ahead, except maybe the lawyers. But it doesn't have to be that way.

How to Fight for Your Money

There are many financial traps on the road to divorce and many people—including your estranged spouse—who may try to take advantage of you. But you can get through it all by being smart and disciplined. The main thing to keep in mind is that your real adversary isn't your spouse, but rather an expensive system that encourages the two of you to run up huge bills by declaring war on each other.

Here's how to make sure that instead of ruining your life, your divorce frees you to restart it.

Consider the Alternatives to All-Out War

Regardless of why you're getting divorced, if you really want to get through it without having your life destroyed (financially and otherwise), you should do everything you can to avoid an all-out war. A contested divorce, involving lawyers and judges, is not only unpleasant but expensive. According to Divorce360.com, an informational web site for people going through marital breakups, the total cost for a typical middle- to upper-middle-class couple can run anywhere from $53,000 to $180,000. So if circumstances permit (meaning you're still speaking to each other), try really hard to agree on taking a less confrontational path.

If you don't have children and a lot of assets, perhaps you could manage a no-lawyer divorce (also called a *pro se* divorce) in which you and your partner work out the terms on your own. For as little as $25, you can purchase a divorce kit (there are dozens available online) that contains all the necessary legal forms along with instructions on how to fill them out. You file the finished documents with the court and make an appearance before a judge to explain your reasoning. The divorce becomes final when the judge signs the documents.

If you are not the do-it-yourself type or your situation is a bit more complicated but still amicable, you might consider an uncontested divorce, where one of you hires a lawyer who produces and files all the paperwork you'll both need to sign. This shouldn't cost you more than a few hundred dollars, and there are plenty of lawyers (with high-volume practices) who will do it for as little as $90.

Another alternative to contested divorce is divorce mediation. Rather than have your respective lawyers go at each other like cats and dogs, you and your partner sit down with a neutral mediator, who helps you work through all the issues you need to resolve before you can go your separate ways. (You can get a referral for a certified divorce mediator from the Association for Conflict Resolution's online referral list at www.acrnet.org/referrals.) Not only does using a mediator save you money on legal fees, but it also can (and usually does) lead to a better understanding of the financial realities you are both going to face as newly single people.

Once you've settled on a general course, if you're not going the *pro se* or mediator routes, you should interview a number of divorce or family-law attorneys. Be sure to have a frank discussion about payment before signing on as a client. Don't be afraid to ask about payment caps and other strategies that can be used to ensure you don't break the bank.

The Drawbacks of the Collaborative Approach

Some states, like New York, now have a process called collaborative law, in which the lawyers for both of the parties agree to try to resolve the conflict using cooperative strategies rather than adversarial techniques and litigation. While this may sound good, it has some drawbacks. Probably the most serious is that when you agree to go the collaborative route, you sign a binding legal agreement that the attorney you're working with cannot represent you in court. If your spouse decides to hire a new attorney and back out of the collaborative process, you will have to get rid of your lawyer and find a new one. You can go into this process with great intentions and then, after spending months and tens of thousands of dollars, find yourself starting over.

How to Hire a Divorce Lawyer

Hiring a divorce lawyer is like hiring any other professional. You need to check credentials and ask a lot of questions. Here's a quick how-to.

ASK AROUND. Without a doubt, the best way to find a great attorney is by getting a recommendation from someone you know who has gone through a difficult divorce but speaks highly of their attorney. So if you are facing a divorce, think about who you may know who has gotten divorced in your city or town in the last few years. You may not know this person well, but don't be afraid to ask. Tell them the truth: "I'm going through a divorce and I recall that you recently went through one too. Were you happy with your divorce attorney, and if so, why? Would you mind referring me?" If you don't know anyone—or if the divorcées you do know didn't like their lawyers—contact your county and state bar associations to see if they have lawyer referral programs. What you're looking for is an attorney who specializes in divorce and knows the judges in your area.

SCHEDULE A CONSULTATION. After you've put together a list of several prospects, call their offices to schedule a consultation. Most divorce attorneys don't charge for a consultation meeting, but some do. So before you go, make sure to ask if there is a cost for the consultation. There is nothing wrong with paying for a consultation, but you want to know up front what it costs. It's usually the attorney's hourly rate, which can range from a few hundred dollars to $700 for a top practitioner.

ASK LOTS OF QUESTIONS. The job your divorce lawyer will be doing is way too crucial for you to take anything about him or her on faith. So don't be shy about peppering him or her with questions. The most important include:

- How long have you been practicing law?

- Have you always specialized in family law?

- What do you charge? How is it billed and when will I be expected to pay? When all is said and done, how much do you think it will cost me?

- Who else might be working on my case with you and what would their role be? What are their credentials and how do you charge for their time?

- Can you give me an idea of how the process works and how long it will take?

- Are most of your cases settled out of court? What percentage wind up going to trial?

ASK WHAT THEY WOULD DO IF THEY REPRESENTED THE OTHER SIDE. One of the most important questions you can ask an attorney you are interviewing is what they would do if they represented your spouse. How would they handle your opponent's case? What would they accuse you of? How much money would they try to get out of you? This will give you real insight into the potential downside—both financial and emotional—that you are facing.

MAKE SURE YOU UNDERSTAND WHAT IT WILL COST. Don't be shy about asking how much this will cost you. A lawyer who is not willing to discuss financial terms clearly and straightforwardly is not a lawyer you want to hire. In addition to finding out exactly how much a prospective attorney charges—and how billing is handled—you should ask about their retainer policy. A retainer is a deposit you pay in advance against future billable hours. Depending on the nature of your case, a retainer can run anywhere from a few thousand dollars to as much as $50,000. But they are almost always negotiable. Make sure you get in writing what happens if the full retainer is not used, including exactly when you can expect to get the unused portion refunded.

TRUST YOUR INSTINCTS. You and your divorce lawyer are going to be discussing the most intimate and painful details of your life, so you need someone you not only can trust but also feel completely comfortable with. No matter how impressive his or her credentials may be, if there is *anything* about a prospective attorney's manner that puts you off—if you feel at all intimidated or patronized—scratch him or her off your list.

TEST THEM. The single biggest complaint that clients often have about their divorce attorneys is they can't get them on the phone. It is very difficult, if not impossible, to test an attorney on this up front. But what you can test for is how fast they respond to your initial request for a consultation and how professional their support staff is. If an attorney doesn't get back to you the same day you make your initial call, it's more than likely they won't get back to you quickly once you've hired them. Keep in mind that the service you receive while they are selling you on using them is bound to be as good as it's ever going to get. So if it's bad up front, expect it will be much worse down the road—and look for someone else. Also, if you find during your initial consultation that an attorney is willing to share lots of "private, off-the-record" information about other clients, assume he or she will do the same with your information, and move on.

SHOP AROUND. I strongly recommend that you meet with at least three to five divorce attorneys before you hire one. You need to see who's out there and whom you feel most comfortable with. Remember, you may be working with this person for at least a year—and in many cases, as long as two or three years.

Consult a Financial Planner

An attorney is not the only professional you should consult. You should also think about hiring a financial planner with expertise in divorce-related issues. When you're facing divorce, it's essential to have a clear picture of your family's finances and what they are likely to look like post-divorce. Among other things, this means running your credit report, gathering a list of assets, computing your net worth, and making copies of bank and investment statements. Particularly if you've left the bookkeeping and bill paying to your partner, having a professional who can help you with all this is a huge advantage.

Both the Association of Divorce Financial Planners (www.divorceand finance.org) and the Institute for Divorce Financial Analysts (www.institute dfa.com) accredit specialists in this area and can provide referrals through their web sites.

If you'd rather not spend the money on a financial consultant, there are many organizations with web sites that offer guidance and tools to help prospective divorcées take control of their finances. Among the most helpful are Divorce360.com, DivorceNet (www.divorcenet.com), and the Women's Institute for Financial Education (www.wife.org).

They Fought for Their Money!

Janice and Fred are a divorcing Minneapolis couple who started out agreeing that Janice should keep the family's $1-million home in order to lessen the disruption on their 10-year-old son, Jake. With the help of a financial planner, they developed a detailed budget—and in the process realized that with all the new expenses that single life would entail for both of them, Janice simply couldn't afford to continue living in such an expensive house.

As a result, they decided to sell the house immediately. Not only did this help their cash flow, but by selling the house before their divorce went through, they were able to take advantage of the $500,000 capital gains exclusion that married couples enjoy when they sell a house they've lived in for at least two years out of the previous five.

Create a Budget

In addition to helping you assess your current financial condition, one of the most important things these sites or a financial planner can do for you is help you create a budget for your new life as a single person.

Whatever else it may be, life after divorce is generally more expensive than life before. Some of the additional expenses are obvious and predictable (like the cost of new furniture and housewares). But a lot aren't. For example, there's the cost of individual health insurance for an ex no longer eligible for their partner's company health plan. If you have kids and are going to be sharing custody, a second set of toys and clothes may have to be purchased.

It's during this budgeting process that you can come to grips with what kind of lifestyle you are going to be able to afford in your post-divorce life.

Untangle Your Finances

This may seem obvious, but many divorcing couples forget how legally and financially tangled up their lives have become—and as a result, they fail to cut all the ties that bind them together.

One common mistake is neglecting to take your name off the deed to your house if it goes to your ex in the settlement. If your name is still on the deed, you could find yourself on the hook in the event your former spouse fails to keep up the mortgage payments. The same goes for credit card accounts. It may not seem fair, but divorce decrees don't carry much weight with credit card companies and mortgage lenders. That shouldn't be surprising. A divorce decree is simply an agreement between the divorcing spouses; it does not relieve either of them of any financial obligations they may have to outside parties.

> Divorce decrees don't carry much weight with credit card companies and mortgage lenders.

So make sure you close all your joint credit accounts, including overdraft protection on your checking account. Do it in writing, especially if your spouse's spending is out of control. If you're not yet legally divorced, notify your spouse in writing of your intent to close these accounts at least 10 days before you do so. If your spouse won't cooperate—or if the credit card companies involved won't close the account on your word alone—simply report the card lost or stolen. This will force the companies to close the account.

At the same time, be sure to establish credit in your own name. This is especially important for women who have left the banking and credit arrangements largely to their husbands—with the result that they have no real credit history of their own. If you lack a credit history, for this or any reason, act quickly to establish one: Open a checking account in your own name and apply for a credit card *before* your divorce goes through.

Pay Attention to Retirement Assets

Although most married people plan for their retirement as a couple, the fact is that one of them usually has a better-paying job and a more substantial nest egg than the other. This imbalance is generally not an issue—until the couple gets divorced. Then the spouse whose name is on the family's IRA or 401(k) accounts may insist that they belong to him or her alone (usually, it's him). But this is not necessarily the case. Just because one spouse's name happens to be on the retirement accounts doesn't mean the other spouse isn't entitled to a share of the proceeds. Simple fairness (not to mention some states' community-property laws) generally dictate a 50-50 split of at least the retirement assets that were accumulated during the course of the marriage.

All too often, when both sides are working out the settlement, the spouse in the weaker financial position will underestimate the importance of retirement savings, telling the lawyer that he or she would rather get an asset that seems more "real" (like the house). Don't make this mistake. Real assets like houses or cars cost money to maintain; retirement savings don't. What's more, if you wind up selling a house that has increased in value over the years, you could get hit with a big capital gains tax bill—and instead of the $500,000 exclusion that married couples enjoy, as a divorced person you'd get to shelter only $250,000. Retirement benefits, on the other hand, grow tax-deferred.

And don't forget that even though you're divorced, you may still be eligible for spousal Social Security benefits. If you are 62 or older, and you were married to your ex for at least 10 years, you are entitled to retirement benefits based on their Social Security contributions. If you've remarried, you get to decide whether you want your benefit figured on the basis of your old or your new spouse's Social Security. (Details are available online at www. socialsecurity.gov. Click on "Questions," then on "Benefits.")

Safeguard Your Check

If you are going to depend on child support or alimony to make ends meet, be sure your settlement includes the purchase of a life insurance policy on the breadwinner—in an amount high enough to cover the value of their lifetime contribution. Consider disability insurance as well.

And make sure you are either the owner or the irrevocable beneficiary of the policy. If you're neither, your ex could stop paying premiums without your knowledge. The policy could thus be canceled without your ever having a clue—until after the breadwinner dies and you file a claim, at which point you are told that the policy lapsed many years earlier. If you are the owner or irrevocable beneficiary, they have to let you know immediately if there are any problems with the policy, such as premiums not being paid.

Don't Stop Before the Work Is Finished

When the divorce is final, your work has really just begun. The divorce process is draining—physically, emotionally, and financially. This causes many people to shut down before they've finished the job. They don't bother to rewrite their will, change names on accounts, revise beneficiaries on life insurance policies and retirement plans, and roll retirement money into an IRA.

Remember—the secret to surviving a divorce financially is the same as the key to surviving it emotionally. You need to stop dwelling on the past and start focusing on the future.

 ## What to Do if Things Go Wrong

Divorce laws vary from state to state, but for the most part, there is relatively little you can do if you come to regret having agreed to any (or all) of the

FAMILY MATTERS | 139

terms of your settlement. You can always ask your ex if he or she would consider renegotiating, but if the answer is no, your options are limited.

In many states, if your economic circumstances change, you can ask the court to modify child support and other child-related arrangements until your youngest child turns 18 or finishes high school. Spousal maintenance can often be reconsidered as well. However, if you belatedly realize that you should have sold the house or divided the assets differently, you're out of luck. Judges generally won't set aside property settlements unless you can prove that the agreement was fundamentally unfair or that your ex committed fraud (such as hiding assets) during the negotiations. Just changing your mind or deciding it was a bad deal isn't enough.

If your divorce went to trial and you are unhappy with the divorce judgment you received, you generally have 60 days to appeal. After that, the judgment is final. Keep in mind that in most states you can appeal only if the judge made an error of law or abused his or her discretion. Moreover, if an issue wasn't raised in the trial, you generally can't raise it in an appeal. In any case, discuss your specific concerns with a divorce attorney and certified financial divorce analyst. And prepare to pay; appeals can be expensive.

Fight for Your Money Action Steps

☐ Try to avoid litigation. Explore cooperative alternatives such as mediation.

☐ If you must hire an attorney, get a referral from someone who's been through a divorce and interview several candidates to find one who's right for you.

☐ Consult a financial planner to help you sort through your family's finances and to get you on track going forward as a single person.

☐ Close all joint accounts in writing—and don't forget to take your name off the deed if your home goes to your ex in the settlement.

☐ Establish your own credit.

☐ Revise your will and update beneficiaries on insurance policies and retirement plans.

Life Insurance

As a financial advisor, I have reviewed hundreds of my clients' insurance policies, and for the most part what I have seen firsthand is that most people and most families are actually underinsured. In all, Americans have more than $20 trillion in life insurance coverage. That may sound like a lot, but it really isn't. According to a study by LIMRA International, the median amount of life insurance coverage is just $130,500 per family—a very small sum when you consider that in most cases your beneficiaries are going to need that money to cover the cost of your funeral, pay off the mortgage and other debts, replace your lost income, and perhaps send the kids to college. In my experience, most people have purchased an insurance policy through work and at best it's somewhere between one to three times their annual income—which, again, for "most people" is not enough to cover expenses for an extended period of time if they have dependents. On the other hand, I have also seen that many single people who don't have dependents are overinsured. So the first key to insurance is determining what you really need as far as amount and type of insurance—we'll cover that in a second—and then what is the smartest way to buy it.

> **Most people with dependents are underinsured. Most people without dependents are overinsured.**

How to Fight for Your Money

When it comes to life insurance, knowing what you don't need is as important as knowing what you do. Here are some basic guidelines.

Term vs. Permanent

There are basically two kinds of life insurance. There's term insurance, where you pay a premium and in return get a set amount of protection for a set period of time. And there's permanent insurance, where part of your premium pays for your protection and part is invested in what amounts to a tax-deferred savings plan. According to the most recent statistics, about 60% of the policies sold in the United States are permanent policies, while about 40% are term. The greater popularity of permanent policies is not surprising, even though consumer advocates agree that term policies make more sense for most people. Permanent policies generally cost five to 10 times more than term policies—meaning insurance agents make a lot more commissions selling them, which is why your "friend in the insurance business" will gladly come to your home at night to discuss it.

Make Sure You Really Need It

If you are single, buying life insurance makes sense only if you are concerned about paying for your funeral expenses and maybe settling some debts that might otherwise fall on your parents or siblings—for example, if you had a joint credit card account or had someone cosign a loan for you. Life insurance for children used to be recommended as a way to save money for college on a tax-deferred basis. But that was before the easy availability of new college savings options like 529 plans (for more information, see SAVING FOR COLLEGE on page 157). If your child is likely to develop health problems, purchasing a life insurance policy for him now will protect him against the possibility that he won't be able to qualify for one in the future. But for most people, buying insurance for a child shouldn't be a priority.

Shop Around

There are three main factors to consider when you're deciding which insurer to buy your policy from—how stable the company is, how well it takes care of policyholders, and how cheap its rates are.

To get an idea of how strong a company's finances are and whether you can count on it to be around for the long haul, check with one of the firms that rate life insurers. The best known are A.M. Best (www.ambest.com), Fitch (www.fitchratings.com), Moody's (www.moodys.com), Standard & Poor's (www.standardandpoors.com), and Weiss (www.weissratings.com).

As far as customer service goes, the National Association of Insurance Commissioners maintains an online Consumer Information Source at www.naic.org/cis/, where you can look up the complaint record of virtually any insurance company in the country.

Once you've satisfied yourself on these two counts, you should look for the best price. The most efficient way to do this is through an online broker such as Accuquote.com, FindMyInsurance.com, and LifeInsure.com. If you prefer to work through an agent, find an independent one who's not tied to just one company.

Buy the Right Amount

Some financial planners will tell you that the size of your life insurance policy should be anywhere from five to 10 times your annual salary. In fact, no simple rule of thumb can possibly take into account all the variables that must be considered when you're trying to decide how big a policy you need. Life insurance is all about protecting your family against financial hardship in the event you die. So you need to base the size of your policy on one of two things: either what your potential earnings would have been if you hadn't died or how much money your family will need in order to stay afloat after you're gone.

The Life and Health Insurance Foundation for Education (LIFE), an industry-supported educational group, has two terrific calculators on its web site that can help you figure this out: a "Human Life Value" calculator (www.lifehappens.org/life-insurance/human-life-value), which estimates what your lost earnings would be worth, and a "Life Insurance Needs" calculator (www.lifehappens.org/life-insurance/life-calculator), which computes how much money your family is likely to need.

Buy the Policy That's Best for You—Not Your Agent

The kind of life insurance that's best for you may not be what's best for your insurance agent—at least not when it comes to his or her commission. So take your agent's advice with a large grain of salt.

> The best deal for most people is what's called level term insurance.

In general, the best deal for most people is what's called level term insurance—in which you're guaranteed that your premium will stay the same for a period of time you select when you sign up (usually anywhere from five to 30 years). If you die during that period, your beneficiaries collect the death benefit. If you outlive the policy or cancel it at any point, no one gets anything. The policy has no cash value, but neither is it particularly expensive.

In general, the older you are, the more expensive term insurance is. And the longer the term, the more expensive it is. The idea is that you pick a term that covers a period of your life in which your family will need a replacement for your income if you die—say, until your kids are out of college. When your term insurance expires, you will presumably be very old, with fewer (if any) family obligations and no longer generating income that needs replacing.

Most insurance agents will talk up the benefits of permanent policies, which *are* expensive but do have a cash value, as a great way to build a nest egg. (Given how expensive these policies are compared to term insurance, they are certainly good for the agent's nest egg.) There are three basic variations: whole life, universal life, and variable universal life. They are called "permanent" because they stay in effect as long as you keep paying the premiums.

WHOLE LIFE. Imagine paying for term insurance but adding a 50% surcharge to the cost of the annual premium and having some of that extra money put in a money-market account, where it can grow tax-deferred into a little nest egg for your old age. That's what whole life is. It's a term policy with a little cash-value basket added onto it. Insurance agents will tell you how great this cash-value basket is, and how safely and soundly the insurance company invests the proceeds. The problem is that the money is invested so conservatively that the policy's cash value grows too slowly to really amount to anything.

UNIVERSAL LIFE. After decades of being sold on whole life insurance, people began to wake up and realize that it was not the great retirement vehicle they had been told it was. So the insurance industry came up with a new angle. "Instead of just putting your extra premium money in a money-market account," the industry told potential customers, "we will invest it more aggressively and pay you a great rate." Insurance agents sold these policies on the promise that policyholders could earn as much as 11% a year. They would flash fancy illustrations showing that if you earned 11% a year, your cash value would be just enormous in 20 years. These illustrations always looked really impressive. The problem was they were just illustrations, not guarantees. Universal life works great when the insurance company invests well, but it can be a disaster when the company doesn't.

VARIABLE UNIVERSAL LIFE. If you feel strongly about purchasing permanent life insurance—which is to say, if you want life insurance that can also double as a retirement vehicle—I'd recommend variable universal life. With variable universal life you get a cash-value policy that allows you to control how the savings portion of your premium is invested. A good variable life policy may offer more than a dozen different high-quality mutual funds from which you can select. If you want to be conservative, you can choose a bond fund. If you want to be aggressive, you can choose growth funds. The point is, you are in charge. What makes this especially nice is that, as with a 401(k) plan or IRA, the cash value of your policy can grow tax-deferred. That is, you can change investments, buying and selling funds as market conditions dictate, without having to pay taxes on any gains. Of course, as with any speculative investment, you can also lose money. There is no guarantee that your cash value will only go up.

Advocates of permanent life insurance tout its tax advantages and the fact that you can borrow against it. But the fact is that permanent policies cost a lot and contain many hidden fees—for example, a recent *Smart Money* article exposed Metropolitan Life for charging their policyholders fees equal to 15% to 20% of the annual premium simply for the privilege of making monthly payments (rather than one lump-sum yearly payment). As the article points out, charges like these are often built into the payments, so you probably won't even realize it.

If you buy a permanent policy, you have a legal right to understand the detailed costs and commission. Ask your insurance agent to provide you in writing what the commission on the policy is, even if you are not paying it up front and the insurance company is paying it. The truth is you are always paying the commission in costs that are added to the policy or penalties if you terminate the policy or stop funding it early. In most cases, you will find that all of the first-year premiums are a commission to the insurance agent selling it to you. There is nothing wrong with an insurance agent earning a living, but you DESERVE to know the truth of the costs you are paying. This cost may impact you financially later on and it may also help you determine if the advice you are being given feels unbiased or self-serving.

You should use permanent insurance as an investment only after you have maxed out your 401(k) or IRA contributions.

Bottom line: If you're looking for an investment vehicle, you'd probably do better to buy a term policy and invest the money you save in a no-load mutual fund. At the very least, you should use permanent insurance as an investment only after you have maxed out your 401(k) or IRA contributions.

Don't Forget Your Company Benefits

Many employers offer *free* life insurance coverage that can be worth as much as, if not more than, your annual salary. So when you're figuring how much insurance you need, don't forget to factor in your workplace benefits.

Keep in mind, too, that some companies also allow employees to purchase additional life insurance through the company's group plan. There are tremendous advantages to this—not least that a doctor's exam is usually NOT required, a huge benefit for workers with medical conditions that could make acquiring insurance on their own difficult or expensive. Additionally, group insurance policies offered through your employer can be significantly cheaper than if you bought one directly and can usually be paid on a pretax basis. If you are young and healthy, however, do a comparison between your employer's group rate and what it would cost you for an individual policy. Because a group policy covers both healthy and unhealthy workers alike, your company's policy could end up being more expensive than an individual policy for a healthy person in the open market.

Make Sure Your Employer Plan Is "Portable"

The most important advice I can give you regarding a group employer policy is to make sure the plan is portable. This means that should you leave your employer, you can take the insurance policy with you (and fund it yourself). The advantage is that you won't have to requalify for the policy and you should be able to keep the group rate that you were paying—which can save you a ton of money.

Look for Premium Discounts

Sometimes buying more insurance can actually cost you less. Most companies offer rate discounts when you surpass certain benchmark amounts. For example, you might actually pay a smaller premium for $500,000 of life insurance than you would for $450,000, because a discount kicks in at the higher insurance amount.

Don't Overlook Your "Free Look" Period

When you're buying life insurance, keep in mind that most states give you the right to a "free look"— usually a period of around 10 days during which you can evaluate a newly issued insurance policy and return it for a full refund if you decide it's not the right product for you. Check with your state insurance regulator to see what the rules are in your state. You'll find a list of insurance regulators in every state on the web site of the National Association of Insurance Commissioners at www.naic.org/state_web_map.htm.

Don't Forget to Update Your Beneficiaries— or to Name One in the First Place

When your life changes, your life insurance should change with it. If you have a new child—or get a new spouse—don't forget to update the beneficiary designations on your life insurance policies. There's nothing wrong with leaving an ex-spouse as a beneficiary if that's what you want to do (or because a judge ordered you to as part of a divorce settlement). But don't do it by accident.

And don't just name a primary beneficiary. You should also list a contingent or secondary beneficiary in the event you outlive your primary beneficiary. Also, don't name your estate as a beneficiary, because if you do, the death benefit will have to go through probate, meaning your heirs won't be able to access the money quickly.

See if Your Old Policy Can Be Improved

If you already have life insurance, now is as good a time as any to see if you can increase the death benefit at no additional cost. This is probably the MOST important advice I can give you today. As I write this in 2008, the cost of life insurance has dropped significantly. Why? Because we're living longer. Since 2000, term life insurance premiums have dropped by more than 4% a year, according to the Insurance Information Institute. In fact, they are now 50% lower than they were a decade ago. In many cases, today you can double your death benefit with a new policy at the exact same price you are currently paying, provided you are still healthy. Or you can cut your annual premiums in half!

> Since 2000, term life insurance premiums have dropped by more than 4% a year. You can cut your annual premiums in half!

Stop Smoking—Live Longer and Save a Fortune!

I pulled some online quotes through **www.accuquote.com** for a 20-year term life insurance policy with a face amount of $500,000. For a healthy 43-year-old male, the lowest quote for a nonsmoker was $495 per year. For someone smoking more than a pack a day, the lowest price more than quadrupled to $2,065 per year. That is simply amazing. So quit now—and you'll already be on your way to saving money on life insurance.

You save $1,570!

What to Do if Things Go Wrong

If you have any kind of a problem with a life insurance company, you should file a complaint with your state's insurance regulator. You can do this online through the web site of the National Association of Insurance Commissioners, which provides links to every state insurance agency that has an online complaint site and contact information for all those that don't. Visit www.naic.org/cis/fileComplaintMap.do.

Fight for Your Money Action Steps

☐ Check with your human resources department at work to see how much life insurance you currently have and what the premium is costing you, if anything.

☐ Calculate how much money your dependents will need to pay your debts and replace your income after you die.

☐ Decide whether to go with a term or permanent policy.

☐ Request quotes online or work through a recommended agent.

☐ Check a provider's rating and customer-service record.

☐ Name your beneficiaries, and keep the names up to date.

☐ If you have a term policy, call your provider to request a lower premium that reflects today's lower rates.

Estate Planning

According to an AARP survey, only about 60% of Americans over the age of 50 have a will. As a result, some 1.5 million Americans pass away each year without leaving behind any legally binding instructions about what should be done with their property, not to mention their remains. What they do leave behind instead is a legacy of problems and heartache for their loved ones, along with a big stack of legal and tax bills.

No one likes to think about this stuff. I know I don't. But if you have people and things in your life that you care about, you need to do some estate planning.

And don't assume your estate won't be worth bothering about. Most people have more assets than they realize—what with even modest homes in some places still going for upward of half a million dollars and lots of companies offering both free life insurance and 401(k) contributions to their employees. More assets generally means more estate taxes—and with the IRS rules on estate taxes going through all sorts of changes, not having a plan could cost your heirs hundreds of thousands of dollars in assessments that could easily have been avoided.

Anyway, even if your estate isn't worth all that much, do you really want to leave it to the government to divide up your stuff and decide who gets what? That's what happens when you die intestate, which is the legal term for not having a will.

What's more, smart estate planning can protect your family from the risk and expense of probate. Generally speaking, when someone dies, you're not allowed to distribute their property until the validity of their will has been confirmed and any claims against their estate have been resolved. The process of doing this is known as probate. In essence, it involves an appointed person notifying your heirs and creditors that you're dead, taking an inventory of your estate, paying any outstanding debts and taxes, and then distributing what's left to your heirs.

Probate is something to avoid if you can. For one thing, it opens all your private affairs to public disclosure. For another, even if things go smoothly, probate is likely to cost your heirs tens of thousands of dollars in legal fees—on average, between 4% and 7% of your estate's total value. Just hope no one contests the will, because if they do, the sky is the limit.

The good news is that it's not hard to avoid this kind of misery. All it takes is a little planning.

How to Fight for Your Money

As I write this in the summer of 2008, the laws covering estate taxes are in a state of total flux. It's still the case that you can leave as much as you want to a spouse or a registered charity without their having to pay any estate taxes on it. But the way the law stands right now, the amount you can leave to anyone else tax-free is on a roller coaster. If you die in 2009, your heirs won't have to pay any taxes on the first $3.5 million of your estate. If you die in 2010, they won't have to pay any estate taxes at all, no matter how much you leave them. But if you die in 2011, they will have to pay estate taxes on everything over $1 million.

> There are a surprising number of middle-class people whose estates could easily be worth more than $3.5 million.

This clearly makes no sense, and Congress is expected to straighten things out with new legislation by 2010, if not sooner. While it's never a good idea to try to predict what Congress may do, it's a safe bet that estate taxes probably won't be going away anytime soon. Indeed, most experts expect Congress to set them at or close to the 2009 level—with the first $3.5 million tax-free and a maximum tax rate of 45% on anything above that.

So does this mean you don't need to worry about estate planning if you're not a multimillionaire?

Unfortunately, it doesn't. Keep in mind that when you add in the value of a house, the death benefit from a decent-size life insurance policy, and the proceeds from brokerage and retirement accounts—all of which count when you're calculating the value of an estate—there are a surprising number of middle-class people whose estates could easily be worth more than $3.5 million.

Anyway, estate planning isn't just about money. It's also about specifying the kind of medical treatment you'll get at the end of your life, picking someone to make decisions about you and your affairs in the event you're incapacitated, and figuring out what's going to happen to your kids.

This is particularly crucial for unmarried couples, whether gay or straight. Without the right documents, your unmarried partner has zero rights in the event of your incapacity or death. The good news is that unmarried partners can enjoy virtually all the protections available to married couples—*if* they plan properly.

So here is what you need to keep in mind.

Think Hard About Setting Up a Living Trust

A living trust is basically a legal document that does two things. First, it allows you to transfer the ownership of any of your assets (your house, your car, your retirement accounts, whatever you like) to a trust while you are still alive. Second, it designates who should be given those assets after you die. By naming yourself the trustee of your trust, and naming someone else as the beneficiary, you can continue to control your assets—which means that as long as you live, the transfer of ownership will have no practical impact on your ability to enjoy and manage your property.

> If you create a living trust properly and fund it correctly, the assets in it won't have to go through probate when you die.

The main advantage a living trust has over a simple will is that if you create a living trust properly and fund it correctly, the assets in it won't have to go through probate when you die. Another big advantage of a trust is that it can save your heirs a lot of money. If your estate is large enough to be taxable, a well-written trust can reduce the tax bill by tens—sometimes hundreds—of thousands of dollars.

There are too many different kinds of trusts for me to be able to list them all. The following five types are among the most common.

REVOCABLE LIVING TRUST. This is one of the most popular trusts. It's designed to protect basic assets like your home, your car, and your bank and brokerage accounts, and to help your estate avoid probate. It is extremely flexible and can be changed or dissolved whenever you like throughout your lifetime.

MARITAL AND BYPASS TRUST. Often referred to as an "A/B" trust, this is used mainly to reduce estate taxes by allowing each spouse to take full advantage of the estate-tax exemption, effectively doubling the amount of money you can leave to your heirs tax-free.

QUALIFIED TERMINABLE INTEREST PROPERTY TRUST. The QTIP trust is often used by wealthy people who've been married more than once. Say you've got a new spouse and want him or her to be provided for, but intend that your family fortune eventually go to your children by a previous marriage. A QTIP trust will provide income to your surviving spouse for the rest of his or her life, then pass the assets to your children (or whomever you happen to name as the ultimate beneficiary).

CHARITABLE REMAINDER TRUST. This trust allows you to continue to live off the proceeds of your estate even after you've donated it all to a charity (and presumably reaped some hefty tax advantages in the process). Typically set up by wealthy families, it can provide you and your designated heirs with income for the rest of your lives, but once you are all gone, the estate will go to the charity.

IRREVOCABLE LIFE INSURANCE TRUST. This is a great way to protect the real value of your life insurance from the brutal impact of estate taxes. If you assign your life insurance policy (term or whole life) to an irrevocable life insurance trust, the death benefit won't be considered part of your estate—meaning it won't be subject to estate taxes. The only drawback is that once you've set it up, it can't be changed, nor can you easily access your policy's cash value (if it has one).

Whatever Else You Do, You Always Need a Will

Even if you've got a fancy trust, you still need a will. That's because you probably have some assets (such as art or antiques) that you couldn't put in the trust or that you forgot to retitle. Even more important, if you have minor children, you also need to name a guardian who will take care of them in case your death leaves them orphaned.

You Also Need a Durable Power of Attorney

A durable power of attorney appoints someone you trust to handle your finances in the event you become incapacitated. (It's called "durable" because it is designed to remain in force even after you are no longer competent.) A lawyer will generally prepare one when he drafts your will or trust, but there are also standard forms that enable you to do it yourself. Giving someone this sort of power over you may be a little scary, but the alternative to a power of attorney is not pretty. If you're incapable of carrying out some essential transaction, your family might have to ask a judge to declare you incompetent and appoint a guardian to take over your affairs.

And You Need a Health Care Directive

In addition to specifying how you want your assets to be treated, you need to specify how you want yourself to be treated. You can do this with two documents that every adult should have: a *health care directive* (also known as a living will) and a *health care power of attorney*. The directive sets out what kind of medical treatment you're going to want at the end of your life (e.g., whether you want to be hooked up to machines if that's what it takes to keep you breathing). The power of attorney appoints someone to make health care decisions for you if you are incapacitated (e.g., when, if ever, they should pull the plug).

These documents come in many varieties, but it's best to use standard forms that were specifically developed to match the laws of your state. You can usually get them free of charge from state bar associations, government offices, health care providers, and agencies that serve the elderly. If what you want to specify is more complicated than the standard form can accommodate, you can have an attorney draw up a directive that explains your precise wishes in as much detail as you need.

If you're wondering how necessary these documents really are, think back to the heartrending (and well-publicized) case of Terri Schiavo. Schiavo was only 26 when she suffered irreversible brain damage and lapsed into a coma in 1990. She spent the next 15 years in what doctors called a persistent vegetative state. Unfortunately, because she never signed a health care directive or power of attorney, her husband and her parents spent the last seven of those years fighting bitterly over her care, what her wishes would have been had she written them down, and who should have the right to make decisions for her. Ultimately, the courts granted her husband's request to have her feeding tube removed, but in the process her family was torn apart.

Doing It Yourself Is Better Than Not Doing It at All

As a rule, you want your estate documents drawn up by a lawyer who specializes in wills and trusts. That said, the fact is that many people may feel they can't afford the $1,000 or so an attorney may charge to draft a basic will or the $2,500 or more it can cost to set up a trust. I would argue that it's a matter of priorities. Maybe before you buy a new flat-screen television, you should consider getting your estate in order. It's certainly not cheap—but believe me, it's worth it.

In the meantime, if you can't afford to get it done professionally, then do some estate planning yourself as soon as possible. There are plenty of online resources, such as LegalZoom.com and Nolo.com, that can explain the fundamentals. And you should definitely read the American Bar Association's "Guide to Wills and Estates," which you can download for free from the ABA's web site at www.abanet.org/publiced/practical/books/wills/home.html.

Help Yourself by Giving Some Assets Away

If you are lucky enough to have more than you need, consider reducing the size of your estate by giving part of it away while you are still alive. You can give up to $1 million to anyone you want over the course of your lifetime without having to pay any gift tax—and if you give away less than $12,000 in any one year, it doesn't count toward the $1 million total. (Recipients of a gift don't have to pay taxes on it.) What's more, you can make unlimited gifts to IRS-recognized charities. Giving while you are still alive offers more than just financial benefits. You get the satisfaction of seeing your bequests put to use and receiving the thanks of those who benefit from your gifts. You also get an income-tax deduction for charitable gifts, although deductions for very large gifts may have to be spread over several years.

What to Watch Out For

Obsolete Beneficiaries

If you get married, get divorced, or your spouse dies, don't forget to update the beneficiary designations on your life insurance policies as well as on all your retirement, brokerage, and bank accounts, not to mention your will and trusts. There's nothing wrong with leaving an ex-spouse as a beneficiary, if that's what you want to do (or because a judge ordered you to as part of a divorce settlement). But don't do it by accident.

Don't Forget to Fund Your Trust

Trusts can't protect your assets if you don't put any assets in them. So if you have a living trust, don't forget to "retitle" your assets. This means that if you buy a house you should make sure it's deeded not to you as an individual but to your trust. The same thing goes for your car, your bank and brokerage accounts, and any other assets you may own—*except* qualified retirement accounts like 401(k)s and IRAs (because with these you designate a beneficiary, so it doesn't go through probate and hence there's no need to put it in a trust).

Pay Attention to the Tax Consequences

Say you have a brokerage account and a 401(k) account, both of which are worth about $400,000. If you leave the brokerage account to your son and the 401(k) to your daughter, have you treated them the same? Not by a long shot.

This is because when you leave someone a brokerage account, the tax basis of the securities in the account is stepped up to their value on the day you died. In other words, there's no capital gains to report, which means your son inherits your $400,000 brokerage account tax-free. Your daughter, on the other hand, will have to pay income tax on any distributions from your 401(k) just as you would have. If she's in the 25% tax bracket, this will reduce the value of her inheritance to $300,000, creating an unintended inequality and the likelihood of hurt feelings.

The point is that you have to be careful about the tax consequences of what you're leaving to your heirs. From a beneficiary's point of view, the best items to inherit are ones with no built-in tax liability, such as Roth IRAs and brokerage accounts. Assets like traditional IRAs, 401(k) accounts, annuities, and savings bonds all carry tax liabilities and are thus less desirable.

> From a beneficiary's point of view, the best items to inherit are ones with no built-in tax liability, such as Roth IRAs and brokerage accounts.

With this in mind, if you want to leave something to an IRS-recognized charity, try to leave one of these tax-burdened assets (such as a traditional IRA). Since charities aren't taxed, they'll get to enjoy the asset's full value. Save your assets that don't carry any tax liabilities for your family or friends, who do have to pay taxes.

GET THE MOST FROM YOUR BEQUESTS

Value of your $100,000 IRA left to your sister:	$75,000
Value if left to an IRS-designated charity:	$100,000

You might also consider helping your heirs by paying off potential tax liabilities yourself while you are still alive—especially if you expect your beneficiaries to be in a higher tax bracket than you're in now. For example, by converting a traditional IRA to a Roth IRA, you turn a taxable legacy into one that will be tax-free for your heirs. (While it's true that taxpayers with six-figure incomes are generally not eligible to open Roth IRAs, there will be a special opportunity in 2010 for all taxpayers regardless of income levels to convert traditional IRAs to Roth.)

Be Wary of "Trust Mills" and "How to Avoid Probate" Seminars

Don't be taken in by firms that claim they can create a living trust that will allow you to avoid paying income taxes or stop paying self-employment taxes or turn your family into a business with thousands of dollars of business-expense deductions. None of this is possible. These "trust mills," as they are known, do a high-volume business selling gullible people predrafted wills, trusts, and other estate-planning documents, often filled with repetitive legal gibberish, that generally turn out to be useless. Even though customers almost never meet with an actual lawyer, their fees are often higher than what an attorney would charge.

Be wary, too, of "How to Avoid Probate" seminars that are not conducted by a lawyer or, if a lawyer is involved, where the advertisements include a disclaimer that he or she "is not offering and does not intend to provide legal services or legal advice." Probate is a legal process, and most seminars that don't involve legal services or legal advice are not seminars at all but rather disguised attempts to sell you annuities or health insurance.

What to Do if Things Go Wrong

If you have problems with a trust attorney, you should file a complaint with your state bar association. The complaint process varies from state to state, but you can generally find all the information you need on the bar association's web site.

If you've been scammed by a trust mill or a phony seminar, contact your state consumer-protection agency (http://www.consumeraction.gov/caw_state_resources.shtml) as well as your state's attorney general. A complete list of state attorneys general offices is available on the web site of the National Association of Attorneys General at www.naag.org/attorneys_general.php.

Fight for Your Money Action Steps

☐ Set up a living trust to avoid having your assets go through probate when you die as well as to save your heirs a lot of money.

☐ Once it's set up, retitle your assets to put them in the trust.

☐ Hire an attorney to draw up a will, a durable power of attorney, and a health care directive.

☐ If you can't afford an attorney, visit www.legalzoom.com or www.nolo.com to find out how you can do this yourself.

Saving for College

Think getting into college is tough? Try scraping up the money to pay for it. The cost of a college education has never been higher—and it's growing more expensive with every passing year. By 2024, the price tag for a bachelor's degree is expected to be more than twice what it was in 2007—and in 2007, it was anything but cheap. According to the College Board, the average cost of a four-year private college education was roughly $130,000 in 2007; for state schools, the figure was around $54,000.

For most of us, the only way to make sure there will be enough money to send our kids to college is to start saving for it as early as possible. The good news is that there are all sorts of programs designed to make this easier—including a wide assortment of government-sponsored savings programs known as 529 plans that allow you to put away as much as $300,000 or more on a tax-deferred basis. These plans are hugely popular. At the beginning of 2008, parents of college-bound kids had invested more than $130 billion in them—and the numbers are expected to keep rising.

The bad news about college saving is that the choices you have to make are often so complicated they don't seem to make any sense. There are pitfalls at every turn, from saving in the wrong account to saving too little to saving in a way that actually hurts your child's chances for financial aid. But if you have college-bound kids—and you don't happen to have a spare two or three hundred thousand dollars lying around—you need to figure it out.

How to Fight for Your Money

Here's a story that illustrates what we're up against.

Doug R. of Englewood, Ohio, was headed to Ohio State University, but he didn't want to go into major debt to pay for it. So before he enrolled, he worked three jobs and saved up $10,000. Then he applied for financial aid, fairly confident he would get some, since his mom made just $13,000 a year as a part-time teacher.

He was turned down flat.

Why? With $10,000 in the bank, the financial-aid bureaucrats felt he could afford to pay his own tuition. As his mother told me: "It seemed like a slap in the face. It was like they were telling him that if he had been irresponsible with his money, they would have helped him pay for college."

Actually, Doug had been victimized by a common misunderstanding that costs needy college students untold millions of dollars in financial aid each year. The fact is that when your child is applying for financial aid, his or her assets are weighted much more heavily than yours in the college's assessment of how much your family can really afford to pay. So if Doug had put his $10,000 into his mother's savings account instead of his own, he probably wouldn't have had a problem. But not realizing the rules cost him a scholarship.

The point is that if you're going to be able to afford to send your kids to college, you're going to need a plan. Exactly what kind of plan is right for you depends on a lot of variables—like how old your kids are, what kind of college or university they have in mind, where tuition levels are likely to be by the time they are ready to go, and what kind of return you can reasonably expect to earn on your savings.

Fortunately, there are lots of web sites with great tools for figuring all this out. One of the best ones is the College Board's Financial Aid EasyPlanner (http://apps.collegeboard.com/fincalc/ep/wizard-home.jsp). It can help you work through every phase of college financial planning—from calculating the likely total cost of Junior's four years at Harvard to comparing financial-aid packages to figuring your estimated family contribution (the amount, based on your income and assets, that a college will expect you to pay out of your own pocket each year).

Another terrific resource is SavingforCollege.com, an informational site filled with useful data—including the Simplest College Calculator (www.savingforcollege.com/college-savings-calculator/). Just enter your child's age and it will tell you how much four years of college is likely to cost you when the time comes and exactly how much you will need to put aside each month to be able to cover that amount.

There's also FinAid (www.finaid.org), a truly comprehensive source of student financial-aid information, advice, and tools. Among other things, FinAid has a terrific checklist of questions to ask yourself before deciding on a savings plan. (You can find it at www.finaid.org/savings/checklist.phtml.)

If you're looking for something more personal, you can hire your very own college-planning consultant. The National Institute of Certified College Planners accredits Certified College Planning Specialists who are financial professionals trained to help parents figure out the best way to save and pay for college. A list of certified planners is available on the Institute's web site (www.niccp.com).

What you will learn from these various resources is that there is an enormous variety of different ways you can save for college. But there are two basic approaches that everyone should consider: 529 plans and education savings accounts.

The Biggest and Best Savings Program—529 Plans

Probably the best way to save for college is to use what are called qualified tuition programs—better known as 529 plans (after the section of the tax code that authorizes them). Every state has its own rules for 529 plans, but they all fall into one of two categories: They are either prepaid tuition programs that let you lock in the cost of your child's future college education at today's prices or they are savings plans that let you set up a tax-deferred savings account on your kid's behalf.

With the prepaid tuition program, you can guarantee yourself a big-time bargain by paying for all or part of your child's college education now—at current rates—even though he or she may not be attending college for another 10 or 15 years. Some prepaid plans allow you to purchase individual tuition credits. Others let you prepay anywhere from one to five years' worth of tuition. You can do this either with a lump-sum payment or on an installment plan.

You may have heard that prepaid tuition plans are good only for state colleges and universities in the state that sponsors the plan. This isn't true. In fact, there is a prepaid tuition plan called the Independent 529 Plan that covers a nationwide consortium of some 275 private colleges and universities—including such elite schools as Princeton, Stanford, and MIT. (Details are available online at www.independent529plan.org.) Anyway, even if you sign up for a state-sponsored plan that is limited to in-state public universities, it's generally not a problem to transfer the value of your contract to both private colleges and out-of-state schools.

PAY TODAY'S RATES FOR TOMORROW'S TUITION AND SAVE

Estimated Cost of One Year of College Education, Including Room and Board, in 2008–2009	
Private four-year:	$37,090
Public four-year:	$17,207

Estimated Cost of One Year of College Education, Including Room and Board, in 2016–2017	
Private four-year:	$54,800
Public four-year:	$25,423

* Source: http://www.pueblo.gsa.gov/cic_text/family/college/college.htm

Only 18 states offer prepaid tuition plans. By contrast, every state except Washington offers 529 savings plans. Generally speaking, 529 savings plans are similar to 401(k) plans and IRAs, except that all the proceeds are supposed to be used for your child's college or graduate school expenses (basically, everything you have to pay for as a condition of enrollment, such as tuition, fees, books, supplies, and equipment—but NOT room and board, living expenses, or transportation).

As with many retirement plans, the contributions you make to a 529 savings plan are invested in mutual funds or similar securities. The nice thing is that you can put in just about as much money as you want (over $300,000 in some plans), as long as the amount doesn't exceed your child's college costs. And while the IRS doesn't let you deduct your contributions, many state governments do. What's more, your 529 plan investments are tax-deferred, meaning they can grow without your having to pay any capital gains taxes along the way. And no taxes are due when you withdraw the money, as long as it's spent on qualified college expenses.

The biggest drawback of 529 savings plans is that if the funds are used for some purpose other than qualified education expenses—say, because you saved too much or because your kid decided not to go to college—they will be subject to ordinary income tax *and* a 10% penalty. Then again, it's easy to move 529 plans from one beneficiary to another. So if your child drops off the college track, you can transfer the account to a sibling—or even a parent or other close relative.

Choosing the Right 529 Plan

With so many different plans to choose from, you'll need to do some serious research to figure out which one makes the most sense for you. Generally speaking, you should purchase a 529 plan directly from a state sponsor that doesn't impose a sales charge and keeps enrollment, maintenance fees, and asset-management fees to a minimum. In all, your annual costs shouldn't be much more than 1%. (Keep in mind that you do not have to be a resident of a particular state to use its 529 plan.)

Each year, both SavingforCollege.com and the investment web site Morningstar (www.morningstar.com) issue lists of the best 529 plans. The SavingforCollege study compares fees, whereas the Morningstar rankings consider fund diversification as well as fees. Another good resource is the College Savings Plan Network, an organization of state officials who administer 529 plans. Its web site (www.collegesavings.org) offers comprehensive information about every 529 plan in the nation and allows you to make side-by-side comparisons.

In Morningstar's 2008 survey, the top five 529 plans were:

- Illinois Bright Start College Savings Program (managed by Oppenheimer Funds)

- Maryland College Investment Plan (managed by T. Rowe Price)

- Virginia CollegeAmerica (managed by American Funds)

- Virginia Education Savings Trust (managed by the Virginia College Savings Plan Board and its executive director)

- Colorado Scholars Choice College Savings Program (managed by Legg Mason)

Other highly regarded plans are the Utah Educational Savings Plan Trust (which offers a choice of Vanguard index funds), Michigan Educational Savings Program (which is run by TIAA and invests in Treasury securities, not stocks), and the College Savings Plan of Nebraska (which offers an unusually wide assortment of investment options).

Education IRAs

There is another sort of tax-deferred college savings plan called Coverdell education savings accounts. You can put up to $2,000 a year in a Coverdell account, where it can grow tax-free until it's withdrawn. Just like 529 plans, you don't pay any taxes when you take the money out, as long as you spend it only on qualified education expenses. Unlike 529 plan funds, Coverdell savings can be used to pay for elementary and secondary school as well as for college.

If your student has earned income of his own, you might also consider having him open a Roth IRA for his college savings. Although Roth IRAs are generally used for retirement savings, contributions can grow and be withdrawn tax-free before retirement age if they are used to pay for qualified education expenses.

What's great about doing this is that the cash value of a Roth IRA is not counted among your assets in the financial aid formulas. Also, you can contribute as much to a Roth as your child earns, up to certain limits. In 2008, the maximum was $5,000; in 2009 and beyond, the ceiling will be indexed to inflation. And if you wind up saving more than you need for qualified expenses, your child can just leave the excess amount in the account to continue growing for his or her eventual retirement.

> The cash value of a Roth IRA is not counted among your assets in the financial-aid formulas.

The only real disadvantage is that when money is distributed from a Roth IRA, the school may consider it income, meaning that it could reduce the amount of financial aid you receive. As a result, your student may want to hold off on using Roth IRA savings until his or her last year of college.

What to Watch Out For

Putting Your Kids First

The single biggest mistake most parents make when it comes to college savings is making Junior's college funding too much of a priority. Saving for your kids' education is important, but you should *not* put it ahead of your own retirement needs. Your security comes first. You shouldn't even consider putting aside money for your kids' college costs unless you are already putting at least 10% of your income into a pretax retirement account.

Why? Because you can borrow for college but you can't borrow for retirement.

The greatest gift you can give your children is to ensure that you won't be a financial burden to them. If money is tight, your kids can always get part-time jobs when they're in high school and start putting aside their own money for college. There are also countless scholarship and loan programs for deserving students. (And there's absolutely nothing wrong with asking for help: Roughly two-thirds of all full-time undergraduates get some sort of financial aid.)

The right order of savings is to fund retirement first, then college. Even paying off high-interest debt should get priority over college savings.

It can be tough for good parents to put their own needs ahead of the kids'—especially when tuition bills are looming and your retirement is still a long way off. But the right order of savings is to fund retirement first, then college. Even paying off high-interest debt should get priority over college savings.

Not Starting Early Enough

Obviously, the longer you wait to start building your college fund, the more you will have to save each month to reach your goal. What you may not realize is that waiting just a little can cost you a lot. If you don't start saving until your child is 12, you'll have to put aside twice as much each month as you would if you'd started when your child was eight. Time really *is* money.

Investing Your College Fund Too Conservatively

Surveys show that nearly a third of all parents would prefer not to take any risk at all with their kids' college funds. That's understandable, but being overly cautious is not necessarily the best plan—especially if your kids aren't yet in their teens. To reach the same financial goal, a family that invests its college funds in super-safe certificates of deposit that pay annual interest of around 2% has to put roughly twice as many dollars into their college fund as one that invests in a mix of stocks and bonds that earns about 8% a year.

If your kids are at least five years away from entering college, you should be willing to tolerate a little risk for the sake of a better return—for example, investing your college savings in a good mutual fund and then gradually shifting into safer fixed-income investments as Junior's freshman year approaches. Playing it too safe can actually wind up hurting you.

Keeping Your Children's College Savings in Their Names

Many parents think that money for Junior's college education can or should be saved in Junior's name. Wrong. As Doug R. discovered, it's usually a much better idea to keep the funds in a parent's or grandparent's name.

This is because most colleges and universities expect parents to contribute between 5% and 6% of their assets toward the cost of their children's education. But the kids are expected to pony up as much as 35% of any savings or other assets they may have.

What Doug should have done is put some of his earnings into a Roth IRA, which isn't counted toward college, and used the remainder to replace his 20-year-old Buick. It may sound crazy, but when your kids are applying for college financial aid, money in the bank is sometimes the last thing they need.

Forgetting to Take Advantage of the Federal Education Tax Credit

To make it easier to pay those huge tuition bills, the federal government provides two tax credits for parents with kids in college—the Hope Credit and the Lifetime Learning Credit. The rules are a little confusing, but if your modified adjusted gross income is less than $57,000 ($114,000 if you file a joint return), you can reduce your tax bill by as much as $2,000 per family with a Lifetime Learning Credit and as much as $1,650 *per student* with a Hope Credit.

So why doesn't everyone who qualifies apply for one of these credits? A lot of people simply don't know about them, and many of those who do are scared off by how complicated they can seem. But with thousands of dollars at stake, they are worth taking the trouble to figure out.

At first glance, the Lifetime Learning Credit looks like the better deal, since the maximum amount is higher and you can qualify for it, year in and year out, as long as you have a child (or other dependent) who is taking at least one college course, whether or not it is meant to lead to a degree. By contrast, you can use the Hope Credit only if your kid is in the first or second year of a degree-granting program.

Then again, if you're one of those lucky parents with more than one child in college at the same time, the Hope Credit may make more sense for you, since you can claim one Hope Credit for each eligible student in the family. (In other words, if you have three kids in college at the same time and you meet the income requirements, you can take three Hope Credits—worth a total of nearly $5,000—off your tax bill.) With the Lifetime Credit, you can take only one credit per tax return, no matter how many kids you've got in college.

Details are available in IRS Publication 970, "Tax Benefits for Education" (www.irs.gov/publications/p970/index.html).

What to Do if Things Go Wrong

If you've spent years saving for your kids' college education in the wrong kind of plan (one with high fees, poor performance, or excessive restrictions), there's not a lot you can do—except switch to the right kind of plan as quickly as possible. But don't despair. If some cases, you may be able to roll over most if not all of your college funds into a more appropriate account. Talk to a tax advisor or financial planner.

Also keep in mind that the IRS allows you to amend your recent tax returns. So if you have a child or other dependent in college and you forgot to claim your federal education tax credit, you can file an amended return that includes the credit—which will probably entitle you to a refund. Just make sure you do so within three years of the date of the return you are amending. (For details on how to file an amended return, check with your tax professional or see IRS "Topic 308—Amended Returns," available online at www.irs.gov/taxtopics/tc308.html.)

Finally, college financial aid officers always tell prospective students and their parents that while the financial aid formula is what it is, the folks running the financial aid offices at colleges do have some leeway to make exceptions. So if you need more assistance than the formula indicates—maybe because you made a mistake in how you handled your college savings plan—explain your situation to a financial-aid officer. You never know—the school might be interested enough in your child to improve their offer.

Fight for Your Money Action Steps

☐ Start saving for college early. Get online and start your "homework" at www.collegeboard.com. Other great sites include www.savingforcollege.com and www.finaid.org.

☐ Find a 529 college savings plan that's right for you. Go to www.morningstar.com, www.savingforcollege.com, and www.collegesavings.org to do your research. Then enroll!

☐ Remember the best order for savings: Fund retirement first, pay off high-interest debt, *then* save for college.

☐ If you have a child in college, take advantage of the Hope Credit or the Lifetime Learning Credit when you file your taxes. If you missed out, file an amended return.

Health Insurance

Health insurance is such a nightmare these days that it's hard to tell who's got the worse deal—the 47 million Americans (including more than 8 million children) who don't have any coverage or the 260 million who pay good money for policies that often turn out to be rip-offs. Obviously, not having health insurance is a recipe for disaster. But having insurance is not always so great either. That's because with total health care spending heading toward $3 trillion a year in the United States—and costs continuing to increase at nearly three times the rate of inflation—it's as if the industry has found it more profitable to work against their customers than with them.

The worst problems are in the individual health insurance market, where companies routinely try to "cherry-pick" the healthiest customers and deny everyone else coverage. They do this by adding huge premium surcharges for people with family histories of health problems, refusing to pay for services needed to treat common ailments, and finding any excuse they can (like a minor error on an application) to deny payments to policyholders who develop medical problems that require expensive therapies.

According to the most recent Census Bureau figures, only about one in 10 Americans buys individual health insurance. Most people who have insurance are covered by group policies provided by their employer or by government programs like Medicare. The problem is that with private insurance costs skyrocketing, a growing number of employers can no longer afford to offer health benefits. As a result, many are forcing employees to pay more of the costs themselves—if they're not eliminating the benefit entirely.

The bottom line is that in what one expert calls "the Wild, Wild West for America's health care consumers" you need to be prepared to fight for what you're entitled to. That's because the insurance companies make money by saying no, even when the answer should be yes.

How to Fight for Your Money

Until recently, whenever someone submitted a claim, it was standard procedure at Blue Cross of California to pore over the person's medical records, looking for some error or inaccuracy that could be used as an excuse to cancel their policy. It took a class-action lawsuit by some 6,000 customers to get Blue Cross to change its practices and agree to rescind policies only if the mistakes were intentional.

In a nutshell, this is what consumers all over the country are up against—insurance companies, as Los Angeles City Attorney Rocky Delgadillo describes them, that "will devise schemes to maximize profit at the expense of health care."

Here's what you need to do to keep them from taking advantage of you.

Understand What You're Choosing

If you're one of the 180 million or so Americans who get their health coverage through an employer, you really have only two basic choices when it comes to health insurance. The first is whether or not to sign up. Generally speaking, this is a no-brainer. Sure, you may have to pay a big chunk of the premium yourself. (The average employee contribution for family coverage totaled $278 a month in 2007.) But the kind of group rates your company can get you are way cheaper than anything you could get on your own.

The other choice you get to make is what kind of coverage you want. Most employer-sponsored health plans offer some combination of the three basic types of care: through a health maintenance organization (HMO), through a preferred provider organization (PPO), and through a point-of-service (POS) plan. Each has its pluses and minuses.

HMO COVERAGE. A health maintenance organization is, in effect, a group of health care providers who have joined together to provide comprehensive health care coverage for subscribers. HMOs are the oldest managed-care systems around and they vary widely in cost and quality of service. Some people love their HMO and will tell you they are the only way to go because they are so affordable and easy to use. Others will complain bitterly about not being able to see the doctors they want or get the treatment they feel they need.

HMOs are certainly among the most restrictive types of health coverage. When you sign up with an HMO, you are given a list of doctors from which you must select a "primary-care physician." Otherwise known as a "gatekeeper," this doctor is the one you must see whenever you have a medical problem, regardless of what the problem might be. If it turns out you need to see a specialist, the gatekeeper will refer you to one within the HMO. If for some reason you want to see a specialist who's not part of your HMO, the visit will not be covered.

The good news about HMOs is that they are relatively inexpensive. Chances are they'll be the cheapest health care option your employer offers.

PPO COVERAGE. A preferred provider organization usually consists of a group of individual physicians, medical practices, and hospitals that have joined together to create a "group network." In some ways, PPOs look and feel a lot like HMOs, but there are some distinct differences. For one thing, PPOs don't require you to have a gatekeeper. You still have a primary-care physician, but if you want to see a specialist, you can go on your own without a referral. Also, you can use a specialist who's not a member of your PPO's group network and the PPO will still cover at least part of the bill. Not surprisingly, PPOs are more expensive than HMOs.

POS COVERAGE. Point-of-service plans offer subscribers the widest array of choices. Combining features from both HMOs and PPOs, the POS plan allows you either to stay within the plan's network of doctors (thus saving money) or to elect to go outside, in which case you have to pay a deductible (as with a PPO). Like an HMO, you pick a primary-care physician when you first get POS coverage. But unlike an HMO, your gatekeeper can refer you to a non-network specialist for treatment. And unlike PPO coverage, a POS plan will pay most, if not all, of the cost. Not surprisingly, POS coverage generally costs the most.

This may sound crazy, but if you work for a company that offers a variety of health care options, it generally makes sense to go with the most expensive choice. That's because in almost every case the most expensive choice will provide you with the most options, and when it comes to your health care, you don't want to cut corners. It's simply not worth it. Eat out less or cancel those premium channels on your TV/cable, and you've probably covered the cost of going with the most expensive health care option that has the most flexibility.

If you work for a company that offers a variety of health care options, it generally makes sense to go with the most expensive choice.

If You're on Your Own, Do Your Homework

Only 60% of all companies offer health coverage to employees, and the number is dropping every day. So more and more of us have to arrange our own health coverage. Before you surrender to the Wild West of the independent insurance market, see if there is any professional or social organization you belong to—or could join—that offers members a group health plan. If not, it's time to do some homework.

There are hundreds of insurance companies offering countless HMO, PPO, and POS plans for individuals and their families. You can start to sort them out by asking people you know—and maybe even an independent insurance agent, if you've got one you trust—for recommendations based on their personal experience. But that shouldn't be the extent of your research. There are all sorts of great web sites you can consult that summarize and rate hundreds of health plans, both private and public.

Among the most informative and user-friendly are:

- J.D. Power's Health Insurance Plan Ratings (www.jdpower.com/healthcare/ratings/health-plan-ratings)

- National Committee for Quality Assurance Health Insurance Plan Ratings and Report Card (http://hprc.ncqa.org/)

- *U.S. News & World Report*'s Best Health Plans Search (www.usnews.com/directories/health-plans/)

- *Consumer Reports*' HMO & PPO Ratings (www.consumerreports.org/health/insurance/health-insurance.htm)

Keep in mind that comparisons can be difficult, since prices and benefit schedules vary widely. Also, the size of the monthly premium is not the only factor you should consider. Deductibles, copay amounts, breadth of coverage—all these are just as important in figuring how good (or bad) a deal you're getting. In the end, you don't want the cheapest plan—you want the plan that will charge you the least for the protection you want.

If you are struggling to make ends meet, are over the age of 65, or have small children, visit www.cms.hhs.gov to see what government programs you may be eligible for and what options you may have.

Know What's in Your Contract—and What Isn't

Not every health insurance plan covers every ailment or therapy. Obesity treatments, acupuncture, cosmetic surgery, mental health care—even prenatal and obstetrical services—are excluded from many plans. So read your health plan contract carefully—particularly the sections that explain exactly what's covered and what's not, as well as how much you will have to pay when you see a doctor, visit a hospital, or get a prescription filled.

Many insurance companies and almost all employer-sponsored health plans provide policyholders with a Summary Plan Description that lays all this out in plain English. The problem is that this summary is not legally binding. The document you want to read is called the "Evidence of Coverage" or "Certificate of Insurance." If you have your own independent health coverage, you should have gotten this document when you bought the policy. If you have company coverage, ask your HR department for a copy.

Use Your Plan to Its Fullest

The great truth about health insurance is that many of us don't actually use all the health insurance we have. We may go to an in-network doctor when we have the option of using a better out-of-network specialist for the same cost. To get the most out of your health insurance, you need to take the time to read the plan documents—and ask questions if you don't understand what it says (which is more than likely, because it's so complicated).

Virtually every plan has complicated rules about what doctors you can see, what procedures must be preapproved (and how), and under what circumstances you can seek treatment from a practitioner or institution that is not part of the plan's network of approved providers. A lot of these rules may strike you as bureaucratic nonsense. And a lot of them are. But you need to know them and play by them if you want to get the best medical coverage possible and have your claims paid.

Consider a Health Savings Account

To be eligible for an HSA, you must be under 65 and have medical coverage under what is called an HDHP, for "high-deductible health plan." As of 2008, an HDHP was defined as any health plan with a deductible of at least $1,100 and out-of-pocket expenses not exceeding $5,600 a year for individuals and twice that for family coverage.

An HSA is like an IRA or 401(k) account dedicated solely to paying for your medical expenses. You fund the account with pretax dollars. (If you save through your employer's plan, your contributions are not counted as part of your taxable compensation; if you have an individual plan, they are tax-deductible.) Also like retirement savings, HSA contributions are invested on a tax-deferred basis (investment options vary by provider), which allows for compounded growth of your savings over time.

Any time you incur qualified medical expenses, you can dip into your HSA to pay them without incurring any tax consequences.

You can continue contributing to your HSA for as long as you are covered by an HDHP. If your coverage ceases, you can no longer make contributions—but you don't lose the contributions you've already made. They roll over from year to year and continue to grow tax-deferred.

What to Watch Out For

Counterfeit Insurance Companies

Just because it looks, sounds, and acts like an insurance company, that doesn't mean it *is* an insurance company. With reasonably priced health insurance increasingly hard to get, phony companies with genuine-sounding names like Employers Mutual, American Benefit Plans, and TRG have been scamming unwary consumers out of millions of dollars—and leaving them liable for hundreds of millions of dollars in unpaid bills.

What they do is hook customers by offering what seems like terrific health insurance coverage at great rates, using marketing materials and policies that look and read like the real thing. They may even pay off a few small claims to quiet any suspicions about their legitimacy. But the fact is that they are unlicensed, counterfeit companies that simply pocket your premium payments and then disappear when the first big claim is filed.

According to government statistics, in one two-year period some 144 phony health insurers followed this pattern, leaving more than 200,000 consumers on the hook for at least $252 million in unpaid claims.

There's a simple way to protect yourself against this sort of scam. Be very skeptical of any policy that seems unusually inexpensive or makes it easy to sign up even if you have a preexisting condition—particularly if it's offered by a company you've never heard of. And even if the name seems familiar, call your state insurance department to confirm that the policy is legitimate. You can find contact information for every state's insurance regulators on the web site of the National Association of Insurance Commissioners at www.naic.org/state_web_map.htm.

Medical Discount Plans

For people who don't have company health insurance and can't afford their own, medical discount plans can seem to be a terrific alternative. For a monthly fee of $100 or so, you get a card that supposedly entitles you to pre-negotiated discounts from a list of participating medical providers.

The problem is that most of these plans are scams. "These are spreading like kudzu all over the country," says James Quiggle of the Coalition Against Insurance Fraud. "They promise huge discounts. They slap on their web sites lists of medical providers who, in fact, have not agreed to participate. You show up for your treatment and say, 'Where's my 30% discount?' and the doctor doesn't know what you're talking about."

Some of these plans are valid, but even then you need to be careful. A 50% discount still means you have to pay 50% of the bill, which for even a short hospital stay can run into the tens of thousands of dollars. If you are tempted by one of these offers, check your state attorney general's office and state insurance department to see if complaints have been filed against the company. Then call your health providers to see if they accept the card.

What to Do if Things Go Wrong

When it comes to health insurance, all those rules and regulations can drive you crazy, but they come in very handy when things go wrong. If you have a problem with a health insurance company—and at one time or another most people do, usually over a disputed claim—there are all kinds of procedures available to help you sort things out.

The most basic—and serious—problem you can encounter with health insurance is being denied coverage. If this happens to you, immediately check to see if your state offers what's called a risk pool sponsored plan. These are subsidized plans that provide health insurance to people who are otherwise uninsurable. Some 33 states have them; for a complete list and more information, visit www.healthinsurancefinders.com/healthinsurance/risk-pools.html.

Claims and Billing Disputes

If your health insurer has denied a claim that you think is legitimate, you should first try to resolve your problem through your insurance company's internal complaint process. Virtually every company has a toll-free customer-service number you can call, but it's better to conduct this conversation in writing so there won't be any question about who said what if things get nasty.

Customer service can tell you the name and address of the specific individual to whom you should send grievances or appeals. Send everything by certified mail, return receipt requested, so that you have a record of when your letters were sent and received.

If you can't work things out with your insurance company directly, most states provide for an "external review" by a panel of independent experts.* For details of how the process works in your state, there is a terrific guide on the web site of the Kaiser Family Foundation at www.kff.org/consumer guide.

If you need assistance getting through the appeal process, whether internal or external, the health care consumer-advocacy group Families USA has an extremely useful state-by-state guide to finding health advocates on its web site, at http://familiesusa.org/resources/state-information. You can also get help from HealthCareCoach.com, an educational web site designed by the nonprofit National Health Law Program to help consumers better understand the health care system.

Phony Policies and Worthless Discount Cards

If you've been victimized by a phony insurance policy or worthless discount card, it's important to make a fuss about it. As James Quiggle of the Coalition Against Insurance Fraud (www.insurancefraud.org) notes: "So often these plans are deceptive but fall short of outright criminality and want to stay in business. Enough public pressure might induce a deceptive plan to make quick concessions, especially when threatened by the attorney general with expulsion from the state plus fines."

This means filing complaints with your state insurance department, attorney general, and consumer-protection agency as well as with state and local law enforcement. Enough such complaints may lead the authorities to seek cease-and-desist orders and impose fines that can be applied to help the victims. You can also keep the pressure on by complaining to the Better Business Bureau (www.bbb.org) as well as to local consumer reporters.

Fighting Back Against Medical Identity Theft

It's hard to know which is more challenging—proving that someone has stolen your medical identity or digging out from under the financial landslide

---

*The external review process is not available to people who are enrolled in a company health plan that is self-funded—meaning that the employer pays all health costs directly rather than buying insurance from an insurance company. Your employer can tell whether this is the case. If it is, your only option is to go through the health plan's internal appeals process—and if you don't like the results, to hire a lawyer and sue them.

they've caused. Many people first discover they've been the victims of medical identity theft when they check their credit report and find a collection notice from some unknown hospital, medical lab, or other health provider. Given that the impostor used your name, Social Security number, and insurance information, it's generally not easy to prove that it wasn't you who incurred this debt. Some victims have been able to prove their innocence by comparing the impostor's medical history with their regular medical files. One Florida woman billed for the amputation of a foot simply showed up in the hospital administrator's office and kicked both her feet up on his desk.

To get the collection notice removed from your credit report, file a police report and send a copy to the credit agencies. (For more information on how to fix errors in a credit report, see page 107 in the section CREDIT SCORES.) You should also use the police report to prove to the health care providers and your insurance company that someone has been impersonating you. Keep in mind that unless you can make your insurance company understand what's going on, the bills the impostor has been racking up will count against your policy's lifetime maximum benefit. You need to work with the insurance company—perhaps with the help of a lawyer—to make sure that the crook's claims are not counted against your cap.

Once you've accomplished this, it's critical to dig in and try to correct—or at least flag—the misinformation that's been inserted in your medical records by your alter ego. The challenge here is that thanks to the privacy provisions of the Health Insurance Portability and Accountability Act (HIPAA), you don't have the same rights to see and correct your records that victims of financial identity theft have.

Still, it can be done. You can get access to your records and the information you need through what's called a "Jane/John Doe file extraction" that allows health care providers to help identity-theft victims while protecting the sanctity of their records. Details on how to do this are available on the web site of the World Privacy Forum (www.worldprivacyforum.org). Just click on its "FAQ for Victims."

You can protect yourself against medical identity theft by carefully reviewing every "Explanation of Benefits" you get from a public or private insurer. If you spot any service, procedure, or item you don't recognize, contact both your insurance company and the health care provider immediately.

Another way to protect yourself is to contact your insurer at the end of every year and request a listing of all benefits paid in your name over the previous twelve months. Some crooks will change your billing address and phone number to keep you from seeing what they're up to. Once you get that annual list, make a point of demanding explanations for any payments you don't recognize.

Many people think it's okay to ignore erroneous insurance notices as long as they indicate no money is owed. That's a big mistake. Blowing this off now could cost you a lot more later on.

Fight for Your Money Action Steps

☐ If your employer offers group health coverage, make sure you sign up—even if it means paying a big chunk of the premiums.

☐ If your employer doesn't offer health insurance or you are self-employed, take advantage of the many user-friendly web sites that can help you sort out your options for individual coverage. The better ones include J.D. Power's Health Insurance Plan Ratings (www.jdpower.com/healthcare/ratings/health-plan-ratings) and *Consumer Reports* (www.consumerreports.org).

☐ Read your policy carefully, and understand the rules that govern it, so you can get maximum value out of your coverage.

Hospital Bills

The single greatest source of financial misery in this country is the cost of health care, and it's not hard to see why. In 2007, Americans—insured as well as uninsured—spent $275 billion out of pocket on doctors and hospitals. This is what we paid above and beyond what our insurance companies covered. And for millions of us it's just too much. Each year, some 700,000 families are forced into bankruptcy because of health care costs, while another 80 million or so Americans struggle with medical bills they can't afford to pay.

Meanwhile, our hospitals are making out like bandits. According to the *Wall Street Journal*, even nonprofit hospitals have become "profit machines," with at least 25 nonprofit hospitals or hospital systems each recording net earnings of more than $250 million a year. In all, income topped expenses at the nation's 50 largest nonprofit hospitals by upward of $4.25 billion in 2006—an eightfold increase over just five years earlier.

As crazy as it sounds, how much a hospital charges for a particular procedure often depends on who is footing the bill.

It might seem hard to believe, but the hospitals charge the highest prices to those least able to pay. As crazy as it sounds, how much a hospital charges for a particular procedure often depends on who is footing the bill. If you're a giant insurance company, you may get charged a relatively low rate. If you're an uninsured individual, you'll probably get hit with a much higher bill.

Same Surgery, Different Price

Take an appendectomy. This routine surgery plus a typical two-night stay rarely costs the hospital more than $5,000. If you're covered by Medicare, the hospital will accept roughly $4,700 for taking care of you. An HMO will bill your insurance plan $7,000 to $8,000, while Blue Cross Blue Shield will pay $9,000 to $10,000. But if you don't have insurance or you mistakenly use an out-of-network provider, forget about it. You can expect to be billed $30,000 to $35,000 for the same appendectomy—more than six times what Medicare would pay.

And don't think they won't try to collect it all. I recently heard from a Florida woman named Paula T. who went into the hospital after having an arm crushed in a motorcycle accident. Paula wound up with four steel plates, 23 screws, and tens of thousands of dollars in hospital bills that she couldn't pay. The hospital's collection agency had no sympathy. "They'd call late at night or early in the morning and say, 'We're going to ruin your credit. We're coming after you. Your family will be on the streets if you don't pay up,'" she recalls.

The sad fact is that the very hospital that might have saved your life will morph into your worst enemy. It will be ruthless in charging you unfair rates, it will likely *over*charge you for services not provided, and it will try to collect its debts when you are most vulnerable, any way it can.

The good news is that you don't have to be a victim. If you know your rights and stand your ground, you can stop this money-mad health system of ours from taking unfair advantage of you.

How to Fight for Your Money

Know Your Insurance—and Don't Be Afraid to Ask for More

Getting sick or injured is bad enough. You don't want to compound your misery by going into the hospital thinking everything is going to be covered by your insurance—only to discover that it's not. So don't wait until it's too late. Today—right now—read through your health insurance policy and make sure you understand what's covered and what isn't. It's also really important to understand your policy's preapproval or authorization rules. Not getting prior approval when it's required can cost you.

This applies to both medical procedures and medical providers. If you are facing surgery or some other procedure and the doctors you are counting on to treat you aren't part of your plan's network, see if you can work out some accommodation with your insurance carrier. When Paula T. learned that the only anesthesiologist working in the hospital where she had to have her surgery wasn't a member of her plan, she persuaded the insurance people that it didn't really make sense for her to be knocked out by another doctor across the street and then carried back for the surgery. So they agreed to cover the $2,000 fee.

Pay Later—and Get Any Promises in Writing

It's sad but true: In the middle of a medical emergency, hospital bean counters will try to take advantage of your desperation, telling you (or the person who brought you in) that you can't be treated unless you turn over your credit card and authorize a charge that could run into the thousands of dollars. *In fact, under federal law, anyone who comes to a hospital emergency room has the right to be treated and stabilized or stabilized and transferred, regardless of whether or not they have any money.* It is against the law for an ER to withhold or delay treatment because of a patient's inability to pay.

> It is against the law for an ER to withhold or delay treatment because of a patient's inability to pay.

If you are insured, the hospital is allowed to collect your copay amount (which in most cases is around $100 or so), but nothing more. If they insist on more, tell them you won't pay unless they put their demand in writing, in the form of a detailed itemized bill. Since they're playing fast and loose with the law, it's likely they'll back off rather than put anything in writing.

There are also times that well-meaning medical staff inadvertently cost patients a lot of money. Say you have a loved one in the intensive-care unit who is ready to be moved to a regular room. If there are no rooms available, rather than send the patient home, a nurse may suggest that he or she remain in the ICU—and that you shouldn't worry about the extra expense because you won't be charged for it. The nurse may not think they will charge you—but believe me, they will. So if you're ever in this situation, have the nurse put in writing that you're not to be charged extra for the additional ICU stay.

Scrutinize Your Bill—Watch for Duplicate Billing

Experts say that 90% of all hospital bills contain mistakes—and they are never in your favor. Back in 2005, the Department of Health and Human Services estimated that billing errors cost consumers more than $31 billion a year. The figure is probably much higher today. Duplicate billing is probably the most common "error." Often, it will involve surgery cases, but it can involve something as simple as a test that was canceled and then rescheduled, resulting in a double charge. Surgical patients are typically charged something like $70 a minute for their use of the operating room. This fee is supposed to cover more than just renting the space. It's also supposed to include the cost of most everything that is routinely used in the operating room, such as gowns, drapes, tubes, gloves, and equipment. But on many bills for surgical patients you'll find both the operating room fee *and* individual line items for all the OR supplies. In other words, you've been billed twice for them.

Scrutinizing your bill may also reveal that you've been victimized by what can only be described as price gouging. Hospitals have been known to ding patients as much as $70 or $80 for a bag of IV saline that actually costs no more than 10 cents. One uninsured woman in her seventies who fell and broke her thighbone was charged $201,000 for a 19-day stay in a New Jersey hospital. Among other things, the hospital billed her nearly $6,000 for a box of nonsterile, disposable latex gloves that you could buy at Staples for $7.99. Another hospital billed a child patient $57.50 for what the bill described as a "cough support device." It was actually an inexpensive teddy bear.

So when you're leaving the hospital, always ask for an itemized bill. When you get it, the first thing you should do is make sure that all the charges seem correct and that you weren't charged for any services you didn't actually receive. Did they slip an "epidural for a C-section" into your husband's stay for heart bypass surgery? Stranger things have happened. Count how many days in your room you're being billed for; you're not supposed to be charged a room fee for the day you were discharged. And look for duplicate charges.

She Fought for Her Money!

One of the most inspiring stories I've come across concerns a woman from Stanford, California, named Laura who found herself on the hook for $40,000 in hospital bills. An ICU nurse herself, Laura knew there was no way she could afford to pay that debt. "So I phoned up the billing department and told them it was impossible for me to pay this bill," she recalls. "Right away they offered me 20% off, but only if I settled the bill in two lump-sum payments. I told them I couldn't do that."

This was the beginning of a back-and-forth between Laura and the hospital that went on for almost a year. By the time it was over, Laura had gotten them to reduce the $40,000 bill down to $10,000, payable in installments over 18 months with no interest.

Don't hesitate to ask for help in interpreting your bill. Hospital bills are notoriously difficult to decipher. If necessary, ask the hospital's billing officer to meet with you to review the charges.

If you find errors, ask the billing department to correct them. If they refuse, request a copy of the hospital's "grievance process" for disputing errors discovered on medical bills.

If the hospital doesn't have any such process, write a letter detailing your grievances to its chief financial officer and the manager of patient accounts. Send a copy to your local consumer-protection agency. (You can find a list of state, county, and city consumer-protection offices on the federal government's Consumer Action web site at www.consumeraction.gov/state.shtml.) Be sure to keep copies of every letter and email. Take notes about dates and times of telephone conversations and the employee with whom you spoke. If anyone agrees to amend your bill, tell them you won't take their offer seriously until they put it in writing.

Don't Be Afraid to Haggle

If you get hit with a hospital bill you can't afford, be like Laura. Haggle with your health care providers for a discount, just as you would with a used-car salesman. Remember that Medicare and the big insurance companies get charged much less than you do. So don't pay sticker price! And don't stop at the first "no" you hear or limit your bargaining to the clerk behind the window in the billing office. Clerks and cashiers are generally authorized to discount bills only to a certain level and within a specific time frame. Ask to speak to that person's supervisor or call to set up a face-to-face meeting with the manager of credit and collections, the manager of patient accounts, or even the hospital's chief financial officer. And just as in buying a car, never accept the first discount they offer you.

If you have some financial resources, you may be able to negotiate a deeper discount in return for a larger up-front payment. But don't agree to anything you're not certain you can afford to pay. And no matter what arrangement you and the hospital work out, make sure you get it in writing.

Don't Accept Medical Credit

Quite often in the course of working out a payment arrangement with a hospital, a credit officer may suggest that you put your outstanding balance on a medical credit card. The terms may seem attractive, but be wary. You may be offered 0% interest for a certain period, just as you would be if you were buying a lawn mower on a Home Depot card. But miss a payment or exceed the no-interest time limit and your interest rate may jump as high as 27%. What's more, your credit score will suffer.

There's an even more compelling reason not to put your hospital bill on any credit card. The moment you do so, you lose any leverage you may have to negotiate any further discounts on your bill. Once the hospital has been paid by the credit card company, it no longer has any interest in bargaining with you. After all, it has now gotten its money. Your issue is now with the credit card company, and they are not likely to have any sympathy for you.

So when the hospital credit officer starts talking credit cards or lines of credit, tell him the only arrangement you will consider is one that involves interest-free payments spread out over a manageable period of time—and that you don't want any information about your medical debt forwarded to any of the credit bureaus. And once again, don't take the word of someone just because they sound friendly and helpful. Get it in writing.

Don't Ignore Your Bill

Even if you can't afford to pay your bill, you should show the hospital that you are making a good-faith effort to handle your obligation. Tell the hospital's billing office that you are working on a payment plan and that you would like them to change the status of your account to "pending." (This will keep your bills from being turned over to a collection agency.) Then check on your insurance situation. If you have coverage and your claim has been denied, appeal it quickly. Your policy should explain how to do this. If you can't work things out with your insurance company directly, check if your state provides for an "external review" by a panel of independent experts. Most do. (For details on how this works, see page 174 in the section HEALTH INSURANCE.)

What to Do if Things Go Wrong

Get an Advocate

What do you do if your kitchen table is piled with hospital bills you can't afford to pay and you don't know where to begin? One solution is to hire a medical-billing advocate. These are trained professionals who will go over your bills to ferret out any errors or overcharges and then negotiate a reasonable payment schedule with insurers, health care providers, facilities, and collection agencies. Fees can range from $50 to $200 an hour to review and renegotiate medical bills. This may seem like a lot, but it's usually a good investment, since a good advocate can save you tens of thousands of dollars.

You can find an advocate in your area or with the particular specialty you may need through the web site of Medical Billing Advocates of America (www.billadvocates.com), a nationwide patient-advocacy network that deciphers hospital bills for consumers and works on behalf of uninsured patients.

Don't Assume You're Not Eligible for Charity Care

While your insurance appeals are pending, check with the hospital to see if you are eligible for public programs or charity care. Even though nonprofit hospitals are required to provide charity care, they usually won't offer it. As Laura, the Stanford nurse who got her bill knocked down by 80%, puts it: "You have to ask for everything. It's there, but you have to ask." And don't assume you won't qualify. The income ceilings for charity care are often much higher than people think, ranging as high as 400% of the federal poverty-income guidelines. And don't assume the hospital staff knows the score. One recent study found that many hospital staff members routinely tell patients not to bother applying for free care, when in fact it is available. Instead, ask the billing office for copies of the hospital's financial assistance and charity care policies.

Hold the Hospital Accountable

Hospitals have come under intense scrutiny—and been hit by dozens of lawsuits—for being too aggressive in trying to collect money from uninsured patients. As a result, the American Hospital Association adopted a "Hospital Billing and Collection Practices Statement of Principles" that calls upon hospitals to be more responsible in their billing practices and more compassionate with patients who cannot afford to pay for the care they receive. More than 4,200 of the nation's hospitals have pledged to abide by those principles. If yours is one and you think it is not living up to them, give a copy of the principles to the billing office. You can download both the Statement of Principles and the list of participating hospitals from the web site of the American Hospital Association at www.aha.org.

You might also want to file a complaint with your local consumer-protection agency (www.consumeraction.gov/state.shtml).

If They Sue You, Sue Back

In some worst-case situations involving unpaid bills, a hospital may threaten to sue you or place a lien on your house. If this should happen to you, consider retaining an attorney to file a countersuit charging what's called discriminatory demand of reimbursement. This entitles your attorney to force the hospital to turn over its original invoices for everything they charged you—a move that often encourages the hospital to drop its suit and sometimes even cancel your bill, since they may not want the public to know how incredibly inflated so many of their charges are.

If no one you know can recommend an appropriate lawyer, you can find one by using the National Association for Consumer Advocates' online lawyer locator at http://members.naca.net/findanattorney.php. And if you can't afford a lawyer, you might qualify for free legal assistance from the federally funded Legal Service Corporation. You can find a list of LSC offices in your area on the organization's web site at www.lsc.gov/map/index.php.

Fight for Your Money Action Steps

☐ Read through your health insurance policy and make sure you understand what's covered and what isn't. Also make sure you understand your policy's preapproval or authorization rules.

☐ When you get your hospital bill, review it CAREFULLY. If you have questions, ASK. If you find an error that the hospital won't correct, file a complaint with your local consumer-protection agency.

☐ If you can't afford the bill, negotiate.

☐ If you are in over your head, hire a medical-billing advocate to work on your behalf.

☐ If the hospital is threatening you with legal action, get a lawyer immediately. If you can't afford one, check with the federally funded Legal Services Corporation (www.lsc.gov/map/index.php).

Health Club Memberships

When it comes to high-pressure salesmanship, health clubs can be surprisingly adept at separating you from your money, particularly the big national chains. The come-ons are always so attractive—huge discounts off the normal enrollment fee, personalized evaluations, free guest passes. It sounds like such a good deal. And when you walk into the place, there's always some incredibly buff guy or really cute girl who seems happy to show you around, tells you how there's never a wait for any of the machines, and reassures you that it's no hassle to quit if you ever change your mind. Before you know it, they've persuaded you to sign a contract that commits you for at least a year to two years and allows them to take their monthly dues directly from your checking account. Worse, many of these contracts have penalty fees should you terminate early or require a few months' notice before termination (otherwise the membership is automatically renewed).

With tactics like these, it's no wonder the health-club industry rakes in revenues of close to $20 billion a year. Nor is it surprising that the Better Business Bureau reports that complaints about health clubs have nearly doubled in recent years.

How to Fight for Your Money

There's no question that among the roughly 30,000 health clubs in the United States today, there are many terrific gyms offering really good deals on really good services. But there are also plenty of rip-offs. The good news is that if you know what to look for, it's not too difficult to separate the good from the bad. Here's how.

Shop Around—and Don't Be Rushed

Start your search by checking with your employer—and your insurance company, too. Many employers now offer group discounts at certain health clubs, and insurance companies sometimes offer full or partial reimbursement of your membership dues. Be aware of what benefits you're entitled to. Additionally, check with your credit card company, which may have special offers for its members, and with membership retailers like Costco.

The fitness business is an incredibly competitive one. Most areas are home to a wide range of workout places—from big chains like 24 Hour Fitness, LifeTime, and Bally, which offer lots of amenities, to community centers like the YMCA and JCC that have fewer bells and whistles but generally lower costs. There are also small, independent clubs, and if you live near a university campus, you may have access to school facilities (possibly even for free, if you're an alumnus).

Having all these choices gives consumers more control. So don't be afraid to push for a good deal. Don't feel you have to sign up for a long-term commitment or pay an initiation fee. If one gym in town is offering a really attractive promotional offer, bring their flyer to another gym you like (or already belong to) and ask them to match it. Check for "new membership specials," and "refer a friend specials"—or anything coming up. Most clubs offer a new promotion each month.

Above all, don't let anyone (no matter how cute they may be) twist your arm to join. Never sign a contract on your first visit to a gym. Instead, take it home, where you can read the fine print without anyone rushing you. And check with your state's consumer-protection agency as well as the Better Business Bureau (www.bbb.org) to see whether a gym you're considering joining has been the subject of many complaints.

If a sales rep gives you a hard time about doing any of this, it's a sure sign you should find another gym.

Be Wary of Automatic Billing

As anyone who's read my bestseller *The Automatic Millionaire* will know, I am a great believer in automating your finances. But I don't recommend the kind of automatic bill-paying most health clubs try to impose on customers.

What a lot of gyms do is include in their contracts a provision that allows them to arrange an electronic funds transfer that takes your monthly payment out of your checking account and automatically sends it to them.

The idea that anybody besides you should have the right to take money out of your account is bad enough. But to give that power to an outfit as untrustworthy as a health club is downright outrageous. Consider this story, which I was told by a young woman named Donna who lives near Minneapolis.

About two years ago, Donna signed up at a local health club for a tanning package that she thought was for one month only. What she didn't realize was that it was an ongoing package that automatically renewed each month—and that the club had the right to take each month's payment directly out of her checking account.

Now, at the time, Donna was living paycheck to paycheck, and before she realized what was happening, the health club's automatic withdrawals had drained her account. As a result, in addition to the unexpected tanning charges, she also got hit with hundreds of dollars in bank overdraft penalties.

When she explained the problem to her bank, they agreed to cancel the overdraft fees. But the gym was not nearly so nice. It refused to release her from her contract unless she agreed to pay it off in full. Feeling she had no choice, she did.

Nevertheless, the health club continued to take money out of Donna's checking account. Finally, she got her bank to place a "stop payment" on her account so that the gym could no longer withdraw money from it. But they keep trying to this day.

For all her trouble, Donna learned two valuable lessons: From now on, anytime she's in a dispute with a company, she'll keep a written record of everyone she speaks to and what they promised. And most important, she will never again sign a contract that gives any business the right to pull money directly from her account.

Sadly, Donna's situation is not unusual, and her advice is worth following. If a gym is not willing to trust you to pay your monthly dues on your own, why should you trust them with the keys to your bank account? Given how competitive the fitness industry is, a reputable gym should be willing to waive the electronic-funds-transfer requirement and invoice you like any other business. If they're not, find another place to work out. And if you feel you

MUST join this gym and they require automatic withdrawal, then do it with your credit card, not your bank account, which can be harder to stop and/or recover if you are debited twice by accident (which happens all the time).

Make Sure It's All in Writing—and Give Yourself an Out

Make sure you read and understand exactly when your contract expires. Health-club salespeople will promise you the moon—especially when it comes to how easy it supposedly is to transfer or cancel your membership. In fact, their promises mean nothing unless they are written into the contract.

When you're dealing with a chain, you should make sure you understand what the contract says about using your membership at different outlets. For instance, a basic membership at L.A. Fitness allows you to use all their branches in your state, but not those elsewhere in the country. And if you're thinking about taking out a long-term membership, pay special attention to the cancellation rules. Don't assume you can get a refund if you decide you don't like the place. It's hard enough getting out of a health-club contract if you get injured or have to move.

In fact, some clubs will allow you to temporarily freeze your membership in the event you're laid up due to illness, injury, or pregnancy, as long as your account is in good standing. But canceling a long-term health-club membership for good—no matter how legitimate the reason—can be horrendously difficult, if not actually impossible. For example, if you move, some fitness chains will refuse to let you out of your contract if they have a branch within 25 miles of your new address.

As a result, it's probably a good idea to avoid signing up for a long-term membership at a club you're joining for the first time. A short-term trial membership may be a little more expensive on a monthly basis, but the extra cost will be more than worth it if your circumstances change or the gym doesn't live up to your expectations. And again, read the small print that explains what it takes to cancel your membership. Many contracts require written notice of cancellation—and have a specific day of the month written notice must be received by or you are billed for the entire month.

Avoid the "Platinum Membership" or Bells and Whistles

Many salespeople will first sell you on the idea of a membership—and then, as soon as you are ready to sign, push to sell you the higher-end membership. Usually, the Platinum or Gold membership will give you access to more clubs (either in the city, state, or country), depending on the club. In reality, most people have a hard enough time going to the gym that's a mile from their house. The extra 10 to 20 bucks a month you may spend to get this added benefit in most cases won't be worth it. And in truth, your club may offer "free passes" you can use later at a club in another city (ask them for a few guest or free passes before you sign on the dotted line). Lastly, before you sign up for, say, the "gym locker membership" that allows you to leave your clothes in the locker and even get them washed, ask yourself: Is it really worth it? It's not "just 10 dollars a month more"—it's $120 more a year, or $240 more if it's a two-year contract. Think about the added costs in annual or two-year time frames and you may rethink adding the extras and save yourself a fortune.

Negotiate Hard Against the New-Membership Fee

Most clubs push for a new-membership fee or a special one-time initiation fee—which in some clubs could run over $100. This fee is a huge profit center for the club—and in almost every case it is negotiable and different, depending on the time of the year. Most clubs offer specials at certain times of the year when the initiation fee is waived. January seems to be peak time for deals like this, since all the gyms are competing for all those New Year's resolution makers.

Don't Forget Your "Cooling-Off Period"

By law, consumers are entitled to a "cooling-off period," during which they have the right to cancel a fitness contract they've just signed. So don't panic if you've gotten talked into signing a health-club contract that you can't afford or otherwise isn't right for you.

In most states, you have three days to change your mind, though in some places it's longer. Rhode Island, for example, gives you 10 days, while in Georgia you get a week. You can find a complete list of what every state offers in the way of consumer protections on the web site of the International Health Racquet and Sportsclub Association, at http://download.ihrsa.org/publicpolicy/statelawsummary10-06.pdf.

What to Watch Out For

Bills That Don't Stop Coming

Ending a health-club membership is hard enough. Getting them to stop billing you can be even harder. The Better Business Bureau reports that fully a quarter of all the billing complaints they get regarding health clubs come from people who continued to have money taken out of their checking accounts even after they felt their contracts had expired or been canceled.

So even though you may be convinced that you no longer belong to a gym, don't assume they feel the same way. Even if they're not pulling money out of your checking account, that doesn't mean you're in the clear. It's entirely possible that your membership wasn't properly terminated, in which case the club may decide that you've skipped out on them and so turn over your account to a collection agency.

> Even though you may be convinced that you no longer belong to a gym, don't assume they feel the same way.

To guard against this happening, double-check with the club that your account is closed. And then, just to be triple sure, check your credit report after a few months to make sure they haven't reported you as a delinquent account. If they have, you will need to dispute the report with the credit agency (see the section CREDIT SCORES on page 107 to learn how) and then straighten things out with the club.

Annual Increase in Fees

Many gyms are now raising their rates, especially as times get tough. You may even receive a written notice of a rate increase. The nice letter lets you know you don't have to do anything. The truth is that one thing you can do is go back into your membership office and find out if they are offering any "new specials" where the monthly fee is lower than the one you signed up for. Some contracts may have guaranteed rates as well, in which case the gym isn't technically allowed to raise your rate during the contract period—so be sure to check. Lastly, you can always threaten to close your account, and when they ask why explain that it's because the fee is being raised and you can't afford it. You may be surprised to find out that they will let you keep your current membership fee for an additional year.

Keep an Eye on Your Valuables

Even at the most upscale places, health-club locker rooms are prime targets for petty thieves. Wallets, credit cards, laptops, cell phones, watches—all are at risk, and the club is not liable for items that are stolen. So when you go to the gym, it's best to bring as few valuables with you as possible. What you can't leave at home, carry with you in a fanny pack. And if you must leave valuable items in a locker, take inventory before you leave the gym. That way, if something is missing, you'll know right away and be able to notify the club and the police immediately.

What to Do if Things Go Wrong

Always start by putting your complaint in writing and addressing it to the head manager of the club where you had the problem. At the same time, copy the CEO of the gym. More than likely, the founder can be found on their web site, as can the company headquarters. Then follow up the letter with a call or meeting with the manager. By starting a paper trail and copying the founder or president of the national company, you will find that you are instantly taken more seriously and also they may be more motivated to help you quickly resolve the problem. If you find yourself in a dispute with a health club that you haven't been able to resolve with them directly, your best bet is to file complaints with both the Better Business Bureau (www. bbb.org) and your state's attorney general. A complete list of state attorneys general offices is available on the web site of the National Association of Attorneys General at www.naag.org/attorneys_general.php.

Fight for Your Money Action Steps

- ☐ Shop around for the best deals in your area—and check with your membership organizations, employer, and insurance company for special discounts and reimbursements.

- ☐ Read the fine print—know for sure when your contract expires and how to cancel.

- ☐ If you absolutely must enroll in automatic payments, charge the fee to a credit card. Do not give your new gym the right to pull money directly from your bank account.

- ☐ Take advantage of the cooling-off period if you sign a contract you immediately regret.

Buying a Home

As I write this at the end of 2008, we're experiencing the most difficult real estate market in more than 20 years. Some will argue it is the most difficult market since the Great Depression. According to the National Association of Realtors (NAR), there are currently over 4.5 million homes listed nationwide, representing a supply of over 11 months. There are also record foreclosures. According to data released by Foreclosures.com, almost 102,000 U.S. homeowners lost their homes to foreclosure in August 2008 alone, an increase of nearly 6% from July 2008 and more than an 80% increase from 2007.

Since the beginning of 2008, lenders have repossessed 656,545 properties nationwide, or 8.6 of every 1,000 households in the United States. By the end of the year, it is estimated that more than 1 million homes will be lost to foreclosure.

Real estate has always been a cyclical business and market. And with all down and difficult markets comes real opportunity. Home prices right now are falling across the country, making homes more affordable in most U.S. cities. According to NAR, the national median existing-home price was $212,400 in July 2008, down 7.1 percent from a year ago when the median was $228,600.

The bottom line for homebuying is that buying a home is more than just an investment—it is, in fact *your home*, where you live, love, and have a life. The good news for most people is that buying a home will ultimately be the best investment you make over your lifetime, because over the long term, real estate values increase. Simply buying a home and paying down the mortgage can provide you with financial security for life.

The other reality is that recent conditions have created what is arguably the best BUYER'S MARKET for real estate in decades.

But even with this buyer's market, buying a home can be complicated and expensive if you do it incorrectly. Whether it's a buyer's market or a seller's market, the fundamental issue for people looking to buy a house is always the same: How can you find a place you love at a price you can afford? And how do you borrow responsibly to make this purchase something you can hold on to? (Be sure to read the next section, on mortgages.) What complicates matters is that in even the simplest real estate transactions there are so many moving parts and so much money involved. As a result, unless you're very careful, you can get taken to the cleaners—not just by the folks you're buying from but also by the very people whose job it is to help you make a deal.

How to Fight for Your Money

Realistically, buying a home is probably the biggest purchase you'll ever make. It's also likely to be the most confusing. Here's how to go about it without getting ripped off.

Hire a Great Real Estate Agent

With all the real estate web sites available on the Internet these days, it's possible for anyone with a computer to do a lot of the stuff that only a real estate agent used to be able to do. Certainly, you don't need a professional in order to locate homes for sale in a particular area or get a good sense of where prices are in the category that interests you. But this kind of research may be the least important thing a great real estate agent can do for you.

I've been a real estate agent myself (specializing in commercial properties), and I've worked with real estate agents on all of my own real estate transactions. I know from personal experience how much they can help you. But I also know that not all real estate agents are created equal. There's a constant stream of newcomers into the field, and in many states it's shockingly easy to get a real estate license.

As of this writing, there are roughly 3.2 million real estate agents in the United States—roughly 60% more than just three years ago. Many of them are great—but not all. So how do you find the one who can guide you through the process intelligently and help you close a great deal? Here's a list of things you should look for.

- A GREAT REAL ESTATE AGENT WILL LISTEN TO YOU CAREFULLY. Great agents are great listeners. They have to be in order to really help you. When a great agent meets you for the first time, he or she will pepper you with questions to find out what you're looking for, what you really want, why you want it, and most important, what you think you can afford.

- A GREAT REAL ESTATE AGENT WILL HELP YOU FIGURE OUT WHAT YOU REALLY *CAN* AFFORD. The first thing a top-notch agent will do is run your numbers and give you a ballpark estimate of what your price range should be. A great agent will also provide you with referrals to lenders who can help you get preapproved for a mortgage.

- A GREAT REAL ESTATE AGENT WILL SAVE YOU TIME BY NARROWING YOUR SEARCH. A great agent won't run you ragged (and waste your time) by dragging you around to countless properties. Rather, the agent will help you figure out what you are looking for, show you a selection online, and allow you to narrow your choices before you actually hit the streets. He or she will then "tour you" to ones you've chosen— and keep track of what you like.

- A GREAT REAL ESTATE AGENT WILL EDUCATE YOU ABOUT THE MARKET. Great real estate agents know more than simply what's for sale in a particular neighborhood. They know the neighborhood. They can tell you all about an area's history, what makes it special, and where they see the market there going. If you're looking at a new development, the agent will know the developer's track record and plans for the future.

- A GREAT REAL ESTATE AGENT WILL SHOW YOU WAYS TO GET MORE VALUE FROM THE PROPERTY. From the moment a great real estate agent first sees a house, he or she is thinking about what could be done to increase its value. Install new kitchen cabinets, redo the floors, knock out the back bedroom and add a master bath—great agents will look at houses and immediately begin suggesting ways you could make it more valuable.

- A GREAT REAL ESTATE AGENT WILL HOLD YOUR HAND AT CLOSING. The closing of a home purchase at the title office can be a scary few hours. Great agents will go over the paperwork with you and your attorney, checking it for errors. They will also work closely with you and your mortgage banker or broker to make sure everything is as it should be.

How to Find a Great Agent

Finding an agent who is ready, willing, and able to do all these things is not as hard as you might think. You should start by asking trusted friends and colleagues for recommendations. If one name keeps cropping up, that's a good sign. Make a note if you see a particular agent's name repeatedly on For Sale signs in the neighborhood where you want to buy. You can also collect business cards from agents you meet at open houses.

As your list of prospective agents begins to take shape, do an Internet search on all the candidates you're considering. Look for articles, chat room or blog posts, and personal web sites to get a feel for their work, their style, their values, and how they market themselves. Also check whether they belong to the National Association of Realtors. About half of all real estate agents do, and membership in NAR (www.realtor.org), which offers advanced training and requires members to follow a code of ethics, is a good sign that they are serious about their profession.

Don't Be Afraid to Ask Tough Questions

When you've narrowed your list to three to five prospects, schedule a meeting with each—and treat your meeting like an actual interview. I recommend that you ask the following questions:

- How long have you been in business?

- How long have you worked in this particular market?

- How many listings (properties for sale where you represent the seller) do you have?

- How many clients are you currently working with?

- How many deals did you do last year in the area I'm interested in?

- Why should I work with you rather than one of your competitors?

- What makes you a good real estate agent?

- What is your process—how do you work with your clients?

- Do you have a team or an assistant? Will I be working with them or you?

- Can you give me the names of three clients you've worked with whose situation was similar to mine?

Based on their responses, ask yourself how you think it would be to work closely with each of them. Does your gut say this person is trustworthy? The

My Free Gift to You!

Visit my web site at **www.finishrich.com** to listen to my free audio on how to hire a real estate agent.

only correct answer is whether the agent feels right for you. It's all about chemistry.

Before you commit to a particular agent, check them out with your state's real estate commission or licensing board. (You'll find a list of every state agency that licenses real estate professionals on the web site of the Association of Real Estate License Law Officials at www.arello.com/index.cfm?fuseaction=RegAgency.) You want to verify that your choice is not only licensed but also that his or her license is in "good standing," meaning the agent has kept current with all educational requirements. You also want to find out whether he or she has any record of complaints or disciplinary actions.

Pick an Area Where You Want to Live and Start Looking

Before you can buy a house, you have to find a house. And the sooner you start looking, the sooner you'll finish. So don't feel you need to wait until you've hired a real estate agent. Get started right away. Just draw a circle on a map that covers an area within five miles of where you want to live. Somewhere within that circle you are going to find a home you like in your price range.

The place to begin your search is the Internet. In fact, that's where 84% of would-be homebuyers start out these days, according to the National Association of Realtors. Given the terrific real estate resources available online, it's not hard to see why. In just a couple of hours at your computer, you can gather information about what's available where and for how much that would have taken you months to assemble 10 years ago. Here's a list of 10 top real estate sites:

AOL Real Estate (http://RealEstate.aol.com)

Coldwell Banker (http://ColdwellBanker.com)

CyberHomes (www.cyberhomes.com)

DotHomes (www.dothomes.com)

Movoto (www.movoto.com)

National Association of Realtors (www.Realtor.com)

ReMax (www.ReMax.com)

Trulia Real Estate Search (www.Trulia.com)

Yahoo! Real Estate (http://RealEstate.Yahoo.com)

Zillow (www.Zillow.com)

Of course, Internet research only goes so far. For all the convenience of online house hunting, nothing beats firsthand experience. So be sure to check the open-house listings in a local newspaper (or online at www.openhouse. com), make a list of the ones in your price range, and then get in your car and go look at them. In a matter of hours, you'll be able to see as many as a dozen properties and get a real sense of what's out there that you can afford.

Run the Comps and Make a Realistic Offer

Once you find a house you love (or at least one you like enough to want to buy), you're going to have to make an offer. As a rule, houses don't have set prices. What they have is an "asking price." It's up to you to respond with an offer, which can be more or less or the same as the asking price.

How do you know how much to offer? This is where a great real estate agent really comes in handy. He or she will help you figure out whether to go high or low, and by how much. Agents do this by assessing how much demand there is for the property, how eager the owner is to sell, and most of all by "running comps"—providing you with an analysis of what comparable properties in the area have been selling for. Your real estate agent will be able to do this for you at no cost. Or check out sites like www.homesmartreports. com, which charges $25 for a solid analysis of sales trends in any given neighborhood. Less detailed comps are available for free from www.zillow.com, www.domania.com, and www.homegain.com, and for $6.95 from www. equifax.com.

Most experts recommend you look back between 90 and 180 days. But it really depends on the market. Real estate is local. Some markets are so hot that you need to gauge the most recent comps possible. Other areas are so slow that you may have to research property sales going back more than a year to get a feeling for the market.

You should run the comps even if you know the neighborhood. Thinking you know what prices are and actually knowing them are two different things. Your purchase decision should be based on hard facts, not hunches.

Knowledge Without Offers Costs Money

If you're not scared when you make an offer on a home, you are definitely the exception, not the rule. Most people get really nervous when they make an offer on a property. There are so many factors to consider—and so much money at stake—that pulling the trigger can be downright nerve-racking.

Having purchased half a dozen properties in the last 10 years, I can tell you that while it does get easier the more you do it, it's never really easy. And I certainly understand what it is like to freeze up and not be able to make a decision. Back in the mid-1990s, I found myself unable to pull the trigger for nearly four years!

As a result, I wound up paying $640,000 for a two-bedroom condo that I probably could have bought for about $300,000 when I first started looking. Learn from my lesson. Spend as long as it takes to find a place that you like. But once you do, STOP LOOKING AND MAKE AN OFFER.

Protect Yourself with a Well-Drafted Purchase Agreement

When you make that offer on a house and then get the great news that it's been accepted, don't think you're done. You still have to close on the purchase, and this can be a complicated process that takes weeks, if not months.

The first step in the closing process is to sign a purchase agreement and put down a deposit (also known as "earnest money"). You'll need to hire a good real estate attorney to draft your purchase agreement. (They often work for a set price.) The purchase agreement commits you to buying the house at a specified price, subject to various contingencies such as your being able to get a mortgage. One thing you should insist on is that the purchase agreement include language that gives you the right to have your earnest money returned in full if for any reason you change your mind about buying the house. Given all the uncertainties that go along with buying a house, you want to give yourself maximum flexibility.

Have the House Inspected by a Professional

Unless you are purchasing a new, custom-built property, you should never close on a house without having it first checked out by a professional home inspector. Some people balk at the cost, which can run anywhere from $250 to $1,000 or more, but that doesn't make sense. Considering how much the house is going to cost you, the inspection fee is a small price to pay to ensure that the biggest purchase of your life doesn't turn out to be a lemon.

A properly performed home inspection will uncover any serious problems involving structural issues, leaks, faulty appliances, electrical and plumbing woes, possible health hazards like lead, and so on. (You might also consider ordering up a termite inspection and, if the property has water tanks or a well, a water inspection, too.) Although a professional inspector will provide you with a written report of his findings, don't just wait for him to submit it. Show up at the house and personally watch him conduct the inspection. Chances are he will do a better job if he knows you are looking over his shoulder.

You should be able to get a referral for a good inspector from your real estate agent or your mortgage lender—preferably from both. And make sure he is either a member of the American Society of Home Inspectors (www.ashi.com) or InterNACHI, the National Association of Certified Home Inspectors (www.findaninspector.us). Many states allow anyone to hang out an inspector's shingle. You want someone who really knows what he's doing.

If You Get a Warranty, Make Sure You Know What It Says

Most newly built houses and condos come with builders' warranties that guarantee against construction defects for anywhere from one to 10 years. But the protection they offer may not be as solid as you think. So before you close on a new home, read the warranty carefully and have a lawyer look it over, too.

Some 30 states have what are known as "right-to-repair" laws, which are meant to encourage sound construction and give builders the opportunity to repair defects. In fact, since most of these laws were shaped by lobbyists for construction interests, what they really do is make it difficult for you to pursue claims against a builder—even if you have warranties. What's more, some right-to-repair laws require homeowners to perform proper upkeep—which means that if you don't follow the maintenance schedule listed in your warranty, your protection could lapse. This is why it's important to know what's in your warranty—and why it's probably a good idea to ask an attorney to review it with you to ensure that you understand your obligations.

What to Watch Out For

Conflicts of Interest

Occasionally, a real estate agent will show you a house that is represented by another agent at his or her firm. If you decide to buy it, the sales contract will more than likely include a line noting that your agent actually does not represent you but rather represents the seller.

In this case, you MUST get an attorney. Don't let "your" agent tell you not to worry about it. If you sign a contract that says your agent represents the seller, you have no protection legally. So get yourself an attorney who can look over the contract—and watch your back—in the deal.

This situation is called "dual agency," and it's a classic conflict of interest that happens all the time in the real estate business. The laws covering dual agency vary from state to state. Only six states—Colorado, Kansas, Maryland, Oklahoma, Texas, and Vermont—actually prohibit agents from representing both sides in a transaction. But even in states where it's legal, agents have an ethical obligation to tell a prospective buyer if they or their firm are also working with the seller. Of course, that doesn't mean they will. A few years back, state investigators in Massachusetts made undercover visits to 45 real estate offices to see if they were giving new clients a dual-agent disclosure form, as the law required. None of them were.

The problem with dual agency is that it's just not realistic to expect one agent (or real estate firm) to do the best possible job getting the lowest price for a buyer at the same time that it's trying to get the highest price for the seller. Even with the most ethical of agents, there are bound to be problems. At the very least, once you express interest in a house that your agent represents, you will probably find him or her becoming a bit more distant and less willing to advise you candidly on what the seller might or might not accept.

The fact is, you need to know that your agent is representing you and you alone. One way to do this is to use a "buyer's agent" who works in an office representing only buyers. You can find agents who work only with buyers through the National Association of Exclusive Buyer Agents (www.naeba. org), a group whose code of ethics requires (among other things) that members avoid all possible conflicts of interest, disclose any referral fees they may get from sellers' agents, and reserve their loyalty exclusively to their buyer clients.

If you do end up working with an agent or firm that also represents sellers, always keep in mind that even though you may really like your agent personally, he or she may not have your interests at heart. So avoid sharing crucial details—such as your bottom-line position in negotiations. You don't want to put your agent in the awkward position of knowing your spending limit when he or she is discussing strategy with the seller.

If you do end up working with an agent or firm that also represents sellers, avoid sharing crucial details—such as your bottom-line position in negotiations.

Rebates, Referral Fees, and Kickbacks

When it comes time to close your purchase, chances are that your real estate agent or mortgage broker will recommend that you use a particular escrow agent, appraiser, and title insurance company. In many cases, that's because they know them and like their work. But sometimes it's because they have a hidden financial interest in steering business to these particular folks.

Under the federal Real Estate Settlement Procedures Act, it's illegal for a real estate agent or mortgage broker to accept "referral fees" or "rebates" in exchange for sending a client to a particular closing agent. Nonetheless, steering clients in exchange for kickbacks happens all the time. A study by the Washington State Insurance Commissioner calls the number of violations "truly astonishing." In New York State alone, a kickback scheme run by the nation's four biggest title insurance firms cost homebuyers hundreds of millions of dollars, according to a federal antitrust suit filed in 2008. Similar charges in California led state regulators to slam the same four companies—which together control more than 90% of the title-insurance business—with $49 million in fines and penalties.

The problem with kickbacks is that when you're steered to a particular closing agent, you're probably not getting a competitive price or the best service. One indication of how much this practice costs consumers is to compare title-insurance rates in a state like California, where kickbacks have been rampant, to those in Iowa, which is the only state in the country where the government runs the title-insurance business. In California, title insurance for a $500,000 home will cost you $1,200 to $2,000. In Iowa, coverage for a $500,000 home costs just $110.

So unless you live in Iowa or have plans to move there in the near future, I strongly advise making it a point to do some comparison shopping. By all means, call the title firm your real estate agent recommends—but also look in the phone book or online for two or three other national companies. Ask each what services they provide and what they charge for them. Then pick the one that you—not your agent—like best.

What to Do if Things Go Wrong

Problems with a Real Estate Agent

If you feel your real estate agent has acted unethically or otherwise short-changed you, complain *in writing* to the agent's supervisor. List specifics. Tell exactly what happened, when it happened, and who was involved. Keep a copy for yourself and send the letter by certified mail, return receipt requested, to provide you with a record of when and to whom you filed your complaint.

If that doesn't resolve the problem, complain to your state real estate licensing board. As I noted earlier, you can find contact information for every state agency that licenses real estate professionals on the web site of the Association of Real Estate License Law Officials at www.arello.com/index. cfm?fuseaction=RegAgency. When you contact the state licensing board, ask them to describe the procedure for filing a complaint, what steps the agency will take to investigate and handle the complaint, how long it will take, and how you will be notified of progress and decisions.

If an ethics issue is involved and the agent is a member of the National Association of Realtors, you should complain to your local Realtors association, with a copy to your state's real estate licensing commission. You can find contact information for every state NAR chapter on the organization's web site at www.realtor.org/leadrshp.nsf/webassoc?OpenView.

Defective Construction and Warranty Problems

Given all the obstacles thrown up by right-to-repair laws, if you buy a newly built home and then discover it has construction defects, your best bet may be to consult Homeowners Against Deficient Dwellings (www.hadd.com), an advocacy group that helps homeowners understand their rights and pursue remedies. Although HADD does not investigate complaints or bring legal action of any kind, it is allied with activist legal and consumer organizations such as Consumer Attorneys, Public Citizen, and Trial Lawyers for Public Justice. Its web site is also a treasure trove of valuable information, including the procedures for filing defective-construction complaints in every state.

Fight for Your Money Action Steps

- ☐ Make a commitment to find yourself a great real estate agent. Schedule interviews with your top three prospects and make a decision.

- ☐ Figure out what kind of home you want to buy and where.

- ☐ Run the comps and make a realistic offer.

- ☐ Hire a great real estate attorney to look out for your best interests, from the purchase agreement all the way through the closing.

☐ Order a complete home inspection.

☐ Read more about the homebuying process in the next chapter, HOME MORTGAGES.

☐ Read *The Automatic Millionaire Homeowner* to create a truly powerful lifetime plan to finish rich as a homeowner.

Home Mortgages

As I write this, CNN has just reported that lenders foreclosed on a record 1.2 million homes in the second quarter of 2008. To make matters worse (or even scarier), another 2.9 million homeowners (or 6.4% of the total) were behind on their payments. What is truly devastating about these numbers is that each and every foreclosure represents a family or individual tragedy.

It is easy to say (and many "experts" have) that the mortgage meltdown was simply the result of lenders pushing homeowners to take on mortgages they couldn't afford. And there is no doubt that millions of people were sold mortgages they couldn't afford. But the foreclosure crisis is not solely the fault of irresponsible lenders. It came about for many reasons—one of which is that too many borrowers were too willing to sign agreements they did not understand.

The most important truth I can share with you on this subject is that you need to understand your mortgage BEFORE you sign on the dotted line and close on a home. And if you are already in a home and have a mortgage, you need to understand NOW what type of mortgage you have and how it truly works.

Unfortunately, a stunning number of homeowners simply do not understand how mortgages work, much less what they currently have. According to a recent study by BankRate.com, one in four people do not know what type of mortgage they have. Considering that for most people, home mortgage payments make up more than 30% of their spending, it's utterly stunning that millions of us simply have no clue as to how our homes are being financed. You cannot let yourself be one of these people.

For years I have stood by one simple axiom about real estate that is very different from other experts':

I believe the old saying that the secret to real estate is "location, location, location" is wrong. The secret to real estate is "FINANCING, FINANCING, FINANCING."

If you get the financing of your home wrong, you may well wind up losing the property entirely. And if you think I'm exaggerating, just look around—it's been happening in millions of cases all over the country.

A Quick History of the Recent Mortgage Meltdown

It's hard to believe now, but mortgages used to be rather simple. You'd hear the word "mortgage" and you'd think things like "stable," "responsible," and "boring." The biggest decision most homeowners had to make when choosing a mortgage was whether to get a 15-year mortgage or a 30-year mortgage. The rate was fixed, and you knew exactly how much you would be paying each month for an extended period of time. The most exotic of mortgages was an adjustable-rate mortgage (known as an "ARM") and that was typically a 30-year mortgage with a fixed rate for the first five, seven, or 10 years.

In the late 1990s, however, mortgage lenders began offering a wide variety of exotic products. There were option mortgages, interest-only mortgages, negative-amortization mortgages, and on and on. Many buyers didn't even try to understand these complicated loans. Instead, they focused on the first month's payment, which was always very low. To make matters worse, lenders created "no documentation" loans—informally known as "liar's loans"—which allowed you to buy a home with little or no money down and no proof of income.

Finally, the industry began pushing what were known as subprime mortgages. These were loans that allowed people with very little (if any) savings and not very good credit to buy a home (often with no down payment). The result was record homebuying and record home-price appreciation. Before long, many people were looking at their homes as if they were stocks that they could buy and flip for quick and easy profits. At the same time, the lenders were handing out home equity loans that allowed a record number of homeowners to borrow against the supposed appreciation of their homes and use the proceeds to pay off their credit cards or buy more things.

For a while, while home prices continued to rise, it worked for millions of Americans. But as always happens, the party eventually came to an end. By the end of 2007, mortgage delinquencies were skyrocketing, real estate values were tumbling, the banks were facing losses of close to a trillion dollars (that's right—a *trillion* with a *t*), and as many as 6 million Americans were in imminent danger of losing their homes to foreclosure.

To put it mildly, mortgages were no longer a simple and straightforward path to homeownership and eventual wealth. Instead, to many homebuyers who could no longer afford their monthly payments (which had doubled and tripled as their adjustable interest rates reset), they had become "toxic."

In the immediate aftermath of the mortgage meltdown, with Congress on the warpath, several big financial institutions in ruins, and most of the nation's major banks taking multibillion-dollar write-downs, lenders finally did what they should have done years earlier. They began to clean up their act. If you had good credit, verifiable income, and the cash to cover at least a 20% down payment, you could get yourself a 15- or 30-year fixed mortgage, no problem. But forget about getting one of those nothing-down, no-documentation, deferred-interest mortgage time bombs. They were history.

At least that's what a lot of people would like to believe.

It would be nice to say that the bad old days are gone for good, that never again will prospective homebuyers have to worry about predatory mortgage lenders offering those tempting deals that seem so affordable up front but in fact contain hidden traps that will eventually bankrupt you. But the fact is that these things go in cycles. Although the exotic mortgage products—and the scam artists who promoted them—are currently out of favor, you can bet that sooner or later they will be back.

So if you're in the market to get a new mortgage or refinance an old one, keep your guard up. In the right hands, a sensible mortgage is still one of the greatest tools ever invented for building wealth. You just need to make sure that a sensible mortgage is what you get.

How to Fight for Your Money

Basically, a home mortgage is a loan you take out to buy a house, the collateral for which is the house itself. (This means that if you fall behind on the payments, the lender can seize your house and kick you out.) In its simplest version, a mortgage loan is repaid over a set period of time (usually 15 or 30 years) with a series of regular payments, part of which go to pay the interest charges and part of which go to pay down the principal. Early in the life of a mortgage, when the loan balance is high, most of the payment goes to pay interest. But as time goes on and the loan balance diminishes, the interest charge declines along with it and more and more of the payment goes to pay down the principal. By the time you get to your last payment, virtually all the money is applied to the principal. This process is what is known as amortization.

The impact of the mortgage crisis is bound to be felt for many years (maybe decades), and until the pain fades, mortgage lenders are likely to be pretty careful about what kind of mortgages and refinancing deals they offer and who they offer them to. This is a good thing, because no one benefits— not the lender, not the national economy, and definitely not the borrower— when a bank or broker lets someone bite off more than he or she can chew.

Still, if we've learned anything from the meltdown, it's that as a borrower you shouldn't expect a mortgage lender to look out for your interests. You've got to do that for yourself. Here's how.

Figure Out How Much You Can Afford

When it comes to buying a place to live, the bottom line isn't how much houses or condos cost. It's how much you can afford to spend.

So how much home can you afford?

The most sensible rule of thumb is probably the one recommended by the Federal Housing Administration, the government agency charged with help- ing Americans become homeowners. It says that most people can afford to spend 29% of their gross income on housing—and as much as 41%, if they have no other debt. The following table shows what price range your income would justify.

WHAT PRICE RANGE IS RIGHT FOR YOU

Annual Gross Income	Monthly Gross	29% of Gross	41% of Gross
$20,000	$1,667	$483	$683
$30,000	$2,500	$725	$1,025
$40,000	$3,333	$967	$1,367
$50,000	$4,176	$1,208	$1,712
$60,000	$5,000	$1,450	$2,050
$70,000	$5,833	$1,692	$2,391
$80,000	$6,667	$1,933	$2,733
$90,000	$7,500	$2,175	$3,075
$100,000	$8,333	$2,417	$3,417

As the table indicates, if you have a household income of $80,000 a year, you should be able to afford to spend somewhere between $1,933 and $2,733 a month on mortgage payments. Whether you should be on the high side or the low side of this range depends on how much debt you are already carrying, what other financial goals or commitments you have (like retirement savings or special medical expenses), how secure your job is, and what your future prospects are. Obviously, if you have little or no debt, few other commitments, and are looking forward to a series of promotions at work, you can comfortably bump up against the 41% ceiling. If things are a little tight, you'll want to stay closer to the 29% floor.

The next table shows what the monthly payments are for different-size 30-year mortgages at different interest rates—in other words, how much house you can get for a monthly payment you can afford.

TYPICAL MORTGAGE PAYMENTS

Mortgage Amount	5.0%	5.5%	6.0%	6.5%	7.0%	7.5%	8.0%
$100,000	$537	$568	$600	$632	$668	$699	$734
$150,000	$805	$852	$899	$948	$998	$1,048	$1,100
$200,000	$1,074	$1,136	$1,199	$1,264	$1,331	$1,398	$1,468
$250,000	$1,342	$1,419	$1,499	$1,580	$1,663	$1,748	$1,834
$300,000	$1,610	$1,703	$1,799	$1,896	$1,996	$2,098	$2,201
$350,000	$1,879	$1,987	$2,098	$2,212	$2,329	$2,447	$2,568
$400,000	$2,147	$2,271	$2,398	$2,528	$2,661	$2,797	$2,935
$450,000	$2,415	$2,555	$2,698	$2,844	$2,994	$3,146	$3,302
$500,000	$2,684	$2,839	$2,998	$3,160	$3,327	$3,496	$3,665

Monthly payments (principal and interest) for 30-year, fixed-rate mortgage

Figuring an interest rate of around 6% (which is where standard 30-year fixed-rate mortgages are as I write this), what the table says is that someone who can afford to spend between $1,933 and $2,733 a month on housing—that is, someone who earns $80,000 a year—could easily carry a $350,000 to $450,000 mortgage. In most parts of the country, that's still more than enough to buy a pretty decent home.

Clean Up Your Credit *Before* You Start Shopping for a Mortgage

The single most important factor in whether you will qualify for the best possible and least expensive mortgage is your credit score—the three-digit number, based on your credit history, that essentially summarizes what kind of credit risk you are. Credit scores range from 300 to 850. A difference of just 50 points can cost you thousands of dollars over the life of your mortgage, and a hundred or more points can be worth tens of thousands to you to lose or keep. So your credit score is truly critical, and if it's not ideal, now is the time to fix it. Ideally, you should start working on your score at least a year before you start shopping for a mortgage, but the good news is you really can raise your score in six months. The section CREDIT SCORES on page 108 explains how credit scores are calculated and what it takes to raise one.

When you're finally ready to start applying for a mortgage, make sure you concentrate all your applications and inquiries into one 30-day period. You need to do this because every time you ask a bank or broker about the possibility of getting a mortgage, they're going to check your credit—and every time someone checks your credit, a few points get shaved off your credit score. Fortunately, the credit-rating agencies that set your credit score don't want to penalize consumers for shopping around for a mortgage, so they count all credit inquiries received from mortgage lenders within the same 30-day period as just one inquiry.

Shop for Your Mortgage Before You Start Shopping for Your House

There's nothing worse than finding the house of your dreams—and not knowing if you'll be able to get the money it's going to take to buy it. Actually, there may be one thing worse: finding the house of your dreams and then making a hasty, ill-informed decision about a mortgage because you're excited and want to close the deal as quickly as you can.

> You should get an ADVANCE COMMITMENT from a lender before you start looking at houses.

Mortgages are complicated, and you want to make your choice calmly and deliberately, not when you're keyed up, stressed, and in a hurry. This is why you should get an ADVANCE COMMITMENT from a lender *before* you start looking at houses.

Basically, a preapproval is a solid commitment from a particular lender to give you a particular mortgage at a particular rate, subject only to your finding a suitable house. You shouldn't confuse this with a prequalification, which doesn't really commit anyone to anything.

When you ask a lender to preapprove you for a mortgage, you are asking him to formally review your financial situation, decide whether you are creditworthy, and then, assuming you are, commit to lending you a certain amount of money on particular terms, subject only to your finding an appropriate property. To do all this, the lender will pull your credit report and score and study your credit history to see whether you can be trusted to pay your bills on time. In addition, the lender will want to verify both your current income and your income history. He will probably want to see copies of your tax returns for the last three years, especially if you are self-employed, and he will want to see a verified list of all your assets and liabilities.

Because this review is so thorough, it may take several days to complete. But once it's done, you'll have a real commitment that you can literally bank on.

Knowing in advance exactly what kind of mortgage you can get will not only make the whole homebuying process more enjoyable, but it could also get you a better deal, since sellers are generally more willing to talk turkey with buyers who have solid financing.

Getting Preapproved: Whom to Ask and Where to Go

So how do you decide whom to ask for a preapproval? Finding a mortgage lender is mainly a matter of shopping around. You should start by meeting with your current bank. If you bank with a national bank, visit your branch and ask to speak with the loan officer. Often, bank customers get preferred rates. You should also get recommendations from your real estate agent (by law, they must provide you with three referrals). And, of course, ask people you trust who have mortgages themselves as well as financial professionals you deal with, such as your accountant or financial advisor. Whittle the list down to a half-dozen or so banks, finance companies, and mortgage brokers, and then start making the rounds.

With your credit report in hand—and a good idea of how much you want to borrow in your head—visit each of the candidates. There are four basic questions you should ask them:

- WHAT'S THE PROCESS LIKE? Applying for a mortgage is a lot like applying to college. There are all kinds of forms to fill out, scores to worry about, and choices to make. Ask the banker or broker to spell out the process he or she will go through to help you do all these things. You should also make sure they can help you get preapproved. If the answer is "No, but I can get you prequalified," this is not a broker or banker you want to work with.

- WHAT KIND OF EXPERIENCE DO YOU HAVE? You want someone who's been in the business for a while with plenty of experience handling what you're looking for. If you are buying your first home and the lender's experience is mainly with refinancing, he or she may not be the right one for you.

- WHAT KIND OF LOANS DO YOU GENERALLY RECOMMEND? Every mortgage lender will tell you that the answer depends on the client's particular needs and situation. So ask which kinds of mortgages he or she favors and why. If you're not comfortable with what you hear, find someone else. And be wary of anyone who talks up adjustable-rate loans or other exotic products.

- DO YOU SPECIALIZE IN A CERTAIN KIND OF CLIENT OR PRODUCT? Some mortgage professionals welcome first-time homebuyers. Others work mainly with sophisticated investors. You want someone who works with the type of borrower you happen to be.

The answers you get to these questions should give you a sense of whether the mortgage professional you're talking to is the right one for you. Chemistry should count for something, too. You're going to be discussing a lot of sensitive personal information, so if you don't feel comfortable, the relationship is not going to work.

If you're satisfied by the answers you get, ask the candidate for a ballpark estimate of the kind of rate and terms their institution would be willing to give you. And don't be shy about pressing for details. Ask all the questions listed on page 211.

This shopping process is a good way to screen out sleazy lenders and abusive loans. Good lenders will give you clear explanations. Predators, on the other hand, never answer your questions clearly. So if you come away from a meeting feeling confused, even if you really like the lender or mortgage broker, don't do business with that lender—keep shopping.

Most likely, each lender will present his proposals in a slightly different way. As a result, you may find it hard to compare competing mortgage offers. One way is to match up each mortgage's APR (annual percentage rate), since that figure takes into account not only the interest rate but also any interest you will be expected to prepay (called "points"), as well as fees and closing costs.

For an even more accurate comparison, there are a number of user-friendly mortgage evaluators available online. MyFico.com has a "Which

Is the Better Loan?" calculator (www.myfico.com/LoanCenter/Mortgage/Calculators/LoanEvaluation.aspx) that will compare the overall costs of any two mortgages and tell you which is the better deal, while Tcalc.com has one that will compare three loans at once (www.tcalc.com/mortgage-comparison-calculator.html).

Once you've figured out which lender's offer is the best, ask that lender for a preapproval. If, after going through the rigorous preapproval process, you're told that you don't qualify for the mortgage they originally offered you, continue to shop around before you accept one with less favorable terms.

Don't Buy a Loan You Don't Understand

As I said earlier, a quarter of all homeowners don't understand what type of mortgages they have. The truth is that in recent years many millions of people were ruthlessly sold mortgages based simply on the initial interest rate. Their lenders told them, "Here's the interest rate and here is what your monthly payment will be at the beginning." I call that ruthless because the size of your initial monthly payment and your initial interest rate isn't nearly enough information for you to understand what the true cost of your home will be.

What you need to know to really understand your mortgage is NOT COMPLICATED. It's just been made more confusing than it needs to be—so much so that even financially sophisticated people have been taken in. Back at the height of the housing bubble, a good friend of mine called me to say that she had been offered "a jumbo mortgage with a 2% interest rate"—and what did I think? My immediate response was to tell her that it had to be a "teaser" rate. At the time, rates for jumbo mortgages were running around 6.5%. "There's NO WAY they can offer you that rate," I said. "My guess is that it adjusts in six months or less."

Armed with that new information and a list of questions, my friend went back to her lender—and sure enough, it turned out that the 2% rate was good for only one month and then would be reset every month after that based on current conditions. Had she not called me, she probably would have bought a home with a mortgage she couldn't possibly afford.

Questions to Ask a Mortgage Lender
Before You Sign on the Dotted Line

- What type of mortgage is it? Is it a fixed rate or adjustable rate?

- How long is the term of the loan (what is the amortization schedule)?

- If it is an adjustable-rate mortgage, how long is the rate locked in? And when it resets, what will it adjust to? Every adjustable-rate mortgage is tied to the movement of a key economic indicator (such as the Treasury Bill index or the London Inter-Bank Rate). So if you have an ARM, ask which index it is tied to, how much over the index your rate will be set, and why that particular index is a good idea for you.

- Is there a prepayment penalty—meaning that if you refinance or pay off the mortgage early, will the lender charge you a penalty fee? And if so, how much is it?

- What happens if I rent out the property, as opposed to living there myself? Do I have to let you know and is there a penalty fee or interest-rate adjustment?

- What is the cost of the loan? Are there up-front fees (known as "points")? How much is the fee?

- If the down payment is less than 20% of the purchase price, how much will I have to pay for private mortgage insurance? And once my equity in the house reaches 20%, how can I get my PMI obligation waived?

- What is the mortgage's APR (its true interest rate)?

If you insist on getting answers to these questions, you will learn more than most people ever do when they get a mortgage—and as a result, you will be prepared to make an educated decision.

What made the subprime mess possible was the fact that millions of people were willing to sign up for mortgages they didn't understand—and, in many cases, didn't really need. More often than not, they did so because they were dazzled by the false prospect of "free" money—the idea, planted by predatory lenders, that they didn't need to worry about the details because rising real estate values would take care of everything.

Obviously, the details do matter. So if there's anything in your mortgage agreement that doesn't make sense to you—or doesn't seem to reflect what you were promised—demand an explanation. And don't believe the banker or broker who tells you, "Don't worry—we'll fix it later." The fact is, later never comes. As one consumer advocate says, "I've never met anyone who actually got the better loan later."

Take a Homeowner Class—Get More Financial Education

I wrote an entire book on homeownership called *The Automatic Millionaire Homeowner*. This book is a true "Homeownership 101" course, and you can find out all about it at my web site at www.finishrich.com. Whether you buy *The Automatic Millionaire Homeowner* or check it out of the library for free, you should read a book like it. And if you are a first-time homeowner, I strongly recommend that you take a course on homeownership. Many lenders today offer "first-time homeowner" classes. You can visit finishrich.com for information about workshops offered in your area or check with the U.S. Department of Housing and Urban Development (better known as HUD) or your local city or county consumer-protection agencies.

In addition to courses, HUD sponsors local counseling agencies that provide housing advisors who can act as your advocate in the lending process, helping you to interpret and evaluate mortgage estimates and documents. There's a list of HUD-approved local agencies in your state on the HUD web site at www.hud.gov/offices/hsg/sfh/hcc/hcs.cfm.

Remember: No matter how nice they may seem, most bankers, mortgage brokers, and real estate agents are paid by commission and earn money when you "close the transaction." While most mortgage advisors are honest, it only takes one "bad apple" to destroy your life financially. So you MUST educate yourself and make sure the advice you get is objective and honest.

Don't Overreach

As I said earlier, the key to real estate is "financing, financing, financing." It's not enough to be able to pay for your home in the beginning—you have to be able to pay for your mortgage for as long as you own it (which may be much longer than you think). Part of what went wrong during the subprime mess was that irresponsible lenders persuaded people to take on mortgages they simply could not afford. They did this because banks don't keep most of the mortgages they make. Rather, they repackage them into what are called mortgage-backed securities, which are sold to institutional investors around the world. As a result, it wasn't their problem if the borrower couldn't make the payments.

The point is that just because a bank or other financial institution might be willing to lend you a certain amount of money doesn't mean you should take it all. Buying a house almost always costs more than you think it will. Not only are there taxes and insurance premiums on top of the mortgage payment—not to mention closing costs—but there are also the costs of moving and decorating. And when you stretch to buy the biggest house you can possibly afford, it's easy to forget that in addition to the higher mortgage payments, you're also going to have to cope with higher maintenance costs, higher utility bills, a higher property-tax assessment—pretty much higher everything.

So think about the *total* cost of ownership. There are a number of calculators available online to help you come up with a realistic estimate; two good ones are www.vertex42.com/ExcelTemplates/home-expense-calculator.html and www.bygpub.com/finance/MortgageRatioCalc.htm. Whatever you do, don't let a real estate agent or mortgage broker convince you to take on bigger payments than you can feel comfortable with. Use the chart on page 209 to guide you instead.

Don't Get Pushed Around

By law, mortgage lenders are required to give you three key documents that can help you understand the mortgage you are buying.

- GOOD-FAITH ESTIMATE. There are a laundry list of administrative and legal fees, taxes, insurance premiums, and other costs you have to pay when you close a mortgage. These generally add up to thousands—and sometimes tens of thousands—of dollars. Within three days of your making a loan application, the lender is required to give you a "good-faith estimate" of what the total is likely to be.

- TRUTH-IN-LENDING STATEMENT. At the same time you get the good-faith estimate, the lender is also supposed to give you a "truth-in-lending disclosure statement." The TIL, as it's called, sets out the terms of the loan—how much you're borrowing, the interest rate and APR, whether the rate is fixed or adjustable, how many payments you'll make and how much they'll be, and so on.

- HUD-1 SETTLEMENT STATEMENT. At least 24 hours before you close on your mortgage, your closing agent or escrow company is supposed to give you a HUD-1 settlement statement—a detailed, close-to-final breakdown of all the costs, fees, and charges of your mortgage. It may not be 100% accurate because the lender may still be calculating a few details, but it must be very close.

There's a simple reason why the law gives consumers early access to these three documents. Whether you're buying or refinancing, real estate transactions are complicated, stressful affairs, and consumers need some breathing room in order to review and understand what they're being asked to sign. For this very reason, some lenders deliberately hold back the documents, hoping they can railroad a questionable deal through.

They Fought for Their Money!

I recently heard a classic story about this sort of thing from a couple in Seattle. June is a lawyer. Her husband, Frank, teaches. A few years back, when mortgage rates dropped really low, they decided to refinance. Their bank was happy to do the deal, but it would not let them look at the loan documents until the closing.

So when they got to the closing, June sat down and did what she always does—she read every page of every document they wanted her to sign. This annoyed the closing agent, but she stood her ground. Sure enough, in the fine print, June found a bunch of things that bothered her. The straw that broke the camel's back was a provision saying that if either June or Frank died, the bank could declare the loan in default and demand full payment.

"That's ridiculous!" June told the loan officer. "Just because one of us dies doesn't mean we can't make the payment. I don't even know if that's legal."

The loan officer told her not to worry about it. "Of course they won't do that," she said.

"Well, I'm not signing any papers saying they can do that," June replied. "So forget it. We're not refinancing." And with that, she and Frank walked out.

A few days later, the loan officer phoned them to say that the bank was refunding their $300 loan-application fee, which was supposed to be non-refundable. She also wanted to know the name of their favorite restaurant, because the bank wanted to give June and Frank a $100 gift certificate for dinner. "It sort of makes you wonder what was going on," June says.

She and Frank did eventually refinance their mortgage—but with another lender.

What happened to June and Frank—being pressured to quickly sign a stack of closing documents that they had never seen before—is not at all uncommon. To prevent this from happening to you, make it clear to both your real estate agent and your lender that you'll want to get as much detail about your mortgage as early as possible and that you intend to take your time reviewing it.

Like June, be prepared to encounter—and politely resist—pressure to move more quickly. Remember, it's your money at stake. You have the legal right—as well as the responsibility to yourself and your family—to take all the time you need to make sure you understand everything you are signing.

If you feel you need more time, don't hesitate to ask your lender to postpone the closing for 24 hours. If they won't agree, do what June did—walk away. Keep in mind that if you were approved for this mortgage, you'll be able to get another somewhere else at similar terms.

What to Watch Out For

Unsolicited Offers

Predatory lenders traditionally target homeowners who are looking to refinance an existing mortgage rather than homebuyers who are looking for a new mortgage. In fact, 90% of the folks who took out subprime loans from 1998 to 2006 were already homeowners. In particular, scam artists go after homeowners with a history of credit problems, counting on their embarrassment to keep them from doing any comparison shopping.

Because all mortgages are publicly recorded, it's easy for unscrupulous lenders to find out your current interest rate. They can then phone you or show up on your doorstep claiming that you're paying too much and that they can get you a better deal. This in itself is a giveaway. As a rule, you should never do business with a mortgage lender who approaches you with an unsolicited offer—whether in person, by phone, or via email.

Keep in mind that if you are pressured into signing a contract to refinance a home loan, you have three business days to cancel it and receive a refund of all closing costs. In fact, when you close the refinancing, you're supposed to get a "Notice of Right to Cancel" that lists the deadline to notify the lender that you've changed your mind. (Unfortunately, there is no such cooling-off period with new mortgages.) In any case, if you think you've been scammed—or want out of a refinancing for any reason—you've got to move fast. Call the lender immediately, and at the same time send him a written notice by certified mail, return receipt requested.

Exotic Mortgages

Starting in the 1990s, there was a huge explosion in the number of different mortgages banks and other lending institutions were offering. By 2005, homebuyers had literally thousands to choose from. There were adjustable-rate mortgages, piggyback mortgages, option mortgages, interest-only mortgages, hybrid mortgages—the list went on and on. Each of these exotic mortgages probably made sense for someone—but not for most of the people who wound up buying them.

As a result of the mortgage meltdown, most mortgage lenders have stopped offering the most dangerous of these products, such as the option mortgages that could leave you owing far more than you borrowed. But many are still around—particularly the adjustable-rate mortgages that got so many people in trouble by enticing them with low introductory rates.

If we've learned anything from the mortgage crisis, it's that these sorts of products should be treated with extreme caution. Generally speaking, if you can't afford a standard 15- or 30-year fixed-rate mortgage, you shouldn't be buying.

Surprises at the Closing

It's always a good idea to bring your lender's good-faith estimate to the closing and compare it with your HUD-1 statement. A few minor differences are to be expected, but if you run into any substantial surprises, that's a sign that something may be very wrong. In fact, the very first tip-off that you are dealing with a predatory lender usually comes when you are about to sign and they suddenly present you with brand-new information. In particular, don't sign a mortgage agreement if the terms change at the last minute or any previously unmentioned products, services, or fees unexpectedly appear on the HUD-1 or in the mortgage contract.

Private Mortgage Insurance

Private mortgage insurance (PMI) is a policy that insures your lender will get paid if you cannot make your mortgage payments. Most lenders require you to buy it if the size of your mortgage exceeds 80% of the value of your house.

The cost of PMI varies, depending on the size of your down payment and the nature of your mortgage, but it's not cheap. Annual premiums typically run around 0.5% of the loan amount for the first few years (so the cost for a $300,000 mortgage would be $1,500 a year).

Given that PMI doesn't help you—just the bank—it's something you want to get rid of as soon as possible. So you should keep a sharp eye on the value of your house and the outstanding balance of your mortgage. By law, on all mortgages signed on or after July 29, 1999, you have the right to request that your PMI be canceled once your loan-to-value ratio falls to 80% based on the original property value. What's more, your lender is required to automatically cancel your PMI when you hit 78%, provided you have a good payment record and don't have a second mortgage or home equity loan on the house. So the moment your loan-to-value ratio reaches 80%, ask your lender to cancel your policy. (Under the law, your mortgage servicer is required to provide you with a telephone number you can call for information about PMI cancellation.) Keep in mind that the mandatory cancellation provision applies only if you've increased your equity by paying down what you owe. If the improvement is a result of rising home values, you can ask for PMI cancellation, but they don't have to agree.

Foreclosure Scams

Traditionally, Americans have been known for doing almost anything to avoid losing their homes to foreclosure. And for good reason: Not only will it ruin your credit rating, but losing your home to foreclosure is one of the scariest experiences a family can go through. Unfortunately, as mortgage delinquency rates rose to record highs in the aftermath of the subprime crisis, scam artists began offering phony foreclosure-prevention schemes that continue to victimize tens of thousands of desperate homeowners. The most common ploys include:

LEASE BUYBACKS, in which a homeowner signs the deed to his home over to a scammer who has promised to rent the place back to him until he can afford to repurchase it; in fact, the homeowner-turned-tenant usually winds up getting kicked out and the scam artist keeps the house.

MORTGAGE-SETTLEMENT FRAUDS, in which homeowners are given documents to sign that will supposedly settle their outstanding mortgage balances but actually transfer ownership of their home to the scammer— something they don't discover until they are served an eviction notice.

FORECLOSURE-PREVENTION SPECIALISTS, who charge ridiculous fees for making a few phone calls and filling out some forms, none of which actually accomplishes anything except to give the scammer access to your personal financial information.

If you're having trouble making your mortgage payment, here's what you should do.

1. CALL YOUR LENDER IMMEDIATELY. The single biggest mistake borrowers make when they fall behind on their mortgage is not contacting their lender. As soon as you realize you have a problem, you've got to make that call. The foreclosure process for most lenders has a set schedule, so the longer you wait the fewer options you'll have.

2. ASK TO SPEAK TO THE "LOSS MITIGATION" DEPARTMENT. See if your monthly statement contains the phone number to the lender's loss mitigation department. If not, call the customer service number and ask for that department. At most lenders, the loss mitigation department helps borrowers determine which workout option they qualify for. Keep in mind, though, that some lenders have their collections departments advise borrowers on workout options, so don't be alarmed if you're sent straight to collections.

3. BE PREPARED TO REVIEW YOUR SITUATION IN DETAIL WITH YOUR LENDER. Your lender will ask a series of questions to assess your financial situation. Some lenders, like Wells Fargo Home Mortgage, have specialists with both the training and technology to prequalify a caller for a workout option right over the phone. If you have the right financial documents in front of you when you make the call, you might be able to get a resolution within minutes. So organize your bills, statements, and anything else that will help give an accurate picture of your current financial status. And resist the temptation to make your financial situation sound better than it really is. All that will accomplish is to get you a workout agreement that won't really help you. (By the same token, don't exaggerate how bad your situation is. That may lead your lender to think there's no way you can keep your house.)

4. KNOW THE WAYS YOUR LENDER CAN HELP YOU AVOID FORECLOSURE. Depending on how serious your situation is, your lender can either offer you retention options (ways to keep your house) or liquidation options (ways to give up your house without going into foreclosure). Retention options include forbearance (which generally lets you pay less than the full amount of your mortgage payment for a temporary period), a repayment plan (where you pay off your overdue mortgage payments in installments), reinstatement (where you agree to pay your lender everything you owe in one lump sum by a specific date), and loan modification (where your interest rate and other loan conditions are changed). Liquidation options include a short sale (where your lender agrees to accept an offer to buy your house for less than the amount you owe—which then cancels the debt), deed in lieu of foreclosure (where you voluntarily transfer your property to your lender), and assumption (which allows a qualified buyer to take over your mortgage and make the payments). If you have an FHA loan, you may have additional options available to you. For example, HUD provides interest-free loans to repay past-due interest and escrow amounts. It's important to check with your lender for details.

5. KNOW WHERE TO TURN IF YOU AREN'T GETTING THE HELP YOU NEED FROM YOUR LENDER. You should start with a HUD-approved housing counselor. You can find one near you by calling HUD toll-free at (800) 569-4287 or through the HUD web site at www.hud.gov/offices/hsg/sfh/hcc/hccprof14.cfm. You might also try the Homeownership Preservation Foundation, a HUD-certified, nonprofit organization that offers advice and resources to help homeowners with financial challenges. You can call them toll-free at (888) 995-HOPE or visit their web site at www.995hope.org. In addition, foreclosure help is available from the Association of Community Organizations for Reform Now (www.acorn.org), the Mortgage Bankers Association's Foreclosure Prevention Resource Center (www.homeloanlearning center.com/YourFinances/ForeclosurePreventionResourceCenter. htm), the National Foundation for Credit Counseling (www.nfcc. org), and NeighborWorks America (www.nw.org).

What to Do if Things Go Wrong

If you feel a mortgage professional has taken advantage of you or otherwise treated you unfairly, the first step, as always, is to write a polite but firm letter to his or her immediate superior—or, if you're dealing with a bank or other large financial institution, to the customer-service department. In it, you should set out the nature of your complaint and what you expect them to do about it.

If this does not lead to a resolution of the problem, it's time to go to the authorities. In general, states regulate mortgage brokers, independent loan servicers, certain mortgage banks, title and escrow companies, appraisers, and real estate agents, while the federal government oversees banks, credit unions, savings and loans, and thrifts.

To file a mortgage-related complaint with state authorities, you'll need to figure out which agency in your state is the right one. This is not always obvious. In Ohio, Washington, Kentucky, and Louisiana, for example, it's the Department of Financial Institutions. In Maine, it's the Bureau of Consumer Credit Protection. California uses two agencies—the Department of Corporations and the Department of Regulatory Agencies. Fortunately, the web site of the American Association of Residential Mortgage Regulators has a complete list of which agency to contact in every state. You can find the list at www.aarmr.org/page04.lasso.

Getting Out of a Bad Mortgage

As I noted earlier, once you sign a mortgage contract, you're on the hook. There's no cooling-off period during which you're allowed to change your mind and pull out of the deal. You cannot cancel it even if you feel the lender has taken unfair advantage of you. But this doesn't mean you're screwed.

What you should do is immediately consult a lawyer with experience in residential mortgage issues. Particularly in cases where there is any basis for a claim that you were victimized by predatory practices, you might be able to renegotiate the contract to get better terms from the lender. If no one you know can recommend an appropriate lawyer, you can find one by using the National Association for Consumer Advocates' online lawyer locator at http://members.naca.net/findanattorney.php. And if you can't afford a lawyer, you might qualify for free legal assistance from the federally funded Legal Service Corporation, which provides free legal help in civil matters like housing and mortgage disputes. You can find a list of LSC offices in your area on the organization's web site at www.lsc.gov/map/index.php.

Fight for Your Money Action Steps

☐ Understand that before you start shopping for a house, you need to shop for a mortgage.

☐ Figure out how much you can afford to spend.

☐ Go to myfico.com to order your credit score and credit report. Then get to work on fixing any errors and raising your score so you qualify for the best mortgage possible.

☐ Shop for a trustworthy lender.

☐ Protect yourself by asking your lender all of the specific questions outlined on page 211.

☐ Become an educated homebuyer. Read *The Automatic Millionaire Homeowner* and visit my web site at www.finishrich.com to find first-time-homebuyer workshops in your area.

Home Building and Remodeling

As a financial advisor helping clients plan for the cost of home-remodeling jobs, the number-one thing I learned was that construction projects always cost more than the estimate—and they ALWAYS take longer than expected. In fact, it's not uncommon for a remodel to cost as much as twice the estimate and take twice as long to complete as planned. The stress that results from this can be phenomenal. I have watched clients lose both their health and their marriages over the course of remodeling jobs.

We have all heard the nightmare stories of contractors who take six months to do a one-month job. Or, even worse, who promise to redo your kitchen for $15,000 and get you to pay them half in advance—only to demolish a wall and half the ceiling, and then disappear for good. Sadly, they are not urban legends.

According to a 2007 Consumer Federation of America survey of 39 consumer-protection agencies in 25 states, home improvement and contractor-related complaints are the second most common consumer problem in the United States—and the fastest-growing category. In California alone, the Contractors State License Board investigates more than 20,000 complaints each year against contractors.

There's no getting around it. If buying a home is the biggest single investment most of us will ever make (and it is), building or remodeling may be the second-biggest financial investment we make BUT the biggest potential headache. If done right, building or redoing a house to meet your own personal specifications can be enormously satisfying. But if you get stuck with a dishonest or incompetent contractor, the project can turn into a "money pit" that will take over your life, drain your savings, and possibly even ruin your marriage.

Despite the risks, more than 100,000 Americans build custom homes each year and millions more undertake remodeling projects. How many of these people get ripped off by dishonest builders is anybody's guess. Given that we spend a total of more than $300 billion annually on home repair and remodeling projects—plus another $50 billion or so on custom home building—it's safe to say that building and remodeling rip-offs cost us tens of billions of dollars a year. So proceed with caution.

How to Fight for Your Money

The number-one predictor of whether your project will go right is choosing a competent and honest contractor. But even if you do, you must still monitor the process closely. Home building is a great example of how fighting for your money can require you to sweat the details.

Whether you are building a new house from the ground up or remodeling an existing one, your ability to get the finished product you want at the price you want will depend on five main factors:

- Hiring good people
- Making—and sticking to—a budget
- Drawing up a well-thought-out plan before construction—and then sticking to it
- Understanding the construction contract you are signing
- Staying on top of the project

It's really that simple. If you can do these five things, you will get your house built or remodeled without going broke (or crazy) in the process. Here are some guidelines to keep in mind.

Making the Plan

All successful construction projects begin with a good plan, and except for the simplest remodels that means the first thing you should do is find yourself an architect. It's one thing to sketch out a plan yourself; it's something else entirely to create workable blueprints that accomplish what you're looking for and comply with building codes. Get referrals from friends and colleagues who've been through projects similar to what you're planning. Particularly if you're building a custom home, make a note of houses you like in your area and find out who designed them. (Records of all new construction, which include the name of the architect, are usually on file and available to the general public at your local city hall.) You can also use the online sources "architect finder" on the web site of the American Institute of Architects at www.aia.org.

As with hiring any professional, you should interview at least two or three candidates. You want to make sure both that their taste matches yours and that you get along. This is also the time to agree on a fee structure (some architects charge by the hour, others set a flat fee for the job), the proposed time frame for the project, and how cost overruns and delays will be handled. The AIA web site contains a list of 20 questions to ask an architect you're considering (including "How busy are you?" and "What sets you apart from other architects?") as well as sample contracts.

Don't Try to Do It Yourself

As crucial as the architect is, the most important decision you will make when you're building or remodeling a home is your choice of contractor. Some people try to save money by acting as their own contractor, but unless you have some experience in the building trades and nothing else to do with your time, this is probably not a good idea.

Lining up materials and subcontractors and overseeing the progress of the job is only part of what a contractor does. Whether you're building a skyscraper or remodeling a kitchen, the success of any construction project depends in large part on your ability to get subcontractors arriving and departing in a smooth flow. The tight scheduling of workers in the correct sequence is essential, and if you don't have the kind of relationships that most established contractors have, you may have trouble getting the subcontractors you need when you need them. Subcontractors tend to show up more reliably when they're called by someone with whom they have worked in the past and for whom they hope to work again in the future. From a subcontractor's point of view, the do-it-yourself contractor represents nothing more than a one-time opportunity— meaning, if they have time, maybe they'll squeeze you in, but don't count on it.

To Find a Good Contractor, Dig, Ask—and Check

Despite what you may have heard, not all contractors are crooks. In fact, there are plenty of responsible, reliable contractors who take great pride in their work. The question is, how do you find one of them?

It's really not that complicated, although it does take a little effort. You begin by asking for recommendations from relatives, friends, and business associates. You should also make a note if you happen to see a custom home or remodeling project that you like. Contractors generally post signs on their job sites with their names and contact information. In the case of a remodel, you might even knock on the door and ask the homeowners if they'd recommend the professionals they are working with. In addition, online services like Angie's List (www.angieslist.com) and Consumers' Checkbook (www.consumerscheckbook.org) rate all sorts of service businesses, including contractors, based on reports submitted by thousands of consumers around the country.

You can also get leads from the National Association of Home Builders (NAHB), which has a directory of certified "Graduate Master Builders," "Graduate Master Remodelers," "Green Professionals," and other credentialed specialists on its web site at www.nahb.org. Just click on "For Consumers," then on "Find a Builder or Remodeler," then on "Builder and Remodeler Online Designation Directory." The National Association of the Remodeling Industry (NARI) has a similar contractor locator on its web site at www.nari.org/homeowners/findapro/.

Your aim should be to compile a list of at least three good candidates you can ask to bid on your job. Once you've got a few names, you should meet personally with all of them in their offices. If a candidate doesn't have an office, scratch him off your list. Not having an office is the definition of fly-by-night, and you want somebody who is established.

The three most important questions you should ask a prospective contractor are: (1) Are you licensed and bonded? (Bonding is a financial guarantee provided by most reputable contractors that they will honor their contracts.) (2) Do you guarantee your work in writing? (3) Can you provide names and telephone numbers of at least three recent clients as well as some suppliers or subcontractors? (You want to talk to his subcontractors or suppliers to make sure he pays his bills—because if he doesn't, you will be responsible for them.)

The only acceptable answers are yes, yes, and yes. And make sure to actually look at his license and call his references. Too much is at stake here to take anything on trust. Ideally, you should ask former clients if you can come to their homes and see the work your candidate did for them. In addition, contact your local Chamber of Commerce and Better Business Bureau (www.bbb.org), as well as your state licensing board (www.clsi.com/state_contractor_license_board.htm), to make sure the contractor has a clean record and the right credentials. You should also check the county courthouse to see if he's been named in any current or past lawsuits.

Figure Out What You Want and What It's Going to Cost

The key to a successful construction project is creating a detailed, specific budget. A good budget not only tells you how much you can expect to have to spend, but you can also use it as the basis for a request for bids from contractors.

The key to a successful construction project is creating a detailed, specific budget.

Start by writing out the scope of the work you want done—describing exactly what the job is, how long you expect it to take, and when you need to have it finished. On a simple project, you can do this yourself. On more complicated projects—and all custom home construction—you do this with your architect. The more detail, the better. Next, list your specifications: How many square feet of floor will be covered? It's good if you can say that you'll use a medium-priced granite for your kitchen countertops. It's better if you can specify exactly which granite product, with the product number.

To get a realistic idea of the prices and options available to you, you should comparison-shop online or in person at hardware and specialty stores. Typically, a remodeler or builder will suggest that you establish an "allowance" for specific items—appliances or bathroom fixtures or flooring, for example. The trouble with this approach is that all too often the allowance doesn't come close to covering the cost of the products you want. You can avoid disappointment—as well as the temptation to spend more than you can afford—by pricing things out in advance.

For custom home-building projects, Building-Cost.Net (www.building-cost.net) has a really terrific cost estimator that takes into account the size and shape of your proposed house, the kind of finishes you want, and where you live. You can also find out average construction costs per square foot for your region from the NAHB's web site (www.nahb.org). Click on "Resources," then on "For Consumers," then on "Building Your Home."

For remodeling jobs, you can get a ballpark idea of costs at home-improvement web sites like The Old House Web (www.oldhouseweb.com/how-to-advice/estimated-remodeling-and-repair-costs.shtml) or by using the online calculators available at ImproveNet (www.improvenet.com/HomeOwner/ProjectTools/), Remodel Estimates (www.remodelestimates.com), and Service Magic (www.servicemagic.com/resources.home-improvement-estimator.html). In addition, RemodelingOnline offers a "Cost vs. Value" report (www.costvsvalue.com) that not only tells what a typical job of the sort you want will cost in your area, but also how much it is likely to add to your home's resale value.

Put Everything in Writing

Once you've selected a contractor and agreed on what he's going to do and how much it's going to cost, you need to put it all in writing. Drawing up a contract actually isn't all that difficult. The American Institute of Architects has created a series of standard contracts for virtually every type of construction project, and most respectable contractors use them.

Whether or not you use an AIA form, your contract should include:

- The contractor's name, license number (if a license is required in your state), company name, and address

- Your design plans

- Detailed specifications of all materials and appliances to be used, right down to the brand name, model, color, and features

- When the work will be started and when it will be finished

- The total price you will pay for the job, including permit fees and sales tax

- A payment schedule (also known as a "draw" schedule), under which specified partial payments are made as the contractor completes specified project milestones and the final payment is contingent on receiving proof that all subcontractors and suppliers have been paid

- How much of the final payment (usually at least 15%) you will withhold until the work is completed to your satisfaction

- A system for authorizing changes in your plans once work has started (known as change orders), a description of the final review and sign-off process, and the plan for cleaning up the work site

- A warranty that guarantees all work for at least one year, including specifics about what is and is not covered, instructions on how to proceed if you have problems, and the name of the individual whom you should contact

The point is that everything should be in writing. If it's not in your contract (or in the change orders that get added to the file over the course of the project), don't expect it to be in your house when the job is done.

Keep an Eye on Things—Inspect, Inspect, Inspect

Construction projects, both big and small, are the ultimate example of Murphy's Law—if something can go wrong, it will. There's also a related law of home construction that a friend of mine who recently built a house told me about: If someone can take advantage of you, they will.

So you need to keep a sharp eye peeled and take nothing for granted. Check credentials and licenses and ask to see a contractor's proof of insurance. Make sure the materials and appliances used in your job are the ones you contracted for.

For bigger jobs, which include all custom home construction, you should have a professional project manager who can ride herd on the contractor and verify that the required work has actually been completed before any payments are made. If you are building a house, your architect can take this role. If he's not willing to or if your project isn't quite that ambitious, it might be worth your while to spend a few more dollars and hire a building inspector. The point is, you need an objective third party who is knowledgeable about construction to make sure things are being done correctly and to sign off before any payments are made.

What to Watch Out For

Unlicensed Contractors

Most states require contractors to be licensed, and there are good reasons for it. Unlicensed contractors generally do shoddy work, rarely have proper insurance, and can actually hold you responsible if they get hurt on the job. What's worse, it's against the law to hire an unlicensed contractor in a state where licensing is mandated, so if you do it and get caught, you could wind up being prosecuted.

> Unlicensed contractors can actually hold you responsible if they get hurt on the job.

To be fair, most people don't deliberately hire unlicensed contractors. They get tricked into it. Here are some warning signs:

- He can't or won't show you his license or supply references.

- He doesn't have an office you can visit.

- He claims he can do the job for much less than anyone else.

- He insists on a large down payment—or even payment in full—before he will start work. (In many states, it's illegal for a contractor on a remodeling job to ask for a down payment greater than $1,000 or 10% of the price, whichever is less.)

- He says you won't need any permits for jobs that involve electrical, plumbing, or structural work, or he asks you to get the permits yourself.

- He suggests you can make it easier for yourself by paying him off the books in cash, or he offers you a discount in return for letting him use your home as an example of his work.

You should be especially wary of contractors who try to pressure you into having home-improvement work done immediately. If they tell you your roof is about to collapse or your water heater to explode, before you sign a contract obligating you to thousands of dollars in repair work, spend a couple of hundred dollars to hire an inspector who can give you an informed, objective second opinion.

Contractors Who Show Up at Your Door

One of the oldest home-repair scams is for a guy to show up at your door claiming he's a licensed contractor who "just finished a job down the street" and noticed something wrong with your house. Don't hire anyone who shows up uninvited at your door, no matter how persuasive they may sound.

And if you do get talked into signing anything, keep in mind that federal law gives you three days to back out of any purchase worth more than $25 that's made at your home or at a temporary place of business, like a fairgrounds or home show. Even worse, if you get talked into writing a check, call your bank immediately and put in a stop-payment order.

Storm Chasers and Disaster Vultures

Contractor scams are especially prevalent after disasters—when government and insurance money is pouring into a region, there's lots of work that needs to be done quickly, and homeowners are desperate for help. As tough as it may be, this is a time to be more careful than ever. In particular, you should beware of anyone claiming to be a FEMA-certified contractor, electrician, roofer, or plumber. The Federal Emergency Management Agency does not certify building trades professionals. What's more, all FEMA staff workers and inspectors carry photo identification; ask to see it if you're approached by a stranger claiming to work for FEMA.

"Cost-Plus" Contracts

Some contractors will try to talk you into what's called a "cost-plus" contract, claiming it will save you money. Don't believe it.

Under a cost-plus contract, instead of setting a fixed price for your project in advance, you agree to pay whatever the contractor's costs turn out to be plus a percentage (usually 8% to 25%) for overhead and profits. The problem, of course, is that with a cost-plus arrangement, the contractor has absolutely no incentive to try to keep expenses down.

What you want is a fixed-price contract. That way, it's in the contractor's interest to watch costs—since the more he spends, the less likely he is to turn a profit.

Losing Your House to a Lien

Most states allow contractors and subcontractors who haven't been paid in full to file what's called a "mechanic's lien" against your home. A mechanic's lien is a legal claim on a piece of real estate made by someone who is owed money for supplying either the labor or materials to improve that real estate. If one is placed on your house, you won't be able to get an occupancy permit until it's cleared. And in the most extreme case, you could be forced into foreclosure.

To guard against this happening to you, you should insist on getting a lien release or waiver every time you pay a bill from a contractor, supplier, and subcontractor. If they won't give you the release, don't give them the check.

On bigger projects, of course, your contractor will be paying most of the bills. But you can still stay on top of the situation. One of the main protections homeowners have is that a subcontractor or supplier can't file a mechanic's lien unless he previously filed a notice of intent when he first started work. In fact, among the most disconcerting aspects of building a house or doing a major remodel is that early on in the project you start getting legal notices from all the suppliers and subcontractors warning that if they are not paid, they will put a lien on your house. The good thing about this is that it gives you a complete record of everyone your contractor is dealing with.

With this knowledge in hand, the most important advice I can share is that you shouldn't make your final payment to your contractor until you have verified he's gotten lien releases from all his subcontractors and suppliers.

What to Do if Things Go Wrong

If you have problems on a remodeling project and your contractor is a member of the National Association of the Remodeling Industry, you can use the group's formal complaint process. An ethics committee referees disputes and helps resolve them. You can file a complaint by calling NARI toll-free at (800) 611-NARI (6274) or by writing to them at:

National Association of the Remodeling Industry
780 Lee Street
Suite 200
Des Plaines, IL 60016

The National Association of Home Builders doesn't investigate complaints against its members.

In general, if you suspect fraud or cannot get a contractor to finish work you've paid or contracted for, complain to your state's attorney general's office. (A complete list of state attorneys general offices is available on the web site of the National Association of Attorneys General at www.naag.org/attorneys_general.php.) You should also complain to your local consumer-protection agency and the local chapter of the Better Business Bureau (www.bbb.org).

Fight for Your Money Action Steps

☐ Hire a reliable, trustworthy team, including an architect and a contractor—and possibly a project manager. Get recommendations, check credentials, and get copies of licenses.

☐ Comparison-shop to make your budget detailed and realistic. Once your budget plan is written up—stick to it!

☐ Have a contract drawn up. Everything needs to be in writing. (See page 229.)

☐ Never make your final payment to your contractor until you have verified that he's gotten lien releases from all his subcontractors.

Home-Based Business Opportunities

We've all seen the ads tacked onto telephone poles, peeking out of the classified section of the newspaper, and popping up on computer screens.

"Make big money without leaving home!"

"Earn $1,400 a week stuffing envelopes!"

"Receive $1,000 or more per day by simply returning phone calls!"

"No selling! No explaining! No meetings!"

"Immediate income! No experience necessary!"

Who wouldn't jump at deals like that? The problem, of course, is that virtually all of them are scams. Instead of enabling you to "make big money fast," as the ads typically promise, they often wind up *costing* you anywhere from several hundred to several thousand dollars—and in some cases, they can even get you mixed up in illegal schemes that could leave you subject to arrest and criminal prosecution.

How to Fight for Your Money

According to the most recent government statistics, more than 2.4 million Americans are duped each year by would-be employers promising work-at-home paydays that never materialized.

Typically, work-at-home rip-offs involve phony opportunities to make big bucks doing simple tasks like stuffing envelopes, assembling small products or crafts, or processing medical insurance claims. What the ads don't tell you is that before you can start "raking in the dough," you've first got to take a training course (which costs you money) and order software or supplies (which costs you even more money). And then all a lot of them do is merely send you a list of potential clients—most of whom have absolutely no interest in hiring home workers to do anything.

Not All Home-Based Businesses Are Scams

The good news is that there actually *are* legitimate home-based business opportunities, where you can make your own schedule, working when you like, as much or as little as you like. None of them will make you a fortune, but they won't swindle you out of any money, either. While I don't personally endorse any companies, legitimate work-at-home jobs include:

CUSTOMER-SERVICE REPRESENTATIVE. We've all heard how big companies have outsourced their call centers to India, but in fact nearly 700,000 Americans earn around $8 an hour handling customer-service calls in their own homes. Companies like Alpine Access (www.alpineaccess.com), LiveOps (www.liveops.com), Arise (www.arise.com), and West at Home (www.westathome.com) are always looking for new blood.

MYSTERY SHOPPING. This may sound like a scam, but market-research firms really do pay people to visit stores posing as typical customers and then provide what are called "customer experience evaluations"— essentially, a review of how you liked the place. Rates can run from $5 to $100 for each evaluation. Among the more reputable mystery-shopping contractors are ICC Decisions Services (www.iccds.com), Corporate Research International Mystery Shops (www.mysteryshops.com), Mystery Guest (www.mysteryguestinc.com), and Service Intelligence Experience Exchange (www.experienceexchange.com).

SURVEY-TAKING. Market-research firms also pay consumers to participate in online surveys and focus groups. The pay isn't great. You might earn $10 to $15 for filling out a long questionnaire. But then, the work is pretty easy. You can sign up online with firms like American Consumer Opinion (www.acop.com), National Family Opinion (www.mysurvey.com), and Survey Savvy (www.surveysavvy.com).

Be Skeptical—Appearances Can Be Deceiving

No matter how legitimate a home-based business opportunity may seem, investigate it thoroughly before you sign on. Don't be taken in by a slick-looking web site or fancy marketing materials. These days, anyone with a laptop and some halfway decent software can make themselves look like a Fortune 500 company.

As a rule, you should check with your local consumer-protection agency, state attorney general's office, and the Better Business Bureau chapters in both your hometown and the city where the company you're considering is located to see if either it or its owner has been the subject of complaints. Of course, not finding any complaints doesn't mean this company is clean. Unscrupulous operators generally change business names or move to avoid detection.

> Unscrupulous operators generally change business names or move to avoid detection.

What this means is that once you've completed the initial checks, it's up to you to ask the promoter some hard questions. What tasks will you have to perform? Will you be paid a salary or commissions? Who will pay you and when can you expect your first check? Will you have to pay for anything, including supplies, training, equipment, and membership fees?

If you don't get specific answers or the promoter tells you that you will have to fork over any money in advance, bail.

What to Watch Out For

Work-at-home scams are generally not that hard to spot. There are almost always at least two dead giveaways:

- They will claim you can make pots of money by doing work that requires very little effort or experience.

- They will ask you to send *them* some money up front for instructions or supplies.

These scams come in numerous varieties, but here are five of the most common ones.

The Old Envelope-Stuffing Scam

Who wouldn't want to earn $350 a week just for stuffing envelopes in the comfort of your own home? Lots of ads say you can. In fact, in 2007, thousands of people around the country responded to a classified ad claiming you could earn at least $17.50 an envelope and be guaranteed a weekly income of as much as $1,400. All you had to do to get started was pay a $45 registration fee.

By the time federal authorities caught up with him, the Florida man who had placed the ad had swindled more than 25,000 people out of more than $1.2 million.

Envelope stuffing happens to be one of the oldest work-at-home scams, dating back to the 1930s. The fact is, there isn't any such business as home-based envelope stuffing. Companies that need envelopes stuffed either do it themselves or outsource it to firms that use sophisticated machinery that works much faster—and more cheaply—than any human being. So don't be taken in.

Phony Medical Claims Processing

I got an email recently from a 62-year-old woman in Lancaster, Ohio, named Anna, who told me about her experience with another classic work-at-home rip-off. Anna is disabled, and when she saw an ad from a "health care services" outfit offering the opportunity to make good money processing medical claims on her home computer, she jumped at it.

The first thing the company told her was that she had to pay $195 for training. So she borrowed money from a friend and signed up.

During her training, which consisted of three 20-minute phone calls, Anna drew constant praise for how quickly she was catching on. But when she finished her training and was ready to start earning the big bucks, the cheers turned to jeers. The company sent her a bunch of claims to process, but each time she turned them in, they said her work was unacceptable and refused to pay her a dime.

Eventually, Anna figured out that there never really was any work. The claims she had been sent to process were phonies. All the company wanted from her was that $195 training fee. As it turned out, she was hardly the only victim of that particular scam. The same "health care services" company also swindled at least 67 other people in central Ohio out of a total of $13,000.

If anything, Anna may have gotten off easy. According to the Federal Trade Commission, medical-billing scammers sometimes charge thousands of dollars for training, software, and what they describe as a list of potential clients. Usually, the "client lists" they provide are nothing more than out-of-date professional directories, not rosters of people who have asked for help. In fact, most doctors' offices process their own claims, and the ones that do contract out their billing use established firms.

Small-Products Assembly

Another popular scam involves work-at-home deals where you're "hired" at some exorbitant piecework rate to assemble small products or crafts—usually things like stuffed clowns, Christmas bells, artisan earrings, crosses, or baby burping pads. The technique here is similar to that of the claims-processing scam. Once you sign up—and pay a fee that's often several hundred dollars—the "employer" will send you supplies and instructions. But when you send back the assembled goods, the company typically refuses to pay—claiming that your work doesn't meet its "standards."

Two Work-at-Home "Opportunities" That Can Get You Arrested

There's actually something worse than being swindled out of your money by a work-at-home scam. It's being swindled out of your money—*and then getting arrested for your trouble.* This really can happen if you fall for one of the two most terrible home-business rip-offs around today: work-at-home shipping and work-at-home payment processing.

In the shipping scam, you're promised big bucks simply to receive, repack, and then reship merchandise, usually to a foreign address. The catch is that the merchandise is stolen goods, usually the result of credit card fraud, and what you're doing by receiving and sending it on is participating in a fencing operation. When the police come knocking on your door—and they usually do before very long—you're going to have a hard time convincing them you didn't know what was going on.

Payment-processing scams are even worse. Scammers recruit unsuspecting people by offering them lucrative home-based opportunities to work as a "sales representative" or "transfer manager" processing payments and transferring funds. The way it works is that you give them your bank information so that money can be transferred into your account and then you use a wire-transfer service to send the proceeds to some other account, usually out of the country. For your trouble, you are promised a commission of as much as 10% of all the transfers you handle.

Sounds simple enough—but what you're really doing is helping criminals launder money.

An even crueler variation on this scam is one in which you are sent certified checks or money orders, which you are instructed to take to your bank and cash. You are then supposed to bring the cash—sometimes tens of thousands of dollars—to the nearest Western Union office and wire it all to an offshore account. In fact, the checks and money orders are actually forgeries, and when the bank discovers this—usually a day or two after you have wired the money to your "employers"—you are the one who will be held responsible for paying it back. In other words, you're now guilty of money laundering, forgery, and theft—*and* you owe the bank several thousand dollars that you may not have any way of repaying.

What to Do if Things Go Wrong

If you find you have been swindled by a phony work-at-home operation, your best chance to recover your money is to make a lot of noise.

Start by calling the company you believe is scamming you and ask for a refund. Let company representatives know that you'll be contacting the authorities—and possibly the media as well—about your experience.

Keep a record of all your conversations and correspondence, as well as the time you spend trying to obtain the refund. Send all correspondence via certified mail, return receipt requested, to document what the company received from you.

If you get the cold shoulder, go to the authorities. This includes your local consumer-protection agency (which you can find at www.consumeraction. gov), your state's attorney general's office, local law enforcement, the Better Business Bureau, and the news media.

You should also file a complaint with the Federal Trade Commission, either through its web site at www.ftccomplaintassistant.gov or by calling toll-free (877) FTC-HELP (877-382-4357), or by writing to them at:

Federal Trade Commission
Consumer Response Center
600 Pennsylvania Ave., NW
Washington, DC 20580

If the mails were involved, complain as well to the U.S. Postal Inspection Service. You can do this online at http://postalinspectors.uspis.gov/contact Us/filecomplaint.aspx or by writing to:

U.S. Postal Inspection Service
Operations Support Group—Chicago
Attention: Fraud Complaints Section
433 West Van Buren St., 7th Floor
Chicago, IL 60607

Being a squeaky wheel really can work. After Anna, the disabled Ohio woman who signed up to process medical claims, took her complaint to the Better Business Bureau, the BBB contacted a local television station, which then called the owner of the company that had swindled her. Two days later, Anna got a check refunding her $195 training fee.

Fight for Your Money Action Steps

☐ If it sounds too good to be true, it usually is. Claims that a work-from-home opportunity will earn you tons of cash with little time, effort, and experience simply aren't true.

☐ If you're asked to send money up front for supplies or instructions, walk away.

☐ Identify legitimate opportunities only after fully checking out the company and getting all your questions answered to your satisfaction.

401(k) Plans

Nothing you do in your lifetime other than buy a home will impact your wealth more than deciding to enroll in a 401(k) retirement savings plan at work. Signing up to have a portion of your paycheck deposited directly into your 401(k) account forces you to Pay Yourself First—and if you start young enough, this alone will make you financially secure. In fact, if you do it right and save enough, paying yourself first this way will make you a millionaire.

There's no getting around it—contributing as much as you can to a 401(k) retirement plan is almost always a true "no-brainer."

Why? Well, for one thing, fewer employers offer traditional pensions anymore. For another, the Social Security system is not something you want to count on. I am confident we will always have some form of Social Security, but think about this: As of August 2008, the average retired worker in this country was receiving a monthly Social Security check of just $1,086.10. This works out to $13,033.20 a year—hardly enough to live your golden years goldenly.

So don't be shortsighted. Think long-term. A 401(k) plan is probably your best shot at being able to enjoy a decent—and potentially fantastic—retirement. (The same goes for its close cousins, the 403(b) plan, which is for teachers, hospital workers, and other nonprofit employees, and the 457 plan, which is for government workers.) This is not just theory. It is real. During my days as a financial planner at Morgan Stanley, I worked closely with many clients who were able to retire as millionaires—in many cases, multi-millionaires—simply because they had signed up for their 401(k) plans early in their careers.

Making the 401(k) Plan "No-Brainer" Decision Intelligently

Just because a 401(k) plan is a "no-brainer" doesn't mean you can sign up and then stop thinking about it. The fact is that the people who run 401(k) plans don't always have your best interests at heart.

Don't misunderstand me here—the basic idea and intention of the 401(k) is a great one and most companies that offer them really want to do something good for their employees. But the big banks, brokerage firms, and insurance companies that administer these plans are in the business for one reason and one reason only—to make as much money as they can.

> **These big financial services companies siphon more than 3% of all the money we've got invested in them.**

And, boy, do they. By confusing us with what the chairman of the Securities and Exchange Commission has called a "witch's brew of hidden fees, conflicts of interest, and complexity," these big financial services companies are able to siphon more than $150 billion a year out of our 401(k) accounts. That's more than 3% of all the money we've got invested in them—meaning that 401(k) participants plans have to earn more than 3% a year just to break even!

How to Fight for Your Money

As of March 2008, some 55 million American workers had more than $4.3 trillion invested in defined-contribution plans like the 401(k) and its cousins. By 2015, experts predict, we'll have nearly twice that much invested. A key feature of these plans is that you get to decide how much money you put in and how it will be invested. Having this kind of control can be great, but it also means there are no guarantees. How much money you will have at retirement will depend mainly on what kind of investment decisions you make along the way. And it's not as if you can count on your employer for help. A lot of employers don't manage their 401(k) plans very well—or if they do, it's with their interests in mind, not yours. This can cost you money—sometimes a *lot* of money. So you've got to pay attention.

Even though they're not perfect, if you are eligible for a 401(k) plan, you should definitely take advantage of the opportunity. One big reason is that they entitle you to FREE MONEY. That's because most companies will match every contribution you make with a contribution of their own. Many offer a match of 50 cents on the dollar (a 50% bonus just for signing up), while some even match contributions dollar-for-dollar (a 100% bonus). This is too good a deal to miss out on.

If that's not enough, all contributions to these plans are tax-deductible and tax-deferred, meaning you don't pay a cent in taxes on the earnings you put into the plan or on any of the returns your money generates over the years. Uncle Sam doesn't ask for his cut until you start taking the money out of the account, which is something you presumably won't do until after you reach retirement age—by which time your contributions will have had the opportunity to make full use of the miracle of compound interest and you will likely be in a lower tax bracket than you are now.

> You don't pay a cent in taxes on the earnings you put into the plan or on any of the returns your money generates over the years.

The impact all this can have on your ability to build wealth is phenomenal. If you're like most people, the government normally grabs about 30 cents from every dollar you earn before you ever even see the money. That leaves you with only about 70 cents. But when you make a contribution to a tax-deferred retirement plan, you get to do so with the entire dollar. It's now the government that gets bypassed. This is what gives tax-deferred investments such a terrific advantage over regular investments. The following table shows just how terrific they are.

	401(k) Retirement Plan (Pretax)	Regular Investment (Taxable)
Gross income	$1.00	$1.00
Taxes deducted	−0	−30%
Amount available to invest	$1.00	$0.70
Annual return	+10%	+10%
Balance after one year	$1.10	$0.77
Are gains taxable?	No	Yes

How much would you rather have after a year—$1.10 or 77 cents? This is a no-brainer. But wait—it might get better. If your company is one of those that offer to match a percentage of employee retirement contributions, you could come out really far ahead.

	Tax-Deferred Retirement Plan (with Employer Match)	Regular Investment (Taxable)
Gross income	$1.00	$1.00
Taxes deducted	−0	−30%
Amount available to invest	$1.00	$0.70
Typical employer match	+25%	0
Amount invested	$1.25	$0.70
Annual return	+10%	+10%
Balance after one year	$1.38	$0.77
Are gains taxable?	No	Yes

Think about it—$1.38 vs. 77 cents. You get almost a 100% increase in your net savings simply by using a pretax retirement account! That's huge—and it's only year one.

The catch, to the extent that there is one, is that if you take out any money before you're 59½, you have to pay a 10% penalty on top of whatever taxes you might owe.

Here are some key tips to making the most of your 401(k) opportunity.

Aim to "Max Out" the Plan

The first decision you have to make when you get your 401(k) sign-up package is how much of your income you're going to contribute to your retirement account every pay period. Every sign-up package contains a form for you to sign authorizing your employer to deduct money from your paycheck to fund your retirement account. Most plans will ask you whether you want the amount deducted from your paycheck to be a set percentage of your income or a specific dollar amount. I always recommend that you go with the percentage. If you pick a specific amount, you'll need to readjust it every time you get a raise. Not only is this a bother, but it also creates the possibil-

Your goal should be to "max out" the plan.

ity that you might forget and, as a result, wind up underpaying yourself.

Most people who sign up for 401(k) plans contribute around 4% of their income. Most people also retire poor, dependent on Social Security or family to survive. So this is not a model you want to follow.

Your goal should be to "max out" the plan. This means making the maximum contribution your company's plan allows. As of 2009, the IRS allows you to put up to $16,500 a year into a 401(k) plan. If you are over age 50, you can contribute up to $22,000 a year. In 2010 and beyond, the ceilings will be adjusted annually to keep up with inflation.

Think about it. If you earn $75,000 a year, 4% of your income is $3,000. Now answer this question: Which would you rather have at retirement—$300,000 or $1.6 million? That's roughly the difference between putting $3,000 a year into a 401(k) plan and maxing it out.*

While you can use these figures as a guide, you should double-check them with your employer's benefits office. If your company has a poor participation rate (meaning not enough of your fellow workers have signed up), your maximum allowable contribution may be lower. Don't guess at this. Check with your benefits office *today*. And recheck the maximums every January so you can take full advantage of any increases that may have been made. The reason you need to recheck is that many plans won't allow you to save more than 15% of your gross income, even if that happens to be less than the IRS-allowed maximum.

Begin by Saving One Hour a Day of Your Income

Even though I just said that your goal should be to "max out" your 401(k) contribution, I am a realist. I know you may read this and say to yourself, "There's no way I can save the maximum that my plan allows." While many plans only allow you to save up to 15% of your salary, some let you save 25% or more—and saving that big a piece of your salary may seem impossible. But you can do it.

The trick is not to think about percentages. Instead, when it comes to funding your retirement plan, think in terms of how many hours you work each week. If you work a 40-hour week, I believe you DESERVE to at least keep one hour a day of your income. That's five hours of income a week—or 12½% of your gross income. If you are starting late on your road to retirement savings, your goal should be to save two hours a day— or 25% of your income.

Right now, most Americans save less than 15 minutes a day of their income. When you consider that we are trading our time for a paycheck, the

*The calculation assumes an average 7% annual rate of return over 30 years.

idea that you deserve to keep at least an hour a day of what you are working for seems to me like the ultimate no-brainer.

If you have to start small and feel the most you can save is, say, 4% of your income (which amounts to just under 20 minutes a day), then make it a goal to increase that percentage periodically—every month, if your plan allows it. Remember, if you started out putting just 1% of your salary into your 401(k) and then raised your contribution rate by 1% each month, within a year you would be at the one-hour-a-day goal I suggested—and you would be saving four to five times what the average American saves.

Automatic Enrollment in Your Plan Is Great— but Pay Attention!

Thanks to the Pension Protection Act of 2006, which made it easier for employers to enroll workers in 401(k) plans without their written authorization, a growing number of companies automatically include new employees in their 401(k) plans unless the employees choose to opt out. This is great, since the participation rate at companies that have automatic enrollment is roughly double that of companies that don't.

But even if you're lucky enough to work for a company that automatically enrolls all its employees in its 401(k) plan, don't think this means you don't need to do anything. The problem is that most automatic-enrollment programs set your contribution level at just 3% of your paycheck, which really isn't enough to build a decent nest egg—and may not even be enough to earn your full company-matching contribution. So check with your human resources department to make sure your contribution level is where you want it to be. And make a point of asking if your plan is one of the new ones that offer what's called "automatic enrollment with automatic increases." With this feature, simply by checking a box on your enrollment form, you can arrange to have your contribution level automatically increased on a preset schedule, just as I suggested above.

Consider the New Roth 401(k) Plan

Since 2006, employers have been able to offer a variation on the traditional 401(k) plan called the Roth 401(k). The major difference between a regular 401(k) and a Roth 401(k) is that with a Roth none of the contributions you put in are tax-deductible—but all the distributions you take out at the other end are tax-free. A regular 401(k) is pretty much the opposite: Your contributions are tax-deductible, but you have to pay income tax on your distributions.

Which is a better deal for you depends on whether you think your tax rate will be higher or lower after you retire. If you think you'll be in the same or a higher tax bracket down the road, then the Roth 401(k) may make sense for you. If you think you'll be in a lower tax bracket, then you should probably stick with the traditional 401(k).

The problem is that there's no sure way to predict your likely tax rate 20 or 30 years from now. Fortunately, the government allows you to contribute to both kinds of 401(k) plans at the same time, so you can hedge your bets. The only catch is that your total contributions can't exceed the IRS limit for a single plan (which is $16,500 in 2009). And, of course, your employer has to offer a Roth 401(k) plan. As of mid-2008, fewer than one in four did.

Put Your Money Where It Will Grow

As a rule, you don't get much help when it comes to figuring out how to invest your 401(k) money. The folks from HR may give you a few pamphlets and the URL of a web site you can check out, but that's pretty much it. So it's no wonder that many people just stash their contributions in a money-market fund and leave it at that. That's too bad, because what they are doing is shortchanging themselves. A money-market fund is safe, but it doesn't generate anywhere near the kind of returns you will need to build up a decent nest egg.

A money-market fund doesn't generate anywhere near the kind of returns you will need to build up a decent nest egg.

You need to put your money where it will grow. So take some time to learn about your investment options and, if you need it, get some professional advice on putting together an investment plan. Your goal should be to diversify your investments with a variety of mutual funds that give you wide exposure to the stock and bond markets, both in the United States and internationally. If all this seems confusing (and it should), ask your benefits office if your investment choices include a "target date" or lifecycle fund. This is a fund specifically designed for retirement savings. You pick a target date close to when you plan to retire, and the fund automatically ensures that you will have the appropriate mix of investments for someone your age—more aggressive when you're younger, gradually becoming more conservative as you approach retirement.

These "set it and forget it" funds have become enormously popular. More than 80% of all 401(k) plans offer them as an option, and as of the middle of 2008, they held more than $204 billion in assets—nearly 100% more than they did in 2006. That still amounted to only about 5% of all 401(k) assets, but target-date funds are growing so fast that some experts believe that by 2013 they will account for 75% of all 401(k) assets.

This concerns some critics, who worry that target-date funds can be riskier than they seem. The basic idea is that as you approach retirement age your investments should be geared less toward growth and more toward capital preservation—meaning that over time you should be moving away from stocks and toward fixed-income securities. The problem is that not everyone agrees on how quickly this shift should occur. In fact, while some funds aim to have just 10% of their assets invested in stocks by the target date, the stock total for others is as high as 65%.

Still, most experts agree that a good target-date fund can do a much better job investing for your future than you can do for yourself. Indeed, a 2008 John Hancock study showed that over the previous ten years 84% of those who handled their own 401(k) investments earned an average annual return two full percentage points lower than they would have gotten by investing their money in a Hancock target-date fund.

> Most experts agree that a good target-date fund can do a much better job investing for your future than you can do for yourself.

As of the summer of 2008, there were roughly 40 companies offering more than 250 individual target-date funds to choose from, with new ones coming onto the market just about every other day. How do you select the right one for you? It's tricky. Because the concept is so new, there is no accepted standard for comparing the performance of different target-date funds. Of course, when it comes to picking one for your 401(k) account, you may not have a choice. Most companies that offer target-date funds to 401(k) participants offer only one family of funds.

If you do have a choice, both Morningstar and Lipper Inc. (another highly regarded fund-tracking firm) give top marks to the low-cost Vanguard family of funds for people who feel most comfortable with index funds that are designed simply to match the market. If you have more of an appetite for risk and like actively managed funds that try to do better than the market as a whole, Morningstar and Lipper both like the more aggressive T. Rowe Price funds.

If your 401(k) plan offers target-date funds managed by some other firm, ask your plan administrator for a copy of their Morningstar and Lipper evaluations.

Don't Borrow Against Your Future

Most large 401(k) plans allow contributors to borrow money from their accounts—usually up to half your vested account balance, to a maximum of $50,000. Some also allow hardship withdrawals. This may be a lifesaver in an emergency, and in fact about one out of four eligible employees have outstanding loans from their 401(k) accounts. But in general, borrowing from your 401(k) is a bad idea.

In general, borrowing from your 401(k) is a bad idea.

To begin with, by borrowing from your account, you are reducing the size of the nest egg you'll have when you're ready to retire. Even if you pay yourself back with interest—which is what you're legally required to do—the interest you pay will probably be a lot less than what your money would have earned had it been invested elsewhere. (According to a calculation that Vanguard did for the *New York Times*, a 35-year-old with $20,000 in his 401(k) who takes out and repays two loans over the next 15 years will end up at age 65 with about $38,000 less than someone who never borrowed.)

What's more, if you aren't able to repay what you borrowed within five years (or, in many cases, if you leave your job before you can pay it off), your "loan" will automatically turn into a withdrawal—and that can mean big trouble. In most cases, any withdrawals you make before you reach the age of 59½ are subject to both income taxes and a 10% penalty. You may say this won't happen to you, but the fact is that your circumstances may change, and this is a terrible risk.

Given all this, you might think that no respectable financial institutions would encourage anyone to borrow from a 401(k). Guess again. One of the worst things the banks have done in recent years is to introduce a debit card connected to your retirement account that you can use to borrow against your 401(k) with a simple swipe.

If your company adopts this scheme—and, fortunately, not that many have—all you have to do is get your plan administrator to approve you for a line of credit, and after that you can borrow at will. Interest starts accruing as soon as the transaction posts, without even any grace period. As one government regulator told Bloomberg News, "This is close to a predatory lending practice." Do yourself a favor and avoid this option.

Don't Cash Out Your Plan!

The single biggest mistake people make with their 401(k) plans is cashing them out when they leave a job. Doing this creates a financial disaster on two levels. To begin with, the taxes and penalties you have to pay when you cash out a 401(k) account early (that is, before you've reached retirement age) can eat up nearly half of your payout. What's worse is that even if you're cashing out only a few thousand dollars, the price you will eventually pay in a diminished nest egg could easily run into the hundreds of thousands.

Nonetheless, according to a 2005 survey by the human resources consulting firm Hewitt Associates, nearly half of all employees cash out their 401(k) plans when they leave a company. Not surprisingly, workers in their twenties have the highest cash-out rates. Nearly two-thirds of them take the money and run. This is a real tragedy. Twentysomethings may think that the relatively small amounts of money in their 401(k) accounts don't really matter—and, anyway, they've got plenty of time to worry about retirement. But the fact is that they are the ones with the most to lose.

When you exit a company where you had a 401(k) plan, there are two sensible things you can do with the money you've saved: (1) you can transfer it to the 401(k) plan at your new employer; or (2) you can roll it over into an IRA.* By doing either, you ensure that your retirement savings continue to grow tax-deferred without interruption. (Leaving funds in an old 401(k) plan simply isn't a good idea. It's too easy to lose control of your money when you do, so take it with you when you go.)

Had you left it alone, that $10,000 you just cashed out would have grown to more than $217,000 by the time you reached 65.

Here's what happens when you don't transfer or roll over your money, but instead ask for your 401(k) balance in cash. Let's say you had $10,000 in your account. To begin with, if you haven't yet reached the age of 59½, the government will hit you with a 10% penalty for making a premature distribution, which in this case will cost you $1,000. You will also have to pay both federal and state income taxes on your $10,000, which could total another $3,500. So right off the bat, your $10,000 has been whittled down to $5,500.

But that's not the half of it. Let's say you're 25 years old and your money was earning 8% a year. Had you left it alone, that $10,000 you just cashed out would have grown to more than $217,000 by the time you reached 65.

So to get $5,500, you gave up $217,000. How much sense does that make?

---

*In some IRA rollovers, your company will liquidate your 401(k) assets and mail a check for the full amount directly to you. If this is the case, you have 60 days to deposit the check into an IRA account. If you take longer than 60 days, the transaction will be considered a withdrawal on which you will owe the government income taxes plus a potential penalty.

What to Watch Out For

Losing Your Nest Egg to Excessive Fees

One argument you often hear in favor of signing up for a 401(k) plan is that in addition to all their other advantages, they are generally free. In fact, nothing is really free—and that includes 401(k) plans.

Most 401(k) participants don't realize it, but a small portion of everyone's account is skimmed off by a shadowy group of brokers, bankers, fund managers, administrators, accountants, lawyers, and consultants. According to experts, when you figure in these fees and other hidden charges, the average 401(k) plan actually costs its participants somewhere between 3% and 3½% of what they've got invested each year. And in some cases the cost is as high as 5%.

It's not that the professionals who run 401(k) plans don't deserve to be paid for their work. But they don't deserve to be overpaid. And since their fees are generally hidden, they can pretty much get away with charging us anything they want.

In a 2008 interview with the NPR radio show *Marketplace,* pension consultant Matthew Hutcheson pointed out that paying an annual fee on your 401(k) that's just a single percentage point higher than it should be could eventually shrink the size of your retirement nest egg by as much as 20%. "Over a regular working lifetime," he said, "we're talking about $80,000, and to make that shortfall up, a person would have to work three or four additional years just to break even."

> Paying an annual fee on your 401(k) that's just a single percentage point higher than it should be could eventually shrink the size of your retirement nest egg by as much as 20%.

There are a number of bills in Congress aimed at forcing 401(k) administrators to do a better job disclosing the real cost of these plans. But until these bills become law, don't be shy about asking your company or 401(k) provider for a breakdown of the fees in your plan. If they total much more than 3%, you're probably being charged too much— and you should complain about it to your employer.

And don't be afraid to make noise and fight for your money. It does bring results. In 2006 and 2008, workers at a number of giant corporations (including Wal-Mart, Boeing, Deere, and General Dynamics) sued their employers for saddling them with unnecessarily expensive investment choices.

What the companies did was to give 401(k) participants a choice of only "retail" mutual funds, which charge relatively high management fees, instead of the lower-priced institutional funds that are available to large clients. Although the differences in fund-management fees can *seem* tiny (most were less than 1%), small differences can add up to big bucks. The suit against Wal-Mart says the company's practices cost its employees $60 million over six years.

Missing Enrollment

Just because your company offers employees a 401(k) plan, don't assume you're automatically enrolled. Although the number of companies offering automatic enrollment is increasing, nearly 60% of employers still require workers to join on their own. So if you don't recall ever enrolling, contact the benefits office at your employer today and ask them for a retirement-account sign-up package. You were probably given one when you first started work—and because it was so thick and boring-looking, you probably stuck it in a drawer somewhere and haven't seen it since.

If that's what you did, by all means go get yourself a new package—and this time fill it out and send it in. (If you work for a big corporation, you may be able to download all the necessary forms from the company web site.)

Investing Too Heavily in Your Own Company's Stock

It's generally never a good idea to put all your eggs in one basket. This is especially true if the eggs are your retirement savings and the basket is your company's stock. If you work for a publicly traded company, they may encourage you to invest your 401(k) money in the company's stock. Be wary. Investing a little is fine, but a lot can be disastrous. Think about it. What happens if most of your 401(k) money is invested in your own company's stock and the company goes out of business? Not only do you lose your job, but you lose your retirement savings at the same time. Talk about a double whammy!

> What happens if most of your 401(k) money is invested in your own company's stock and the company goes out of business? Not only do you lose your job, but you lose your retirement savings at the same time.

That's just what happened to thousands of workers at ill-fated Enron Corp. When the company was flying high in the late 1990s, most of them had loaded up their 401(k) accounts with Enron stock. Then, in 2001, Enron collapsed, costing them their jobs—and nearly 60% of their retirement assets. Some 7,000 employees of the fallen Wall Street giant

Bear Stearns suffered the same fate in 2008, losing both their jobs and a big chunk of their life savings as the value of their company stock plunged from nearly $170 a share to less than $10. And look what happened to Lehman Brothers, whose stock went from $82 a share in the summer of 2007 to zero a year later. Institutions like Washington Mutual, Fannie Mae, and Freddie Mac suffered similar collapses. All went from being considered rock-solid, long-term performers to virtually worthless in a very short period of time. I have said for years that you simply cannot afford to have more than 5% to 10% of your net worth in one stock. In the aftermath of the 2008 meltdown, I now feel this more strongly than ever.

An Overly Long Vesting Schedule

While your own 401(k) contributions always belong to you, the money your employer puts in your 401(k) account may not really be yours until you have worked for the company for a certain number of years. If you leave the company before then, you may be entitled to take only part of your employer's contributions with you—and in some cases, none of it at all. This is called vesting.

Typically, it takes only two or three years for you to be "fully vested"— that is, to enjoy full ownership of your employer's contributions. But some companies stretch out the process for as long as six or seven years. Make sure you understand your company's vesting schedule. And don't count on that money until it's really yours.

And when you leave your company, double-check that you received every penny of your vested funds. Don't assume your employer will calculate the amount correctly. This is one reason why it is essential that you keep copies of all your 401(k) statements. They are the only way you'll be able to prove anything if your employer did make a mistake.

What to Do if Things Go Wrong

Be alert for mistakes on your retirement account. Check your 401(k) statements regularly to make sure your contributions are being properly credited to your account. Notify your employer at the first sign of a problem, and always do it in writing. If you can't get the issue resolved, or if you suspect that your employer is stealing money from the plan, complain to the Employee Benefits Security Administration of the U.S. Department of Labor. You can telephone them toll-free at (800) 444-3272 or write them at:

Employee Benefits Security Administration
U.S. Department of Labor
200 Constitution Avenue, NW, Suite N-5668
Washington, DC 20210

You can also contact the Employee Benefits Security Administration online at www.dol.gov/ebsa. To find the regional office serving your state, visit www.dol.gov/ebsa/aboutebsa/org_chart.html#section13.

Fight for Your Money Action Steps

☐ Make the decision to Pay Yourself First!

☐ Make sure you're signed up for your retirement plan at work.

☐ Start contributing at least one hour a day of your income, with the ultimate aim of maxing out your plan.

☐ Investigate your investment options and allocate your savings wisely in order to build up your nest egg.

☐ Avoid borrowing money from your account—and don't cash it out when you leave an employer!

IRAs

One of the most shocking statistics I know is that according to the Internal Revenue Service, only about 10% of the people eligible to contribute to individual retirement accounts actually do so. In other words, there are millions of working people in this country who are throwing away what may be the best chance they have for a decent retirement.

There is no getting around it. If you don't work for a company that offers a 401(k) plan, you must get yourself an IRA and "max it out"—meaning that you make the maximum allowable annual contribution. Thanks to the miracle of compound interest—plus the huge advantage you get from the fact that you don't pay any taxes on your IRA contributions until you start withdrawing them (presumably after you've retired)—even relatively modest savings of a few thousand dollars a year can be transformed into a huge nest egg.

So why do so few people take advantage of this great opportunity? In most cases, it's probably because they think they can't afford to. In fact, if you look at the numbers—and consider how little you're going to get from Social Security (for most of us, the equivalent of roughly $13,000 a year)—you'll realize that if you're not participating in some other kind of tax-deferred retirement plan, you can't afford *not* to have an IRA.

Invest in an IRA Today!

Average Social Security benefit in 2008: $13,000
Is that enough to live on?

How to Fight for Your Money

IRAs come in four flavors, but all have one thing in common—they give you tax breaks that make it much easier to save for retirement. Here's how they differ.

- TRADITIONAL DEDUCTIBLE IRA. Your contributions are deductible and your savings grow tax-deferred, but your withdrawals are taxable.

- TRADITIONAL NONDEDUCTIBLE IRA. Your contributions aren't deductible, but they grow tax-deferred and only part of your withdrawals are taxable.

- ROTH IRA. Your contributions aren't deductible, but if you follow the rules, they grow tax-deferred and all your withdrawals are tax-free.

- SPOUSAL IRA. If you're unemployed or retired, but your spouse is still working, you can contribute to a spousal IRA as long as your spouse has enough earned income to cover the contribution and you file a joint return. As long as your joint adjusted gross income is less than $166,000, your contribution is fully deductible.

In short, anyone who earns a taxable income or files a joint return with a spouse who earns an income can contribute to an IRA. But if you earn too much, you can't contribute to a Roth IRA or deduct a contribution to a traditional IRA. (In 2009, your eligibility to contribute to a Roth IRA phases out for couples with a combined gross income (AGI) between $166,000 and $176,000, and for single filers with an AGI between $105,000 and $120,000.)

As long as you're eligible, you can have as many IRAs as you want—though there is a limit on how much you can contribute in total. In 2009, the maximum was $5,000 a year plus an extra $1,000 "catch-up contribution" for people 50 or older. In 2010 and beyond, the limits rise with inflation in $500 increments.

Some people think that $5,000 or $6,000 a year is not enough to really amount to anything. In fact, if you do it right, even a relatively modest contribution of a few thousand dollars a year can grow into a nest egg worth hundreds of thousands—even millions—of dollars. Here's how to do it right.

Start Early, Start Now—Save Until You Retire

How much you'll have in your IRA at retirement depends mainly on three things—how much you contribute, how much your investments earn, and how many years your money has the chance to compound. It's never too late to start, but the earlier you start, the better.

THE TIME VALUE OF MONEY
Invest Now Rather Than Later

SUSAN Investing at age 19 (10% Annual Return)				KIM Investing at age 27 (10% Annual Return)		
AGE	INVESTMENT	TOTAL VALUE		AGE	INVESTMENT	TOTAL VALUE
19	$2,000	$2,200		19	0	0
20	2,000	4,620		20	0	0
21	2,000	7,282		21	0	0
22	2,000	10,210		22	0	0
23	2,000	13,431		23	0	0
24	2,000	16,974		24	0	0
25	2,000	20,871		25	0	0
26	2,000	25,158		26	0	0
27	0	27,674		27	$2,000	$2,200
28	0	30,442		28	2,000	4,620
29	0	33,486		29	2,000	7,282
30	0	36,834		30	2,000	10,210
31	0	40,518		31	2,000	13,431
32	0	44,570		32	2,000	16,974
33	0	48,027		33	2,000	20,871
34	0	53,929		34	2,000	25,158
35	0	59,322		35	2,000	29,874
36	0	65,256		36	2,000	35,072
37	0	71,780		37	2,000	40,768
38	0	78,958		38	2,000	47,045
39	0	86,854		39	2,000	53,949
40	0	95,540		40	2,000	61,544
41	0	105,094		41	2,000	69,899
42	0	115,603		42	2,000	79,089
43	0	127,163		43	2,000	89,198
44	0	139,880		44	2,000	100,318
45	0	153,868		45	2,000	112,550
46	0	169,255		46	2,000	126,005
47	0	188,180		47	2,000	140,805
48	0	204,798		48	2,000	157,086
49	0	226,278		49	2,000	174,094
50	0	247,806		50	2,000	194,694
51	0	272,586		51	2,000	216,363
52	0	299,845		52	2,000	240,199
53	0	329,830		53	2,000	266,419
54	0	362,813		54	2,000	295,261
55	0	399,094		55	2,000	326,988
56	0	439,003		56	2,000	361,886
57	0	482,904		57	2,000	400,275
58	0	531,194		58	2,000	442,503
59	0	584,314		59	2,000	488,953
60	0	642,745		60	2,000	540,048
61	0	707,020		61	2,000	596,253
62	0	777,722		62	2,000	658,078
63	0	855,494		63	2,000	726,086
64	0	941,043		64	2,000	800,895
65	0	1,035,148		65	2,000	883,185

The large center text reads: **SEE THE DIFFERENCE**

EARNINGS BEYOND INVESTMENT $1,019,148

EARNINGS BEYOND INVESTMENT $805,185

SUSAN EARNS	$1,019,148
KIM EARNS	$805,185
SUSAN EARNS MORE	$213,963

Susan invested one fifth the dollars but has 25% more to show.
START INVESTING EARLY!

Suppose you contribute $5,000 a year to an IRA, earn an 8% annual return, and want to retire at 65. If you were to start at age 55, you'd contribute a total of $50,000 in the 10 years before you retire, at which point your account would be worth $72,433. By contrast, if you started at 25, you'd contribute $200,000 over the next 40 years—and by the time you retired, your account would be worth $1.3 million. In other words, by starting at 25, you'd wind up contributing four times as much as you would have if you'd started at 55, but when you retired you'd have more than *17 times* as much money. In fact, if you started at 25 and contributed the $5,000 a year for only the first 10 years and then never contributed another dime, you'd still have more than 10 times what you'd have if you'd started at 55—nearly $729,000 in all. That's what 30 extra years of compounding can do.

Be Smart About Which Type of IRA You Choose

The standard advice you'll hear from most "experts" is that which type of IRA you should open depends on whether you think the tax bracket you'll be in when you retire will be higher or lower than the one you're in now. If you think you'll be in a higher tax bracket, you should choose a nondeductible Roth IRA. If you think you'll be in a lower tax bracket, you should choose a traditional deductible IRA. (Pretty much everyone agrees that a nondeductible traditional IRA makes sense only if you aren't eligible for any of the other IRA options.)

This may seem simple enough, but predicting your tax bracket isn't that easy. Most people assume they'll be in a lower bracket because they won't be working anymore. But how safe is that assumption? Surveys show that slightly more than half of all baby boomers—that giant generation that's currently reaching retirement age—do *not* plan to quit their jobs when they hit 65. In fact, three out of four current retirees still do some sort of work. And in any case, don't forget that your Social Security benefits are taxable. So your taxable income may be higher than you think.

What's more, who knows what tax rates will be when you retire? It's certainly conceivable that they could be much higher than they are now—meaning that even if you were earning less, you wouldn't necessarily be in a lower bracket.

So how do you decide? Well, one thing you can predict with a fair degree of certainty is how long your money will have a chance to compound in your IRA. This is an important thing to know, because it happens to be a fact that the longer the time frame, the better off you are likely to be with a Roth IRA. That's because, with enough time to do its magic, the miracle of compound interest will put you so far ahead that not having to pay taxes on your withdrawals after you retire is bound to be worth a lot more to you than being able to deduct your contributions now.

So if you're relatively young (say, under 35) and have decent prospects, a Roth is generally the way to go. If you're between 35 and 50, your decision should depend mainly on how badly you could use the $1,000 or so in tax savings you'd realize from the up-front deduction that a traditional IRA lets you take. If you could live without the money (and you meet the income requirements), you'd probably be better off making your contribution to a nondeductible Roth and reaping your rewards down the road. But if you're 50 or over, the traditional deductible IRA is almost always a better deal.

> So if you're relatively young (say, under 35), a Roth is generally the way to go. If you're 50 or over, the traditional deductible IRA is almost always a better deal.

Be Careful How You Invest

One of the great things about an IRA is that you can invest the proceeds pretty much any way you want—not just in the choices your employer provides through a 401(k). As is the case with 401(k) plans, your goal should be to diversify your investments with a variety of mutual funds that give you wide exposure to the stock and bond markets, both in the United States and internationally. If all this seems confusing (and it should), ask your bank or broker about "target date" or lifecycle funds. These are funds specifically designed for retirement savings. You pick a target date close to when you plan to retire, and the fund automatically ensures that you will have the appropriate mix of investments for someone your age—more aggressive when you're younger, gradually becoming more conservative as you approach retirement.

While there is no one "right" investment for an IRA, there are some types of investments that are clearly not appropriate. Some, like life insurance and antiques, are not allowed. Others are just a bad idea. For example, take tax-deferred investments such as municipal bonds or annuities. Because of their tax advantages, investors pay a premium for these kinds of investments in the form of reduced yields or higher fees. But any investment you put in your IRA is automatically tax-deferred, so you'd be paying this premium for an advantage you already have.

You also should think long and hard before you put investments in an IRA that cannot be easily valued and sold, such as real estate, limited partnerships, or business partnerships, especially if you are getting close to the age of 70½, when you are required to start making withdrawals. These kinds of assets generally have to be appraised, which will cost you money, and if they can't be broken up easily, you may find yourself forced to withdraw the entire investment in order to meet minimum distribution requirements.

Avoid Those Penalties

As a rule, it's best to leave your money in your IRA until you are ready to retire. But if you do need to take money out and you are younger than 59½, be sure to do it in a way that avoids getting hit with the 10% penalty that the IRS generally charges for premature withdrawals. The penalty exceptions include:

- ROTH IRA CONTRIBUTIONS. Because you've already paid income taxes on the money, you can always withdraw the amount of your own contributions (but not any profits) to a Roth IRA without incurring taxes or penalties.

- HOMEBUYING. You can make a penalty-free withdrawal of up to $10,000 from both a traditional and a Roth IRA for a "first-time" home purchase. The good news here is that the IRS defines a "first-time buyer" as anyone who hasn't owned a home for at least two years. However, you can take advantage of this exception only once.

- DEDUCTIBLE MEDICAL EXPENSES. If you itemize your taxes, the IRS allows you to deduct all unreimbursed medical expenses that exceed 7.5% of your adjusted gross income. It also allows you to withdraw an equivalent amount of money from a traditional IRA without penalty—whether or not you itemized.

- MEDICAL INSURANCE PREMIUMS. If you lose your job and qualify for unemployment compensation for at least 12 weeks, you can make a withdrawal from both a traditional and a Roth IRA equal to whatever medical insurance premiums you paid that year for yourself or your family.

- HIGHER EDUCATION EXPENSES. If any member of your immediate family (including grandchildren) is attending an accredited college or university, you can make a penalty-free withdrawal from both a traditional and a Roth IRA to cover "qualified" education expenses, which include tuition, fees, books, supplies, and equipment.

When You Start Withdrawing Depends on Your Circumstances

The law permits you to start taking distributions from your IRA when you're 59½. But that doesn't mean you have to start then. Just when you begin withdrawing your funds depends on your circumstances.

If you're in a high tax bracket, you should postpone taxable IRA withdrawals as long as possible. On the other hand, if you're in a low bracket, you might want to immediately start taking out as much as you can without bumping yourself into a higher bracket. If you don't need to spend the money, you can pay the income taxes on it and then put it into a Roth IRA.

Tap Your IRA Before Your Social Security

Cash-strapped seniors who are tempted to start collecting their Social Security benefits early would probably do better to spend down their IRA instead. It's extremely unlikely that leaving your IRA money untouched would earn you anywhere near as much as what you'd gain in greater Social Security benefits by waiting until you reach full retirement age.

Keep an Eye on the Calendar

The worst IRA penalty of all is for failing to make the required minimum distribution when you turn 70½. Anyone guilty of that forfeits *half* of what they should have taken out but didn't. Don't let this happen to you. The rules governing minimum distributions are complicated. (They basically mandate a payout schedule based on your life expectancy and that of your beneficiary.) So talk to your accountant or read IRS publication 590, "Individual Retirement Arrangements," which you can find on the IRS web site at www.irs.gov/publications/p590/—and make sure you understand them.

What to Do if Things Go Wrong

If you have any problem with a bank or a brokerage firm with which you've opened an IRA, or any brokers or salesmen who've sold you investments for your IRA—say, your contributions have not been properly credited or your instructions haven't been followed—there are any number of government agencies you can go to for help. Of course, you should first try to resolve the problem directly with the financial institution in question. But if that doesn't work, don't hesitate to contact your state's department of banking, insurance, or securities, depending on the nature of your issue.

You can find your state banking regulator on the web site of the Conference of State Bank Supervisors at www.csbs.org. (Click on "State Banking Commissioners" on the list of "Quick Clicks.") A complete list of state insurance regulators is on the web site of the National Association of Insurance Commissioners at www.naic.org/state_web_map.htm. Contact information for your state's securities regulator can be found on the web site of the North American Securities Administrators Association at www.nasaa. org/QuickLinks/ContactYourRegulator.cfm.

You should also file a complaint with federal authorities. For a complete list of federal bank regulators, see page 77 in the section BANK ACCOUNTS. If your problem is with a broker or securities firm, file a complaint with the Securities and Exchange Commission either online at www.sec.gov or by calling their complaint center toll-free at (800) 732-0330. You can also write to them at:

SEC Complaint Center
100 F Street, NE
Washington, D.C. 20549-0213

Complaints about brokers can also be directed to the Financial Industry Regulatory Authority (www.finra.org), a nongovernmental agency created in 2007 by the National Association of Securities Dealers and the New York Stock Exchange to oversee brokers and brokerage firms. You can file a complaint online through FINRA's Investor Complaint Center at https://apps. finra.org/Investor_Information/Complaints/complaintCenter.asp.

When making a complaint, be sure to include your name, address, telephone number, and email address as well as those of the institution or individual you are complaining about. Include specific details about your problem and copies of relevant documents (never the originals). If you don't have any luck with this approach and a significant sum of money is involved, talk to a lawyer about your problem.

Fight for Your Money Action Steps

☐ Set up an IRA today and aim to max it out.

☐ Decide if you'd be better off in a traditional IRA or Roth IRA.

☐ There are literally hundreds of banks, brokerage firms, and mutual-fund companies you can choose from to help you open an IRA. The following five firms make the process really easy. They are all large companies that offer online services with phone support.

TD Ameritrade
www.tdameritrade.com
800-669-3900

ING Direct
www.ingdirect.com
800-ING-DIRECT

Sharebuilder
www.sharebuilder.com
800-747-2537

Fidelity
www.fidelity.com
800-343-3548

Vanguard
www.vanguard.com
877-662-7447

Pension Plans

The traditional pension plan is generally a great deal. You don't have to contribute anything yourself and, as long as you put in a certain number of years on the job, once you retire you're guaranteed a set monthly benefit for the rest of your life.

Unfortunately, like most great deals, traditional pension plans are no longer as common as they used to be. While four out of five government workers are still covered by them, the ratio in private industry is exactly the reverse. Only one out of five private-sector workers is entitled to a pension—typically, someone who is covered by a union contract or works for a very large, very old company. In all, some 44 million American workers are covered by some 30,000 defined-benefit plans backed by a total of more than $6 trillion in assets.

If you do have a pension coming to you, you definitely have a leg up on retirement. But don't assume your golden years are all set. As millions of workers have discovered in recent years, just because you're entitled to a pension doesn't mean you're actually going to get it. Faced with tough economic conditions, an increasing number of companies are cutting back their pension plans or getting rid of them entirely. Although a company can't take away benefits you've already earned, it can eliminate those you were expecting to earn in the future. This is particularly a risk when companies merge.

According to the Pension Rights Center, some 74 major companies—including such household names as Boeing, Coca-Cola, Dupont, and IBM—either stopped offering pensions to new employees or terminated their plans entirely between 2005 and 2008. Back in 1998, 90 of the Fortune 100 companies offered guaranteed pensions to new hires; these days, reports the consulting firm Watson Wyatt, fewer than 60 do.

Moreover, your plan may be seriously underfunded, which means it may not have enough money to pay out all the benefits it is supposed to. Four out of five state pension plans are currently underfunded, with one in five having less than 70% of the assets it will need to be able to meet its obligations. Underfunding also is a major problem in the auto, airline, and steel industries. And there are continuing worries about whether the federal Pension Benefit Guaranty Corp. has the resources to protect all the workers covered by these shaky plans.

The good news is that you don't have to be a victim. There are steps you can take to protect yourself. It's simply a matter of educating yourself and asking the right questions.

How to Fight for Your Money

Make Sure You Know the Rules— Get the Summary Plan Description

Every pension plan is different, so it's important to know the rules governing yours. When you go to work for a company or government agency that offers workers a pension plan, you're supposed to be given a copy of something called the Summary Plan Description. It describes how your pension plan works—what your benefits are, how they're calculated, what you need to do to earn them, and so on. Make sure to read this document and then put it in a safe place. (If your employer never gave you one, or if you can't find it, ask your plan administrator for a copy.) You should also read and save any notices you get from your employer about changes to the plan. The old rules will still apply to the benefits you've already accrued, but the new rules will govern all future benefits. If you want to know more about how your plan works—especially if you have concerns about how it's being managed— ask your plan administrator for a copy of the full plan document.

Keep a Record of Your Work History

Since your pension benefits depend largely on how long you worked for your employer and how much you earned, it's vital that you keep as complete a record of your work history as possible. Don't assume that the HR department will have an accurate record.

You need to keep your own records in case you wind up in a dispute with your employer. Keeping each year's final pay stub is generally the easiest way to do this. If you started or stopped employment during the year, note that on the stub. If you have lost your paperwork (or never kept it in the first place), you can get a record of the companies you worked for by filing a "Request for Social Security Earnings Information" with the Social Security Administration (www.ssa.gov). The service isn't free (fees start at $15 to research one year and rise as high as $80 for 40 years), but it can be invaluable.

Know the Vesting Rules

Employers almost always require you to work a certain number of years before you are entitled to full pension benefits. This requirement is known as vesting. Every employer has its own vesting policy, and it's essential that you understand yours if you want to be able to make an intelligent decision about when to retire or otherwise leave your job.

Some companies have what's called "cliff vesting," which means you become vested all at once. For example, if your company has a policy of five-year cliff vesting, you're entitled to zero benefits if you don't stay at least five years, and full benefits once you do. Other companies practice "graded vesting," under which your benefit entitlement increases gradually—typically, over a seven-year period—until you are 100% vested.

Many pension plans also have other service thresholds that confer additional benefits. For example, if you stay at least 20 years, you may be entitled to start collecting full benefits at age 59, rather than 65. After 30 years, you might be entitled to retire with full benefits whenever you like, regardless of how old you are.

Sometimes staying in a job just a few months longer than you planned can be worth tens of thousands of dollars.

So if you're considering leaving a job that comes with a pension plan, make sure you figure your employer's vesting rules into your calculations. Sometimes staying in a job just a few months longer than you planned can be worth tens of thousands of dollars in additional pension benefits.

Use the Pension Formula to Your Advantage

Most pension benefits are calculated using your most recent earnings, such as the average of the highest three out of the last five years or the highest five out of the last 15. With this in mind, you may be able to increase your pension by ramping up overtime work that increases your total compensation during those crucial years. Similarly, you may want to avoid doing anything that will decrease compensation during those years—such as switching to part-time status. Check your plan description and consult with your plan administrator to see what makes sense for you.

Review Your Payout Options *Very* Carefully

Deciding how you want your pension benefits paid out to you is one of the most important decisions you will make for the rest of your life. Consider getting professional advice from an unbiased source before doing anything other than taking a joint benefit that will include survivors' benefits for your spouse.

If you are offered the option of taking a lump-sum payout (as opposed to monthly payments for the rest of your life), ask an accountant or financial planner to compare its value to the value of regular payments. A lump sum can be a smart choice if you manage the money well, but this requires a detailed review of whether or not your money-management efforts generate a better return than the fixed payment offered by the pension plan. It can also be smart if your pension fund is underfunded and you have doubts about whether you'll actually receive all the benefits to which you're entitled. Then again, if you opt for a lump sum with the idea of investing it and living off the proceeds, you have to be prepared for the risk of losses as well as gains. And you may be giving up such valuable benefits as cost-of-living adjustments and health insurance.

You will also have to decide between a "single-life" benefit, which you get as long as you live but ends when you die, or a "joint and survivor" payout, which your spouse would continue to receive even if you were to die before him or her. The single-life benefit generally gives you a bigger monthly check, which makes it a reasonable choice if you expect to outlive your spouse. But if you expect to leave your spouse behind, the lower joint payment makes more sense. Given that women tend to live longer than men, it's not surprising that 69% of married women go for the single-life payment, while 72% of married men choose the joint payment option.

Insurance agents often suggest that if you expect your spouse to outlive you, there is a way you can take the more lucrative single payout and still protect your surviving spouse. What they propose is that you protect your spouse by using the extra income from the single-life benefit to buy a life insurance policy that will provide your spouse with a lump-sum payout that, if managed correctly, could be worth a lot more than the continuing joint pension benefit. It's a clever idea, but be wary. Would your spouse really be able to manage a lump-sum insurance payout to produce the same income as the survivor benefit? What's more, under this scheme, your surviving spouse would miss out on the health insurance and other advantages that often go along with a survivor's benefit.

Don't Give Up Your Spousal Benefits Without a Fight

A spouse must agree to give up his or her survivor benefits. If your spouse is the one with the pension and he or she wants to take the single-life option, don't sign away your rights without getting the opinion of an unbiased advisor. There are times it makes sense and times that it doesn't. One time it definitely doesn't is if you are getting divorced, in which case you should make sure your spouse's pension is part of the negotiations. In the event you are awarded part of the pension, don't forget to get the appropriate court order to enforce the judgment. (For private pensions, it's what's known as a Qualified Domestic Relations Order.) It is *not* enough that it says you are entitled to it in the divorce order.

What to Watch Out For

Employer Mistakes

Employers can and do make mistakes when figuring pension benefits, especially when there have been changes in plan rules over the course of your employment. So when you receive your pension-plan statements, double-check the pension calculations.

Often, a company that has reduced the size of its annual pension contribution (say, from 1.5% of a participant's salary to just 1%) will mistakenly calculate retirees' pension benefits as if the lower percentage applied to all their years of service even if they worked some of them when the higher rate was still in effect. Other common errors include inaccurate or incomplete records, such as an incorrect date of birth or failing to include bonuses in the participant's total compensation. Since even a "small" error can cost you tens or even hundreds of thousands of dollars in benefits, go over your statements carefully.

Shaky Finances

Given the growing concern about pension-plan underfunding, it's a good idea to learn as much as you can about the state of your plan's finances. As

I noted earlier, if they are shaky and you're approaching retirement, you might want to consider taking your benefits in the form of a lump-sum payout.

If you work for a government agency, you can generally get information about your pension plans directly from your agency's plan administrator. You can also consult independent research firms such as Wilshire Consulting (www.wilshire.com) that regularly evaluate state retirement systems and other large government pension plans.

If you're a private-sector worker with a pension plan, you have even more options. Starting in 2009, all private plans were required to send participants an annual funding notice that lists their assets and liabilities, funded status over the past three years, and how their assets are invested. You can learn even more about the status of your plan by looking at the report your company's pension plan is required to file annually with the IRS. Ask your plan administrator for a copy of the report (it's called a "Form 5500") or look it up online at www.freeerisa.com. If your company is publicly held, additional information about its pension-plan finances will be included in filings with the Securities and Exchange Commission.

If you find anything in these reports that troubles or confuses you, ask your plan administrator for a full explanation.

Losing Touch with an Old Employer's Plan

You don't have to work for someone until you're 65 to be entitled to a pension. As long as you worked long enough to be vested, you may be eligible for a pension benefit from an employer you left many years before you reached retirement age. So once you've been vested, make sure you always keep your employer informed of your current address, regardless of whether or not you still work for him.

You may be eligible for a pension benefit from an employer you left many years before.

If you've neglected to do this, write to the company's pension-plan administrator today. If the company is no longer around—or if it claims to have no record that you ever worked for it—a great place to get help is the web site of PensionHelp America (www.pensionhelp.net), which has links to many resources, including the Pension Rights Project. You can also find out if your former employer's pension plan was discontinued by checking the web site of the federal Pension Benefit Guaranty Corp. (www.pbgc.gov), which was set up to protect employees when a failing company can no longer fund its pension plan.

The Limits of Government Protection— What You Must Know Now!

The federal government created the Pension Benefit Guaranty Corp. in 1978 to protect workers covered by private pension programs. The PBGC basically offers insurance that guarantees that if your pension plan goes under or otherwise can't meet its obligations, you will still receive a benefit—though you probably won't get as much as you were originally supposed to get. As a rule, when the PBGC steps in, workers and retirees with large pensions can expect to see their benefits cut—sometimes drastically. Indeed, airline pilots saw their benefits reduced by as much as 75% when Delta, United, U.S. Airways, and Aloha Airlines all ended their pension plans.

> As a rule, when the PBGC steps in, workers and retirees with large pensions can expect to see their benefits cut—sometimes drastically.

The maximum PBGC benefit for plans that ended in 2008 was $51,750 for those retiring at 65 and $23,288 for those retiring at 55. Moreover, once a plan ends, workers can no longer accrue additional benefits. And nonmonetary retirement benefits, such as health insurance, are not protected at all. So if your company's pension plan seems to be on shaky ground, you should definitely start thinking about alternative ways of funding your retirement—like IRAs.

I have serious concerns (as do many experts) about whether or not the PBGC can ultimately protect the bulk of pension plans that are currently underfunded. The fact is, as of 2007, the PBGC's long-term obligations exceeded its assets by some $14 billion. This represented a considerable improvement over 2004, when the PBGC's deficit was more than $23 billion, but it still raises the prospect of a pending financial crisis of epic proportion for many Americans. This is why when it comes time to decide between taking a lump-sum payment or a fixed monthly benefit, I would lean toward the lump sum. Remember, you can always create your own "lifetime payment plan" with a tax-deferred fixed annuity that you own and control.

What to Do if Things Go Wrong

If you are in a government plan and have problems that cannot be resolved with your plan administrator, your best bet may be to contact your local or state legislator or U.S. congressman, depending on whether it is a state or federal plan.

Private-sector pension plans are regulated by the IRS and the Employee Benefits Security Administration at the U.S. Department of Labor. If you have a problem with a company pension that your plan administrator is not willing or able to resolve, you should file a complaint with the Employee Benefits Security Administration, either through its web site at www.dol.gov/ebsa or by calling toll-free (866) 444-3272.

For all pension issues, whether public or private, you should also contact PensionHelp America (www.pensionhelp.net), an advocacy group with an impressive record of sorting out pension issues. Another valuable resource is the Pension Rights Center in Washington, which has links to local pension-rights groups all over the country. You can contact them online at www.pensionrights.org, by phone at (202) 296-3776, or by mail at:

Pension Rights Center
1350 Connecticut Avenue, NW
Suite 206
Washington, DC 20036-1739

Fight for Your Money Action Steps

☐ Pull out a copy of your Summary Plan Description. If you don't have it, get a copy from your plan administrator.

☐ Create a work history file for your records.

☐ Know your vesting schedule.

☐ Educate yourself on the state of your plan's finances.

☐ Consult an accountant or financial planner to understand your pay-out options when you are considering retirement.

☐ If you're eligible for a pension with a former employer, be sure to be in touch with the plan administrator. For help, visit PensionHelp America at www.pensionhelp.com.

Social Security

The U.S. Social Security program is the largest government program in the world. In 2008, it paid out $608 billion in benefits—nearly 21% of the entire federal budget and more than 4% of the nation's gross domestic product. While the average benefit is only slightly more than $13,000 a year, that's enough to keep an estimated 40% of all Americans age 65 or older, who would otherwise be struggling, out of poverty.

Pundits of Social Security will have you believe that the program is going bankrupt. It can seem that way if you factor in the estimates that by 2017 Social Security will be paying out more in retirement benefits than it collects in payroll taxes—meaning that it will have to begin dipping into its reserves to make ends meet. Moreover, by 2041, the experts say, those reserves will be gone and, unless new revenue sources are found, the system will have only enough money to pay retirees about three-quarters of what it pays them now. Personally, I believe a big part of the problem will be solved simply by raising the age at which we become eligible to start collecting Social Security retirement benefits.

You can now begin collecting a partial Social Security benefit at age 62, but the age at which you are eligible for full benefits is gradually increasing. A 1983 law raised it from 65 to 67 for people born after 1960, and in 2008 the American Academy of Actuaries urged Congress to increase full retirement age by another two years to 69. "Holding the retirement age constant is a certain prescription for future financial problems," the academy said in a rare "public interest" statement. "Raising it . . . would contribute to solving those problems."

Due to economic pressures, the rules are constantly changing, and you need to know how those changes affect you.

How to Fight for Your Money

When it comes to complicated regulations and massive bureaucracy, Social Security is right up there with the IRS and the DMV. But if you want to get the most out of all those payroll taxes you paid over the years, you can't let it intimidate you or ignore your benefits and rights. Nobody is *giving* you any benefits—you earned them. So don't be reluctant to stand up for your rights.

Most people still assume that the "official" retirement age—the age at which you qualify for full Social Security benefits—is 65. In fact, for people born after January 1, 1967, it's now 67. So if you were born in, say, 1970 and were counting on being able to collect a full benefit when you turn 65 in 2035, you may have to rethink your plans. (You can find the complete retirement schedule on the Social Security Administration's web site at www.ssa. gov/retire2/agereduction.htm.)

Here are some other important tips to keep in mind.

Make Sure Your Earnings Record Is Accurate

The size of your Social Security retirement benefit is largely based on how much you paid over the years in Social Security taxes. (That's the dreaded "FICA" deduction on your payroll check.*) So it's vitally important that your earnings record is accurate. Every year, the Social Security Administration is supposed to send you a statement listing your Social Security wages over the course of your working life. Make sure the SSA's numbers match the numbers on your pay stubs or W-2 forms. Call the Social Security Administration right away if you find any errors or if any years are missing (other than the most recent year, which may not yet have been recorded). The toll-free number is (800) 772-1213.

While I was working on this book, I double-checked my most recent Social Security statement and, sure enough, my 2006 earnings were not credited correctly! This is why you must check this carefully—every year.

Keep in mind that there is a limit each year on the earnings that are subject to Social Security tax. Anything you earn above that amount is not included in your Social Security earnings.

---

*FICA stands for Federal Insurance Contributions Act, the law that authorizes Social Security withholding.

Figure Out When You Want to Start Collecting

The longer you continue working, the higher your retirement benefit will be. So to get the maximum benefit, you should delay retiring as long as you can. Here's how it works.

Your retirement benefit is based on your best 35 years of earnings. (Earnings in early years are adjusted for inflation.) If you work fewer than 35 years, the missing years will be counted as ones in which you earned zero income. This will bring down your average and reduce your benefit. Replacing those zeroes with earnings, on the other hand, will increase your benefit.

Moreover, the longer you wait to start receiving benefits (up to age 70), the bigger your benefit will be. For example, say you were born after 1967 and your benefit at full retirement (age 67) would be $1,000 a month. If you chose to start collecting Social Security at age 62, you would get only $700 a month. Plus, if you were still earning money, your benefit would be cut even further if your earnings exceeded a fairly modest ceiling ($13,560 in 2008). On the other hand, if you waited until you were 70 to claim your benefits, you would get $1,240 a month. And you could earn as much as you want without its impacting the size of your Social Security check.

Based on this, you might think that waiting until 70 to start collecting benefits is a no-brainer. But that's not necessarily the case. It's true that most people who make it to retirement age will probably live into at least their early eighties. (According to the Census Bureau, the average life expectancy for men who reach 65 is another 17 years, while for women it's another 20 years.) Nonetheless, I have always advised most of my clients to start collecting their Social Security benefits as early as possible.

Why? Because even though most people will live long enough to take it later, many won't. Or if they do, they will struggle financially in the meantime. So I believe that even if you can live without your Social Security benefit when you're 62, you should take it anyway. Use the money to help your grandchildren save for college. Take your family on a vacation. Enjoy your life with the extra money! And if you do need the money—well, even though it's only 70% of what it might be if you waited another five years, 70% is better than nothing.

> I believe that even if you can live without your Social Security benefit when you're 62, you should take it anyway.

Many experts disagree with this approach. But the bottom line is that the question of when to start taking Social Security is a very personal one. You need to look at your life and what impact taking the money early versus taking it later will have. Then weigh if waiting makes sense.

Take Advantage of the Quirks

Although the Social Security system is complicated and quirky, sometimes those quirks can work for you. In particular, there is one that every married couple should take advantage of.

According to the Social Security rules, if both spouses have been receiving benefits and one of them dies, the surviving spouse will continue to receive whichever of the two benefits was bigger. (In other words, if you were receiving $750 a month and your spouse was receiving $1,000 a month, your benefit would increase to $1,000 a month after your spouse died.) Because of this rule, it often makes sense for the lower-earning spouse in a two-income couple to start collecting benefits at 62, while the higher-earning spouse waits until age 70. Not only is the couple's joint net income likely to be higher this way, but regardless of which spouse dies first, the survivor will get the higher benefit for the rest of his or her life. Get a financial advisor to run the numbers before making a decision. Another little-known rule that can be really helpful involves survivors' benefits. When one spouse dies, the surviving spouse may be able to start collecting survivors' benefits as young as age 60, as long as he or she hasn't remarried. This can be true in some cases even if you're divorced. (You can start collecting at age 50 if you're disabled and at an even younger age if you're caring for a child.)

If you are eligible for both a spousal benefit and a benefit based on your own earnings, Social Security assumes you'll take the higher benefit. But once you reach full retirement age, you have a choice—and sometimes taking the lower benefit makes more sense. For example, it's generally a better idea to take the spousal benefit even if it's lower than the retirement benefit, since you will ultimately get more money if you wait until you're 70 to claim your retirement benefit.

The thing to keep in mind is that if you want to collect on a deceased spouse or former spouse's benefits, wait until you are least 60 to remarry. Otherwise, you won't be eligible. For a full explanation of Social Security programs, visit www.socialsecurity.gov/pubs/10035.html.

Be Prepared to Fight for Disability Benefits

One of the most unfortunate side effects of Social Security's fiscal crisis is that it's tougher than ever for disabled people to claim benefits. The fact is that regardless of their circumstances, most people who apply for Social Security disability benefits these days are rejected initially. So if you are disabled, be prepared to fight for your rights.

Most people who apply for Social Security disability benefits these days are rejected initially.

Under the law, you're entitled to disability benefits if you are permanently disabled and have worked long enough to qualify. What's more, after two years of eligibility, you are also entitled to valuable health care coverage under Medicare.

The problem is that disability claims have doubled since 2001 and the Social Security Administration is swamped with a backlog of cases. As a result, most initial disability applications are routinely denied, requiring applicants to file an appeal if they are to have any hope of ever collecting the benefits they deserve. Here are some ways to improve your chances of success:

- Ask your own doctors to provide evidence supporting your disability claim, rather than depending on the doctors assigned by Social Security.

- Get a lawyer who is experienced in handling Social Security disability appeals to assist you.

- Fill out all forms completely, noting all your health issues (including psychological/mental issues) and prior work experience.

- Call your representatives in Congress if your claim is unreasonably denied.

Consider Taking a "Do-Over"

When I was a kid and I made a mistake in a game I was playing, I could sometimes ask for a "do-over." Amazingly, Social Security gives you the same second chance. If you claimed your Social Security benefits early and then wished you hadn't, you have the option of paying back all the money you received (without interest!) and starting over at a later date with a higher benefit. Details on how to do this are available on the Social Security web site (www.ssa.gov), but basically it involves withdrawing your application for benefits, waiting for Social Security to tell you how much you have to repay, and then reapplying for benefits.

See If You Qualify For SSI

Supplemental Security Income (SSI) is a federal program that provides cash for basic needs like food, clothing, and shelter to aged, blind, and disabled people who have little or no income. You may think of SSI as something only for the very poor, but you'd be surprised at how many people qualify. If you have very few assets (less than $3,000 for a couple, not including your home and a car) and you are disabled or 65 or older, you may be eligible for SSI. So check with your local SSA office if there's a chance you might be. (To locate the nearest office, go to the SSA web site at www.ssa.gov and click on "Find a Social Security Office.")

What to Do if Things Go Wrong

In a very real sense, things have already gone wrong with Social Security. There is no getting around the fact that unless big changes are made, many of today's workers will not get all the retirement benefits they've been promised. So we need to keep the politicians' feet to the fire. If you are concerned about your future Social Security benefits, let your representatives in Washington know about it. Make it clear to them that "kicking the can down the road" and leaving the problem to some future Congress to solve is simply not acceptable. We need responsible action now.

You can find contact information for your congressman on the web site of the U.S. House of Representatives at www.house.gov; just click on "House Directory." To get contact information for members of the U.S. Senate, go to the Senate's web site at www.senate.gov and click on "Senators."

For individual problems with Social Security, your best bet if you have an issue that needs resolving is to go to your local SSA office in person. Because of budget cuts, it's extremely difficult to get through to a live person on the SSA's toll-free complaint lines. Once you get to the office, ask if you can make an appointment to come back on a designated day and time to minimize waiting. Write down the claim number you're assigned and the name of every person you speak with. Dealing with a bureaucracy can be extremely frustrating, but if you keep good records and stay focused, you can generally get your issue resolved.

If you can't, hire a lawyer experienced in dealing with Social Security and don't hesitate to contact your representative in Congress.

Fight for Your Money Action Steps

☐ Check your Social Security statement diligently every year. Errors in your earnings history should be addressed as soon as possible with the Social Security Administration.

☐ Know the exact year that you'll be eligible for full Social Security benefits. Visit the site at www.socialsecurity.gov for a full schedule.

☐ Weigh your options when it comes to deciding whether to collect your Social Security benefit sooner versus later.

☐ If you're disabled, stand your ground and file an appeal if you are initially denied Social Security benefits.

Annuities

With more and more baby boomers heading into their sixties—and stock market returns no longer looking like a "sure thing"—annuities are becoming an increasingly popular investment vehicle for retirees. Sales of individual annuities totaled a record $258 billion in 2007, according to LIMRA International, a research firm whose figures are considered authoritative. This represented an 8% increase over 2006, and it increased the total amount Americans had invested in annuities to just over $2 trillion.

Basically, an annuity is a contract between you and an insurance company. You give them a bunch of money to invest and, depending on what kind of annuity you are buying, they promise you a regular stream of monthly payments that could last anywhere from a few years to the rest of your life and beyond. What's supposed to make annuities a good deal is that the investments the insurance company makes for you are tax-deferred (meaning you don't pay any tax on the earnings until they are distributed to you). Even better, annuities usually come with some sort of guarantee. In some cases, it may be a particular rate of return or a pledge that no matter how badly the stock market does, your investment will never decrease in value; in others, it's a promise that the company will pay out at least as much as you put in (if not to you, then to your heirs).

There's no getting around it—annuities are complicated. There are literally hundreds of different kinds and making comparisons is very difficult. One thing all annuities have in common is they are all either *immediate* (meaning they start paying out right away) or *deferred* (meaning you have to wait a set period of time before the payments start). They are also either *fixed* (meaning they offer a guaranteed interest rate for a set number of years, much like a certificate of deposit) or *variable* (meaning your money is invested in stocks and bonds, as a result of which your rate of return will rise and fall with the market).

What makes annuities different from other kinds of investments is the insurance component—the fact that different kinds of protections can be built in for the investor. Some annuities will guarantee you a monthly payment for the rest of your life—no matter how long you live. Others will guarantee you a minimum rate of return or that your principal will never decline in value or that your survivors will receive certain benefits. In general, the more protection you try to build into your annuity plan, the more it will cost you. Not surprisingly, salespeople love to push the more complicated plans that include all sorts of bells and whistles—and hence are much more expensive.

The Securities and Exchange Commission estimates that some 5 million older Americans are talked into buying annuities that are hazardous to their wealth and unsuited to their needs.

Insurance companies pay hefty commissions (sometimes as high as 15%) to agents who can convince people to pull hundreds of thousands of dollars in retirement savings out of other investments and put them into annuities. Some unscrupulous agents prey on the elderly, calling themselves "elder advisors" or "senior specialists"—though as one securities industry official points out, "the training they receive is often nothing more than marketing and selling techniques targeting the elderly." In all, the Securities and Exchange Commission estimates that some 5 million older Americans are talked into buying annuities that are hazardous to their wealth and unsuited to their needs.

This doesn't mean you should avoid annuities, but it does mean you need to be careful.

▶ How to Fight for Your Money

The simplest annuity is what's called a **fixed lifetime immediate annuity**—a **life annuity**, for short. This is the plain vanilla of annuities and it's meant for retirees who don't have a pension and are afraid of outliving their savings. It's also good for people who do have pensions but aren't sure they can count on them and so choose to collect their benefit in one lump-sum payment. You invest a chunk of your savings (or your lump-sum payout) and, starting right away, the insurance company sends you a check every month for the rest of your life. The insurance company, of course, is betting that you will die before they start losing money on the deal. If you don't—well, the law of averages says that enough other customers will probably die prematurely to keep the company ahead of the game.

A life annuity can be an effective substitute for a traditional pension, but it does have drawbacks. One catch—and it's an important one—is that like any immediate annuity, it locks you in. Once you sign off on the payment schedule and the checks start arriving, that's it—you can't get your money out any faster. So don't go this route if there's any chance you're going to need the cash sooner than the schedule calls for.

Another problem with fixed annuities is that you are trusting the insurance company or bank that sold it to you to do a good job managing your money. While it's true that a fixed annuity comes with a guaranteed rate of return, that guarantee is only as good as the company that stands behind it—and as we saw in 2008, even the biggest and most reputable insurance companies can stumble badly and even collapse.

One way to maintain some control over how your annuity is invested is to get what's called a **variable annuity.** This is an annuity where your money is invested in a portfolio of investments that you choose yourself. It offers a guaranteed payment like a fixed annuity, but also the chance to earn more if your investments perform well. The key word here is "choice." There are variable annuities that allow you to choose from as many as 30 of the best mutual funds around. So you can pretty much custom-tailor your portfolio to what suits you best.

Because this sort of investing can be risky, the insurance company will be more than happy to sell you all sorts of protections that limit (or even eliminate) your downside. And because you may not live long enough to actually see any of the proceeds, they will be happy to write insurance guaranteeing that your heirs will receive at least as much money as you paid in.

> Total fees for variable deferred annuities average nearly 2½% of assets. This is more than twice what most mutual funds charge!

The downside for variable annuities is that they can be expensive. That's because you have to pay both an insurance fee and a money-management fee for each investment you select. According to Morningstar, total fees for variable deferred annuities average nearly 2½% of assets. This is more than *twice* what most mutual funds charge! And sometimes they exceed 4%!

On top of this, there are **surrender charges** to consider. Most deferred annuities let you withdraw 10% to 15% of your principal each year, but if you need to pull out more than that (say, because you've encountered an unexpected medical expense), you may get hit with what is known as a surrender charge. In most cases, you are subject to surrender charges for the first six to eight years you own the annuity, but many of the worst annuities have surrender fees that last 10 years or longer. These fees, which typically start out at around 6% or 7% of the amount you are withdrawing, are at their highest in the first year and then taper down each succeeding year, eventually reaching zero.

The good news is that a number of major investment and brokerage firms offer **"no-load" annuities** that come with extremely low management fees and without sales commissions or surrender fees. Fidelity (www.fidelity.com), Vanguard (www.vanguard.com), and TIAA-CREF (www.tiaa-cref.org) are among the most competitive. But don't expect to get something for nothing: No-load annuities lack many of the features, such as a guaranteed minimum benefit or guaranteed lifetime payments, that make variable annuities so attractive to investors.

Annuities Can Be Tax Time Bombs

Another problem with variable annuities is that they can be tax time bombs. If you own stocks or mutual funds in a regular brokerage account, your earnings are taxed at the capital gains rate—and when you die, your heirs won't have any capital gains liability at all, since the basis on which capital gains are calculated is automatically "stepped up" from your original purchase price to what the investments were worth at the time of your death.

> Don't even think about a deferred annuity until you have exhausted all your other retirement savings options.

Withdrawals from variable annuities are not treated so nicely. When investment earnings from an annuity are paid out to you, they are taxed at the ordinary income rate—which is much higher than the long-term capital gains rate—and when you die, whoever inherits your annuity will not enjoy any step-up; he or she will have to pay income tax on all the gains the same way you did. What's more, withdrawals before age 59½ are subject to stiff penalties.

This doesn't mean you shouldn't buy a variable annuity. They can be a great way to grow your nest egg tax-deferred. But you should consider buying one ONLY if you meet the following four conditions:

1. You have maxed out contributions to all other retirement plans, such as 401(k) accounts and IRAs.

2. You are planning to buy from a low-cost provider.

3. You are currently in a high tax bracket and expect to be in a lower one after you retire.

4. Withdrawal time is still quite a few years away.

The first condition is probably the most important. Don't even think about a deferred annuity until you have exhausted all your other retirement savings options. That means you're already maxing out your 401(k) and IRA contributions.

Here are some other tips to keep in mind when considering annuities.

Don't Be Bamboozled by the Bells and Whistles

According to a survey by AARP Financial, nearly a third of us are guilty of making an investment we shouldn't have because we really didn't understand what we were buying. This is particularly true when it comes to annuities. The fact is that unscrupulous salespeople love to push complicated products like equity index annuities simply because they are so difficult to figure out.

They Fought for Their Money!

This is the story of Kevin and Diane Brown, a retired couple from New Port Richey, Florida, who thought they could increase their income without incurring any taxes by getting rid of their old annuity and buying a new one. There is a way to do this: You arrange with the insurance company to have the assets in the old annuity transferred directly to the new one. Unfortunately, that's not what the Browns did. Based on bad advice from their sales agent, they cashed in their old annuity and used the proceeds to write a check for the new one. Because the money went through their hands, the IRS hit them up for nearly $5,000 in taxes that they hadn't anticipated.

It was a nasty shock, made all the worse by the fact that the agent who gave them the bad advice refused to return their calls once the transaction had been completed. "He was such a nice young man, so personable," says Mrs. Brown. "He really gained our confidence." Furious, the couple complained to the manager of the insurance agency, the Florida Department of Financial Services, and the local newspaper. "It was a case of desperation," Mr. Brown said. "We had no way of coming up with $5,000 for taxes."

In the end, things worked out for them. Wanting to avoid bad publicity, the insurance agency cut them a check for $5,000. But there were a lot of sleepless nights before that happened. The moral: Don't trust a sales agent to give you tax advice. Talk to an accountant or independent financial advisor.

Don't let yourself be bamboozled. Don't buy an annuity unless you really understand exactly what you are getting. With all the talk of bonus interest rates and no downside risk, it's easy to miss the fact that you're getting stuck with outsize fees or ridiculous surrender penalties that can cost you all of your gains if you need to make an early withdrawal. Read the contract carefully and make sure you understand it all. And even if you do, take it to an accountant or financial advisor for a second opinion before you write anyone a check.

Understand How Annuities Are Taxed to Avoid Being Blindsided

Annuities are like IRAs or 401(k) plans. You can move funds from one to another, but if you don't do it correctly, you could get hit with a nasty tax surprise. In order to swap one annuity for another, do a direct company-to-company transfer (it's called a 1035 exchange) to avoid a nasty tax surprise.

Never Put an Annuity in an IRA or Other Tax-Deferred Retirement Account

The assets in your IRA or 401(k) account are sheltered from taxes, so there is no real point to shifting any of them into an annuity while you are still saving for retirement. Some insurance agents will try to get you to do this. Ignore them. You'll just wind up paying fees for tax deferral that you already have. On the other hand, when you are ready to start withdrawing your retirement funds, it may be appropriate to use at least part of your nest egg to buy a life annuity.

Never Put All Your Savings in an Annuity

Annuities are best used in combination with other investments. Putting all your eggs in one basket is never a good idea, and putting them in one with extended surrender penalties is particularly risky because you might need access to the money.

Trust, but Verify

Back in the 1980s, Ronald Reagan used a famous phrase to describe his attitude toward negotiating arms agreements with the Soviets: "Trust, but verify." That's good advice for dealing with annuity providers. Before you do business with an agent who wants to sell you an annuity, check with your state insurance department to verify that he or she is properly licensed. And ask them whether the agent has ever been disciplined for improper behavior. You should also verify the financial strength and stability of the company that's providing the annuity. You can do this through your state's insurance department or through a credit-rating company like A.M. Best Co. (www.ambest.com).

What to Watch Out For

Salespeople Who Call Themselves "Financial Advisors"

The folks who hawk annuities often call themselves financial advisors or retirement consultants, but they are generally just insurance agents who are not licensed to sell anything but insurance products. That's why no matter what your financial situation and goals may happen to be, their solution is always the same—buy an annuity! Given the high commissions they generally earn from selling annuities, you should take their advice with a huge grain of salt.

Salespeople Who Won't Tell You How Much Commission They Earn from Selling You an Annuity

Insurance agents often tell customers they shouldn't worry about how much commission they make from selling annuities since the customer isn't the one who has to pay it. But like so many other things they say, that's not really true. Yes, insurance companies do pay agents up-front commissions as high as 15% of the amount of every annuity they sell (meaning they can pocket as much as $37,500 cash for selling you a $250,000 annuity). But the cost of that commission is passed right back to you in the form of smaller payouts and higher fees—particularly surrender charges. As a rule, if the agent's commission is higher than 4%, the terms of your annuity will probably be lousy. So it's important to know how much your agent stands to earn. And if he or she won't tell you, it means you're probably getting a bad deal.

> As a rule, if the agent's commission is higher than 4%, the terms of your annuity will probably be lousy.

You can usually figure out how much the commission was by looking at your annuity's surrender charge. As a rule, the surrender charge for the first year is almost always just a bit higher than the commission that your broker or financial advisor got when he sold you the annuity.

Promises of Huge Gains

Variable annuities are like any other investment: They can go up and they can go down. While it's true that for an extra charge (usually a substantial one), you can buy an annuity that is guaranteed to maintain some minimum value, there is no way an insurance company or anyone else can guarantee you huge returns. Of course, that doesn't stop unscrupulous salespeople from claiming they can.

Colleen and Rich Powell, a retired couple from Spring Hill, Florida, had never invested in anything but certificates of deposit, until a friend recommended her "financial advisor" to them. The advisor, who was really an insurance agent, immediately began pushing the idea of a variable annuity. "We stressed we could not afford to lose any principal," Mrs. Powell says. "We also told him we were completely naïve about investing and the stock market. He said his own parents had the variable annuities he was recommending for us. He was so convincing, but still we hesitated. And then he told us we'd never make less than 11% a year, and could make as much as 25%. It sounded like an answer to our prayers. We foolishly trusted him."

Needless to say, the Powells never made anywhere near the gains the salesman promised. In fact, the value of their account began falling almost immediately. They filed an arbitration complaint against their broker and eventually won a $50,000 award, but there was no happy ending for them. The broker filed for bankruptcy and, as Mrs. Powell notes sadly, "We've yet to collect a penny."

Getting Trapped in a Low-Yielding Annuity

If you're considering a fixed annuity that guarantees you a relatively good interest rate for the first several years, make sure that the interest-rate guarantee lasts at least as long as the surrender-charge period. With many fixed annuities, the interest they pay falls sharply as soon as the guarantee expires, and if you've still got a surrender charge hanging over your head at that point, you could find yourself stuck in a low-yielding investment with no easy exit.

The Switch-and-Roll

Some advisors will push you to roll over your assets to a new annuity as soon as your surrender period is up. They will give you all sorts of reasons why this makes sense—for example, that you may be able to lock in a higher death benefit or get some new special feature—but the real reason they want you to "switch and roll" is that if you buy a new annuity, they will earn a new commission. So before you agree—and in the process subject yourself to a new six or eight years of surrender fees—make sure the "new" bells and whistles you're getting aren't already provided by your current policy. You should find this out by calling your current annuity company and asking them directly; don't just take an agent's word for it.

What to Do if Things Go Wrong

There aren't many businesses more heavily regulated than insurance— except maybe the securities industry. Since annuities involve both insurance and securities, there are an awful lot of places you can go for help if you think you've been scammed, swindled, or otherwise mistreated in the course of buying one.

You should probably start by contacting the brokerage that employs the person who sold you the annuity. Talk to the salesperson's supervisor. If the supervisor agrees the sale was inappropriate, he or she may be able to cancel the transaction. Your next call should be to the insurance company or bank that issued the annuity. Start with customer service and work your way up the chain to someone with the authority to unwind your annuity. Explain politely but firmly just how you were misled and make it clear that although you have no desire to sue anybody for fraud, you will have no choice but to do just that if the situation can't be resolved amicably.

If this doesn't produce results, it may be time to call in the big guns. Complaints about fixed annuities and insurance agents should go to your state's department of insurance. You can find contact information for the insurance regulator in your state on the web site of the National Association of Insurance Commissioners at www.naic.org/state_web_map.htm. If you bought your annuity from a bank, there are a variety of bank regulatory agencies you can call. Which one is right depends on whether the bank is federally chartered, state chartered, a savings and loan, a credit union, and so on. You can find contact information for all the appropriate banking agencies in the section BANK ACCOUNTS (page 67).

If your problem involves a variable annuity and/or a broker, you should complain to the Securities and Exchange Commission (www.sec.gov). You can call the SEC Complaint Center toll-free at (800) 732-0330. Or you can write them at:

SEC Complaint Center
100 F Street, NE
Washington, DC 20549-0213

Individual states also have securities regulators to whom you can complain. You can find contact information for your state's securities regulator on the web site of the North American Securities Administrators Association at www.nasaa.org/QuickLinks/ContactYourRegulator.cfm.

Complaints about brokers can also be directed to the Financial Industry Regulatory Authority (www.finra.org), a nongovernmental agency created in 2007 by the National Association of Securities Dealers and the New York Stock Exchange to oversee brokers and brokerage firms. You can file a complaint online through FINRA's Investor Complaint Center at https://apps.finra.org/Investor_Information/Complaints/complaintCenter.asp.

Fight for Your Money Action Steps

☐ Review the four conditions laid out on page 282 to determine if it makes sense for you to invest in an annuity.

☐ Get the advice of an accountant or financial advisor before investing in an annuity—and remember, the agent who sells annuities is not a financial advisor!

☐ Check your agent's credentials with your state insurance department and check out if they've ever been disciplined for improper behavior.

☐ Bottom line—don't buy an annuity unless you really understand what you're getting.

Online Shopping and Auctions

Who doesn't buy stuff on the Internet these days? In 2007, Internet commerce totaled $175 billion, according to a survey conducted by Forrester Research for the National Retail Federation. That's a nearly fivefold increase since 2000. Online shopping has exploded because it's quick, easy, and convenient. But all that convenience comes at a price. Internet sales scams—particularly those involving online auctions—are among the fastest-growing category of consumer complaints. According to the Internet Crime Complaint Center (IC3), a joint operation between the FBI and the Justice Department's National White Collar Crime Center, nearly 207,000 Americans lost roughly $240 million to scam artists and other Internet criminals in 2007. And that's just the people who filed complaints. The actual total is probably several times that.

How to Fight for Your Money

About half of all the complaints about online shopping involve problems related to Internet auctions, and there's no question that sites like eBay and

Ubid are a world unto themselves. But whether you're bidding for something at an online auction or buying a fixed-price item from an Internet merchant, the ways scam artists try to rip you off are similar. Here's how to protect yourself.

Know Your Seller

Where possible, buy from sites you know. If you're buying from a site that's unfamiliar, research them before you place an order. Virtually anyone can set up a shop online and start doing business. Try calling the seller's phone number to make sure you can reach them. Type the site's name in a search engine to see if you can find any reviews. For auction sites like eBay, check the seller's feedback rating. Steer clear of those with less than positive ratings . . . or no ratings at all. Be aware, however, that feedback ratings can be manipulated. To protect yourself, always check the seller's history to make sure he or she has previously sold items similar to what you're think-ing of buying. As one expert says: "If it's all been for very low-priced items and suddenly the person is selling laptops, for example, you should be very suspicious." You should also look for the "Buy Safe" seal. Buy Safe (www. buysafe.com) is an independent company that certifies online merchants as being trustworthy and reliable.

Make Sure Your Internet Connection Is Secure

It's easy to tell whether a site is encrypted. Your browser will display a small icon of a closed padlock or unbroken key.

Before you buy anything from an e-commerce site, make sure it uses encryption technology, which scrambles sensitive information such as your credit card number to keep computer hackers from steal-ing it. It's easy to tell whether or not a site is en-crypted. Just look at the web address in your browser display. If it begins with "https" instead of "http," the site is encrypted. In addition, your browser will display a small icon of a closed padlock or unbroken key. (You can usually find this icon in either the lower right-hand corner of the browser or in its address bar.)

Most reputable e-commerce sites also display the words "Secure Sockets Layer (SSL)" or a pop-up box that says you are entering a secure area. The most secure sites will display something called Extended Validation (EV) SSL Certificates. A site with one of these has had its authenticity verified by a reputable authority such as VeriSign. If a web site doesn't have a security certificate, it's probably too risky to shop there.

Make Online Purchases with a Credit Card— Not with a Debit Card or Check

If something goes wrong with an online transaction—like, say, you get cheated—you'll be glad you paid with a credit card. Thanks to the Fair Credit Billing Act, when you charge something to a credit card, you have the right to have the charge reversed if the item turns out to be defective or simply never arrives. You can also stop payment if you are dissatisfied with the quality of any goods and services you've purchased with a credit card. (For more details, see the section CREDIT CARDS on page 89.) When you pay with a debit card, you have no such protections.

And never pay with a personal check. That's an open invitation to identity theft, since it contains your bank account number and home address.

If you're buying something from an individual who is unable to accept a credit card charge, insist on paying through an online payment service like Escrow.com or PayPal.com, which protect buyers against fraud. (But if the seller suggests a service other than Escrow.com or PayPal, check them out carefully. There have been cases where scammers have set up phony escrow services to con both buyers and sellers out of their money.)

Guard Your Privacy

Be wary if an online merchant asks for information that's not pertinent to your purchase, such as your date of birth, Social Security number, or annual income. When you're filling out an order form, provide only the basic information that is required (usually it's marked with an asterisk) and don't volunteer anything beyond that. (Some outfits sell this information to marketers; others may be fronts for identity theft.) And never share your passwords with anyone. In fact, if you ever set up accounts with online merchants, make a point of using different passwords for different web sites.

Be Careful When You're Bidding

Before you place a bid for anything at an online auction, read the description of the item carefully. Ask questions if you're uncertain about any aspect of the transaction—especially the item's condition. Find out who pays for shipping and delivery. Generally, sellers specify shipping cost and give buyers the option to pay for faster delivery. Check the seller's return policy. Can you return the item for a full refund if you're not satisfied? If you do return it, will you be required to pay shipping costs or a restocking fee?

Don't place a bid until all your questions have been answered to your satisfaction. And before you start bidding, figure out the maximum price you're willing to pay for the item and don't go beyond it. This approach will protect you from being fooled into paying an inflated price by "shill bidding"—a scam in which confederates of the seller try to bid up an item way beyond what it's really worth. In any case, never bid on anything unless it's an item you really want, since if you turn out to be the highest bidder, you will be obligated to buy it.

Keep Your Receipts

Receipts are always important, regardless of where or how you bought something. But they are especially crucial when you're shopping in the virtual world, where it's often difficult to know whom you're dealing with. So whenever you complete an online purchase, always print and save the confirmation page. In fact, until you actually receive the merchandise you ordered, keep all the associated documents, including the product description and price as well as copies of any emails you may have exchanged with the seller or merchant.

Know Your Rights

Federal regulations require online merchants to honor their promises to ship goods by a certain date—or, if they didn't specify how long it would take, then within 30 days of when you placed the order. If the goods aren't shipped by then, the seller must notify you and give you a chance to cancel your order and receive a refund. What's more, you have the right to reject merchandise if it turns out to be defective or not what was promised.

What to Watch Out For

Wire-Transfer Requests

Be suspicious if a seller insists that you pay by wire transfer. Even if he is an individual (as opposed to a business) and so has no way of processing a credit card charge, there is absolutely no reason why he can't accept payment through an online payment service like Escrow.com or PayPal.com. Except, of course, if he is trying to scam you.

Foreign-Based Sellers

Be extra cautious when dealing with sellers or buyers located outside the United States. U.S. consumer-protection laws and regulations do not apply to them, and you will have little if any recourse if they rip you off.

Discount Prices for Designer Labels

In June 2008, a French court ordered eBay to pay a $63-million judgment for allowing counterfeit Louis Vuitton bags, Christian Dior clothing, and Guerlain, Kenzo, and Givenchy perfume to be sold on its site. Luxury brands like Hermès and Rolex won similar cases against eBay in previous years. Counterfeit designer goods are a problem everywhere, but especially online. So be extremely skeptical of any seller who is offering designer products at bargain-basement prices. Chances are, they're fakes.

Sellers Who Want Direct Contact

Online auction sites generally provide bidders with the seller's direct contact information *after* they make a bid. So be wary of a seller who puts his address or phone number in the description of the item he's trying to sell. Chances are he's trying to get around the site's antifraud protections.

Suspicious Photos

The kind of photos used in an online auction listing can often tell you more than the seller may intend. Look at them carefully. You want them to be of the actual item the seller is offering—NOT stock photos of the product from the manufacturer's web site—unless perhaps the item is being sold as over-stock. The use of stock photos generally means that the item is in lousy condition, is a fake—or doesn't even exist.

Being Phished to a Phony Site to Be Swindled

If you receive an unsolicited email from an Internet merchant and you're interested in what he has to sell, don't click on any links that may be embedded in the message. Instead, find your own way to the merchant's web site by using a good search engine like Google or Yahoo. Online scammers often pose as reputable merchants and send out email solicitations containing what are called "spoofed links"—links that look like they'll take you to a good vendor but in fact direct you to a phony site where they can "phish" your personal data.

What to Do if Things Go Wrong

If you have problems during a transaction, you should first try to work them out directly with the seller or site operator. If that doesn't work and you paid with a credit card, contact the credit card company to dispute the charge. (For details on how to do this, see page 100 in the chapter CREDIT CARDS.) You should also complain to your state's consumer-protection agency (see the list on the federal government's Consumer Action Website at www. consumeraction.gov/state.shtml), the local chapter of the Better Business Bureau (www.bbb.org), and the Federal Trade Commission (through its online complaint form at www.ftccomplaintassistant.gov).

If you've been victimized by any kind of Internet scam, file a complaint online with the Internet Crime Complaint Center at www.ic3.gov/complaint. Include your name, mailing address, and telephone number as well as the name, mailing address, and web address of the person or business that defrauded you. You should also include specific details of how you were defrauded and any other relevant supporting information. After you file the complaint, you'll be assigned a complaint ID and password so you can update your complaint as you get new information. After reviewing your complaint, analysts with the IC3 may refer it to appropriate federal, state, and local authorities.

Fight for Your Money Action Steps

☐ Make sure your online purchase is from a legitimate merchant.

☐ Buy only from secure sites.

☐ Use a major credit card.

☐ Check the seller's rating before placing a bid on an auction item. Has he sold similarly priced items before?

☐ Keep your receipts and correspondence.

Appliance Protection Plans/Extended Warranties

E very time I buy a new computer, iPod, cell phone, DVD player, or even a microwave, I go through the same drama. I've finally figured out which model I want to get and I tell the salesman to write it up, and then he stops me cold by saying: "And you're going to want the extended warranty, right? I mean, you never know with these things. It's worth it just for the peace of mind."

But is it really worth spending 10% to 20% of the purchase price for a plan you may never use, for coverage you may already have?

Americans buy upward of 100 million appliance protection plans and extended warranties each year, spending a total of more than $9 billion annually to get extra protection for everything from $20 toasters to $90,000 SUVs. The irony is that in the vast majority of cases we are shelling out good money for protection we already have or don't really need.

This is why, except for computer purchases for my company, I almost never purchase an extended warranty. Experience has taught me that when you do buy an extended warranty, the hassle of actually using it (returning the defective product, paying the shipping and restocking fees, pulling together all the paperwork) simply isn't worth the time and trouble it takes. In fact, it's often cheaper to buy a brand-new product than to pay the deductible on an extended warranty for an old product that they may or may not be able to fix to my satisfaction. So when the salesman asks me if I want the extended warranty, my answer is: "No, thank you!"

A Good Deal for the Retailer—but What About You?

Extended warranties are definitely a great deal for the folks who sell us the products we're paying to cover. A retailer typically keeps at least half—and often more—of the purchase price of every extended warranty he or she sells. On a $500 service contract for a $3,000 flat-screen TV, that can mean at least $250 in pure profit for the dealer—which is why you'll rarely get out of a store without being subjected to a strong sales pitch for the extra coverage.

But the fact is that, with a few exceptions, most consumer products are so reliable these days that they rarely break down during the period covered by most extended warranties. As a result, the cost of the warranty is almost always far higher than any repair bills you are likely to incur. Indeed, according to a 2007 *Consumer Reports* survey, two out of three new-car buyers who bought extended warranties said they had spent a lot more on the warranty than they saved in repair costs. Fewer than one in 20 said they actually came out ahead.

When it comes to electronics and appliances, the situation is even worse. Experts estimate that for every 100 warranties sold on electronics and appliances, only 15 people ever file a claim. And most of those problems are not the result of defective workmanship but rather of consumers not reading the directions properly.

> Two out of three new-car buyers who bought extended warranties said they had spent a lot more on the warranty than they saved in repair costs. Fewer than one in 20 said they actually came out ahead.

How to Fight for Your Money

As a rule, if a product is so unreliable that you need to supplement the manufacturer's warranty with additional protection, you probably shouldn't be buying it in the first place. That said, there are some items—like laptop computers and rear-projection TVs—for which extended warranties may make sense. Here's what you should keep in mind.

You May Already Be Protected

Virtually every consumer product comes with a manufacturer's warranty that offers protection for anywhere from 30 days to three years. On top of this, many credit card companies will give you as much as a year's additional coverage if you buy the product with their card, while some big retailers automatically tack an extra year or two of warranty coverage onto products they sell. And most homeowner's insurance policies cover accidental damage, loss, or theft of household items, including electronics. So before you fork over any additional dollars for an extended warranty or protection plan, make sure you really need it.

Make Sure You Know What's Covered

Most warranties are loaded with fine print, and it's important to understand in advance what's covered and what's not. According to the *Los Angeles Times*, Amazon.com's extended warranty lists 35 cases in which protection

I Fought for My Money!

A few years ago, I bought a top-of-the-line computer at a top-tier store in Manhattan with a renowned reputation for service. Because things often do go wrong with laptops, I forked over $500 for a three-year extended warranty. Sure enough, in the third year, my screen died. I immediately dug out the paperwork and sent the computer back to the retailer. Three weeks later, they sent the computer back to me with a note saying that the computer had water damage that was not covered by the warranty and that it would cost me $850 to get it fixed. I knew there was no water damage, so I fought back—hard. I insisted the problem was covered by the warranty; they insisted it wasn't. Finally, after eight phone calls, half a dozen emails, and a letter to the manager sent via both certified mail and fax, they relented and agreed to fix the computer.

It would have been very easy for me to give up on my computer. This is exactly what the stores that sell these warranties count on. They know you are busy, and so they will attempt to stonewall you. This did not work with me—and it shouldn't work with you. If you ever buy an extended warranty and get the runaround like I did—FIGHT BACK! Don't ever give up, speak to management, and put your complaint in writing.

doesn't apply, including "plasma TVs used in altitude levels above 6,000 feet above sea level." When it comes to major appliances or large items like flat-screen TVs, it's crucial to know what kind of service the warranty provides. Will they come to you to fix it or will you have to bring it to them? And when it's fixed, will they hook it back up? Also, keep in mind that while the salesman may insist that *everything* is covered, including your three-year-old flushing your cell phone down the toilet, his verbal assurances are worthless. If it's not in the warranty contract, you're out of luck.

And find out about the deductible. Many warranties make you pay the first $25, $50, or $100 of each repair. When you add in shipping fees, service fees, and the like, a deductible can render an extended warranty pretty much worthless.

Consider Who's Protecting You

Some extended warranties are administered by the manufacturer, some by the retailer, and some by third-party warranty companies. When you buy this kind of protection, it's important to know who stands behind it—especially in tough economic times. That's because if the company goes out of business, your warranty may disappear along with it. In 2007, an Ohio-based company called Ultimate Warranty went bankrupt, leaving nearly 140,000 customers who had paid upward of $45 million for extended warranties holding contracts not worth the paper they were printed on. So find out who is actually guaranteeing your warranty and make sure you're comfortable that they'll be around to honor it.

Take Your Time

Because their profit margins are so huge, most retailers will do everything they can to keep you from leaving their store without buying an extended warranty. But the fact is that there's no reason you have to decide right then and there. Typically, you have 30 days from the date of purchase to buy an extended warranty. So if you think you may need one, take your time. At the very least, take the contract home and read it carefully BEFORE you hand over any money.

Pay Attention to the Calendar

Most extended warranties go into effect the day you purchase the product, so at the beginning at least they will merely duplicate the manufacturer's warranty coverage that comes with the product. What this means is that if your product has a one-year warranty, a three-year extended warranty will give you only two years of extra coverage.

Don't Pay Too Much

As a rule, a warranty costing more than 15% of the price for three years of coverage is not worth it.

Most three-year extended warranties go for somewhere between 10% and 20% of the product's price. Given the likelihood that you'll never use the protection, you want to pay as little as possible for it. As a rule, anything more than 15% of the price for three years of coverage is not worth it.

Consider the Extras

Extended warranties don't provide for repairs only if a product turns out to be defective, they sometimes also include valuable extras such as tech support. This can make a protection plan worthwhile for items like computers. For example, Apple offers first-rate tech support for its Macs, but it's free for only the first 90 days. After that, the company charges $49 for every phone call—unless you buy its three-year AppleCare warranty, in which case you can make as many tech-support calls as you want for no extra charge. Given that AppleCare costs only $169 for an iMac, you'll be ahead of the game if you make just three or four tech-support calls.

What to Do if Things Go Wrong

If you have an issue with your extended warranty or appliance protection program, you should first try to resolve the problem with the retailer who sold you the defective product. If that doesn't work, contact the manufacturer. It's usually best to do this in writing, with a letter sent by certified mail in which you detail the nature of your problem and how you would like to see it rectified. Include copies (not originals) of your sales receipt and other relevant documents.

If the manufacturer doesn't help, file a complaint with your state or local consumer-protection office. You should also complain to your local chapter of the Better Business Bureau (www.bbb.org) and to the Federal Trade Commission, either by telephoning its Consumer Response Center toll-free at (877) 382-4357 or through its online complaint form at www.ftc complaintassistant.gov.

Finally, you should consider taking legal action. Disputes involving less than $750 can usually be handled without lawyers in small-claims court.

Fight for Your Money Action Steps

☐ Find out what kind of manufacturer's warranty is already included with the product.

☐ Find out if the retailer offers an additional warranty free of charge.

☐ Call your credit card company in advance to determine what kind of coverage you'll have through them if you purchase the product on your card.

☐ Know what's covered through your homeowner's insurance.

☐ Check reliability statistics of the product through *Consumer Reports* or J.D. Power and Associates.

☐ If you're leaning toward buying the extended warranty after all, find out what the deductible is and who the warranty is actually through— the manufacturer, the retailer, or a third party.

Gift Cards

G ift cards may be the perfect solution for that hard-to-please teenager or guy-who-has-everything uncle on your Christmas or birthday list, but in general they are a much better deal for the banks and retailers who issue them than they are for you. For one thing, when you buy a gift card, you're basically lending money interest-free to the merchant who sold it to you. For another, gift cards are often so difficult or inconvenient to redeem that millions of recipients wind up throwing them away—in effect, turning your interest-free loan into an outright gift *to the merchant*!

In 2007, nearly 200 million Americans spent roughly $97 billion on gift cards. But the recipients of those cards used them to make only about $89 billion worth of purchases—meaning that gift-card issuers wound up pocketing nearly $8 billion.

How to Fight for Your Money

For all the convenience they offer, gift cards are often incredibly frustrating to use. Indeed, in an effort to protect consumers, 29 states have passed laws imposing restrictions on gift cards. (A complete list of state laws governing gift cards can be found on the web site of the National Conference of State Legislators at www.ncsl.org/programs/banking/GiftCardsandCerts.htm.) Still, the rules governing them remain tricky and hard to follow. So if you're thinking of buying a gift card—or if someone has given you one—here are some tips to keep in mind.

Read the Fine Print

If you think that a gift card is as good as cash, think again. Not only do some of them have expiration dates, but many also charge a laundry list of fees for all sorts of routine services—and in some cases for doing nothing—that can reduce a card's value sharply. To make matters worse, many merchants restrict how and where their cards can be used. For example, Starbucks gift cards are not good at many Starbucks outlets in airports, supermarkets, and bookstores. And some bank-issued gift cards aren't accepted at gas stations, car-rental agencies, and cruise lines.

> The worst offenders in terms of fees and expiration dates are the bank-issued Visa and MasterCard gift cards.

The worst offenders in terms of fees and expiration dates are the bank-issued Visa and MasterCard gift cards. For example, if you buy a Visa-branded US Bank gift card online, you'll be charged $6.95 for delivery. You'll get to check your balance by phone twice for free, but after that it's 50 cents a call—$1 if you insist on talking to a human being. After six months, if you haven't used the card, what's called a dormancy fee kicks in. In this case, it's $2.50 a month—meaning your card's value will be reduced by $2.50 every month until you either use it or it expires.

The point is that when you receive a gift card, you should read the fine print to make sure you fully understand expiration dates, fee schedules, and other rules that could affect your ability to redeem the card. If the person who gave you the card didn't include this information with it, check the retailer's web site or call them for a copy of all the applicable terms and conditions.

Use Them or Lose Them

The worst thing you can do with a gift card is to throw it in a drawer somewhere and forget about it. I've been guilty of this myself and now I always make an effort to use the card immediately. Gift cards may be made out of plastic, but they do not last forever. Even if yours doesn't have an expiration date, the merchant that issued it might. When Sharper Image declared bankruptcy in 2008, it stopped accepting its gift cards—leaving consumers stuck with an estimated $25 million of suddenly worthless plastic.

So if you're given a gift card, use it as soon as you can.

Don't Expect Change

If you use a $50 gift card to buy a $40 item, don't expect to get back any change. The $10 will stay on the gift card. And don't assume that you can put it toward another purchase of something that costs more than $10. If you're using a retailer's card, "split tender" transactions—where you pay for part of a purchase with a gift card and the rest in cash—are usually not a problem. But some merchants will not let you do that with a bank-issued gift card. So if you're the recipient of one of these, keep in mind that you probably won't be able to use it to buy anything that costs more than the card's face value, so do your best to buy something as close to the value of the card as possible.

Don't Throw Away the Paperwork

Pretty much the worst thing that can happen to a gift card is that it gets lost or stolen. If yours goes missing, you can usually get a replacement card from the issuer—for a fee of $15 or so—if you know the card number and can provide some proof (such as a receipt) that you actually owned it. So when you are given a gift card, don't throw away the paperwork. Keep the receipt that came with it, make a copy of both sides of the card or write down the card's ID number, and make a note of the customer-service telephone number on the card's back. (Keep in mind that you must report a loss right away. As far as the issuers are concerned, you are responsible for any transactions on the card before it was reported missing.)

Get the Most Out of Your Card by Registering It

A growing number of issuers will let you register your gift card. Indeed, some—such as Crate & Barrel and Starbucks—won't replace a lost or stolen card unless it's been registered. But you can also register your gift cards at a number of consumer web sites designed to help you manage and protect them. Probably the best of these is GiftCardTracker.com, a totally free service that's been around since 2004. Its founder, a Virginia native named Ken Hawkins, got the idea after he walked into his local Office Max with a $50 gift card he had been given two years earlier—only to learn that it was no longer worth anything. In addition to keeping track of your gift-card account numbers, customer-service contact information, and other key data, GiftCardTracker.com will send you email reminders when your card is nearing its expiration date and keep you up to date on the latest offers involving thousands of gift cards.

If You Don't Want It, Swap It

If you've gotten a gift card from a store you don't like, there's a better alternative to throwing it away. You can swap it online for a gift card from a store you do like. Sites such as Swapagift.com, CertificateSwap.com, and CardAvenue.com provide a marketplace where you can trade cards with other dissatisfied recipients, put your card up for sale, or purchase one at a discount.

What to Do if Things Go Wrong

If a gift-card issuer doesn't seem to be following his own rules or otherwise drops the ball, you should first try to resolve the problem directly with him. If that doesn't work, you should go to the authorities.

If the card was issued by a retailer, file a complaint with your state's attorney general as well as with the Federal Trade Commission. You can find a complete list of state attorneys general offices on the web site of the National Association of Attorneys General at www.naag.org. Complaints to the FTC can be filed online at www.FTCComplaintAssistant.gov or by calling toll-free (877) FTC-HELP (877-382-4357), or by writing to them at:

Federal Trade Commission
Consumer Response Center
600 Pennsylvania Ave., NW
Washington, DC 20580

You should also report your gripe to the Better Business Bureau at www.bbb.org.

If the card was issued by a national bank, complain to the Office of the Comptroller of the Currency at www.helpwithmybank.gov/complaints, or by calling toll-free (800) 613-6743 or by writing to them at:

Comptroller of the Currency
Customer Assistance Group
1301 McKinney Street
Suite 3450
Houston, TX 77010

Fight for Your Money Action Steps

☐ When you receive a gift card, read the fine print!

☐ Make a photocopy of the front and back of the card and file it in a safe place along with the receipt. (And when you give a gift card, always include the receipt.)

☐ Go the extra step and register your card.

☐ This weekend, you're going shopping! Pull out all those cards that are stashed away—and use them before they expire.

☐ Never give a bank card. Write a check instead.

Rebate Offers

How many times have you been talked into buying some expensive new product—say, a new microwave oven or a digital camera—mainly because the manufacturer is offering a rebate that will knock 40 or 50 or maybe even 100 bucks off the price? But when you get home, the forms you're supposed to complete and the instructions on what part of the box you're supposed to cut out and send in are so confusing that you can't be sure you've done any of it right. So you wind up doing one of two things. Either you stuff the forms in a drawer, telling yourself you'll get to it some other time (which, of course, you never do). Or you send in all the paperwork, fingers crossed—and nothing happens.

Then, to add insult to injury, when you contact the manufacturer to find out what happened to your rebate check, he tells you they have no record of your ever applying for one, and anyway the program expired months ago.

Rebates are the deal that consumers love to hate—and for good reason. As New York senator Charles Schumer put it in a letter to the Federal Trade Commission a few Christmases ago: "[R]ebates unfailingly bring in billions in excess profits for companies that offer them, but when it comes to saving the shopper a dime, as rebates claim to do, they fail the consumer more often than not."

REBATES ARE RIGGED TO FAIL YOU

Value of products sold with a rebate offer:	$8 billion
Percentage that is ever redeemed:	20%

That's no exaggeration. According to experts, an attractive-sounding rebate can goose the sales of a product by as much as 500%. So every year companies offer some 400 million of them worth roughly $8 billion on products ranging from cars to cell phones to computer software to food. But according to the Promotional Marketing Association, four out of five rebates never get redeemed. And that's not because consumers are lazy. As Senator Schumer correctly noted, it's because of the "scrambling to meet deadlines," the "extremely fine print," and the "unclear instructions."

How to Fight for Your Money

Why do manufacturers make it so hard to redeem rebates? The answer is simple: greed. The fewer customers who qualify for rebates, the more money the companies get to keep. As one industry expert told the *Wall Street Journal*, "Rebates are a good business plan only when consumers fail to claim them."

So how do you protect yourself when the game is rigged against you? Here are some basic tips.

Don't Forget to Apply for It

That sounds simple enough, but once you get your new purchase home, open the box, and misplace the receipt, it's easy to zone out on the whole rebate process. If you are counting on a rebate to make the price you paid affordable, take care of it as soon as possible. Dallas entrepreneur Daniel Pentecost, who successfully cashes in on six to eight rebates a year, told *U.S. News & World Report* that he tracks his rebates in a spreadsheet. "As soon as I have the product in my hands," he said, "the very first thing I do before I use it is I cut off the UPC code, then put it in the envelope. I know that if I don't, it will slip my mind."

Read the Fine Print

Then read it again. And then once more for good measure. Manufacturers all have different rules, which makes the rebate game hard to master. Most rebates require some proof of purchase and a receipt, but what exactly you need to send in varies from one company to another. Some require the original receipt, while others will be fine with a copy. Some might ask for the UPC code, which can be confusing when merchants put their own bar codes on packaging. So don't throw out the box until your rebate check arrives, just in case you mailed in the wrong proof of purchase.

He Fought for His Money!

Chris, a photographer from Atlanta, Georgia, makes a practice of using certified mail with return receipt whenever he files for a rebate worth more than $20. "That way I have proof of when they received it and who signed for it," he says, which makes it tougher for companies to claim they never got anything.

Chris' vigilance paid off when a rebate he filed for a Netgear computer router apparently fell into a black hole. After waiting six months, he went to Fry's Electronics, the retailer that sold him the router. "Since I had copies of everything I'd submitted," he says, "including a return receipt showing that the fulfillment house had received my paperwork before the cutoff date, Fry's agreed to refund me the amount of the rebate."

Also, pay attention to the dates. Deferred rebates don't start until weeks after you purchase the item. It's possible, too, that the promotion is over but the store hasn't removed the materials yet.

Document Everything

The key to rebate success is good record-keeping. Keep notes on exactly when you mailed in which rebate applications, make copies of everything you send, and be sure to keep the initial rebate offer containing contact information. All this will come in very handy if you get into a dispute over an unpaid rebate.

The key to rebate success is good record-keeping.

Beware of the "Check Card" Scam

One of the biggest rip-offs associated with rebates is what I call the "check card" scam. What happens is that you apply for your rebate, but instead of receiving a check that you can deposit or cash, you get a "check card" that has all kinds of ridiculous rules about when it can and can't be used.

This happened not too long ago to a good friend of mine named Nicola, who bought an AT&T cell phone that came with a $100 rebate. Sure enough, after she sent in all the paperwork, AT&T didn't send her a check for the amount, but rather a $100 Visa check card. So Nicola took the card to a restaurant and tried to use it to pay for a meal. It was rejected. Then she took it to a nail salon. Same thing. She was finally able to use it a few times at a grocery store. But when the remaining balance on the card was down to $3, she decided it wasn't worth the hassle anymore and she threw it away—thereby saving AT&T $3.

Multiply this by the tens (or hundreds) of thousands of customers who probably do the same thing and you'll see why companies like AT&T pay their rebates with check cards instead of checks. Indeed, even a quick search online will turn up countless stories from people like Nicola who have had bad experiences with rebate check cards. Many of them complain that these cards are almost impossible to activate and are often declined for what seems like no reason at all.

If that's not bad enough, many of the companies that do pay their rebates by check use checks that expire in 90 days or less. So if you're lucky enough to actually get a rebate check, make sure you deposit or cash it before it expires.

Don't Be Too Patient—and Don't Give Up

Too many consumers are too patient. If your rebate is overdue, don't just sit there. According to the Federal Trade Commission, "By law, companies are required to send rebates within the time frame promised, or if no time is specified, within a 'reasonable' time," which the FTC defines as 30 days. And if they tell you your application has been turned down because you missed a deadline that you know you made or failed to send them documentation that you know you sent, fight back. Rebate rejections can be reversed if you are persistent. As Chris the photographer notes: "Rebates are a game and you have to play it in order to get paid. But if you play it, you will get your money."

▶ What to Do if Things Go Wrong

If more than a month has gone by and you haven't received your check, make a fuss. The way to start is with a call to the manufacturer or the fulfillment house the manufacturer uses to handle its rebate programs. Contact information is usually included in the original rebate offer, which is why you should make sure to keep it. If you haven't, check with the retailer who sold you the product or go online and do a search for "rebate contact information" along with the name of the company that offered the rebate you want to inquire about.

When you reach a customer-service representative, explain that you followed all the instructions but haven't yet received your rebate and would like to know why. Be prepared to have him or her ask you to resend all the documentation you originally sent. (This is why it's essential to keep copies.) If they tell you there's nothing they can do or are otherwise unhelpful, ask to speak with a manager.

If the phone call does not get you any results, you should write a polite letter to the manufacturer, setting out the details of what you bought, where you bought it and when, and noting that your decision to purchase the product was based on their offer of a rebate. Add that your purchase of the product constituted an acceptance of their offer, and that if you don't get your rebate check within 30 days, you will complain to the authorities and begin legal action for breach of contract. (You'll find a sample letter you can use as a model on page 394 of the FFYM Toolkit.)

Send copies of the letter to regulators such as the FTC as well as the attorneys general of both your state and the state in which the company is headquartered. If another 30 days goes by and the company still hasn't sent you a check, file complaints with the FTC and the Better Business Bureau as well as local consumer-protection agencies. You can complain to the FTC either through its online complaint form at www.FTCComplaintAssistant.gov or by calling toll-free 877-FTC-HELP (877-382-4357), or by writing to them at:

Federal Trade Commission
Consumer Response Center
600 Pennsylvania Ave., NW
Washington, DC 20580

You can file a complaint with the Better Business Bureau through its Online Complaint System at https://odr.bbb.org/odrweb/public/GetStarted. aspx.

Fight for Your Money Action Steps

☐ Apply for the rebate as soon as possible.

☐ Read the fine print.

☐ Keep all packaging, proofs of purchase, and receipts.

☐ Know the dates of the promotion.

☐ Keep good records. Keep notes on exactly when you mailed in which rebate applications, make copies of everything you send, and be sure to keep the initial rebate offer containing contact information.

☐ Use certified mail with return receipt for rebates over $20.

☐ Follow up if you don't receive your rebate within a month. Be diligent!

☐ Organize and keep track of your rebate submissions at www. rebatetracker.com.

Tax Preparation

Tax preparation is a huge business. In all, we spend up-ward of $11 billion on it each year. Six in 10 taxpayers hire someone to help them fill out the forms and calcu-late what they owe, while millions more rely on com-puter programs like TurboTax. Unfortunately, taxpayers don't always get their money's worth.

It's not hard to understand why. The tax code is so complicated and hard to understand that even if your finances are relatively simple, filing your in-come taxes can still be a nightmare. Back in 2002, the General Accounting Office estimated that filers were paying nearly $1 billion a year more than they should have because they used the standard deduction instead of item-izing. And that's just one common error.

How to Fight for Your Money

I'm a huge believer in having your taxes done professionally—especially if your income exceeds $50,000 a year. In my experience, the savings you real-ize from a professionally done return will more than cover the cost. In fact, the savings are usually somewhere between five and 10 times your invest-ment. So if you spend $500 having your tax return done, you will more than likely shave $2,500 to $5,000 off your tax bill.

That said, deciding whether to prepare your taxes yourself or to hire a pro pretty much depends on how much time and patience you have and how complicated your finances are. If you're self-employed or have just inherited money, purchased rental property, exercised stock options, or gone through a major life change (like getting married or divorced or becoming a parent), it's almost always worth your while to pay a professional to do your taxes.

> If you spend $500 having your tax return done, you will more than likely shave $2,500 to $5,000 off your tax bill.

The catch is that pretty much anyone can hang up a shingle and call themselves a tax preparer. In fact, only two states, California and Oregon, require tax preparers to be licensed. As Senator Chuck Grassley of Iowa put it during a 2006 Senate hearing on the subject: "It's incredible that we have legal requirements for a barber to cut your hair, but there are no requirements for someone to prepare your taxes. The worst that can happen when you get a lousy barber is a bad hair day. But if you get bad tax advice, you may be audited, owe thousands of dollars, and even face jail time."

Tax preparers range from the guy who sets up a desk in the local real estate office every winter, to the big storefront chains like H&R Block, to professional accountants and enrolled agents. Here's how to pick a good one.

Bigger Doesn't Always Mean Better

Those national chains such as H&R Block (www.hrblock.com), Jackson Hewitt (www.jacksonhewitt.com), and Liberty Tax Service (www.libertytax.com) may seem like a good bet. After all, they process millions of returns annually, they have thousands of retail locations where you can meet with someone face-to-face, they have fancy web sites,

> Many firms just use a software questionnaire similar to the kind of program you can buy for yourself for $50.

and everybody's heard of them. But the fact that these companies are well known doesn't guarantee success. That's because at the end of the day, how well your return is prepared depends on who actually does the work. In a 2006 investigation, the Government Accountability Office sent staffers to 19 different chain outlets to have an imaginary couple's taxes done. According to its report, "nearly all of the returns prepared for us were incorrect to some degree."

That's not really surprising, because many firms use high school graduates (as opposed to more expensive college graduates) to process your return. They just use a software questionnaire similar to the kind of program you can buy for yourself for $50. If you don't like the idea of a part-time employee with only a high school diploma doing your taxes (and you shouldn't), make sure you ask up front about who will be doing your return and what kind of experience he or she has.

Look for Real Professionals

Your best bet for quality tax-preparation help is to use a certified professional. Professional tax preparers are certainly more expensive than the chains—an accountant will typically charge $100 to $300 an hour, versus a total fee of $200 or so for an itemized return at H&R Block—but spotting just one missed deduction or credit (say, the deduction for interest on a student loan or the alternative motor vehicle credit, if you own a hybrid car) can easily save you the difference.

There are two kinds of professionals you should consider: enrolled agents and certified public accountants.

ENROLLED AGENTS are the only federally licensed tax specialists. They must pass an IRS-administered exam as well as a background check, and to keep their licenses they must take 24 hours of continuing education courses each year. Many are former IRS employees, so they generally know the unwritten IRS rules that govern what sort of deductions are likely to trigger an audit. To find an EA in your area, visit the web site of the National Association of Enrolled Agents (www.naea.org) or the National Association of Tax Professionals (www.natptax.com).

CERTIFIED PUBLIC ACCOUNTANTS (CPAS) also must pass a licensing exam, but theirs covers a much wider range of topics than just tax matters, including accounting, auditing, and personal financial planning. You should probably use a CPA to handle business tax matters or more complicated individual returns. You can find contact information for CPAs in your area on the web sites of the American Institute of Certified Public Accountants (www.aicpa.org) and the National Society of Accountants (www.nsacct.org).

Ask for Referrals

The best credential any tax preparer can have is a steady stream of satisfied, repeat customers. So ask for recommendations from relatives, friends, and coworkers who are in roughly the same financial circumstances as you are. If someone you know and trust swears by their tax preparer, make an appointment and check him or her out.

Reputable professionals never promise you a big refund before they have reviewed your situation and run your numbers. They also never ask you to sign a blank tax form or other tax document.

Basically, you want to make sure they have experience in the kind of issues your taxes typically involve. You also want to know that they're up to speed on the latest tax changes. Ask what publications they read, whether they attend continuing education courses, and how many of their clients are audited. And in this age of identity theft, find out how they safeguard your personal information.

Look for Protection

A problem with a tax preparer often means a problem with the IRS. So before you hire one, find out what (if any) protection you will have in the event they make a mistake. The big chains typically promise to cover any fines, penalties, and interest you might get hit with as a result of their work. Many CPAs and EAs will do the same. But this is not something you can just assume. So make a point of asking about it in advance. And if they tell you that nothing is guaranteed, take your business elsewhere.

Don't Wait Until the Last Minute

If you start looking for a tax professional after the beginning of February, chances are you're not going to have much luck. All the good ones are usually fully booked up by then. The time to start shopping is in the fall, when a top preparer will have the time to consider your situation and discuss what he or she might be able to do for you.

You May Be Eligible for Free Tax Assistance

Many low- to moderate-income tax filers can qualify for free tax assistance through the federal VITA program (for Volunteer Income Tax Assistance) program or, if you're over 60, Tax Counseling for the Elderly. Military members can also receive help through the Armed Forces Tax Council. You can find more information about these programs on the IRS web site at www.irs.gov/individuals/article/0,,id=119845,00.html. And anyone, regardless of age or income, can get tax help from the IRS by calling toll-free (800) 829-1040.

If Your Situation Is Relatively Simple, Do It Yourself with Software

If you're a wage earner with run-of-the-mill deductions like mortgage inter-est, property taxes, and child care or educational expenses, there's no reason you can't do your taxes yourself with one of the many brands of tax-prepara-tion software you can buy today. There are dozens of programs and online tax-prep services to pick from, but your best bet is to stick with one of the three bestsellers: TurboTax (http://turbotax.intuit.com), TaxCut (www.tax-cut.com), and TaxACT (www.taxact.com).

They each cost between $20 and $50, and all work pretty much the same. They lead you through a long list of questions about your income, personal finances, spending, and family situation. On the basis of your answers, the software then fills out the appropriate federal and state forms, prints them out, and even helps you file it all electronically (which speeds up any refunds you may be entitled to).

TurboTax, by Intuit (which also makes the hugely popular Quicken per-sonal-finance software), dominates the market. An estimated 75% of all electronic filers use TurboTax, and it was rated the best tax-prep software by both *USA Today* and *PC* magazine. The other two big sellers are TaxCut from H&R Block and 2nd Story Software's TaxACT, which is affiliated with the well-known tax-guide publisher J. K. Lasser.

Regardless of which brand you choose, don't pay full price. Tax software is often discounted or bundled with other finance-related software at an af-fordable price from New Year's Day right through the middle of tax season. Surf the web and check ads in the Sunday paper for the best deals.

Take Advantage of "Free File"

To convince more people to file electronically, the IRS has partnered with several tax-prep software companies to offer free electronic tax filing to low- and moderate-income individuals. (In 2007, you had to have an adjusted gross income of $54,000 or less to qualify.) To access the list of providers, go to the IRS web site at www.irs.gov and click on the "Free File" icon. And make sure you read the fine print when you're selecting a provider. While the federal return is always free, some charge a fee for filing state returns and not all providers handle every state. Others have lower income ceilings or age requirements. Given that there are nearly 20 providers to choose from, your best bet may be to use the IRS's interactive "Guide Me To A Company" tool to narrow down the field.

What to Watch Out For

Unannounced Outsourcing

Some accounting firms outsource their tax-prep work to chains. Others send returns to overseas subcontractors in places like India, where they can be

> Some accounting firms outsource their tax-prep work to chains.

processed overnight for as little as $50. Either way, you're being ripped off—*and* subjected to the danger of identity theft. As Beth Givens, director of the Privacy Rights Clearinghouse, told *Smart Money* magazine, tax returns contain so much data "in one bright, shiny package"—everything from your Social Security number to your date of birth to your bank and brokerage account numbers—that sending them anywhere, no less halfway around the world, is "a great gift to the identity thief." So make sure your return will be prepared in-house. If your preparer won't guarantee that, find another one—or, at a minimum, find out how they protect your Social Security number and other sensitive information.

"Related" Products You Don't Really Need

Many preparers make their real money not by filling out tax returns but by selling you related products such as insurance and loans. One of the biggest rip-offs is the refund anticipation loan, which can seem incredibly convenient but in fact comes with hidden service fees and finance charges that combine to produce APRs as high as 700% or more. (For details, see the section REFUND ANTICIPATION LOANS on page 321.) Avoid these products like the plague, and be wary of a preparer who tries to sell you on them.

Software "Up-Selling"

Just about every brand of tax-prep software has a web site where they allow you to start filling out your tax return free of charge using a bare-bones version of their program. But along the way, they will try to get you to buy a more sophisticated version. This is called "up-selling"—and the added bells and whistles are not always worth the price. A friend of mine who was doing her taxes on the TurboTax site was persuaded to upgrade from TurboTax's $49.95 Deluxe version to its $74.95 Premier version because she had sold some stock during the year. The difference? Premier asked her two questions about her stock sale that Deluxe didn't, and it made absolutely no difference in the amount of tax she wound up owing. In other words, she paid $25 more than she needed to for no reduction of her tax bill. Companies will try to up-sell you at every turn. Think hard before you take the bait.

What to Do if Things Go Wrong

When you get lousy service from a tax preparer, the problem is compounded by the fact that you still have to deal with the IRS. Remember, even if some-one else prepared your return, you are still responsible for what's in it. So if you think it was done inaccurately or incorrectly, don't just send it in. In-stead, redo it—and if there isn't enough time to do it correctly before April 15, then file for an extension. You can do this online or through the regular mail; download instructions and the required forms from the IRS web site at www.irs.gov/pub/irs-pdf/f4868.pdf.

If you believe your tax preparer has acted unprofessionally—whether by treating you badly or abusing the law—you should report him or her to the IRS. If your preparer is a certified professional (that is, a CPA, EA, or tax at-torney), you should write a letter to the IRS's Office of Professional Respon-sibility, in which you detail just what your preparer did (or didn't do). The letter should also include any documents that support your claim, along with the practitioner's address, telephone number, and professional desig-nation (CPA, EA, or whatever).

You can either fax the letter to (202) 622-2207 or mail it to:

Internal Revenue Service
Office of Professional Responsibility
SE:OPR, Room 7238/IR
1111 Constitution Avenue, NW
Washington, DC 20224

If your preparer is not a certified professional but rather what the IRS calls an "unenrolled" preparer (say, some college kid working at a storefront chain), you should file your complaint by filling out the IRS's Informational Referral Form 3949-A. You can download the form from the IRS web site at www.irs.gov/pub/irs-pdf/f3949a.pdf. Once you've completed the form, you should mail it to:

Internal Revenue Service
Fresno, CA 93888

You should also complain to the Better Business Bureau (www.bbb.org) and, if your preparer is an EA or CPA, to the appropriate professional organization.

Fight for Your Money Action Steps

☐ If you're going to outsource your tax preparation, hire an enrolled agent or a certified public accountant.

☐ Start your search early.

☐ Get a recommendation for a professional from someone you know and trust, but make your final decision after you've interviewed him or her.

☐ Find out what their guarantee is if mistakes are made on your return—and how your privacy will be protected, too.

☐ If your finances aren't complicated, consider filing your taxes yourself with TurboTax, TaxCut, or TaxACT.

Refund Anticipation Loans

Get money fast when you file your taxes with us. Receive up to the amount of your anticipated federal tax refund (minus bank fees)... on the spot after filing your return. Plus... your tax preparation fees are paid out of the loan, so you pay nothing out-of-pocket.

—*H&R Block Tax Offices*

Refund anticipation loans (or RALs, as they are called) sure sound like a good deal. That's probably why about 9 million of us sign up for them each year. But it's the banks and the tax-preparation firms that benefit, not us. They rake in more than $1 billion a year providing these virtually riskless loans. How? By imposing exorbitant service fees and finance charges that combine to produce APRs as high as 1,200% or more. That's a pretty steep price to pay for convenience.

How to Fight for Your Money

Most RALs advertise an APR of 36% and that's technically true. But when you add in all the fees, the effective rate goes through the roof.

Take the terms offered by H&R Block, one of the nation's best-known tax-preparation firms. In addition to charging you 36% annual interest on your RAL, they also tack on a $29.95 activation fee and a $20 check-processing fee. Let's say you're expecting a refund of $500 and you don't want to wait for the government to send it to you. Figuring in the $49.95 in fees and a finance charge of $15 or so, you'll be paying around $65 to borrow $500 from H&R Block for maybe a month, which is how long it usually takes the IRS to mail you a refund. This amounts to an APR of more than 150%.

FIGHT FOR YOUR REBATE

Your refund if you take a RAL:	$435
E-file instead and receive:	$500
You gain:	**$65**

You'd do a lot better taking a cash advance on your Visa card or Master-Card. After all, they'll probably charge you "only" 29.99%.

Even H&R Block says the best option is to file electronically with the IRS rather than taking out a RAL.

If you're desperate to get your tax refund quickly, file your taxes electronically and check off the box that tells the government to deposit your refund directly into your bank account. Even H&R Block agrees. As a spokesman for the company told MSNBC.com, "We believe the best option for our clients is to file electronically with the IRS and to receive an IRS direct deposit rather than taking out a RAL."

And don't be scared off by warnings that the only way to file electronically is through a professional tax preparer, who will charge you for the privilege. If your annual adjusted income is less than a certain amount (the ceiling in 2008 was $54,000), the IRS provides a service called Free File, which allows you to file both your federal and state income-tax returns electronically without charge. Details are available online at www.irs.gov/efile. There is also a service called I-Can E-File (www.icanefile.org), provided by the Legal Aid Society of Orange County, California, that allows anyone anywhere in the country, regardless of their income, to file their federal return electronically for free.

What to Do if Things Go Wrong

If you've been misled by a tax-preparation firm or bank that sold you a RAL, contact your city or state consumer-protection agency as well as the Better

Business Bureau (www.bbb.org). If a bank was involved, file a complaint with the appropriate regulatory agency. (For a complete list, see the entry BANK ACCOUNTS on page 67.) You should also complain to the Federal Trade Commission either through its web site at www.ftc.gov, by calling toll-free 877-FTC-HELP (877-382-4357), or by writing to them at:

Federal Trade Commission
Consumer Response Center
600 Pennsylvania Ave., NW
Washington, DC 20580

Fight for Your Money Action Steps

☐ Just say "No" to refund anticipation loans.

☐ To get your tax refund quickly, file your taxes electronically and get your refund deposited directly into your bank account.

Charitable Giving

Practically every morning when I walk from my apartment to my office in downtown Manhattan, I'm stopped by at least half a dozen people asking for contributions to some worthy cause. Some claim they're raising money to protect the environment. Others say they're collecting for battered women. Still others mention hurricane relief or Darfur.

For all I know, they're all telling the truth. But I still don't give them any money.

It's not that I'm cheap. I actually believe deeply in the importance of giving. In fact, in most of my books I tell readers that tithing—giving at least 10% of your income to charity—should be part of everyone's financial plan. It's certainly been part of mine for years. But I want the money I donate to really do some good. I don't want it to be wasted.

The fact is that not all charities are legitimate—and even among the legitimate ones some are more efficient and effective than others. According to an investigation by the *Los Angeles Times*, only 46 cents out of every dollar collected by commercial fund-raisers actually gets to the charities they're supposedly representing. In California alone, the newspaper found, middlemen wound up pocketing more than $1.4 billion in charitable contributions between 1997 and 2006.

So unless you're careful, the hard-earned dollars you contribute to charity could be wasted—or, worse, wind up lining some scam artist's pocket.

How to Fight for Your Money

U.S. charities raise more than $300 billion a year in pledges and donations by tugging at our heartstrings with moving stories about the important work they do and the desperate needs they fill. And it's hard to resist tales of woe and photos of needy children. But if you really want to do good with your money, you need to give smart. Here's how.

Develop a Plan

Be a thoughtful, informed giver. Ask yourself what causes are most important to you and what charities fit best with your interests and sympathies. Then figure out how much you can afford to donate and make that an item in your budget. Not only will this make it more likely that you will actually follow through on your good intentions, but when some telemarketer phones you at dinnertime asking for a contribution to some charity you never heard of, you can politely and truthfully end the conversation by explaining that you have a charity budget and they are not on it.

When some telemarketer phones you at dinnertime, explain that you have a charity budget and they are not on it.

Do Some Research

Before you start writing any checks to a specific charity (no matter how worthy it may seem), you should do some research about how it handles its finances. A rule of thumb in the nonprofit world is that no more than 30% of the money a charity collects should go to administrative costs and fund-raising expenses—meaning that at least 70% of every donation should go to support the cause itself (whether it's feeding hungry kids in Africa or buying books for inner-city libraries).

The Internet makes it easy to find out this kind of information. There are numerous rating organizations with web sites that provide extensive information about how virtually every major charity and countless minor ones raise and spend money.

Three of the best information sources are:

Better Business Bureau's Wise Giving Alliance
4200 Wilson Boulevard, Suite 800
Arlington, VA 22203
(703) 276-0100
www.give.org

American Institute of Philanthropy
P.O. Box 578460
Chicago, IL 60657
(773) 529-2300
www.charitywatch.org

GuideStar
4801 Courthouse Street, Suite 220
Williamsburg, VA 23188
(757) 229-4631
www.guidestar.org

If none of these organizations can provide data about the charity of your choice (or if the information they do have is incomplete), check with the government agency responsible for registering charities in your state. You can find a complete list of these on the web site of the Better Business Bureau's Wise Giving Alliance at www.give.org. (Click on "Resource Library," then on "Helpful Resources for Donors.")

You should also ask the charity itself for a copy of its IRS Form 990. This is a tax document that all but the smallest nonprofits (those with less than $25,000 in annual revenues) are required to file. Generally speaking, it can provide a nice snapshot of an organization's financial health.

Of course, financial statements can be hard to interpret and figures can be manipulated. So rather than relying solely on IRS filings by a group you're thinking of supporting, call them up directly and ask to speak to someone in the development office. Explain that you are considering making a donation and then pepper them with a lot of questions. Which of their programs need money the most? How do they monitor the effectiveness of their programs? Who is on their board? Do any board members make money by providing services to the organization?

If a charity doesn't want to talk about its mission statement, its spending habits, or its financial health, think twice about making a donation. Your willingness to give money gives you the right to ask questions and receive straightforward answers about a charity's health.

Be Wary of Telephone Solicitations

You should be particularly skeptical of telephone solicitations. Don't be afraid to question the person on the phone about his or her relationship with the charity they are touting. It's not uncommon for telemarketers calling on behalf of charities to pocket as much as two-thirds of all the donations they manage to bring in. So if it turns out that the solicitor works for a telemarketing firm, ask what percentage of your contribution will actually go to the charity itself. If you don't like the answer—or if they refuse to tell you—hang up. (If the cause they're touting happens to be one you want to support, you can always contact the charity directly for information about how to make your contribution without going through a middleman.)

It's not uncommon for telemarketers calling on behalf of charities to pocket as much as two-thirds of all the donations they manage to bring in.

Take Advantage of the Tax Breaks— But Not Everything Is Deductible

People will tell you that the great thing about charitable contributions is that they allow you to do good *and* reduce your income-tax bill at the same time. But don't be fooled—not all charitable donations are tax-deductible.

Maybe you gave money to a sick friend at a benefit or to one of those police organizations that call you up and solicit for funds. Or maybe you donated to a political campaign or spent $50 on raffle tickets for your child's after-school program. These are all worthy causes, but that alone doesn't cut any ice with the IRS. Unless the recipient is a registered public charity— officially known as a 501(c)(3) organization—your contribution is *not* tax-deductible. (And don't be misled by organizations that describe themselves as tax-exempt. All that means is that *they* don't have to pay taxes; it doesn't necessarily mean that contributions to them are tax-deductible.)

So if your goal in charitable giving is at least partly a tax deduction, make sure the recipient of your donation is a 501(c)(3) organization. And if you don't want to get in trouble with the IRS, make sure you subtract from your deduction the value of any goods or services you received in return for your contribution.

For instance, say you got a copy of your favorite band's latest CD as a premium for contributing to your local public-radio station's pledge drive. If so, you can't deduct the entire amount of your contribution. You've got to subtract the cost of the CD. Or say you spent $100 on tickets to a charitable gala; if the food and entertainment were worth $30, you can claim only a $70 deduction on your taxes.

How do you know how much to subtract? The charitable group should provide you with a letter telling you the value of any goods or services you may have received in connection with your contribution. If they don't, ask them for it.

Be Careful About Donating Noncash Gifts

Of course, money isn't the only thing you can give to a charity. You can also donate cars and boats, household goods and clothing, stocks and bonds, mutual funds, you name it—if it has value, some charity will probably be happy to take it.

Deducting the value of noncash contributions can be tricky. If you're one of those people who think that donating old junk is a great way to clean out your attic and cut your tax bill at the same time, think again. In recent years, the IRS has tightened up the regulations regarding deductions for noncash charitable gifts.

To begin with, donated goods must be assessed not at what you think they're worth but at fair market value, which is the price that a seller could actually get a buyer to pay.

For stocks, mutual funds, and other securities, that's relatively straightforward. You are entitled to deduct 100% of whatever amount the security happens to be trading at on the day you make the donation. This can be a terrific deal taxwise if you are donating a long-term investment that is worth a lot more than you originally paid for it. By transferring the security directly to the charity (as opposed to selling it and donating the proceeds), you avoid having to pay any capital gains tax, yet you get to deduct the investment's full market value on your tax return.

The benefits are slightly less generous when you donate stuff you own— like appliances or books or clothing. Items worth more than $500 must be professionally appraised. Figuring the fair market value of property worth less than $500 is your responsibility—and you can't claim your old TV or tennis racquet is worth what it would cost you to buy a new one, or even what you originally paid for it. The IRS suggests using thrift-store or consignment-store prices as a gauge of what your donated item is really worth. eBay is another acceptable source of prices for used goods. You can also find a valuation guide for clothing and many household items on the Salvation Army's web site (www.salvationarmyusa.org).

The IRS is especially strict when it comes to donations of clothing and household items. No matter what their sentimental value, in order to be tax-deductible, clothing and household items must be in good condition or better.

The government has also cracked down on the deduction you can take for donating an old car. Until 2005, you were allowed to deduct the full Kelley Blue Book or NADA Guide value of any vehicle you donated to a registered charity. These days, you can deduct only the amount the charity actually receives if and when it sells your donated car—which is usually quite a bit less than the "official" price. There are three exceptions: You can deduct the full Blue Book or NADA price if you give your car to a charity that (1) doesn't intend to sell it; (2) intends to fix it up before selling it; or (3) intends to sell it to a needy person at a discount.

If you are unsure of the rules, go the IRS's web site (www.irs.gov) and download Publication 526, "Charitable Giving." And whatever else you do, be sure to keep good records. The IRS requires a receipt or canceled check for any donation, no matter how small the amount. So when you're giving money, try to pay by check or with a credit card. Actual cash is not only hard to track, but it can too easily wind up in the wrong person's pocket.

What to Do if Things Go Wrong

When it comes to supporting charities, you can't afford to let your guard down. It's sad, but there are scammers out there eager to take advantage of those of us who want to make a difference and support a cause. So be skeptical if you receive an unsolicited phone call or email from an organization asking for money or from an individual claiming to be a victim—particularly around the holidays or in the aftermath of a major disaster. At the very least, never provide any credit card or bank information unless you are absolutely sure that the solicitor is legitimate.

If you have any suspicions that a solicitor is falsely posing as a representative of a well-known charity like the Salvation Army, United Way, or American Red Cross, you should contact the real charity directly. They will either verify the solicitor's affiliation with them and deal with any complaints you may have about his or her behavior—or they will take steps to deal with the scam.

If you suspect a solicitor of shilling for a nonexistent charity, you should contact a law-enforcement agency such as your local police, the Federal Bureau of Investigation (www.fbi.gov), or the U.S. Postal Inspection Service (http://postalinspectors.uspis.gov/).

Complaints about the behavior or management practices of existing charitable organizations should go to the Federal Trade Commission in Washington, D.C. You can contact the FTC through its charity fraud Web page (www.ftc.gov/charityfraud). You should also notify the Better Business Bureau's Wise Giving Alliance through its online complaint page at www.give.org/inquire/complaint.asp.

Fight for Your Money Action Steps

☐ Be proactive. Figure out what issues are most important to you and how much you can afford to donate, then go on a charity-rating web site and find out which organizations that work on these issues are the most financially sound.

☐ If getting a tax deduction is important to you, make sure you are donating to a registered public charity, known as a 501(c)(3) organization.

☐ Follow the rules for valuing noncash donations when you deduct them from your taxes.

☐ If you suspect charity fraud, report it.

Cable and Satellite TV

able TV service is truly a joke. On any given night, you may have 150 channels to choose from and for the most part there is nothing on any of them that's worth watching. (Is it just me—or do you feel this way too?) One of the first things I always do when I prepare a money makeover for a TV show is look at how much the family is spending on cable. In my experience, it is often more than $100 a month. One hundred dollars a month is $1,200 a year. Do you know what that means? Figuring the taxes you have to pay, you have to earn nearly $2,500 a year to pay the cost of receiving 150 stations you don't watch! There are families right now in America that literally work a full month every year just to pay their cable bill.

> There are families right now in America that literally work a full month every year just to pay their cable bill.

The good news, I guess, is that if you really love television, you now have a lot to choose from and many more ways to get it.

What Do You Really Watch— and Do You Really Need It?

For a nation of TV watchers, the explosion of channels available to us over cable and satellite TV in recent years might seem like a great thing. And for some people, it is. But for most of us, it's a huge rip-off.

I'm not talking about bad programs. That's a matter of taste. If you don't like what's on, you don't have to watch—and you certainly don't have to shell out $100 a month for cable or satellite service. But if there are programs you do like, then chances are you are going to be ripped off. That's because in order to get the channels that carry them, you'll also have to subscribe to dozens—if not hundreds—of other channels that you may have no interest in watching.

As most cable and satellite TV subscribers know, you can't really pick and choose the channels you get. You have to order them in blocks (or "tiers," as some of the companies call them), starting with a basic lineup of 50 to 75 channels. So if all you're interested in is CNN and the Weather Channel, that's too bad—you're still going to get ESPN, MTV, Comedy Central, and Lifetime as well.

According to a Nielsen Co. survey, the average U.S. home receives 104 television channels—but only watches about 15 of them with any regularity. What's so terrible about getting channels that you don't watch? Well, nothing really—*except that you're paying for them*. In all, some experts estimate, we consumers fork out as much as $6 billion a year more than we should for channels we don't want and wouldn't subscribe to if we could choose on an à la carte basis.

This doesn't mean you should throw your cable or satellite box out the window. But don't be fooled into thinking that you're getting a great bargain from any of the cable or satellite companies.

How to Fight for Your Money

For all that the lack of à la carte pricing is a rip-off, there's no question that consumers have benefited from the bitter competition between the two systems. While prices are still relatively high (cable rates have nearly doubled since Congress deregulated them in the mid-1990s), they are no longer increasing the way they used to. And the variety and quality of services you can get—from high-definition programming to video on demand to built-in digital recorders—is nothing short of amazing.

It may seem as if everyone with a TV has either cable or satellite service, but the fact is that some 15 million U.S. households still get their TV the old-fashioned way—with an over-the-air antenna. But they are a dying breed. Roughly 65 million of the nation's 110 million TV households are wired for cable, while around 30 million homes subscribe to one of the nation's two DBS (for direct satellite broadcast) services, DirecTV and EcoStar's Dish Network. And as of 2008, the latest entry into the video delivery business—the competing fiber-optic networks being built mainly by Verizon and AT&T—had attracted around a half-million subscribers.

If you're fortunate enough to live in one of the areas where fiber-optic service is already available, you should probably give it serious consideration, since its huge bandwidth gives it the ability to offer superior picture quality, better interactive services (like video on demand), and more HD channels than either cable or satellite. The catch is that it will be years before it will be available everywhere—or even in most places.* So, for the time being at least, the real choice for most of us is between cable and satellite.

Here are their pros and cons.

Cable

PROS: Simplicity, economy, versatility. You don't need to buy any equipment (except for a TV), and if you're willing to forgo all premium and HD channels, you can get a bare-bones basic package for as little as $30 a month. With a digital box (which will cost you an extra $10 or so a month), you can sign up for all sorts of more costly premium programming, such as HBO and Showtime, as well as for video on demand and elaborate HD packages.

CONS: Lack of competition. More than 98% of all communities wired for cable are served by only one provider. So if you want cable but don't like the company that has the franchise for your area, you're out of luck. This may be why customer-service problems (like waiting for days for the cable guy to show up) are legendary. Also, cable is not available in some rural areas.

Satellite

PROS: High customer-satisfaction ratings—perhaps because no matter where you are, you have a choice between DirecTV and Dish. Phenomenal sports offerings (for example, DirecTV's NFL Sunday Ticket Super-Fan offers more than 200 games a season for about $350). Dozens of HD channels (Dish has 150; DirecTV has 130).

CONS: Substantial up-front costs to buy or lease equipment and pay for installation, including around $250 for an HD dish and as much as $750 for a high-def DVR setup (though rebates can reduce or eliminate many

*As of this writing, Verizon's FiOS fiber-optic TV service is available only in parts of California, Delaware, Florida, Maryland, Massachusetts, New Jersey, New York, Pennsylvania, Texas, and Virginia, while you can get AT&T's U-verse service in just 21 cities in California, Connecticut, Indiana, Kansas, Michigan, Texas, and Wisconsin.

of these charges). Local broadcast channels are not always available, and there is no true video on demand (because satellite systems are not interactive like digital cable). You also need to be able to mount an 18-inch dish on your house with an unobstructed view of the southern horizon, and even then your signal can be distorted in bad weather. (The start-up costs are not a problem if you live in an apartment complex or condominium building already wired with a dish. But even then, most companies still charge you an "activation fee.")

Don't Panic—You Really Have Only Three Companies to Choose From

Given all the sports, movie, and HD packages the cable and satellite companies offer—not to mention the countless rebates, credits, and different kinds of contract commitments—picking a provider can seem to be a hugely complicated deal. The thing to remember is that you really have only three choices: whatever company has your local cable franchise or DirecTV or Dish. And if you've decided you'd prefer cable to satellite, you have only one.

This doesn't mean you're at their mercy. In fact, the opposite is true. The competition between the satellite and cable providers is so intense—and they're all so worried about the challenge posed by the new fiber-optic networks—that they are often willing to wheel and deal. This is particularly true when it comes to keeping existing customers from defecting. So if you currently have cable service, don't be afraid to call the company and tell them

He Fought for His Money!

I worked with one couple on a money-makeover TV show and the first thing we did was exactly that. They were paying nearly $80 a month for cable—more than $1,000 a year. The husband insisted he needed ESPN. I convinced him he didn't need it—that he could save $500 a year by living without it. Then we called the cable company and asked for a better package. Just dropping the sports-channel tier cut his bill in half. Later, I had him call back a second time and tell the cable company that he had just gotten a coupon from a satellite TV company offering introductory service at $19.95 a month for six months. Guess what happened? His cable company matched the offer—and threw in ESPN for free, for a total savings of nearly $400!

you're thinking of switching to satellite TV. They may offer to reduce your rates in order to keep your business.

Negotiate, Negotiate, Negotiate

In my experience, there is almost nothing easier than lowering your cable or satellite bill. Usually, you can do it with one phone call. That's because what you are paying now is almost certainly more than what a new customer would pay for the same service if they signed up today and took advantage of one of the many "new-customer specials" that cable and satellite companies constantly offer.

> There is almost nothing easier than lowering your cable or satellite bill.

So open your junk mail this week and see what is being offered in your area. Check your newspaper, too, and go online. The competition between cable and satellite TV providers is brutal—and their willingness to make deals is especially great in areas where the new fiber-optic service is available. Take advantage of the situation. Call your cable company and negotiate your bill down. If they won't work with you, threaten to cancel. And if that doesn't work, then SWITCH SERVICES to get yourself a better deal.

Don't Pay for Remotes You Don't Use!

Many people these days have universal remote controls. If you're one of them, think about returning the remotes that the cable company provides. Remember, they charge you $2 or $3 a month for each remote. Why pay for something you don't need? (Just make sure they remove the remote-control charge from your bill.)

What to Do if Things Go Wrong

The first place to go if you have a service or billing problem with your cable TV provider is the company itself. Call the customer-service number listed on your bill and see if you can work it out with them.

One thing to keep in mind when dealing with cable-company call-center employees is that they are often expected to handle all complaint calls they receive within a certain period of time or they get into trouble. As a result, they've been known to make promises that just aren't true, or even hang up on a customer who won't take no for an answer. In fact, these frontline customer-service representatives often don't have the authority to fix your problem; their instructions are to make excuses or even lie. So when you call, don't waste your time with the person who picks up the phone; instead, ask to speak to a supervisor.

If you can't resolve your problem with the company, you should file a complaint with your local government. Cable companies generally operate under franchises granted by local municipalities, and each municipality with a cable franchise designates one of its officials to handle complaints from residents. Contact information for this official should be listed on your cable bill. If you can't find it, call City Hall or the county courthouse and ask who your local government has named as cable liaison. It might be the city manager or a public works officer.

If your problem involves poor service (as opposed to a billing error), you should also complain to the Federal Communications Commission—and encourage other customers to do the same. If enough people file similar complaints, the agency will mount an investigation. You can file your complaint online through the FCC's web site at http://esupport.fcc.gov/complaints.htm. You can also contact the FCC by telephoning them toll-free at 888-CALL-FCC (888-225-5322) or writing to them at:

Federal Communications Commission
Consumer & Governmental Affairs Bureau
Consumer Inquiries and Complaints Division
455 12th Street, SW
Washington, DC 20554

In addition, you should contact the local chapter of the Better Business Bureau (www.bbb.org) as well as your local consumer-protection agency or state attorney general's office. You can find a complete list of state attorneys general offices on the web site of the National Association of Attorneys General at www.naag.org/attorneys_general.php.

The same goes for a problem with DirecTV or Dish—except that there is no point in complaining to your local government, since the satellite companies do not operate under local franchises.

Fight for Your Money Action Steps

☐ Ask yourself—can you make do with fewer channels?

☐ Gather together any promotions you can find from competing services in your area—check your mail and newspaper, and search online. Then get out your current bill and call your current provider.

- ☐ Review your current service with your provider, ask about other packages that might make more sense for you, then compare offers from their competitors.

- ☐ Negotiate! Let your current provider know that you're switching to the competition if they're not willing to offer a better deal.

Cell Phone Plans

remember my friend David's first cell phone. David had one in 1985, and when we took it into a restaurant, every single person in the place stared at us. Never mind that the phone was as big as a brick. It was portable, and no one had them yet.

Fast-forward to today. There are now 3.3 billion cell phones—enough for every other person on the planet. Never in history has a technological device become such an essential part of our lives so completely. As I write this in the summer of 2008, there are more than 262 million wireless subscribers in the United States—roughly 86% of the population—yakking away on their cell phones an average of 23 minutes a day.

In all, Americans spend nearly $150 billion a year on wireless phone services. The average bill runs $48.54 a month. This may not sound like very much, but it's a lot bigger than it needs to be. Why? Because most of us have the wrong cell phone plan—as a result of which we wind up buying a lot more minutes than we really need. Indeed, while reliable figures are hard to come by, some experts estimate that the average cell phone user lets 40% of his plan minutes go to waste.

Why do we do this? Well, even though we all depend on cell phones to keep our lives on track, the fact is that most of us hate having to pick a cell phone provider and figure out the billing plan that makes the most sense for us. And for good reason. The five major cell phone carriers—Alltel, AT&T, Sprint, T-Mobile, and Verizon—offer such a confusing array of features, services, and pricing plans that it's often difficult to figure out who has the best deal.

The good news is that after years of phenomenal growth—the cell phone population exploded by nearly 700% between 1995 and 2007—we're reaching the point where just about everybody who wants a cell phone already has one. As a result, the number of new customers signing up for cell phone service in the United States finally seems to be leveling out.

Why is this good news? Because with the market for new cell phone users pretty much tapped out, the only way a cell phone company can continue to grow is by stealing business from its competitors. And as one marketing expert told *USA Today*, "When operators have no choice but to try to take customers away from each other, they have a natural inclination to sharpen the pencils and make the best offer they can."

In other words, if you know what to look for, this may be the best time ever to be in the market for a good cell phone plan. Just saving $10 a month on a plan could help you pocket more than $120 this year! And if you are a family and aim to save $30 a month, that's $360 a year in savings. Chances are you can do this in an hour with just a little research and a little negotiating with your current provider.

How to Fight for Your Money

The key to getting a good cell phone plan is knowing what you really need it for. Ask yourself the following:

- Do you live on your cell or do you keep one just for emergencies?

- Do you call all sorts of different people or mainly the same ones over and over again?

- Are most of your calls local or do you have friends and relatives in a different part of the country that you call a lot?

- Are you a single twentysomething who texts as much as you talk or do you have a family (and, hence, a need for several phones)?

- Do you often travel outside the country or do you stick close to home?

Your answers to these and other similar questions about the way you use your cell phone should determine which of the countless service plans out there is right for you. A good plan meets your needs. A bad one forces you to change your behavior in order to achieve savings or keep from being penalized. Here's how to determine which is which.

Don't Buy a Bigger Plan Than You Need

There are three kinds of cell phone users. Low-volume users generally use their cell phones only for emergencies or to give to their kids so they can call if they get stuck somewhere. Typically, they are on their cell phones less than 300 minutes a month. Medium-volume users, who use their phones to keep in touch with friends and family but don't spend half their lives on them, are in the 300- to 1,000-minutes-a-month range. And then there are high-volume users, who log north of 1,000 minutes a month—and whose phones are basically attached to their heads.

When in doubt, go for the smaller plan. The key to getting a good deal on a cell phone plan is never to buy a bigger plan than you need. Most people worry too much about the excess fees they will have to pay if they go over their plan's limit. It's certainly true that most carriers will charge you as much as 45 cents a minute for any time in excess of what your plan includes. But this is less of a problem than being locked into a plan that's bigger than you need. If you find yourself using more minutes than your plan allows, most carriers will be happy to let you upgrade. But they might not let you downsize if the reverse turns out to be the case. So be conservative. When in doubt, go for the smaller plan.

If You Are a Low-Volume Caller, Go with a Basic Plan for as Little as $10 a Month

If you're a low-volume user, you should probably get one of the basic plans offered by the major providers. For $30 to $40 a month, most big carriers will give you at least 300 minutes with no long-distance or roaming charges plus a free phone. If that's too much, you can get really inexpensive service from a specialty provider like Great Call. For as little as $10 a month, Great Call's super-simple Jitterbug phone (designed for elderly users) comes with no minutes but allows you to make emergency calls for free; non-emergency calls cost 35 cents a minute. (See their web site at www.jitterbug.com for more information.)

You might also consider a prepaid plan, where you pay in advance and are charged only for the time you actually use the phone (often as little as 10 cents a minute). Verizon has one prepaid plan that charges just two cents a minute, though it also charges you a $2.99 access fee for each day you use the phone. Prepaid plans also make sense if your credit is bad or you have teenage children whose phone usage you want to limit. All the major carriers offer them. Maybe you don't need a phone at all—maybe a phone card would do!

For medium-volume callers, there are plenty of good plans offering up to 1,000 minutes for between $40 and $80 a month, while high-volume users can get absolutely unlimited domestic calling (that is, as many calls as you want for as long as you want anywhere in the United States) for $100 a month. Keep in mind that these figures cover only regular phone calls. Extra services—such as text, photo, and video messaging—will cost you extra.

Think About Who You'll Be Calling

Most people tend to make most of their calls to the same small group of numbers—their home, their office, their spouse or sweetheart, their best buddies, and so on. If this is true of you, you should probably consider a plan like Alltel's My Circle or T-Mobile's myFaves, which allows you unlimited calling to several specific numbers that you pick in advance. (Alltel lets you choose up to 20 numbers; T-Mobile limits it to five.) In many cases, this feature can make it possible for a high-volume caller to use a less expensive medium-volume plan without going over the monthly usage limit.

Think About Where You'll Be Calling

All the major carriers put most of their marketing efforts into pushing national calling plans that let you phone anywhere in the United States without incurring any long-distance or roaming charges. These are generally terrific deals if you make a fair number of long-distance calls. But if you don't, you might want to consider getting a local or regional plan, where in return for agreeing to pay extra for long distance, you get extra-cheap rates for calls within your home city or region. (Local plans generally cover a single metropolitan area, while regional plans may include several states.)

Basically, the smaller your coverage area, the less your plan will cost—but the more you will have to pay for out-of-area calls. For example, while T-Mobile's basic national plan gives you 1,000 minutes for $49.95 a month, its regional plan gives you 3,000 minutes for the same price—though calls made from outside the region or to a number outside the region will cost you 49 cents a minute. Similarly, for $39.99 you can get a national plan from Alltel that includes 500 minutes or a regional one that gives you 700 minutes.

At the opposite end of the spectrum, if you travel outside the country a lot—or make a lot of overseas calls—you'll want to pick a carrier with good international calling capabilities. Ideally, you want one that uses Global System for Mobile (GSM) technology, so its phones can also be used outside the United States—which means either AT&T or T-Mobile. (Alltel, Sprint, and Verizon all use what's known as CMDA—for "code division multiple access"—technology, which is very efficient but is not compatible with the cellular networks in most other countries.)

Don't Forget About the Cost of Nonvoice Features

The thing about cell phones is that telephone conversations are the least of their uses these days. If we're not texting or sending photos to friends, we're using our phones to access our favorite web site, play games, or listen to music. Unfortunately, it's easy to forget that none of this is free. So if you think you might be using any of these nonvoice features—and chances are you will be—make sure you get a plan that includes them. Texting can cost as much as 15 cents a message if your plan doesn't include it—and as little as a penny per message when it does.

Before You Pick a Carrier, Check Out Their Coverage

Location, location, location!

Just like in real estate, location is critically important when it comes to cell phone service. Though all of the major carriers provide what's described as nationwide service, the coverage they offer varies considerably from region to region. And in some places, it's nonexistent. So before you pick a provider, you should find out what kind of on-the-ground coverage they have in areas that matter to you—like your house or apartment, your neighborhood, your workplace, and places you often visit.

All the major providers offer coverage maps on their web sites, but take them with a grain of salt. The carriers' maps tend to be fairly general and they don't always show the random dead spots that drive most cell phone users crazy. So always check with friends and neighbors about their experiences and visit such independent web sites as www.deadcellzones.com and www.cellreception.com, where you can punch in your address or zip code and see reports on what kind of coverage you're really going to get.

If You Have a Family, Get a Family Plan

All the major carriers offer family plans, where Mom, Dad, and the kids all have separate phones with separate numbers but share the same pool of monthly minutes. The advantage is that under the family plan, the separate lines cost you far less than if everyone had his or her own individual account. If you have a family—or for any other reason need more than one cell phone—signing up for a family plan is as close to a no-brainer as anything you'll find in the cellular universe.

CHEAPER BY THE DOZEN

Two separate cell numbers:	$79.98 a month
Two numbers on a family plan:	$69.99 a month
You save:	**$9.99 a month**
Three separate cell numbers:	$119.97 a month
Three numbers on a family plan:	$79.98 a month
You save:	**$39.99 a month**

Choose Your Carrier Before You Choose Your Phone

Each carrier has a specific set of cell phones that work with its network. So do you pick a phone and then see which carriers support it? Or do you pick a carrier and then see which phones it allows? If you think about it for a minute, you'll realize that the best phone in the world isn't worth very much if your carrier has spotty coverage and lousy customer service. In other words, the chicken in this chicken-and-egg problem is the carrier. So make sure you've found yourself a good carrier before you worry about whether your phone will come preloaded with a sufficient number of cool ringtones.

How the "Big 5" Compare

The five major cell phone service providers (soon to be four if Verizon's proposed merger with Alltel is approved by regulatory authorities) all offer similar menus of individual, family, basic, and premium plans at roughly the same prices. The devil, of course, is in the details. Each has strengths and weaknesses you should consider when figuring which company to choose.

In a nutshell, here is how they stack up.

ALLTEL (www.alltel.com; 800-255-8351). Though it's probably the least widely available of the major carriers, Alltel gets top marks for connectivity and customer service. Perhaps because its coverage is so good, it automatically credits customers for dropped calls. And its My Circle plan, which allows unlimited free calls to up to 20 designated phone numbers (whether or not they're in the Alltel network), is the best such offering in the business.

AT&T (http://www.wireless.att.com; 888-333-6651). As a result of its merger with Cingular, AT&T is now the nation's largest cell phone carrier. But bigger isn't always better. Though AT&T is the exclusive carrier for Apple's much-coveted iPhone, its customer service is considered mediocre and its coverage is below average, particularly in the West. On the plus side, it is the only carrier to offer what it calls Rollover Minutes, which allow you to carry over unused minutes from month to month for up to 12 billing periods. Parents will also appreciate its Smart Limits plan, which allows you to control your kids' use of their cell phones.

SPRINT (www.sprint.com; 866-866-7509). Both *Consumer Reports* and J.D. Power and Associates rate Sprint's coverage and call quality as below average virtually everywhere in the United States. Its customer service also gets low marks. (In one scary indication of how it deals with customers, Sprint terminated 1,000 subscribers in 2007 for complaining too much.) That said, it is strong in data services, such as text messaging and mobile video, and its pricing is competitive. For example, it offers unlimited calling at night and on weekends like all the other carriers—but its "night" begins at 7 P.M., two hours earlier than everyone else's.

T-MOBILE (www.t-mobile.com; 800-T-MOBILE). Particularly for high-volume callers, T-Mobile has the best rate structure of all the big carriers, with the most free minutes for the money. It also charges the least for Web access and for photo and video messaging. Its myFaves plans, which allow unlimited free calls to any five numbers in the United States, may not be as extensive as Alltel's My Circle, but nobody else is even in the game. And its customer service is first-rate. T-Mobile's main weakness is coverage, which can be spotty in parts of New York, Georgia, California, and Oregon.

VERIZON (www.verizonwireless.com; 800-256-4646). Most people agree that Verizon has the best call quality among the major carriers, with fewer dropped calls and circuit overloads. In addition to reliability, it also offers excellent customer service. On the other hand, its pricing tends to be higher than the competitions', and in many areas of the country its "national" coverage depends on what is called "extended service"— meaning you have to pay roaming charges.

Always Ask for a Trial Period

Given that it's so hard to get out of cell phone contracts—and that there are so many variables involved in cell phone service—it's always a good idea to ask for a trial period to test the service. There is really no substitute for real-world experience when it comes to knowing how well you'll be able to talk to the kids at school, your spouse at home or work, and friends and colleagues wherever they may be. AT&T, Sprint, and Verizon all offer 30-day trial periods, after which, if you're not satisfied with the service, you can return your phone and get out of your contract without having to pay an early-termination fee. If the carrier you're leaning toward doesn't offer any sort of test drive, see if you can sign up for service on a month-to-month basis—that is, without having to commit yourself for one or two years of service.

You May Not Have to Sign a Contract

To read the carriers' ads and visit their web sites, you'd think the only way you can get a decent cell phone and decent cell phone plan is to sign a contract that commits you to at least two years' of service. In fact, most carriers will give you a monthly service plan without a long-term commitment as long as you're willing to forgo some of the more attractive come-ons—like free phones and special data services. If you don't like the idea of paying full price for a phone (which, depending on the model, can easily run to several hundred dollars), ask if you can sign a contract for one year rather than two. You'll have to pay part of the cost of the phone (typically between $50 and $100), but the flexibility you get is worth it.

What to Watch Out For

Early-Termination Fees

Aside from dropped calls, nothing bugs cell phone customers more than the early-termination fees carriers force you to pay if you want to get out of your contract before it expires. With penalties running as high as $200 per phone line, it's hardly surprising that in a survey conducted by *Consumer Reports*, one in seven cell phone subscribers said that if it weren't for the early-termination fee, they would have left their current carrier long ago.

It used to be that you would be charged the full termination fee regardless of whether you quit at the beginning of your contract or the day before its expiration date. But as a result of a series of class-action lawsuits filed against a number of the major carriers, all of them have begun prorating their fees—meaning that the further along you are in your contract, the lower the fee.

Of course, this doesn't help much if you want to drop your service near the beginning of your contract. But there are ways to get out of a cell phone contract without paying a termination fee.

For one thing, the contracts of nearly all carriers include what's called a "material adverse change" clause. In plain English, this means that anytime your carrier adds a new charge to your plan—which happens all the time—you have the right to cancel your contract without penalty within 14 days. The carriers obviously know this, and they interpret the clause as strictly as possible. So if you try to go this route, make sure you follow the contract provisions closely. You'll probably get an argument from the company, but it's one you have a good chance of winning.

> Anytime your carrier adds a new charge to your plan, you have the right to cancel your contract without penalty within 14 days.

Another way to avoid a termination fee is to transfer your cell phone contract to someone else. All the major carriers allow customers to do this, though their rules for how it must be done differ slightly. Finding someone to take over your contract is simpler than you might think. For a fee of around $20, web sites like CellSwapper (www.cellswapper.com) and Celltrade (www.celltradeusa.com) will hook you up with consumers who are eager to get a cell phone account without having to pay an activation fee.

Mandatory Contract Extensions

The big carriers used to be notorious for extending service contracts (often without proper notification) every time a customer asked for a change in their service plan—and, in some extreme cases, even when they simply called customer service to get new batteries or file a complaint. This outrageous behavior led to fraud investigations by a number of states, as a result of which all the major companies have stopped requiring contract extensions for plan changes. But this doesn't mean you can let your guard down.

Once your initial contract ends, you are free to continue service on a month-to-month basis. The companies, however, will do everything they can to get you to sign a new contract. Their main tactic is to try to hook you by offering you a "free" new phone or sexy new data service. Buried in the fine print that accompanies these offers are provisions that say your contract will automatically be extended if you take the deal. So be skeptical of promotional come-ons. If you like your carrier and don't mind having your contract extended, then by all means take advantage of the offers. But make sure you know what you're agreeing to when you sign up for one of these "free" deals.

Unnecessary Phone Insurance

Cell phones may be free, but they are not cheap. As a result, many consumers are tempted to buy the cell phone insurance that all the major carriers offer. It's a temptation you should resist. That's because unless you wind up putting in a claim within the first few months, these policies are far more likely to cost you money than save you money. The problem is that the premiums generally total around $60 a year, while the deductibles run as high as $100. So if you lose or break your phone after having the policy for a year, you'll be out around $160—which is pretty much what you would have had to spend on a new phone if you didn't have any insurance.

What They Mean by "Unlimited Nationwide Calling"

One of the most attractive developments in cell phone pricing in recent years is the wide availability of national calling plans that allow you to call "nationwide" without incurring any roaming charges. But not all "nationwide" calling plans are alike.

The problem is that not everyone defines the word "nationwide" the same way. While you may think that "nationwide" means anywhere in the country, some providers define "nationwide" as meaning anywhere within their network. So before you start traveling with your phone, check with your carrier to make sure your definition of "nationwide" agrees with theirs. Otherwise, even if you never leave the good old USA, you could find some hefty roaming charges on your next bill if you happen to make a call from somewhere outside your carrier's coverage area.

Roaming Charges for Overseas Calls

Roaming charges can be a huge issue if you travel outside of the country with your cell phones. Calls placed from foreign countries can easily cost you upward of $1 per minute. So before you travel abroad, you should call your carrier and find out the costs and see if they have an overseas plan you can sign up for. In many cases, you can add this service just for the time you'll be traveling.

What to Do if Things Go Wrong

There are basically two kinds of problems with cell phone service providers—contract issues and service issues. Your first stop in the event of either kind of problem should be with the carrier itself. Either call their customer-service number or visit one of their stores. If you can't resolve the problem with them, you should file a complaint with the government.

Issues involving your cell phone contract—say, early-termination fees or mandatory extensions—are the province of your state's utility regulators and the consumer-protection arm of your state attorney general's office. You can find contact information for each state's utility regulators on the web site of the National Association of Regulatory Utility Commissioners at www.naruc.org/commissions.cfm. And you can find a complete list of state attorneys general offices on the web site of the National Association of Attorneys General at www.naag.org/attorneys_general.php.

If you have a service issue—say, a problem with the way your carrier handles your calls or how much it charges for certain services—you should complain to the Federal Communications Commission. You can file a complaint online through the FCC's web site at www.fcc.gov/cgb/complaints.html or by calling toll-free 888-TELL-FCC (888-835-5322). You can also write to the FCC's consumer office at:

Federal Communications Commission
Consumer & Governmental Affairs Bureau
Consumer Inquiries and Complaints Division
445 12th Street, SW
Washington, DC 20554

If you write to the FCC, your complaint should include the following:

- Your name, address, mailing address, and phone number where you can be reached

- All telephone and account numbers that are the subject of your complaint

- The names and phone numbers of all companies involved with your complaint

- The amount of any disputed charges, whether you paid them, whether you received a refund or adjustment to your bill, and the amount of any adjustment or refund you have received

- The details of your complaint, including any additional relevant information

If Your Cell Phone Is Lost or Stolen, 10 Steps to Protect Yourself

I recently saw a TV report that prompted me to write an entire article about what to do when your cell phone is lost or stolen. If this happens to you, you could get stuck with a *huge* bill for unauthorized charges—unless you know how to fight back. Consider what happened to San Francisco resident Wendy N., who was hit with a bill for $26,000 after her cell phone, unbeknownst to her, was stolen before she left for an overseas vacation. Cingular held her responsible for charges incurred after the phone was taken, up until the time Wendy discovered the theft and called the carrier.

Wendy was able to prove via airline and passport documents that she was out of the country and couldn't possibly have made the unauthorized calls from San Francisco during that time, but Cingular still held Wendy accountable for all charges. Not only that, they advised Wendy that if she couldn't pay the bill she should consider filing for bankruptcy!

CAN THIS BE LEGAL?

If you dig through all the fine print in your cell phone contract, you'll most likely discover a statement that reads something like this: "Should your cell phone be lost or stolen, you are responsible for any costs incurred for unauthorized calls made prior to reporting the cell phone missing."

Unlike a credit card, cellular contracts are not required to limit liability for fraudulent charges. But it's also important to realize that the extent of your liability as stated in your contract is your provider's policy—it's not a law.

The laws that give consumers the right to dispute unauthorized charges vary from state to state. In states where the laws do exist, they're not doing much good because there's no single independent agency set up to review evidence, enforce the laws, and provide a timely resolution.

Why? It all comes down to money. In California, for instance, the significant financial contributions made by the wireless industry to state government give the telecommunications industry enormous influence over entities like the Public Utilities Commission. In effect, this allows the wireless industry to make up its own rules.

AVOIDING AND RESPONDING TO A THEFT

Are we at the mercy of an unregulated industry that's free of consequences and penalties? Not if we learn how to defend ourselves.

Last year, an estimated 600,000 cell phones were reported lost or stolen. Here are the 10 things you need to know to protect yourself from cell phone theft and fraudulent charges:

1. GUARD YOUR CELL PHONE AS YOU WOULD YOUR WALLET.
   Yes, this is obvious advice, but frankly the best way to not get stuck with fraudulent charges is to do what you can to prevent unauthorized calls in the first place.

On a related note, think twice about what information you store on your device. A stolen cell phone can lead not only to a huge bill, but to identity theft as well.

2. PASSWORD-PROTECT YOUR DEVICE.
Check the user guide that came with your phone and start using the "lock" or "password" feature to potentially prevent a thief from making unauthorized calls. There are ways to override passwords, but at the very least you might be buying yourself some time until you discover the loss and call your provider.

3. DON'T BE FOOLED BY CELL PHONE INSURANCE.
Purchasing cell phone insurance will provide coverage for the device itself, but it won't protect you against charges for unauthorized calls.

4. CALL YOUR CELL PHONE PROVIDER AS SOON AS YOU DISCOVER THE LOSS.
Report your missing device, and be sure to keep meticulous records, including the date and time you called your carrier, the name and ID number of the representative to whom you spoke, and what you were told.

Also note the state or region of their call center, plus their telephone extension number. Finally, ask for confirmation in writing that your device has been disabled. Some companies can even email this to you.

5. FILE A POLICE REPORT.
This may not help your chances of getting the stolen phone back, but it still provides an official record of the crime. Your carrier may even require the police report number when you phone in the loss.

6. OPEN AN INVESTIGATION WITH YOUR CARRIER IF NECESSARY.
If you find that you're not getting an immediate resolution, don't waste another minute. Call your carrier and request an investigation, then follow up in writing. Generally, requesting an investigation gives you a better chance of preventing any formal collections action from being taken and should also delay reporting to any of the credit bureaus.

When you request an investigation, advise your carrier that you'll be filing a complaint with the Federal Communications Commission (FCC), your state attorney general's office, and your state's public utility commission (PUC). Your carrier is more likely to pay closer attention to you when they know you're an informed consumer.

7. CONTACT THE FCC.

The FCC will forward your complaint to your service provider, requiring a response from them within 30 days. You can contact them via their web site or call them directly at (888) 225-5322.

8. CONTACT YOUR STATE ATTORNEY GENERAL'S OFFICE.

According to ConsumersUnion.org, state attorneys general offices will handle complaints about cell phone fraud and contract disputes. They have filed lawsuits against wireless companies based on consumer complaints, resulting in refunds to consumers and agreements by some companies to reform certain practices.

Find the contact information for your state attorney general's office at: http://www.naag.org.

9. CONTACT YOUR STATE'S PUC.

Each state has a government agency, usually called a public utility commission, that oversees telephone companies. To locate your state's PUC online and to file a complaint, visit the National Association of Regulatory Utility Commissioners web site at http://www.naruc.org/.

10. WHEN ALL ELSE FAILS, CONTACT THE MEDIA.

The wireless companies are particularly adverse to negative media attention, so until effective laws are put into place you may have to resort to contacting your local TV station.

In Wendy's case, that's just what she did, and her story has a happy ending. After many months of persistent determination and follow-up, all fraudulent charges were dropped. It seems the wireless industry wants to do the right thing after all—as long as they're forced to by the media.

Ultimately, CBS 5 ConsumerWatch played a huge role in getting the situation resolved. But don't be tempted to skip steps 7 through 9. The FCC, state attorneys general offices, and PUCs all need to see how serious a problem this is, so formal complaints serve an important purpose.

Fight for Your Money Action Steps

☐ Figure out the size of the plan that's right for you (and your family), then comparison-shop among the major providers. Be conservative. When in doubt, go for the smaller plan.

☐ Consider a prepaid plan if you're a low-volume user, have bad credit, or have children who need a phone for emergency purposes.

☐ If you don't make a lot of long-distance calls, opt for a regional or local plan, which can get you more minutes for less money.

☐ Check out the coverage area before you decide on a carrier.

☐ Choose your carrier, then choose your phone.

☐ Ask for a trial period. This is a great way to make sure the plan and the phone work for you before signing on the dotted line.

☐ If you change your service in any way, be sure your contract isn't being extended without your knowledge.

☐ If your phone is lost or stolen, contact your carrier immediately.

Residential Phone Service

I f you go strictly by the numbers, dumping your landline can seem like a no-brainer. After all, most of us already have a cell phone, so why pay for a landline too? Canceling it can save you $50 bucks a month, which adds up to a quick $600 a year back in your pocket.

Unfortunately, it's not that simple. Landlines are convenient, and many people live in places where cell phone reception isn't good. I live in New York City, which has to be one of the best-served cell phone areas in the world, but my cell phone does not work in my building. So I have to have a landline.

The fact is, in this wireless world of ours, millions of homes are still hooked up with landline service—where signals travel from a central exchange along copper wires that snake into our bedrooms and kitchens and plug directly into our telephones.

If it sounds old-fashioned, that's because it is. The number of landline phone subscribers in the United States peaked in 2000 at just under 188 million and has been declining ever since. Early in 2004, the number of cell phone subscribers zoomed past the number of people with landline phones. By 2006, the most recent year for which figures are available, there were barely more than 140 million landline numbers in the United States. These days, cell phones probably outnumber landlines by a two-to-one margin.

Still, even if it's no longer the mainstay it used to be, landline service is a part of our lives, and for many of us it's not going away. For one thing, it's often cheaper than wireless service. For another, regular phones are generally more comfortable to use than cellular handsets, especially on longer calls. And because they have their own power supply (which comes in over the phone lines), landline phones are not as vulnerable to power outages as computer-based systems or cell towers.

One thing landline phones have in common with their wireless counterparts is the confusing maze of choices you have to sort through when you're picking a service provider. Once upon a time, the phone company was a monopoly. This definitely had its disadvantages, but it did make the selection process very simple. Today, after thirty years of deregulation, there are literally thousands of telephone companies angling for both your local and long-distance business. The trick is to figure out which one is right for you.

How to Fight for Your Money

To get residential phone service these days, you need to pick a local carrier for local phone service and a long-distance carrier for long-distance service. You can use the same company for both or you can use different companies for each. Even if you use different companies, you can get both your local and long-distance charges on one bill (the one issued by your local carrier). But since carriers are allowed to charge what's called a "single bill" fee for this convenience, savvy consumers who use different local and long-distance carriers ask their long-distance carrier to bill them separately.

Savvy consumers ask their long-distance carrier to bill them separately.

In one sense, picking your local and long-distance phone companies is not very different from picking a cell phone carrier. Your decision should be based on what kind of telephone consumer you are. If you make a lot of local calls or use a dial-up Internet service, you should look for a "flat rate" plan that gives you unlimited local calling. On the other hand, if you don't use much local service, you should go for a basic "measured service" plan, in which you pay only for the calls you make. The same goes for your long-distance choice. Figure out how many minutes you're likely to need (dig out a few old bills if you're not sure) and look for a plan that provides them at a rock-bottom rate. An easy way to do this is to call your current carrier and have them analyze your current usage. Tell them: "I'm looking to save money. Based on my usage, am I on the best plan? What else can you offer me?"

Even if you're not in the market for new service, I strongly recommend that right now (as soon as you finish this chapter) you give your current plans a fresh look—especially if you've had them for a while. Do you really know how much you're paying for local and long-distance calls? Review some recent bills and do the math. If you're paying more than 5 cents a minute for anything, you might want to think about switching to a new plan—or a new provider.

I can't emphasize enough that the best way to save money NOW is to call your current carrier and simply ask for a better deal. Have them sell you on your current plan and push them to look at what special offers they have and how they can save you money by providing you the best plan based on your current usage. They know exactly how much you use, and they know that they can save you money. Trust me on this—they will not be calling you with ideas about how you can save money. You have to call them. (It's called Fighting for Your Money.)

> If you're paying more than 5 cents a minute for anything, you might want to think about switching.

The great news is that one thing landline users have these days is choice. According to the latest FCC statistics, there are more than 3,100 local phone companies and 1,600 long-distance providers competing in the marketplace today. The giant companies like AT&T, Verizon, and Qwest have the lion's share of the business, but they don't always have the best deals.

For Local Service, It Pays to Stay Local

When it comes to local service, four out of five residential phone customers stick with the established local company—which in most places these days is one of the telecommunication giants. That's not surprising, since in addition to reliable service, they all offer a variety of local calling plans, some bundled with long-distance packages, some separate, some including special features like call waiting, voice mail, and caller ID. Typically, you should be able to get basic unlimited local calling from your local provider for less than $20 a month.

But that doesn't mean you shouldn't check out the competition. One way to find potential alternatives is to log on to your favorite Internet search engine and type in the words "local phone service" along with the name of your city or town. Or you can visit a comparison web site like AllConnect (www.allconnect.com) or ConnectMyPhone (www.connectmyphone.com).

What you'll discover is that some of these companies are simply repackaging and reselling the local telephone company's service, while others offer broadband phone service, otherwise known as VoIP, for Voice Over Internet Protocol. (More about this later.) In general, their prices tend to be lower than the big boys', but they don't always offer all the special features the big companies do. And most worrisome, many lack repair and maintenance capabilities.

For Long Distance, It Pays to Play the Field

The long-distance situation is slightly different. There are real bargains to be had from a wide variety of companies with names you've probably never heard of, like ECG, CogniState, Pioneer, Unitel, and Total Call International. What these outfits do is buy phone time from the big boys at wholesale rates and then resell it to you and me at what amount to discount prices. They can do this because they aren't spending tons of money on giant marketing campaigns (which is why you've never heard of most of them), nor do they have huge corporate infrastructures to support. But their calls go over the same fiber-optic networks as those of AT&T and Verizon, so the level of quality they provide is just as good as the giants'.

You can find which of these outfits offers service in your area—and how much (or little) they charge—by visiting such web sites as LongDistance Smart (www.longdistancesmart.com), PhoneRateFinder (www.phonerate finder.com), SaveOnPhone.com (www.saveonphone.com), Telcompare (www.telcompare.com), and TollChaser (www.tollchaser.com). Many of these companies provide long-distance service at less than 4 cents a minute, without the sizable monthly fees that AT&T and Verizon charge.

Focus on the Services You Actually Use

Most long-distance carriers make a point of emphasizing their interstate rates—that is, the rate for placing a call in one state to a number in another state. But what if you make a lot of long-distance calls *within* your state—say, from Los Angeles to San Francisco, or from Dallas to Houston? Just because a particular plan has a low interstate rate doesn't mean its intrastate rate will also be low. The point is that you should know the rates for the services you actually use—not just the services the company wants to brag about. And if one of the services you use a lot is making overseas calls, be sure to get a flat-rate plan.

Always Review Your Bill—and Make Sure You Understand It

The more complicated and confusing your phone bill gets, the more tempting it is to just pay the darn thing without trying to figure out whether or not it's really accurate. This is a huge mistake. Precisely because phone bills have gotten so complicated—because they include so many different charges, fees, and rates—the odds are very good that the phone company has gotten something wrong. There is also a chance that someone may be deliberately trying to scam you.

Especially if you are a new customer or just switched some aspect of your service, you should make sure that you are being charged the rates you agreed to for the services you signed up for. Among the questions to ask yourself are the following:

- Are there any companies listed on my bill whose names I don't recognize?

- Are there any charges for calls I didn't place or services I didn't authorize?

- Are the rates and the line items not what the company told me they'd be?

If your answer to any of these questions is yes, you should contact your phone company immediately and demand a full explanation.

The VoIP Alternative

One way to save big-time on residential phone service is not to use the phone lines at all. Instead, you can make your calls over the Internet, using what's called Voice Over Internet Protocol, or VoIP. From the user's point of view, VoIP is pretty much indistinguishable from regular phone service. The phones are the same, the voice quality is the same, and you can get all the same special services such as caller ID, voice mail, and call waiting. The big difference is the cost—particularly on international calls. Companies like Lingo, Packet8, VoIP.com, and Vonage offer unlimited local and long-distance calling for around $25 a month. And most offer incredibly cheap—in some cases, free—international calling as well.

Of course, there's a catch. To be able to use VoIP, you need a high-speed Internet connection and all the equipment that goes along with it. This is likely to cost you around $40 a month, which wipes out at least part of the savings (particularly if you don't make a lot of calls). Moreover, not all VoIP providers offer full 911 emergency service. And if your power ever goes out or you lose your Internet connection, your phone service will be gone too— which is why it's probably a good idea to keep at least one basic landline, even if you don't use it much.

And Then There's Skype

An even cheaper—and increasingly popular—alternative to standard VoIP is Skype, an Internet phone service that lets you make and receive calls through your computer. (Most people use either their computer's built-in microphone and speakers or a Skype-friendly headset, but you can also buy regular phones that work with Skype.) Once you've downloaded the free

> With Skype, you can make unlimited calls to anywhere in the United States and Canada for just $2.95 a month.

software from Skype's web site (www.skype.com), you can make unlimited calls to anywhere in the United States and Canada for just $2.95 a month. What's more, for $9.95 a month you can make unlimited calls to 34 other countries, including most of Europe, Australia, New Zealand, Chile, China, Japan, and Korea. Even better, calls to any other Skype subscriber anywhere in the world are free.

Skype is not the only service of its type. Vonage and Packet8 also offer similar service, but they charge as much as $25 a month for it. The drawbacks are the same as with VoIP—plus your computer needs to be turned on and connected to the Internet for you to make or receive calls. Still, given how cheap it is, if you already have a computer and a broadband connection, Skype is a much better deal than even the cheapest landline long-distance service.

What to Watch Out For

Slamming

Given the intense competition among phone companies, it's probably not surprising that some unscrupulous operators try to take advantage of the fact that most consumers don't bother to review their bills. What these rip-off artists do is switch you, without your permission, from the local or long-distance provider you selected to some other company—usually their own. They count on the fact that most consumers won't realize they're now paying a different company—and that their rates may have gone up a bit—and so will never complain.

This practice is called slamming, and it is most definitely illegal. The best way to protect yourself from it is to check your phone bill every month. If the name of your telephone company seems to have changed, call the number on the bill and ask them what's going on.

Another way to protect yourself is to be very careful when dealing with telemarketers who are selling phone services, telephone survey-takers who ask you about your phone service, or sweepstakes forms you may receive in the mail. Quite often, slammers will try to trick you into authorizing a service change without your realizing it. So be careful about what you say over the phone and read the fine print before you sign up for any sweepstakes or drawings. To be extra safe, you can ask your selected carriers to "freeze" your account—meaning that they shouldn't allow your service to be transferred to any other company without direct written or verbal authorization from you.

And if you get a postcard in the mail asking you to "verify" a switch that you didn't authorize, don't ignore it. Instead, call your phone company immediately to let them know you haven't authorized any changes in your service. You should also contact the sender of the postcard and let them know the same thing.

If you discover you've already been slammed, call the slammer and tell them you want your original service restored. Also call your preferred company and tell them you want to be reinstated to the same calling plan you had before the slam. And insist that your bill be wiped clean of any "change of carrier charges" (which are generally imposed when a customer switches companies).

Keep in mind that you DO NOT have to pay anyone—neither the slammer nor your selected company—for service for up to 30 days after being slammed. If you unknowingly paid a slammer, you will be entitled to a full refund. After the initial 30 days, you must pay your authorized company for any service you've received, but at its rates, not the slammer's rates.

Cramming

An even more widespread scam than slamming is what's known as cramming—in which rip-off artists try to slip all sorts of unauthorized charges onto your phone bill. Like slammers, they count on the fact that bills today are so complicated and confusing that you won't notice another small item amid all the other legitimate fees and charges.

A tip-off that you may have been victimized by cramming is the appearance on your bill of small charges (often just $2 or $3) with vague descriptions such as "service fee," "service charge," "monthly fee," "other fees," "mail server," "calling plan," "psychic," and "membership." If you see any charge on your bill that you don't recognize, immediately call the company that billed it, ask for an explanation, and demand that your bill be adjusted. Also call your own phone company and find out the procedure for having an incorrect charge removed from your bill. Keep in mind that even if you did authorize a service, it's considered cramming if the provider misled you about its actual cost. A typical cramming technique is to get victims to authorize a service that they are led to believe is free.

What to Do if Things Go Wrong

The first place to go if you have a problem with any aspect of your home phone service is to the company that provided it. There are customer-service numbers on every bill you receive from your various service providers, as well as contact information on the companies' web sites.

If you can't sort out your issues with the company directly, there are a number of state and federal agencies to which you can complain. Basically, the Federal Communications Commission handles complaints related to interstate or international phone services, while your state public service commission covers issues regarding local service (that is, phone services within your state).

Long-Distance and International Calling Issues

Complaints about interstate or international service can be filed over the Internet through the FCC's online complaint form at esupport.fcc.gov/complaints.htm. You can also telephone the FCC toll-free at 888-CALL-FCC (888-225-5322) or write to them at:

Federal Communications Commission
Consumer & Governmental Affairs Bureau
Consumer Inquiries and Complaints Division
445 12th Street, SW
Washington, DC 20554

The FCC recommends that you use their online complaint form to ensure that they get all the information they need. If you choose to write them instead, make sure your letter includes the following:

- Your name, address, mailing address, and phone number where you can be reached

- All telephone and account numbers that are the subject of your complaint

- The names and phone numbers of all companies involved with your complaint

- The amount of any disputed charges, whether you paid them, whether you received a refund or adjustment to your bill, and the amount of any adjustment or refund you have received

- The details of your complaint, including any additional relevant information

Local Calling Issues

Complaints about local telephone service should be directed to your state public service commission. You can find contact information for each state's public service commission in the government section of your local telephone directory, on the FCC web site at www.fcc.gov/wcb/iatd/state_puc.html, and on the web site of the National Association of Regulatory Utility Commissioners at www.naruc.org/commissions.cfm.

If your issue involves fraudulent or deceptive practices, contact your state attorney general's office. You can find a complete list of state attorneys general offices on the web site of the National Association of Attorneys General at www.naag.org/attorneys_general.php.

Slamming Complaints

If you've got a complaint about slamming, the place to go in 37 states plus the District of Columbia and Puerto Rico is the state public service commission. (You can find a list of which 37 states—along with the contact information for their commissions—on the FCC web site at www.fcc.gov/slamming.) If you don't live in one of these states, file your complaint with the FCC. Again, the FCC recommends that you use its online complaint form at esupport.fcc.gov/complaints.htm. But you can also email your complaint to slamming@fcc.gov or write to:

Federal Communications Commission
Consumer & Governmental Affairs Bureau
ATTN: SLAM TEAM
Room CY-A257
445 12th Street, SW
Washington, DC 20554

If you send a letter to the FCC, in addition to detailing the nature of your problem and providing contact information for everyone involved, you MUST include a copy of any bill you are complaining about. You should mark the copy to show the name of the unauthorized phone company and the amount of the disputed charges.

Cramming Complaints

If you can't resolve a cramming problem with the company that supposedly provided the unauthorized services—and your own phone company won't take the charge off your phone bill—you should complain to the proper authorities. If the charges are related to interstate or international calling, that's the FCC. If they involve local service, it's your state public service commission. If your complaint concerns nontelephone services on your phone bill, you should contact the Federal Trade Commission, either by telephoning its Consumer Response Center toll-free at (877) 382-4357 or through its online complaint form at www.ftccomplaintassistant.gov.

Fight for Your Money Action Steps

☐ Call your carrier to have your current usage analyzed and ask them for a better deal.

☐ Compare deals online for both local phone service and long-distance phone service.

☐ Review your bill every month, not only for errors but to avoid slamming and cramming.

☐ Consider VoIP services or SKYPE, which will usually save you a bundle—especially if you make a lot of long-distance calls.

Bundled-Service Plans

I f your mailbox is anything like mine, it's been filled lately with pitches from your cable TV company, your telephone company, and your Internet provider—all of them trying to steal each other's business. They're all pushing the same idea: that we should get all our telecom services—TV, phone, and Internet—from the same place.

It's called bundling, and the theory is that getting all three services together (a "tripleplay" in the industry's jargon) should be a better deal for you than buying them separately. It's certainly a big deal for the companies. According to some projections, by 2010 roughly one out of every three U.S. households will subscribe to at least a triple-play service and a growing number of us will have quadruple play, which adds cell phone service to the mix. In all, Americans are expected to be spending nearly $120 billion a year on bundled services by then.

But aside from getting one monthly bill instead of three, are there real advantages to bundling? As usual, the answer is that it depends. If you're a big telecom consumer—someone who regularly phones all over the country, is used to watching a lot more than basic cable, and needs the speed of a broadband Internet connection—bundling can deliver real value. But if you're not, it probably won't.

How to Fight for Your Money

When I was a financial planner, I used to urge my clients to diversify their investments. "Remember what your mother told you," I would say. "Don't

364 | FIGHT FOR YOUR MONEY

put all your eggs in one basket." Bundling is putting all your eggs in one basket—big-time. It's bad enough when your cable goes out, but how would you feel if every time it did, you also lost your Internet and phone service?

Then again, most providers offer unlimited calling anywhere in the United States, 100 channels or more of digital cable, and high-speed broadband Internet connections—all for around $100 a month (at least for the first few months). Purchased separately, this kind of phone, cable, and Internet service could easily run twice that. For example, my friend Allan spends about $150 a month on telephone service from Verizon, $175 a month on cable TV service from Charter, and $50 a month on high-speed Internet service from Earthlink—for a total of $375 a month. If he got all those services from Verizon, which offers a variety of bundled packages, it would cost him just $250 a month. So in his case, bundling could save him $1,500 a year. And even if you aren't as big a telecom consumer as Allan, bundling could still save you hundreds of dollars a year.

Here's what to keep in mind if you're considering it.

Price Is Everything

If you're not going to save money as a result of bundling, there is no point in doing it. So evaluate your current phone, TV, and Internet usage realistically. Unless you're really going to use all the services you're going to get, why bother? For instance, if you live in an apartment, your building may offer wireless service at a much cheaper rate than you would pay if you were to purchase your own plan.

You should also make sure you know exactly what the bundled services are going to cost you. Not just the list price, but the *total* price—including taxes and surcharges, which can easily add as much as $15 or $20 a month to your bill. Are there extra fees for cable boxes, DVRs, modems, and remote controls? (Most cable companies basically rent you all the required hardware.) Will there be installation or activation fees? Will your first bill include a charge for an additional month of service (because most companies bill in advance)? Are these charges negotiable? Will the company waive them entirely? Will you have to agree to conditions—say, automatic bill paying? Are you comfortable with that? Since the telecom market is so competitive right now, you actually do have strong negotiating power. If the customer rep can't or won't tell you what your total monthly bill is going to be, including all taxes and fees, think long and hard before signing up.

> Since the telecom market is so competitive right now, you have strong negotiating power.

Don't Confuse Introductory Rates with Real Rates

Those $100-a-month rates certainly sound great, but when you read the fine print you generally find that they are good only for the first few months. So make sure you know how long that low introductory rate will last and how much it might rise once the initial period ends. A good way to ensure transparency before you actually make the switch, especially if you are discussing the plan over the phone with a customer-service rep, is to ask for exactly what you talked about in an email or letter.

Don't assume you have to sign a contract.

This way you always have something to refer back to. Some companies, like WOW and Time Warner, have been offering price guarantees to customers willing to sign long-term contracts (typically, at least 24 months). But what if you move? Or need to drop one of the three services? Or your situation changes and you can't afford the monthly charge? Don't assume you have to sign a contract; you may have more wiggle room than you think. You just have to be open to asking questions and know which questions to ask.

Find Out About Service Limits

When telecom companies say they will provide users with unlimited service, they are generally talking about "normal" users. Customers who make an unusually large number of phone calls or who routinely download a lot of big files may suddenly find themselves saddled with restrictions on their "unlimited" telephone calling privileges or Internet upload and download speeds. So if you make a lot of calls and you download a lot of movies, be sure to find out in advance the provider's policy regarding usage limits. Any restrictions should be noted prominently in your contract, but if you don't see them, don't assume you're in the clear—call customer service and ask.

Hang on to Your Old Phone Number

By law, most companies must allow you to continue to use your old telephone number when you switch to a new service—even if you're going from a traditional landline to VoIP (Voice Over Internet Protocol) service. Still, some charge a fee to transfer (or "port") a number. If your provider does, ask them to waive it. Chances are, they will.

Check Your Bill—and Be Prepared to Fight

Even though the companies are always talking up the convenience of getting just one bill for all your telecom needs, the fact is that one of the most common consumer complaints about bundling is that the bills are confusing, difficult to read, and sometimes just plain wrong—and that it can take weeks or months to get them straightened out. In part, this is because the various telecom companies all offer so many different plans that even they get confused about what they're doing. According to *Consumer Reports,* at one point in 2007, Verizon was offering New York customers six different bundles, two of which appeared to be identical. So go over your bill carefully, and be prepared for a lengthy battle if you find mistakes.

What to Do if Things Go Wrong

If you have a problem with a bundled-service provider, your first step should be to contact the company's customer-service representative. If you can't resolve the problem with them, you should file a complaint with your state's public utility commission. You can find contact information for every state commission on the web site of the National Association of Regulatory Commissioners at www.naruc.org/commissions.cfm.

If your issue involves deceptive or unfair business practices, you should also complain to the Federal Trade Commission, either by telephoning its Consumer Response Center toll-free at (877) 382-4357 or through its online complaint form at www.ftccomplaintassistant.gov.

Fight for Your Money Action Steps

- ☐ Always inquire about total charges, including taxes, surcharges, and extras like cable boxes and remote controls.

- ☐ Find out what the installation and activation fees are and work them into your comparison or ask that they be waived.

- ☐ Understand what your *real* rate will be after the introductory rate expires. Get it in writing.

Air Travel

For most of the last decade, I have virtually lived on airplanes. I have the frequent-flier points, the "Platinum Level" memberships, and the scars to prove it. Now, don't get me wrong—I have a lot of sympathy for the flight attendants, gate agents, baggage handlers, and everyone else who is employed by the airlines. They are, for the most part, overworked and underpaid. But there is no getting around the fact that I have come to hate the airlines. It's not just that traveling by air has become a brutal, miserable experience that gets worse with each passing day. It's that in addition to collecting hundreds—sometimes thousands—of dollars for a ticket, the airlines now charge you extra for just about everything except the wings and your seat belt.

You want to make a reservation over the telephone? That can add $25 to the cost of your flight. Planning to check luggage? On most of the major carriers, checking one bag will cost you at least $15, maybe more. Checking a second piece could set you back as much as an additional $80. Sending your unaccompanied child to visit the grandparents? Prepare to fork over an extra $40. And unless you're flying first or business class, forget about free drinks and hot meals. Figure on at least $2 for a soft drink and $5 for a cold sandwich. Some airlines even charge extra for water!

The Airlines Are in a Terrible Squeeze— and They Want Us to Pay

It sometimes seems as if the airlines are deliberately doing everything they can these days to make the skies as unfriendly as possible. Fares are higher than ever, planes are more crowded and uncomfortable, and schedules are less convenient. With more people flying to more places than ever before (nearly 212 million people traveled on domestic U.S. carriers in the summer of 2008), flights are more likely to be overbooked, departures are more likely to be delayed (nearly 30% of domestic U.S. flights failed to arrive on time in 2008), connections are more likely to be missed, and luggage is more likely to go astray.

To be fair, the airlines have been caught in a terrible squeeze. Even before the run-up in oil prices sent the cost of jet fuel soaring (it nearly doubled between 2007 and 2008), the nation's major carriers had been losing money for a decade.

That's their problem, you say? You're right. But it becomes ours when they try to solve it on our backs. And that's what the airlines have been doing.

Airfares jumped by 20% in 2008 and are expected to climb another 40% by 2012. And as I just noted, most major carriers now make a practice of charging extra for services and amenities that they used to provide for free.

Some people accuse the airlines of nickel-and-diming passengers, but this sort of thing adds up to an awful lot of nickels and dimes. You don't even have to count the fare increases. The new baggage fees alone cost travelers close to a *billion dollars a year*.

How to Fight for Your Money

Go Online to Find Real Bargains

Air travel may no longer seem like a bargain, but there are bargains to be had *if you shop around*. Online travel sites like Expedia (www.expedia. com), Hotwire.com (www.hotwire.com), Kayak (www.kayak.com), Orbitz (www.orbitz.com), Priceline (www.priceline.com), SideStep (www.sidestep. com), and Travelocity (www.travelocity.com) can find you airfares for a fraction of the airlines' own published tariffs. But not all the best bargain-priced carriers, like Southwest and JetBlue, show up on the independent sites, so don't neglect the airlines' own sites. And comparison sites like Farecast (www.farecast.com) and FareCompare (www.farecompare.com) can offer solid advice not only on where to get the best deals but also on whether prices for your particular destination are trending up or down, so you can figure out whether it's worth your while to book now or wait awhile.

Subscribe to the airline weekly newsletters and you could wind up being offered discounts of 25% or more.

Some deals are truly amazing. For example, in a May 2008 special promotion, Spirit Airlines was selling tickets for a flight from Los Angeles to Fort Lauderdale for just $18.

You won't find these sorts of special deals on the big travel sites like Expedia or Orbitz. Most airlines limit them to members of their frequent-flier programs or travelers who subscribe to their weekly newsletters. So if you're thinking of booking a trip, go to the airline web sites and sign up. There's generally no charge, and you could wind up being offered discounts of 25% or more.

Look for an Unexpected Carrier or Airport

Another way to cut the cost of air travel is to look for airlines you wouldn't expect to service the destination you're headed to. For example, on a trip from Los Angeles to London, you could save $200 to $300 by taking Air France or Air New Zealand, rather than the more obvious British Airways or American Airlines. Similarly, Air India could get you from LA to Frankfurt for $400 less than Germany's flagship carrier, Lufthansa.

FLY THE UN-OBVIOUS SKIES

New York to London Economy Fare	
On British Airways:	$942
On Air India:	$689
You save:	**$253**

(one-way fare; as of September 2008)

You can also save as much as a third on airline fares by using unexpected airports—usually smaller, regional airports that serve the same market as a big international hub. If you're heading for Chicago, try Midway instead of O'Hare, or if your destination is Los Angeles, think of Burbank or Ontario rather than LAX.

Finding these unexpected carriers and airports is easier than you might think. There's a web site called FlightStats (www.flightstats.com) that can tell you every airline that flies to any particular destination from any U.S. airport.

Don't Buy Tickets in Bunches— Buying One at a Time Can Be Cheaper

One of the most maddening things about air travel is that similar seats on the same flights are often sold for wildly different prices. That's because airlines use complicated pricing formulas that calculate the most efficient way to ensure that every seat gets sold. Usually, only a handful of seats are available at the lowest fare. This can be particularly frustrating if you're shopping for several seats all at once—say, because you're traveling with your family.

Most likely, there won't be enough cheap seats available to fill your whole order. But instead of selling you as many cheap seats as they have and then charging you more for the rest, most airline reservation systems will simply kick your booking up to the next price level and charge you a higher fare for *all* your tickets. The way to beat this system is simple: Shop for your tickets one at a time. For example, when I searched for four tickets for a July 2008 trip from Los Angeles to New York, the American Airlines web site quoted me a fare of $619; when I searched for just one, the price for the same flight came up at only $344.

Instead of selling you as many cheap seats as they have, most airline reservation systems will charge you a higher fare for *all* your tickets.

THE SINGLE ADVANTAGE

LA-to-NY Reservation for Four Seats:	$619 EACH
LA-to-NY Reservation for One Seat:	$344
You Save:	**$275 per ticket**

Avoid Being Bumped by Nailing Down Your Seat Assignment

There's probably only one thing worse than getting a bad seat on a plane (say, one that doesn't recline or is right next to the galley). That's not getting a seat at all, even though you have bought and paid for a ticket. Most airlines routinely overbook particular flights based on the statistical probability that a certain number of travelers will not show up to claim their reservations. Occasionally, these calculations turn out to be wrong and there aren't enough seats to go around. What happens next can be ugly. If no one volunteers to give up his or her seat, the carrier will start bumping passengers— that is, denying them a seat on the flight even though they have a confirmed reservation.

There are a number of criteria the airlines use to decide who gets bumped first, but generally the most vulnerable passengers are those who don't yet have their seat assignments. So one simple way to minimize the odds that you'll ever be bumped from an overbooked flight is to make sure you get a confirmed seat assignment at the time you make your reservation.

This is also the best way to make sure you won't get stuck in a terrible seat or, if you're traveling with relatives or friends, that you will all be able to sit together.

Most airline web sites provide seating charts that show you exactly which seats are available on any given flight and where exactly on the plane they are located. To ensure you make the right choice, check with SeatGuru (www.seat guru.com), which provides seat maps for 300 different aircraft on 45 different airlines, along with expert commentary on which seats are best and which you should definitely avoid. It's a great resource for any air traveler who needs extra legroom or has vowed never to get seated next to a restroom ever again.

What to Watch Out For

Nontransparent Pricing

Once upon a time, the price of an airplane ticket included all sorts of services and amenities. Not anymore.

Needless to say, most carriers don't provide comprehensive lists of the extra fees they plan to charge. Nor when they quote you a ticket price do they spell out how much is for the airfare and how much is for the various extra charges already built in. (Delta is one of the few major carriers that does. American and United make you search for the information.)

So the smart air traveler needs to ask a lot of questions about baggage allowances, check-in services, cabin amenities, and the like. Specifically, make sure you know how many bags (if any) you are allowed to check for free, how many you can carry on, and at what weight and dimensions. To keep from getting dinged too badly, plan on bringing your own food, pack as light and tight as you can, and unless your trip involves some horrendously complicated connections, try to book it yourself online through the airline's own web site or through one of the major booking sites like Travelocity, Expedia, or Orbitz.

One web site that does a good job of keeping up with the extra charges is SeatGuru. In addition to providing seat maps, it also compiles the latest data on baggage allowances and restrictions as well as many of the fees you might get charged.

Incomprehensible Fare Rules

The rules governing airline fares can make the tax code look simple. Some fares apply only if you make your reservation at least 21 days in advance;

others require that you actually buy the ticket within a certain amount of time after you make the reservation; still others require a Saturday-night stopover. Some allow you to change your flight but not cancel it entirely; others permit cancellations but assess a penalty fee.

In addition to being complicated and often hard to understand, the rules also change constantly. So before you buy an airline ticket, make sure to ask the following questions:

- Is there a penalty if I need to change my flight time or date?

- What happens if I need to cancel the trip entirely?

- If the fare is nonrefundable, can I apply it to another trip at another time?

- If I decide not to use it, can I transfer my ticket to someone else?

As a rule, the cheaper the ticket, the more restricted it probably is—meaning that the less you pay, the more locked in to a specific flight you're likely to be. If your plans are not likely to change, that's fine. But if you need flexibility, be prepared to pay for it.

Paying by Check and Buying Too Far in Advance

If you pay for your ticket with cash or a check, you're out of luck in the event something goes wrong with your flight—like, say, the airline goes bankrupt and ceases operations. Buying your ticket with a credit card, on the other hand, protects you, since credit card companies will not force you to pay for a service you did not receive.

> If something goes wrong with your flight, buying your ticket with a credit card protects you.

There is one catch with this. Most credit card companies will cancel a disputed charge only if you file a complaint within 60 days of when it first appeared on your bill. What this means is that if you buy an airline ticket six months in advance and then the carrier goes out of business the day before you're scheduled to take off, you're out of luck. So don't buy airline tickets too far in advance. Reserve them if you have to—but try to avoid paying for them until you reach the 60-day window. If you're concerned about locking in a low fare, check with a web site like Farecast or FareCompare to get an indication of whether fares on the route you're traveling are likely to rise or fall in the near future.

What to Do if Things Go Wrong

In general, if you have any sort of problem with an airline, you should register your complaint as soon as possible—ideally, giving them the chance to resolve your issue on the spot. If you're in flight and find a fly in your orange juice, don't wait until you get home to file a complaint; ring for the head flight attendant and simply ask for a new drink. If you're at the airport, you should ask for the airline's customer-service representative or a manager with the authority to address your problem.

If you cannot resolve your problem on the spot, start taking notes. Write down all the pertinent information that will help you accurately describe what occurred—names of airline employees involved, time and date of the incident, flight number, airport, exactly what happened, and contact information for any witnesses. You'll also want to hang on to receipts for any extra expenses (such as hotel stays, car rental, or meals) that you incur as a result of the problem.

For the most part, it's best to file a complaint in the form of a letter or email to the carrier's customer-relations manager. You can usually find the manager's name and address by going to the carrier's web site and searching for "customer relations." Or you can go to www.airlinecomplaints.org and click on "airline contacts."

Although complaining by telephone may seem easier and more convenient, it's always better to put things in writing. That way there's never any question about who said what to whom and when. Your letter should be clear about who or what caused your problem and what you would regard as a reasonable resolution. Include photocopies of all relevant documents (boarding pass, baggage checks, etc.). And always keep a copy for your files.

If you keep the text professional and to the point, chances are the airline will do its best to make you happy.

If you don't get any satisfaction from the airline, you should file a complaint with the Department of Transportation's Aviation Consumer Protection Division. They don't mediate individual disputes, but they do keep the airlines on their toes by keeping track of all the complaints they receive and issuing public reports that compare how the various carriers stack up when it comes to customer satisfaction. You can file a complaint with the DOT online at http://airconsumer.ost.dot.gov/escomplaint/es.cfm, or you can write to them at:

Aviation Consumer Protection Division, C-75
U.S. Department of Transportation

1200 New Jersey Ave., SE
Washington, DC 20590

Complaints filed with the DOT should include a concise description of your problem, including your name, contact information, airline, flight date and number, origin and destination cities of your trip, and copies of any tickets.

Safety-related airline complaints should go to the Federal Aviation Administration. You can telephone them at 866-TELL-FAA (866-835-5322). Or you can write them at:

Federal Aviation Administration
Consumer Hotline, AOA-20
800 Independence Avenue, SW
Washington, DC 20591

If you have a complaint related to aviation security, you should contact the Transportation Security Administration by phone at the TSA Contact Center (866-289-9673) or by email at tsa-contactcenter@dhs.gov.

Fight for Your Money Action Steps

☐ Shop around—and go online to find real bargains.

☐ Save additional money by using unexpected airports or carriers.

☐ Protect yourself against being bumped by nailing down your seat assignment early.

☐ Always pay for your ticket with a credit card—never by cash, check, or debit card.

☐ Make sure you know the rules regarding checked baggage and other no-longer-free services.

Hotels

Staying in a hotel these days can be a lot like traveling on an airline. The service is indifferent, the facilities aren't always shipshape, and if you're not careful, they will ding you with all kinds of unexpected extra charges—some of which are nothing short of outrageous. One guy I know got charged $16 just for taking a bottle of water out of a hotel-room minibar and then putting it back. It turned out the hotel tracked minibar usage with electronic sensors, and when my friend moved the bottle, the fridge rang it up as a sale. And don't get me started on the Internet charges and the $200 telephone calls.

Unlike the airlines, the hotel industry is solidly profitable. It earned an impressive pretax net of $28 billion on total revenues of $139 billion in 2007. So there's really no excuse for its habit of ripping off travelers. And make no mistake about it—hotels try to get away with whatever they can. According to a study by Corporate Lodging Consultants, which negotiates hotel rates for hundreds of companies, between billing "errors" and hidden fees, they routinely overcharge business travelers by as much as $500 million a year. Another study by American Express found that hotel reservation systems quoted the wrong rates more than half the time—and the "mistakes" were almost always in the hotels' favor.

As one travel consultant told *USA Today* not too long ago, "These mistakes don't occasionally happen—they regularly happen." Here's how to keep them from happening to you.

How to Fight for Your Money

Don't Be Afraid to Haggle

For all the traveling that Americans do, more than a third of all U.S. hotel rooms sit empty every night. As a result, most hotels will cut you a deal—if you ask for it. In a 2007 survey, *Consumer Reports* found that 70% of travelers who asked for a better deal succeeded in getting either a rate reduction or room upgrade. This was the case even at the most expensive hotels. So don't hesitate to speak up and inquire, because chances are it will be worth your while.

I live by this rule. The fact is, many hotels are like used-car lots. I recently stood at the front desk of a hotel in Las Vegas negotiating with the desk clerk, who kept running back and forth to his manager in the back room. Was it worth it? I ended up with a 2,500-square-foot penthouse suite for $500 a night. (The standard room they'd originally offered me was priced at $395.) So, yes, it was worth it!

I get an upgrade at almost every hotel I check into simply by negotiating at the front desk and asking for one. I've been doing this since I was 18 years old, when I stayed in a hotel with my parents and wound up with a better room than they got. Trust me—this works.

And whenever you call to make a hotel reservation, be sure to tell the clerk you'd like the lowest rate he or she can give you. A lot of hotels will offer their discounted "corporate" rate to anyone who asks—whether or not you're traveling on business or even work for a corporation.

Book Early—and Then Book Again at the Last Minute

Since many hotels offer discounted rates for advance bookings, it's generally a good idea to make your reservation as early as you can. But hotels also sometimes drop their prices at the last minute in an effort to fill vacancies. So you should call again a day or two before your trip to see if you can get an even better rate. In most cases, you'll be able to cancel your original reservation and get yourself a new one at the lower rate without having to pay any kind of penalty.

Make Sure You Know What You've Booked

As with the airlines, you can get all kinds of great hotel deals by booking online through travel sites such as Expedia (www.expedia.com), Hotwire.com (www.

hotwire.com), Kayak (www.kayak.com), Orbitz (www.orbitz.com), Priceline (www.priceline.com), SideStep (www.sidestep.com), and Travelocity (www.travelocity.com). But particularly if you are using a less-well-known site, you want to make sure that the room you booked actually exists.

The daughter of a friend of mine, a college student named Ellen, learned this the hard way not too long ago. While spending a semester in Europe, she arranged to meet three friends in Dublin for a few days. The place where she wanted to stay was booked, so she surfed the web for a while until she found a slick-looking travel site that claimed to specialize in hostels for students. Ellen used it to reserve a room with four beds for her and her friends in a hostel called The Shining, using her credit card to put down a 10% deposit. But when the young women arrived in Dublin, it turned out that The Shining had no reservation for them. Nor did it have any four-bed rooms—nor any record of Ellen's 10% deposit.

There's a simple way to guard against this sort of disaster—or even the less dire but still extremely annoying problem of showing up at a hotel and discovering it's not nearly as nice as it looked in the photos. Whenever you're planning to stay at a hotel you've never been to before, go online to a traveler-based review site like Boo.com, Gusto.com, IgoUgo.com, or TripAdvisor.com, to see what real travelers who've been there have to say about the place. You can even ask questions on the message boards.

Regardless of where you're going and whether you've made your reservation through a third party or with the hotel directly, always phone the hotel to confirm your booking a few days before you start your trip. And double-check that the room rate you were quoted by the reservations clerk is the rate you're going to be charged.

If There's a Problem, Don't Leave the Front Desk Until It's Resolved

Even if you book through legitimate channels and have a confirmed reservation, it's not uncommon to arrive at a front desk and be told there's no room in the inn. Again like the airlines, hotels sometimes deliberately overbook. Unfortunately, unlike airline passengers, hotel guests don't have a federal law that protects them in the event they are bumped.

Most lawyers agree that it's a breach of contract if you've guaranteed your reservation with a credit card and the desk clerk tells you that the hotel doesn't have a room for you. To make sure no one questions the validity of your claim, you should always travel with copies of whatever emails or letters you may have received from the hotel or travel agency confirming your reservation.

In such cases, the policy at most major hotels is to find you another room at a comparable place nearby—and if the room there is more expensive than the one you reserved, to reimburse you for the difference. Customarily, the hotel that's turned you away will also pay for your first night at the other place, provide transportation there, and give you free phone service so you can call your family and business associates to let them know about the change. If the hotel fails to offer you any of these amenities, don't be shy about asking for them.

> **Customarily, the hotel that's turned you away will pay for your first night at the other place.**

Above all, do not leave the front desk until your situation has been resolved to your satisfaction. The front-desk staff will probably ask you to step aside so they can register another guest or answer someone else's question. Don't let them push you around. Until you're taken care of, you have to remain the squeaky wheel who needs to be dealt with now. If the clerks say there's nothing they can do, ask to speak with the general manager or the manager on duty so you're dealing with someone who has the authority to assist you. But keep in mind that raised voices and sharp words are not likely to get you anywhere. The clerks at the front desk most likely didn't cause your problem—but if you are polite, as well as persistent, they may be the ones to solve it.

Watch Out for Those Outrageous Charges

Most hotels these days charge you for virtually every amenity they offer. Some are obvious and easy to avoid, but increasingly they sneak up on you—and the tab can be considerable. In all, hotel surcharges picked nearly $1.8 billion out of travelers' pockets in 2008. The most outrageous rip-offs include:

MINIBARS. With their $8 cans of Coke and their $12 bags of mixed nuts, hotel minibars have been ripping off travelers ever since they first appeared in the early 1970s. These days they're worse than ever, thanks to modern electronics. As my friend with the $16 bottle of water discovered, many have been equipped with sensors. If you even *move* a soda can or candy bar, it signals the desk that you should be billed for it.

RESORT FEES. Many hotels charge "resort fees" of $15 to $25 a day for facilities such as gyms and tennis courts that you may never use. There's generally no way to avoid them, except to ask, when you make your reservation, whether the daily rate covers everything. Mandatory tipping may also be another "resort fee" that you are unaware of, so ask before you leave tips (otherwise you are double tipping).

ROOM SERVICE. When is a cheeseburger and fries worth $30 plus tip? When you have it delivered to your room by a room-service waiter in most big hotels. Let's face it—if you are a business traveler and get in late in the day, ordering room service is more than likely the only way you'll get something to eat. But watch out for the double and triple tip factor. Most room-service bills include both a delivery charge and gratuity—but when the bill is handed to you, there's a blank line labeled "Tip." If you write in a tip here—on top of the delivery fee and gratuity that have already been included—you may wind up paying as much in service fees as you paid for the food.

TELEPHONE CALLS. The rates hotels charge for using their phones are nothing short of amazing. What really boggles my mind is not that hotels routinely charge five times what the phone company does for calls—or that they even charge you for toll-free calls to an 800 number. No, what I still have trouble believing is that some hotels will charge you upward of $7 just for picking up the phone *whether or not you complete a call!* So unless it's an emergency, never use a hotel phone. Make all your calls on your cell or a public phone.

IT'S WORTH THE ELEVATOR RIDE

Two-minute local call from your room, Waldorf Astoria:	$3.90
Cost from a pay phone in the lobby:	$0.25
You save:	**$3.65**

INTERNET CONNECTIONS. Virtually every decent hotel makes a big deal of advertising the availability of broadband Internet connections. But most of them charge you through the nose for it—often as much as $14.95 a day. (You can avoid this charge by using a nearby wireless hotspot. There are a number of online directories—such as www.jiwire.com, www.wififreespot.com, and www.wi-fihotspotlist.com—that can point you to the nearest one.)

PARKING. Particularly in urban locations, hotel parking is another huge rip-off. The hotel garage may be convenient, but at anywhere from $20 to $50 a night, it's probably the most expensive parking spot in town. You're generally much better off looking for a municipal lot nearby.

Review Your Bill Carefully

With all these surcharges and special fees, it's not surprising that hotel bills are often riddled with errors. So when you check out, be sure to review your bill carefully. I never leave a hotel without getting a printout of the bill and going through it line by line.

First and foremost, I check to make sure the room price matches what I was told. (Trust me—it often doesn't.) Next, I check every single charge against my receipts to make sure the bills from the restaurants, room service, bar, pool—you name it—match what I signed for. Did I rent a movie? Why were there two charges for a movie when I know I watched only one?

I almost never leave a hotel without finding a mistake in their favor, and I always get it fixed—that is, credited back to me—before I check out. The moral here is simple. Check your bill, verify, and rectify! When you check out is the time to argue—politely—if you find a charge you don't recognize. The

> I almost never leave a hotel without finding a mistake on my bill—in their favor.

longer you wait to dispute a bill, the less likely you are to prevail—which is one reason why you might want to think twice about taking advantage of the "express checkout" option so many hotels now offer. Express checkout can be great when you're

rushing to catch a plane, but when you do it, you might not see your hotel bill for several days or weeks. By then, it may be too late to sort out a dispute—if you even remember which charges are right and which aren't.

What to Do if Things Go Wrong

If you have a problem with your bill—or any other issue, for that matter—and the front-desk clerk can't resolve it to your satisfaction, discuss it with the manager on duty. If this gets you nowhere, settle your bill with a credit card and then dispute the charge with the credit card company when your next statement arrives. (For details on how to do this, see the section CREDIT CARDS on page 89.)

In general, any problem you can't resolve with the hotel manager should be brought to the attention of the hotel's owner—which in most cases will be a national chain that has a customer-relations department listed on its web site. Most chains are fairly protective of their brand reputation, so unless your complaint is totally unreasonable, they'll probably try to make it up to you—if only by giving you vouchers good toward the cost of a future stay at one of their properties. Whether or not you'll ever want to use the vouchers depends on how bad your experience with them was.

In the case of really bad treatment, you should also file a complaint with your local Better Business Bureau (www.bbb.org), your state's consumer-protection office (which is often part of the state attorney general's office), and the Federal Trade Commission (through its online complaint form at www.ftccomplaintassistant.gov).

Fight for Your Money Action Steps

☐ Negotiate for a better rate.

☐ Book online for great deals, but always confirm your reservation and rate directly with the hotel.

☐ If your hotel has overbooked or has lost your reservation, see what is offered as a resolution. And if nothing is offered—ask.

☐ Be aware that hotels add mandatory extra fees to the room rate for almost all amenities. Ask if you're not sure, in order to calculate the real cost of your stay.

☐ Check your bill line by line and resolve any errors before you check out.

Travel Packages

B ack in 1999, the Federal Trade Commission and 21 federal and state law-enforcement authorities sprung "Operation Trip Trap," a crackdown on 25 crooked travel companies that were swindling consumers with phony or misleading vacation packages. The rip-offs were all classics. The scammers promised consumers "luxury" accommodations that turned out to be vermin-infested shacks. They told people they had won free trips and then hit them with all sorts of hidden fees. And they charged travelers for products and services they never received.

The sweep generated a lot of headlines. Several of the companies wound up refunding hundreds of thousands of dollars to the victims. A dozen or so scam artists were barred from continuing to work in the travel business. And business went on as usual.

In fact, a decade later all that's changed when it comes to travel scams is that instead of sending potential victims postcards, the scammers now send them emails.

So if you're planning a vacation, don't let down your guard. Of the 3,900 industries for which the U.S. Better Business Bureau fields complaints, the travel industry consistently ranks in or near the top 25. In all, says the BBB, vacation scams cost consumers more than $10 billion a year.

How to Fight for Your Money

Increased enforcement by the U.S. Postal Inspection Service may have made travel scammers wary of using the mails to solicit victims. But the Internet is

Don't Be Fooled

Check out the sample site that the FTC has up at: **http://wemarket4u. net/eztrvltrip/index.html** to get an idea of what a fraudulent travel site looks like.

not subject to government regulation, and slick web sites and well-crafted emails offering too-good-to-be-true deals on trips and tours continue to snag unwary bargain-hunters. Here's how to avoid being taken.

Be Careful About Prepaying

Scam artists are well aware that most major credit card companies give customers only 60 days to dispute a charge. As a result, once they've gotten you to pay for some "dream" vacation, they will take their time providing you with written confirmation of your reservation. When you finally do get it—invariably, after the 60-day dispute period has ended—you'll find a different price from the one you agreed to on the phone or online, as well as a list of mandatory extra charges you were never warned about. And when you try to cancel, you'll be told it's too late—if anyone bothers to respond to your complaints at all.

So be wary of deals that require you to pay more than 60 days in advance. At most, don't put down more than a deposit. In particular, be skeptical of any tour operator who tells you that you have to buy your tickets now because the deal is only good today. And if you are persuaded to put down a deposit, insist on getting a confirmation number along with immediate written confirmation of the terms, including how far in advance you can cancel your reservations and still get a full refund. If it is not forthcoming, send a certified letter canceling your trip and demanding a refund. And do this well before the 60-day deadline so you can dispute the charge if they refuse to return your money.

Never Pay by Check

A tour operator who insists on payment by check and refuses to accept credit cards or PayPal is a tour operator you should avoid. Once you write a check, your money is gone. And be aware that you do not get credit card purchase protection when you pay for something using those low-interest cash-advance checks that come with your credit card statement.

Ask Questions if You Prepay

Make a point of finding out what happens to the money you prepay. Is it held in escrow somewhere? What's the name of the bank? If the travel agency is a member of the United States Tour Operators Association, you will be protected by a $1-million bond all USTOA members are required to post. If it's not a member, before you hand over any money, ask the tour operator for some references—ideally, names and numbers of former customers as well as travel agents who have booked trips with him—and check them out.

Double-Check Your Reservations

To be certain that you're not being scammed, check directly with the airlines and hotels the tour operator claims he is booking for your trip. Is there a confirmed reservation in your name? If not, demand an explanation from the tour operator, and if it sounds fishy, cancel. Ask the hotel sales department if they know the tour operator and what kind of reputation he has. Make sure you receive copies of each vendor's cancellation and refund policies.

Ask the hotel sales department if they know the tour operator and what kind of reputation he has.

Beware of Phony Travel Agent ID Cards

One of the most devious travel scams involves what are known as "card mills" that sell phony "travel agent" ID cards. These supposedly entitle the holder to all the discounts, upgrades, and other perks airlines and hotels usually offer real travel agents, and they are not cheap. They usually sell for close to $500—though rarely more than that, since $500 is the threshold that triggers applicable federal and state laws. In fact, they are worthless.

Be skeptical of anyone who offers to sell you a card that will allow you to "travel like a travel agent," when your only "client" is yourself.

What most real travel agents have is an ID issued by the International Airlines Travel Agency Network (IATAN). The IATAN ID card is the only form of identification most airlines and other travel suppliers will accept for discounts or free tickets. Back in the 1990s, it was relatively easy to get one of these cards. But in recent years, the industry has cracked down. As legendary travel guru Arthur Frommer has noted: "Much more than an ID card is now required to qualify people for travel discounts. And companies that take $400 or $500 from you for an ID, without offering real instruction or operating a chain of active retail agencies, are scam artists."

As IATAN itself makes clear, to get an IATAN ID card, you have to meet a series of stringent criteria, including working at least 20 hours a week selling travel and earning at least $5,000 a year in salary and commissions. So be skeptical of anyone who offers to sell you a card that will allow you to "travel like a travel agent," even if your only "client" is yourself. If you qualify for an IATAN card, the annual fee is only $30. If you don't qualify, it doesn't matter how much you pay—you can't get real travel agency credentials if you are not a real travel agent.

Don't Fall for Those "Free" Timeshare Trips

One of the most common travel-package scams is the "free vacation" that is constantly being offered by timeshare promoters. At first glance, these deals usually seem great. To get what's described as a free trip to resort destinations like Orlando or Cancún, all you have to do is agree to sit through a 60- or 90-minute sales presentation for the timeshare resort they're pushing. The problem is that most of these deals don't include transportation, the accommodations they do provide can be dicey, and those 60-minute presentations often turn out to be all-day ordeals in which you're badgered by a team of high-pressure salesmen who won't take "No, thank you" for an answer. So while it's true that you are under no obligation to buy anything when you accept one of these offers, you still usually wind up paying a real price for that supposedly "free" trip.

Legitimate Travel Packages Do Exist

If you're looking for a vacation deal, I recommend doing some comparison searches on the major travel sites, like www.expedia.com, www. Travelocity. com, www.orbitz.com, www.priceline.com, www.sidestep.com, and www. kayak.com. Click on "Vacation Packages" to see what specials are being offered. For last-minute getaways, visit www.lastminute.com.

What to Do if Things Go Wrong

When fighting to get your money back, you first want to try to resolve the problem with the vendor, whether it's a hotel, an airline, or a car-rental agency. Tell them exactly what happened, why you are dissatisfied, and what you want done to rectify the situation.

As you work your way through the complaint process, keep copies of all relevant receipts, emails, letters, and notes on phone conversations, along with a narrative of who said what to you and when. Send everyone copies of your confirmation information and travel documents, but never send the originals.

If this does not resolve the problem, you should dispute the charge through your credit card company. In addition, you should complain to the Better Business Bureau (www.bbb.org). Within two days after you've filed a complaint with your local BBB chapter, the group will forward your dispute to the vendor, allowing him 14 days to respond.

You should also file a complaint with the FTC as well as with any professional association your tour agency happens to belong to, such as the USTOA (www.ustoa.com) or the American Society of Travel Agents (www.asta.org).

You can complain to the FTC either by telephoning its Consumer Response Center toll-free at (877) 382-4357 or through its online complaint form at www.ftccomplaintassistant.gov.

You can contact USTOA either by phone at (212) 599-6599 or by writing to:

United States Tour Operators Association
275 Madison Avenue
Suite 2014
New York, NY 10016

You can contact the American Society of Travel Agents by phone at (703) 706-0387, by email at consumeraffairs@asta.org, or by regular mail at:

ASTA
Consumer Affairs Department
1101 King Street
Alexandria, VA 22314

Fight for Your Money Action Steps

☐ Don't fall for vacation offers from telemarketers or spam email.

☐ If you are pressured to make a quick decision, just say no. It's most likely a scam.

☐ Get all terms and conditions in writing, including date restrictions and cancellation policies.

☐ Confirm bookings directly with hotels, airlines, and rental-car agencies.

☐ Use a credit card for payment, never cash or a check.

Conclusion

You have reached the end of this book, but your FIGHT FOR YOUR MONEY is just beginning.

You have now read more about smart spending than most people will read in a lifetime. As a result, you now possess the ability to take more control over your financial life than most people ever will have.

As I said in the Introduction, you deserve to be in control of your money and not be ripped off. But as we've seen, the battle to protect the money you have worked so hard to earn is a battle you have to fight every day. And this battle for your money is not going to end anytime soon. If anything, it is likely to get harder.

The good news is that you are now wiser financially—and wisdom makes you strong. You no longer have to be a victim, either of circumstances or of legal scams perpetrated by big business to separate you from your paycheck. You have become an insider who knows the tricks that companies play. You know how to read the paperwork before you sign anything, how to calculate the real cost of what you're being offered, and how to negotiate for a better deal.

Live for Your Life

As I put the final touches on this book in the fall of 2008, the world is going through some of the most difficult financial times since the Great Depression.

By the time you read this, that crisis will have been dealt with. No doubt others will be unfolding. The fact is that financial crises are a part of life and a part of history. And how we deal with them is also predictable. A lot of us complain about how unfair it all is and blame the politicians (many of whom deserve to be blamed), while the news media jump up and down, looking for heroes and goats as if they were covering a sporting event.

The most important thing I can say to you as your financial coach and advocate is this: At the end of the day, the only one who really controls your financial life is YOU. And when you control your money, you control your life. This is a truth you can feel in your heart. It is why it is so crucial that you make use of the knowledge and the tools this book provides.

You are the one person with the best chance of helping you and your family when it comes to your money. It is not about which political party is in the White House or which leader says what to whom. It is not about new rules and regulations to "protect us." It's ultimately about YOU and what YOU do to protect yourself.

The fact that big business has no compunctions about doing whatever it can to separate you from your money does not have to be your downfall. You are now too smart to let others take advantage of you. This book has covered your entire financial life from automobiles to taxes, and then some. There are certainly more topics to be covered—and there will certainly be more games played on us—but I am confident that if you use the information you have gotten from this book to FIGHT FOR YOUR MONEY, no one will be able to take advantage of you financially.

Remember this: No one can control our future if we don't let them.

I wrote this book to give you the insight and advantage that millions of people simply don't have when it comes to their money. Now please go use it and share it. I congratulate you on your desire to live and finish rich by fighting for your money.

If this book has touched you, inspired you, and gotten you to take action, please let us know. I truly love and live to hear from my readers. Every day, I wake up to your emails and letters. It is your successes and challenges that motivate me and my team to keep doing what we do every day. You inspire us by your success and you force us to work harder when we hear about your hardships. You can reach me at success@finishrich.com.

Until we meet again, enjoy your journey—and make it joyful.

Your friend,
David Bach

APPENDIX:
FIGHT FOR YOUR MONEY TOOLKIT

Airline Complaint Letter

[insert date]

Customer Service
[insert airline name]
[insert address] [Note: The appropriate address can usually be found on the airline's web site. If not, call the airline to find out where customer-service complaints should be sent.]

Dear [insert contact name],

I'm writing to report an incident that occurred during [insert flight information and date]. I have always been a loyal patron of [insert airline name], but this recent incident, which involved [briefly state problem], has left me with no choice but to file a formal complaint and request that you [insert what you want—e.g., give me a 50% discount on my next flight] in compensation for the poor treatment to which I was subjected.

What happened was this. [Describe the incident as clearly and succinctly as possible. Do not whine or use abusive language. Rather, tell the story logically and methodically, with an eye to proving why you should be compensated.]

In view of what happened, I think it is only fair that you [state, clearly and specifically, what kind of compensation you want].

Please contact me to confirm that my requests will be honored. My daytime phone number is [insert number with area code] and my email address is [insert email address]. If I do not hear from you by [insert date], I will report this incident to the Department of Transportation's Aviation Consumer Protection Division, the FAA, and the Better Business Bureau.

Sincerely,

[your name]
[your address]

Enclosures: [List what you are enclosing—e.g., your airline ticket—and provide copies of those supporting documents.]

Source: Executive Travel Magazine, 2008. www.executivetravelmagazine.com

General Complaint Letter for Defective Product or Inadequate Service

[insert date]

[insert name of contact person (if available)]
[insert title (if available)]
[insert company name]
Consumer Complaint Division (if you have no specific contact)
[insert address]

Dear [insert contact name],

On [insert date], I purchased [or had repaired] a [insert name of the product with the serial or model number or service performed]. I made this purchase at [insert location, date, and other important details of the transaction].

Unfortunately, your product [or service] has not performed well [or the service was inadequate]. Instead of [describe what should have happened], it [explain what did happen].

To resolve this issue, I would appreciate your [insert the specific action you want]. Enclosed are copies of my records [receipts, guarantees, warranties, canceled checks, contracts, model and serial numbers, and any other documents].

I look forward to your reply and a resolution to my problem no later than [insert time limit]. If I do not hear from you by then, I will seek assistance from a consumer-protection agency or the Better Business Bureau. Please contact me at the above address or by phone [insert home or office numbers with area codes].

Sincerely,

[insert your name]
[insert your address]

Enclosures: [List what you are enclosing and provide copies of those supporting documents.]

New Car "Lemon Law" Letter

[insert date]
[insert manufacturer's name]
[insert address]
BY CERTIFIED MAIL
RETURN RECEIPT REQUESTED

Dear [insert contact name if available],

I am writing to notify you of the problems I have had with my [insert year, make, model, and VIN# of car] pursuant to [cite your state's lemon law].

I purchased my car from [insert name of dealership] on [insert date of purchase]. Approximately [insert amount of time] after purchase, I began having trouble with [insert description of problem]. I took my car back to the dealer on [insert dates of repair attempts] to have this problem corrected, but to date, the dealer has been unable to do so. Thus far, my car has been out of service for a total of [insert number] days/a dealership has attempted to repair this problem [insert number] times. Attached are copies of the repair orders that document the dealership's attempts to repair my car.

This problem substantially impairs both the use and value of my car. Therefore, unless you are able to correct this problem within 30 days of your receipt of this letter, I request that you [repurchase or replace] my vehicle under the provisions of [your state's lemon law].

Please contact me at the address below or by telephone at [insert number with area code] to arrange a mutually convenient date and time for you to inspect my car and make the necessary repairs.

Sincerely,

[insert your name]
[insert your address]

Enclosures. [List what you are enclosing and provide copies of those supporting documents.]

Source: http://www.oag.state.md.us

Credit Card Charge in Error

[insert date]
[insert name of creditor]
Billing Inquiries
[insert address]

Dear [insert contact name if available]:

I am writing to dispute a billing error in the amount of [insert amount] on my account. The amount is inaccurate because [describe the problem]. I am requesting that the error be corrected, that any finance and other charges related to the disputed amount be credited as well, and that I receive an accurate statement.

Enclosed are copies of [use this sentence to describe any enclosed information, such as sales slips and payment records] supporting my position. Please investigate this matter and correct the billing error as soon as possible.

Please contact me at the address listed below within 30 days as per the Fair Credit Billing Act.

Sincerely,

[insert your name]
[insert your address]

Enclosures: [List what you are enclosing and provide copies of those supporting documents.]

Source: www.FTC.gov

Letter to Correct Credit Report Errors

[insert date]
[insert name of credit agency]
[insert address]
RE: Request to correct errors in credit report # [insert file number on your credit report].

Dear [insert name]:

In reviewing the credit report you sent me on [insert date], I have noticed the following errors:

1. [Describe the first error—e.g., "You list my date of birth as Jan. 1, 1900."]

This is incorrect. The correct information is: [be very specific here and accompany it with proof if you have it—e.g., "As the enclosed copy of my birth certificate shows, my date of birth is July 25, 1963."].

2. [Describe the second error—e.g., "You list me as having an active charge account with Sears."]

This is incorrect. The correct information is: [be very specific here and accompany it with proof if you have it—e.g., "I closed this account on March 15, 2001. Please note the enclosed copy of the letter I sent Sears instructing them to close the account."].

3. [Describe the third error—e.g., "You list me as having made two late payments on my Bank of America home mortgage."]

This is incorrect. The correct information is: [be very specific here and accompany it with proof if you have it—e.g., "I have made all my mortgage payments on time. Please note the enclosed copy of my latest mortgage statement as well as a letter from Bank of America confirming this fact."].

According to the Fair Credit Reporting Act, you are required to respond to my request within 30 days. My contact information is: [insert mailing address and phone number].

Sincerely yours,

[insert your name]

Disputing a Rebate Rejection

[insert date]
[insert company name]
ATTENTION: Rebate Processing Department
[insert address]
RE: Failure to Receive Rebate by Offer Date

Dear [insert name]:

I purchased a [insert product details] on [insert date] at [insert store name] in [insert city and state]. My decision to purchase this product was based upon your offer of a mail-in rebate of [insert dollar amount] ("offer"). My purchase of the product constituted my acceptance ("acceptance") of your offer, creating a binding and enforceable contract between us.

I have performed my obligations under the contract. I paid the full purchase price and then proceeded to fill in the rebate form provided by you. I included all information requested to process my rebate, but to date I have not received a check in the amount of [insert dollar amount].

I respectfully request you process payment and mail it to me at the address indicated within 30 days. I have reattached all information originally sent for your convenience.

If I do not receive payment in full by [insert date 30 days from mailing], I will begin legal proceedings against you and will file complaint reports with the Federal Trade Commission, the attorneys general of the states of [insert your state] and [insert the company's state], as well as selected consumer-advocacy publications and local and state consumer affairs departments.

I am sending copies of this letter to these agencies and organizations to encourage your compliance. I am also filing a report with Consumer Affairs.com for inclusion on their web site.

Thank you for your prompt attention and resolution of this matter.

Sincerely,

[insert your name]

cc: Federal Trade Commission
6th & Pennsylvania Avenue, NW
Washington, DC 20580

Hon. (name of attorney general)
Attorney General, State of (state)
(address)

Hon. (name of attorney general)
Attorney General, State of (state)
(address)

ConsumerAffairs.com
11400 West Olympic Boulevard
Suite 200
Los Angeles, CA 90064

Source: www.consumeraffairs.com

INTRODUCTION

In a single week this month (October 2008), the U.S. stock market plunged more than 18 percent: Tim Paradis, "Stocks end wild session mixed, Dow falls 128," Associated Press, October 10, 2008, http://biz.yahoo.com/ap/081010/wall_street.html.

while at the same time real estate prices in many cities across America were down 20% or more from their peak in 2005 and 2006: Rex Nutting, "Home prices falling faster in July, Case-Shiller says," *MarketWatch,* September 30, 2008, www.marketwatch.com/news/story/home-prices-falling-faster-july/story.aspx?guid=%7BFA9E2E3B-97CB-4E29-9E73-9A52A3DF220A%7D.

In 2008, nearly 25% of the population (nearly 60 million people in all) either delayed or did without needed medical care because they couldn't afford the bills: Aliza Marcus, "Medical Bills Burden 72 Million Working-Age Adults in U.S.," Bloomberg, August 20, 2008, www.bloomberg.com/apps/news?pid=20601124&refer=home&sid=abot1XN3T0J0.

the 20 biggest health insurers recorded total profits in excess of $17 billion. The year before, the CEO of CIGNA Corp., the nation's fifth largest health insurer, personally earned more than $24 million: Google Finance, http://finance.google.com/finance?catid=52935503; "2007 Executive Compensation at Publicly Traded Managed Care Firms," *Health Plan Week,* May 12, 2008, www.aishealth.com/ManagedCare/CompanyIntel/ExecComp.html.

Telemarketing scams alone cost us an estimated $40 billion a year: U.S. Postal Inspection Service, "Want to Get Rich Quick? It could cost you plenty," http://postalinspectors.uspis.gov/radDocs/consumer/dial4dol.htm.

BUYING A NEW CAR

Americans still buy roughly 14 million new cars, minivans, SUVs, and pick-up trucks each year: "GM, Ford Sales Slump Puts Buyers in Driver's Seat," Bloomberg, November 17, 2008, http://www.bloomberg.com/apps/news?pid=20601213&sid=aQ7RWtaAlpZA&refer=home.

extended warranties alone bring in upwards of $5 billion a year—three-quarters of which is pure profit: Common Rights Law Blog, http://ohiolemonlaw.blogspot.com/2007/05/extended-warranty-ripoffs.html.

new cars take their biggest depreciation hit in the

first year after they roll off the dealer's lot, typically losing 25% to 30% of their value: Philip Reed, "Drive a (Nearly) New Car for (Almost) Free!" Edmunds.com, http://www.edmunds.com/advice/strategies/articles/77147/article.html.

There are roughly 21,000 new-car dealers in the United States: National Automobile Dealers Association, "Annual Contributions of the United State's New Vehicle Dealers," http://www.nada.org/NR/rdonlyres/E51CEDC3-E39D-4C70-AD75-3ACCB5685251/0/StateeconomiesAnnual Contributions.pdf.

the invoice price of a car is not the dealer's true cost, since it generally includes what's called a holdback—a fee (usually 2% to 4% of the MSRP) that most car manufacturers pay their dealers each time they sell a car: Edmunds.com, Buyer Tips/Dealer Holdback, http://www.edmunds.com/advice/incentives/holdback/index.html.

2009 VW Jetta costs: MSRP, invoice and dealer's cost figures from Edmunds.com, August 2008, www.edmunds.com.

More than a quarter of car-dealers' profits come from what they call F&I—finance and insurance: AutoExec.com, "F&I, Service Contracts," May 2007, posted at www.nada.org/NR/rdonlyres/03470866-3B06-49A7-8412-1749A3C11CE1/0/NADA_DATA_2007_FI_Service_Contracts.pdf.

The automakers spend literally billions of dollars each year on advertising designed to: TNS press release, 3/25/08, www.tnsglobal.com/news/news-B1FAE5AC1091484FA02D8B7F4F7EDDAD.aspx; TNS press release, 9/24/08, www.businesswire.com/portal/site/google/?ndmViewId=news_view&newsId=20080924005132&newsLang=en.

though most new cars come with six-year/100,000-mile rust warranties, many dealers will try to sell you on an $800 rust-proofing treatment that costs them all of $40: Doug Newcomb, "Dealer Options to Avoid," MSN Autos, http://editorial.autos.msn.com/article.aspx?cp-documentid=476382.

Cost of dealer's "Fabric Protection Package": $300 Edmunds.com, consumer discussions, www.edmunds.com/dealerships/Chevrolet/Ohio/Seneca County/OldFort.html.

more new-car buyers than ever before—more than a third these days, compared to only one out of five in the late 1990s—get suckered into purchasing extended service agreements: "Extended Car Warranties—Don't be a Pushover," *Consumer Reports,* March 17, 2008, http://blogs.consumerreports.org/cars/2008/03/ex-car-warranty.html.

The price tag on these plans average around $1,000, while the total repair costs they actually wind up absorbing are typically just $250 or so: Consumers Union press release, March 21, 2003, http://www.consumersunion.org/finance/extend-warr-pr.htm.

BUYING A USED CAR

Americans bought 41.4 million used cars in 2007, two-thirds of them from dealers (as opposed to private individuals): Bureau of Transportation Statistics, http://www.bts.gov/publications/national_transportation_statistics/html/table_01_17.html.

an average profit of roughly $300 per vehicle, which works out to more than $8.3 billion in all: John O'Dell, "Used-Car Profit Engine," Los Angeles Times, 11/14/04, http://articles.latimes.com/2004/nov/14/business/fi-auction14.

. . . the fact is that most modern cars will easily give you 200,000 miles or more: Herb Weisbaum, "What's the Life Expectancy of My Car?" MSNBC, 3/28/06, http://www.msnbc.msn.com/id/12040753/.

Craigslist carries ads for upwards of 3 million used cars each month. For its part, eBay welcomes 11 million visitors each month and sells upwards of about $18 billion worth of cars and related products each year: Jim Kneiszel, "Going Once, Going Twice," Edmunds.com, www.edmunds.com/advice/selling/articles/74786/article.html.

rental cars are among the best-maintained vehicles on the road today: https://www.edmunds.com/advice/buying/articles/46537/article.html; Robbie Woliver, "Drive a Bargain with a Former Rental Car," Bankrate.com, March 18, 2003, http://www.bankrate.com/brm/news/auto/20000126.asp.

one out of every ten used cars sold these days has had its odometer rolled back. According to U.S. government figures, this illegal practice costs car-buyers more than $1 billion each year in inflated prices: Ralph Vartabedian, "Making Inroads Against Threat of Odometer Fraud," Los Angeles Times, July 17, 2002, http://articles.latimes.com/2002/jul/17/autos/hy-wheels17.

As many as 10% of all the cars and trucks in Louisiana and Mississippi—some 571,000 vehicles in all—were ruined by Hurricane Katrina in August 2005: "Water Damaged Katrina Cars Hit the Market," Consumer Affairs, February 1, 2006, http://www.consumeraffairs.com/news04/2006/02/flood_cars.html.

CAR LEASING

car dealers average twice as much profit on a lease as they do on a conventional purchase: CarInfo.com, "Auto Leasing Secrets," http://www.carinfo.com/autoleasing.html.

Given that roughly 25% of all new cars (and more than 85% of some luxury models) are leased rather than bought, we're talking about a lot of money—as much as $10 billion a year in excess profits, according to some estimates: Bureau of Transportation Statistics, www.bts.gov/publications/national_transportation_statistics/html/table_01_17.html; CNW Research, Retail Automotive Survey, June 16, 2008; "Drive an Expensive Import? You Probably Lease It," BusinessWeek, August 26, 2008.

Since a Honda typically depreciates by 40% over three years, the car will be worth just $15,000 or so when your lease ends: James R. Healey, "Driving off the lot: Watch out for the cliff," USA Today, October 8, 2004, www.usatoday.com/money/perfi/basics/2004-10-08-mym-autos_x.htm.

. . . basically, 58.5 cents for every business-related mile they drive: Internal Revenue Service, www.irs.gov/taxpros/article/0,,id=156624,00.html.

In the first year or two, leasing usually costs you less, but around the third year the balance begins to shift in favor of buying: "Comparing auto financing options," Consumer Reports, April 2008, www.consumerreports.org/cro/money/credit-loan/auto-lease-or-buy-4-08/overview/auto-lease-or-buy-ov.htm.

CAR RENTALS

All together, they take in more than $20 billion a year: www.carrentalexpress.com/theproof.htm; NauCarrental.com, April 24, 2008, http://naucarrental.com/article.cfm/id/284920.

Costs for renting a Ford Taurus and extras at Chicago O'Hare Airport: Hertz Car Rental, August 2008, www.hertz.com.

Save 25% with your Costco card at National, Alamo and Avis; or 20% at Hertz and Budget: Costco Travel, http://www.costcotravel.com/#11_rentalCars.

Save 20% with your AAA membership card on Premium car classes at Hertz or 15% on Economy through Full Size: American Automobile Association, www.AAA.com.

Houston's George Bush Intercontinental Airport had the most outrageous charges—its taxes increased the cost of renting by more than 66%: Travelocity press release, 3/29/05, http://news.travelocity.com/phoenix.zhtml?c=75787&p=irol-newsArticle&ID=689486.

Renting a Chevy Impala comparison between Minneapolis/St. Paul and Maplewood, MN: Rental rates from www.avis.com in September 2008. Cab fare rates from www.msairport.com. Cab fares are metered at a rate of $1.90 per mile as of September 2008 plus a $2.75 trip fee that is added to the final metered fare. Calculations based on 12 mile trip from MSP airport to Maplewood, MN.

Roughly a third of all rental-car customers sign up for it—paying as much as $40 a day for coverage most of them don't need: Gary Stoller, "Should you say yes to car rental insurance? It depends," *USA Today*, December 14, 2007, www.usatoday. com/money/perfi/insurance/2007-12-10-car-rental-insurance_N.htm.

At Hertz you'll pay $7 a day more to rent a Toyota Prius over a Ford Explorer. But you'll get more than double the gas mileage!: Hertz Car Rental, September 2008, www.hertz.com.

Cost of GPS per weekly rental: $59.75: Hertz Car Rental, JFK International Airport, NY, September 2008, www.hertz.com.

CAR REPAIRS

Car repair shops consistently rank among the Better Business Bureau's Top 10 most complained about industries: Better Business Bureau, http://us.bbb.org/WWWRoot/SitePage.aspx?site=113&id=ec2f39d2-b948-4f54-9959-01130dde2f61.

forced Sears to pay a $46 million settlement after it was sued for conning customers into unnecessary auto repairs and service in the 1990s: Ted Orme, "Keeping your car like new," *Kiplinger's New Cars and Trucks*, 1999, http://findarticles.com/p/articles/mi_m0BUZ/is_1999_Annual/ai_56203073/pg_2.

BANK ACCOUNTS

There are more bank branches in the United States than there are movie theaters or shopping malls—upwards of 91,000 by the most recent count: Federal Deposit Insurance Corporation, www.fdic. gov/bank/statistical/stats/2008jun/industry.html.

In all, there are more than 8,400 different banks with more than $10 trillion in assets and more than $1 trillion in capital: American Bankers Association, www.aba.com/Press+Room/banking_overview.htm.

Between 2000 and 2006, the total amount of fees U.S. banks collected from checking and savings customers climbed from $24 billion to $36 billion—a whopping 50% increase in just six years: David Ellis, "Americans in the dark over bank fees," CNNMoney.com, March 3, 2008, http://money. cnn.com/2008/03/03/news/companies/bank_fees/index.htm.

. . . the GAO investigators couldn't get complete answers at more than 20% of the branches they visited: Carolyn B. Maloney press release, "New GAO Report Finds Bank Fees Rising, Banks Failing to Provide Consumers with Info on Fees," March 3, 2008, http://maloney.house.gov/index.php?option=content&task=view&id=1579&Itemid=61.

the Federal Deposit Insurance Corp., which insures depositors against bank failures, is said to have a "watch list" of 117 institutions it regards as particularly risky: "FDIC Troubled Banks Rise to 117, Most in Five Years," CNBC, Reuters, August 26, 2008, http://www.cnbc.com/id/26408785.

It's called the Federal Deposit Insurance Corporation and it insures about $4.2 trillion worth of deposits at 8,451 banks and savings associations: "Then and Now: Changes Since the FDIC's Creation in 1933," FDIC Consumer News, Winter 2007/2008, www.fdic.gov/CONSUMERS/consumer/news/cnwin0708/thenandnow.html.

. . . as of August 2008, the FDIC had only about $45 billion in its Deposit Insurance Fund—just a bit more than 1% of those $4.2 trillion in deposits it is supposed to be protecting: FDIC press release, "Insured Bank and Thrift Earnings Fell to $5.0 Billion in Second Quarter," August 26, 2008, www.fdic.gov/news/news/press/2008/pr08070.html.

a transfer fee that could run anywhere from $5 (which is what Chase charges): Jessica Dickler, "Raw Deal: Overdraft protection," CNNMoney. com, August 20, 2008, http://money.cnn.com/2008/08/12/pf/raw_deal_overdraft/index.htm.

What most of the nation's biggest banks do is process them in the order of size, starting with the largest dollar amount and working down to the smallest: Kathy Chu, "Banks' check-clearing policies could leave you with overdrafts," *USA Today*, November 20, 2006, www.usatoday.com/money/industries/banking/2006-11-19-bank-usat_x.htm.

If you bank with BofA but make a withdrawal through, say, a Chase ATM, the transaction could cost you $5: $3 from Chase for using one of their machines—and $2 from BofA for not using one of theirs. In all, U.S. banks raked in $4.4 billion in ATM fees in 2007: Jessica Dickler, "Breaking the bank: ATM fees," CNNMoney.com, September 26, 2007, http://money.cnn.com/2007/09/17/pf/raw_deals_atm/index.htm.

Erroneous and fraudulent bank charges: "Answers about Bank Errors," Comptroller of the Currency Administrator of National Banks, www. helpwithmybank.gov/faqs/banking_errors.html#top.

DEBIT CARDS

In 2006, we used debit cards nearly 20% more often than credit cards—roughly 26 billion times in all. And the numbers have been growing steadily. Debit card purchases now total well over $1 trillion a year, accounting for two-thirds of all Visa transactions and half of Visa's dollar volume: "Debit-card Smarts," *Kiplinger's Personal Finance* magazine, August 2007; "The dark secrets of debit," *Consumer Reports*, September 2007, http://www.consumerreports.org/cro/money/

credit-loan/debit-cards/the-dark-secrets-of-debit-9-07/overview/the-dark-secrets-of-debit-ov.htm.

Debit cards are particularly popular among young people between the ages of 18 and 25 who use them instead of cash, even for small purchases. (Around 60% of debit card transactions involve less than $25.): "Debit-card Smarts," *Kiplinger's Personal Finance* magazine, August 2007.

According to calculations by Consumer Reports, *a typical overdraft fee on a debit card purchase translates to an annual interest rate in excess of 1,000%!* "The dark secrets of debit," *Consumer Reports,* September 2007, http://www.consumerreports.org/cro/money/credit-loan/debit-cards/the-dark-secrets-of-debit-9-07/overview/the-dark-secrets-of-debit-ov.htm.

According to the Center for Responsible Lending, on average the typical debit card transaction that spurs a $34 overdraft fee is for a $20 purchase!: Consumer Federation of America, http://www.consumerfed.org/pdfs/DOD_MLA_comments.pdf.

Wachovia Bank suggested in a direct mail promotion, "for ALL of your everyday purchases": "Debit rewards: More glitter than gold," *Consumer Reports,* http://www.consumerreports.org/cro/money/credit-loan/debit-cards/the-dark-secrets-of-debit-9-07/debit-rewards/the-dark-secrets-of-debit-debit-rewards.htm.

The overdraft fees alone that they generate bring in close to $9 billion a year. "The dark secrets of debit," *Consumer Reports,* September 2007, http://www.consumerreports.org/cro/money/credit-loan/debit-cards/the-dark-secrets-of-debit-9-07/overview/the-dark-secrets-of-debit-ov.htm.

Truth in Lending Act (Regulation Z): FDIC, http://www.fdic.gov/regulations/laws/rules/6500-1400.html.

Electronic Funds Transfer Act (Regulation E): FDIC, http://www.fdic.gov/regulations/laws/rules/6500-3100.html.

Last year, the Wall Street Journal *ran an article on an increasingly common debit card scam:* Joseph Pereira, "Thieves are using skimmers to target debit card readers," *Wall Street Journal,* March 18, 2007, http://findarticles.com/p/articles/mi_qn4188/is_/ai_n18741385.

As one expert put it to Consumer Reports: *"Debit cards may be fine for buying a cup of coffee but not so good to use for rental cars or hotel bills, where blocking can tie up hundreds of dollars.":* "The dark secrets of debit," *Consumer Reports,* September 2007, http://www.consumerreports.org/cro/money/credit-loan/debit-cards/the-dark-secrets-of-debit-9-07/overview/the-dark-secrets-of-debit-ov.htm.

CREDIT CARDS

As I write this in the summer of 2008, roughly 53 million American households are carrying nearly $1 trillion in credit card debt: Tim Westrich, "Problems with Plastic: Credit Card Debt Hits Record High," 4/18/08, www.americanprogress.org/issues/2008/04/plastic_problems.html; CardTrak.com www.cardtrak.com/press/2007.05.31.

In 2007 alone, those interest charges totaled $116 billion, while fees added another $23 billion to the industry's coffers: "Can credit card companies afford customers who don't carry a balance?" *Newsday,* January 18, 2008, www.newsday.com/news/columnists/ny-bzbrenner0120,0,2241008.column.

Credit card companies send out about 6 billion such solicitations a year: Tim Westrich, "Problems with Plastic: Credit Card Debt Hits Record High," April 18, 2008, www.americanprogress.org/issues/2008/04/plastic_problems.html.

... but more than a third of the credit-issuing banks in the United States do something even worse. They practice what's called double-cycle billing: Senator Carl Levin press release, November 3, 2006, http://levin.senate.gov/newsroom/release.cfm?id=265688.

... many card issuers have a daily cutoff—often 3 p.m. Eastern Standard Time—after which they will no longer credit your payment that day. And many won't process payments made on a holiday or a weekend until the following business day: Jennifer Wheary and Tamara Draut, "Who Pays? The Winners and Losers of Credit Card Deregulation," Demos.org, www.demos-usa.org/pubs/whopays_web.pdf.

Information relating to billing rights: Federal Trade Commission, http://www.ftc.gov/os/statutes/fcb/fcb.pdf; http://www.ftc.gov/bcp/edu/pubs/consumer/credit/cre16.shtm.

And you can only invoke this right if what you bought with your card cost more than $50 and was purchased within 100 miles of your mailing address: Lucy Lazarony, "The Basics: How to Dispute a Credit Card Purchase," Bankrate.com, http://moneycentral.msn.com/content/Banking/creditcardsmarts/P79885.asp.

CREDIT SCORES

As of 2008, the median FICO score in the U.S. was 723—meaning that half of all Americans scored higher than that and half scored lower: MyFICO, www.myfico.com.

... if it turns out you're right, the credit agency must correct or delete the bad information within 30 days: Equifax, www.equifax.com/answers/correct-credit-report-errors/en_cp.

PAYDAY LOANS

So she did what 19 million or so other Americans do every year: "Credit Unions Seek Payday Loan Consumers," NPR, October 15, 2007,www.npr. org/templates/story/story.php?storyId=15276522.

With upwards of 25,000 outlets across the country—more than Starbucks and McDonald's combined—payday lenders claim they are helping out cash-strapped wage earners by providing some $40 billion a year in short-term loans: "Financial Quicksand," Center for Responsible Lending, 11/30/06,www.responsiblelending.org/pdfs/rr012-Financial_Quicksand-1106.pdf.

typically with APRs as high as 400%—and sometimes more than 1,000%: Michelle Singletary, "Extend 'Payday Loan' Protections to All Borrowers," *Washington Post,* October 12, 2006, www.washingtonpost.com/wp-yn/content/ article/2006/10/11/AR2006101101453.html.

payday lenders charge around $17.50 for every $100 you borrow . . . some of these guys charge as much as $30 for a $100: "Beware Payday Loans," About.com, http://financialplan.about.com/od/ creditanddebt/a/PaydayLoan.htm.

IDENTITY THEFT

In 2007, identity theft was the Federal Trade Commission's No. 1 consumer complaint—for the eighth year in a row: Federal Trade Commission press release, February 3, 2008, http://www.ftc. gov/opa/2008/02/fraud.shtm.

It's an epidemic that affects roughly 10 million Americans who have their identities stolen each year, at a cost of nearly $50 billion: George John, "Prevent Identity Theft: Know the Facts," March 3, 2008, http://article.abc-directory.com/ article/3926; Federal Trade Commission, www.ftc. gov/bcp/edu/microsites/idtheft/consumers/about-identity-theft.html.

Each year Javelin Strategy & Research publishes their Identity Fraud Survey Report—said to be the largest, most up-to-date study of ID fraud in the U.S.: "2008 Identity Fraud Survey Report," Javelin Strategy and Research, February 2008, http://www.idsafety.net/803.R_2008%20Identity% 20Fraud%20Survey%20Report_Consumer%20 Version.pdf.

. . . a scam dubbed "vishing" is even less sophisticated and low tech yet has increased from 3% of identity theft in 2006 to 40% in 2007: "2008 Identity Fraud Survey Report," Javelin Strategy and Research, February 2008, http://www.idsafety. net/803.R_2008%20Identity%20Fraud%20Survey%20 Report_Consumer%20Version.pdf.

The Washington Post *recently ran an article on mobile phones—specifically "smartphones" like the Palm Treo and BlackBerry—that was quite an*

eye-opener: Ellen Nakashima. "Used Cell Phones Hold Trove of Secrets That Can Be Hard to Erase," *Wall Street Journal,* October 21, 2006, http://www.washingtonpost.com/wp-dyn/content/ article/2006/10/20/AR2006102001647_pf.html.

There are over 24 million customers who subscribe to credit monitoring through services like those offered by Equifax, Experian or TransUnion—paying between $60 to $180 a year for the peace of mind they may offer: "2008 Identity Fraud Survey Report," *Javelin Strategy and Research,* February 2008, http://www.idsafety.net/803.R_2008%20 Identity%20Fraud%20Survey%20Report_Consumer %20Version.pdf.

DIVORCE

The average woman experiences a 45% decrease in her standard of living after going through a divorce: Kay Bell, "Gather Documents and Know Assets to Keep from Losing Money in Divorce," Divorce 360, www.divorce360.com/articles/56/ financial-tips-for-women.aspx.

. . . the average man experiences a 15% improvement in his standard of living: Nathan Dawson, "Rebuilding Your Finances after Divorce," 101 Family Matters, http://101familymatters.com/7/ rebuilding-your-finances-after-divorce/.

Over the long term, U.S. government data show that a divorce reduces the average man's ability to earn a living as much as 40% below his married counterparts: Mark A. Fine & John H. Harvey, *Handbook of Divorce and Relationship Dissolution,* Routledge (2005), p. 393.

Judges generally won't set aside property settlements unless you can prove that the agreement was fundamentally unfair or that your ex committed fraud (such as hiding assets) during the negotiations: Jeanne M. Hammer, Family Lawyer, http:// traversecityfamilylaw.com/Pages/Property.htm.

LIFE INSURANCE

Americans have more than $20 trillion in life insurance coverage: "Life insurance basics," Insure. com, February 9, 2008, www.insure.com/articles/ lifeinsurance/basics.html.

According to the most recent statistics, about 60% of the policies sold in the U.S. are permanent policies, while about 40% are term: "2007 Life Insurers Fact Book," American Council of Life Insurers, October 25, 2007, www.acli.com/ACLI/ Tools/Industry+Facts/Life+Insurers+Fact+Book/ GR07-079.htm.

. . . a Smart Money *article exposed Metropolitan Life for charging their policyholders fees equal to 15% to 20% of the annual premium simply for the privilege of making monthly payments (rather than one lump sum yearly payment.):* Smart Money, "Ten Ways to Save on Life Insurance,"

September 2000, http://www.smartmoney.com/
personal-finance/insurance/10-ways-to-save-on-life-
insurance-8010/?page=all.

*. . . they are now 50 percent lower than they were a
decade ago:* Alan Lavine, "Term Insurance Premiums Falling," InsuranceNewsNet.com, August 19, 2008, http://www.insurancenewsnet.com/
article.asp?a=top_lh&id=97487.

ESTATE PLANNING

*If you die in 2009, your heirs won't have to pay any
taxes on the first $3.5 million of your estate. If you
die in 2010, they won't have to pay any estate taxes
at all, no matter how much you leave them. But if
you die in 2011, they will have to pay estate taxes
on everything over $1 million:* "Will You Owe
Estate Taxes?" *Smart Money* magazine, 1/9/07,
http://www.smartmoney.com/tax/homefamily/index.
cfm?story=estatetax; "Estate tax in the United
States"; Wikipedia, http://en.wikipedia.org/wiki/
Estate_tax_in_the_United_States.

*You can give up to $1 million to anyone you want
over the course of your lifetime without having to
pay any gift tax—and if you give away less than
$12,000 in any one year, it doesn't count towards
the $1-million total:* Internal Revenue Service,
www.irs.gov/businesses/small/article/0,,id=
108139,00.html.

SAVING FOR COLLEGE

*By 2024, the price tag for a bachelor's degree is ex-
pected to be more than twice what it was in 2007—
and in 2007, it was anything but cheap:*
"2007–2008 College Costs: Keep Rising Prices in
Perspective," College Board, http://www.college
board.com/parents/csearch/know-the-options/
21385.html; "Huge Gap Between College Costs,
What Families Save; Tax Deferred College Savings Plans Underused," Business Wire, April 30,
2001, http://findarticles.com/p/articles/mi_m0EIN/
is_/ai_73818312.

*These plans are hugely popular. At the beginning of
2008, parents of college-bound kids had invested
nearly $130 billion in them—and the numbers are
expected to keep rising:* College Savings Plans Network, www.collegesavings.org/didYouKnows.aspx.

HEALTH INSURANCE

*47 million Americans (including more than
8 million children) who don't have any coverage:*
"US health insurance costs rise nearly twice as
fast as pay: survey," AFP, September 12, 2007,
http://afp.google.com/article/ALeqM5gKHT3OO579
Mudwlh8Qt4ks51BBLQ.

*260 million who pay good money for policies that
often turn out to be rip-offs:* Current U.S. population is 305 million, according to www.census.gov/
population/www/popclockus.html. Less the 47

million who don't have health insurance leaves
260 million.

*. . . total health-care spending heading towards $3
trillion a year in the U.S.—and costs continuing to
increase at nearly three times the rate of inflation:*
"U.S. Health-Care Costs to Top $4 Trillion by
2016," *Forbes*, February 21, 2007, www.forbes.
com/forbeslife/health/feeds/hscout/2007/02/21/
hscout602078.html.

*. . . whenever someone submitted a claim, it was
standard procedure at Blue Cross of California to
pore over the person's medical records, looking for
some error or inaccuracy that could be used as an
excuse to cancel their policy. It took a class-action
lawsuit by 6,000 customers to get Blue Cross to
change its practices and agree to rescind policies
only if the mistakes were intentional:* "Blue Cross
Reaches Deal in Lawsuit over Policy Cancellations," *Medical News Today*, May 16, 2007,
www.medicalnewstoday.com/articles/70902.php.

*If you're one of the 180 million or so Americans
who get their health coverage through an employer:*
"Health Insurance in the United States,"
Wikipedia, http://en.wikipedia.org/wiki/Health_
insurance#Health_insurance_in_the_United_States.

*The average employee contribution for family
coverage totaled $278 a month in 2007:* "Health
Insurance Costs," National Coalition of Health
Care, www.nchc.org/facts/cost.shtml.

*Only 60% of all companies offer health coverage
to employees, and the number is dropping every
day:* "Health Insurance in the United States,"
Wikipedia, en.wikipedia.org/wiki/Health_
insurance#Health_insurance_in_the_United_States.

All HSA rules and details: Internal Revenue Service, www.irs.gov/publications/p969/index.html.

*Employers Mutual, American Benefit Plans, and
TRG have been scamming unwary consumers
out of millions of dollars:* Julie Appleby, "More
patients get stuck with the bills," *USA Today*,
5/1/02, www.fldfs.com/Consumers/unlicensed_
entities/ue_clips/5-01-02morepatients.html.

*According to government statistics, in one two-year
period some 144 phony health insurers followed
this pattern, leaving more than 200,000 consumers
on the hook for at least $252 million in unpaid
claims:* "Private Health Insurance: Unauthorized
or Bogus Entities Have Exploited Employers and
Individuals Seeking Affordable Coverage," U.S.
Government Accountability Office, 3/3/04,
www.gao.gov/products/GAO-04-512T.

HOSPITAL BILLS

*In 2007, Americans—insured as well as unin-
sured—spent $275 billion out of pocket on doctors
and hospitals:* C. Eugene Steuerle and Randall R.
Bovbjerg, "Health and Budget Reform as

Handmaidens," *Health Affairs*, http://content.
healthaffairs.org/cgi/content/abstract/27/3/633.

*Each year, some 700,000 families are forced into
bankruptcy because of health-care costs, while
another 80 million or so Americans struggle with
medical bills they can't afford to pay:* Maggie Fox,
"Half of Bankruptcy Due to Medical Bills—U.S.
Study," Reuters, February 2, 2005, www.common
dreams.org/headlines05/0202-08.htm; Amanda
Gardner. "79 Million Americans Struggle to Pay
Medical Bills," *Washington Post*, August 20,
2008, www.washingtonpost.com/wp-dyn/content/
article/2008/08/20/AR2008082001109.html.

*This routine surgery plus a typical two-night stay
rarely costs the hospital more than $5,000. If you're
covered by Medicare, the hospital will accept
roughly $4,700 for taking care of you. An HMO
will bill your insurance plan $7,000 to $8,000,
while Blue Cross Blue Shield will pay $9,000 to
$10,000:* Nora Johnson, medical billing advocate.
Interview with *FFYM* researcher Diana Dawson,
June 2008.

*You can expect to be billed $30,000 to $35,000 for
the same appendectomy—more than six times
what Medicare would pay.* Johnson interview,
June 2008.

*Experts say that 90% of all hospital bills contain
mistakes:* U.S. Securities and Exchange Commission, www.sec.gov/comments/s7-11-06/s71106-5.pdf.

*Surgical patients are typically charged something
like $70 a minute for their use of the operating
room:* Johnson interview, June 2008.

*Hospitals have been known to ding patients as
much as $70 or $80 for a bag of IV saline that actually costs no more than 10 cents. One uninsured
woman in her seventies who fell and broke her
thighbone was charged $201,000 for a 19-day stay
in a New Jersey hospital. Among other things, the
hospital billed her nearly $6,000 for a box of non-
sterile, disposable latex gloves that you could buy at
Staples for $7.99. Another hospital billed a child
patient $57.50 for what the bill described as a
"cough support device." It was actually an inexpensive teddy bear.* Johnson interview, June 2008.

*The income ceilings for charity care are often much
higher than people think, ranging as high as 400%
of the federal poverty income guidelines:* Kaiser
Permanente. members.kaiserpermanente.org/
kpweb/pdf/feature/092communityinvolve/ policy_
financial.pdf.

*And don't assume the hospital staff knows the
score. One recent study:* "Options for Avoiding
and Managing Medical Debt," National Endow-
ment for Financial Education, 2006, http://
healthinsuranceinfo.net/managing-medical-bills/
Avoid_and_Manage_Medical_Debt.pdf.

*More than 4,200 of the nation's hospitals have
pledged to abide by those principles:* American
Hospital Association, www.aha.org/aha_app/
issues/BCC/index.jsp.

HEALTH CLUB MEMBERSHIPS

*the health-club industry rakes in revenues of close
to $20 billion a year. Nor is it surprising that the
Better Business Bureau reports that complaints
about health clubs have nearly doubled in recent
years:* Jackie Crosby, "Pumping up the fitness
franchises," *StarTribune*, July 19, 2008, www.
startribune.com/business/25627784.html?page=
3&c=y; "Joining a Gym? Complaints to BBB reveal how to get fit while avoiding the pitfalls,"
Better Business Bureau, December 27, 2008,
http://us.bbb.org/WWWRoot/SitePage.aspx?site=113
&id=1869d6a9-82aa-49a1-8419-40a8251fa916&
art=2709.

roughly 30,000 health clubs in the U.S. today:
International Health, Racquet and Sportsclub
Association, http://cms.ihrsa.org/index.cfm?
fuseaction=Page.viewPage&pageId=19547&
nodeID=15.

*a quarter of all the billing complaints they get
regarding health clubs come from people who continued to have money taken out of their checking
accounts even after they felt their contracts had
expired or been cancelled:* "Joining a Gym?
Complaints to BBB reveal how to get fit while
avoiding the pitfalls," Better Business Bureau,
December 28, 2007, http://us.bbb.org/WWWRoot/
SitePage.aspx?site=113&id=1869d6a9-82aa-49a1-
8419-40a8251fa916&art=2709.

BUYING A HOME

*there are roughly 3.2 million real estate agents in
the United States—roughly 60% more than just
three years ago:* The Association of Real Estate
License Law Officials, www.arello.org/Common_
Area/default.cfm.

*Only six states—Colorado, Kansas, Maryland,
Oklahoma, Texas, and Vermont—actually prohibit agents from representing both sides in a
transaction:* Aaron Cahall, "Real estate double
agents represent buyer and seller," Columbia
News Service, May 8, 2007, http://jscms.jrn.
columbia.edu/cns/2007-05-08/cahall-doubleagents.

*state investigators in Massachusetts made under-
cover visits to 45 real estate offices to see if they
were giving new clients a dual-agent disclosure
form, as the law required. None of them were:*
Tina Cassidy and Karen Curran, "Realtors
breaking state's disclosure laws," *Boston Globe*,
March 29, 1997, www.realtyplan.com/homes/press/
theotherguys.htm.

*In New York State alone, a kickback scheme run by
the nation's four biggest title insurance firms cost*

homebuyers hundreds of millions of dollars, according to a federal antitrust suit filed in 2008: John R. Wilke, "Scrutiny tightens for title insurers," *Denver Post*, 2/12/08, www.denverpost.com/ci_8239825?source=rss.

Similar charges in California led state regulators to slam the same four companies—which together control more than 90% of the title-insurance business—with $49 million in fines and penalties: "The Title insurance toll," *Los Angeles Times*, February 10, 2008, http://articles.latimes.com/2008/feb/10/business/fi-title10.

In California, title insurance for a $500,000 home will cost you $1,200 to $2,000. In Iowa, coverage for a $500,000 home costs just $110: "The Title insurance toll," *Los Angeles Times*, February 10, 2008, http://articles.latimes.com/2008/feb/10/business/fi-title10.

HOME MORTGAGES

By the end of 2007, mortgage delinquencies were skyrocketing, real estate values were tumbling, the banks were facing losses of close to a trillion and as many as 6 million Americans were in imminent danger of losing their homes to foreclosure: Anna Bahney, "Housing rescue bill may fall short; who benefits?" *USA Today*, July 28, 2008, www.usatoday.com/money/economy/housing/2008-07-26-housing-bailout-bill_N.htm.

. . . which is where standard 30-year fixed-rate mortgages are as I write this: Bankrate.com, www.bankrate.com/brm/rate/mtg_home.asp.

90% of the folks who took out sub-prime loans from 1998 to 2006 were already homeowners: Maura Reynolds, "Refinancing spurred subprime crisis," *Los Angeles Times*, July 5, 2008, http://www.latimes.com/business/la-fi-refi5-2008jul05,0,7891725.story.

Annual premiums typically run around 0.5% of the loan amount for the first few years (so the cost for a $300,000 mortgage would be $1,500 a year): Mortgage QnA, www.mortgageqna.com/mortgage-insurance/private-mortgage-insurance-pmi-rates.html.

By law, on all mortgages signed on or after July 29, 1999, you have the right to request that your PMI be cancelled once your LTV falls to 80% based on the original property value. What's more, your lender is required to automatically cancel your PMI when you hit 78%, provided you have a good payment record and don't have a second mortgage or home equity loan on the house: Federal Trade Commission, www.ftc.gov/bcp/conline/pubs/alerts/pmialrt.shtm.

HOME BUILDING AND REMODELING

According to a 2007 Consumer Federation of America survey of 39 consumer-protection agencies in 25 states, home improvement and contractor-related complaints are the second most common consumer problem in the U.S.—and the fastest growing category: "2007 Consumer Complaint Survey Report," Consumer Federation of America, July 30, 2008, www.consumerfed.org/pdfs/07_complaint_report.pdf.

In California alone, the Contractors State License Board investigates more than 20,000 complaints each year against contractors: Jane Hulse, "Digging: You're your job," *Los Angeles Times*, July 13, 2008, http://articles.latimes.com/2008/jul/13/realestate/re-contractor13.

Despite the risks, more than 100,000 Americans build custom homes each year and millions more undertake remodeling projects: "New Privately Owned Housing Units Started in the United States by Purpose and Design," U.S. Census Bureau, www.census.gov/const/www/quarterly_starts_completions.pdf.

Given that we spend a total of more than $300 billion annually on home repair and remodeling projects—plus another $50 billion or so on custom home building: Construction Spending August 2008, U.S. Census Bureau, www.census.gov/constructionspending.

One of the main protections homeowners have is that a subcontractor or supplier can't file a mechanic's lien unless he previously filed a notice of intent when he first started work: Leon A. Frechette, "Lien Laws," AskToolTalk.com, www.asktooltalk.com/articles/construction/contractor/lien.php; Paul Peterson, "Mechanics' Lien Issues," American Bar Association, www.abanet.org/rppt/meetings_cle/2005/fall/PauPeterson.pdf.

HOME-BASED BUSINESS OPPORTUNITIES

According to the most recent government statistics, more than 2.4 million Americans are duped each year by would-be employers promising work-at-home paydays that never materialized: "Consumer Fraud in the United States," Federal Trade Commission, October 2007, www.ftc.gov/opa/2007/10/fraud.pdf.

In fact, in 2007, thousands of people around the country responded to a classified ad claiming you could earn at least $17.50 an envelope and be guaranteed a weekly income of as much as $1,400. All you had to do to get started was pay a $45 registration fee. By the time federal authorities caught up with him, the Florida man who had placed the ad had swindled more than 25,000 people out of more than $1.2 million: Federal Trade Commission news release, "Work-at-Home Marketer Settles FTC Charges in Envelope Stuffing Scheme," 4/28/08, www.ftc.gov/opa/2008/04/workathome.shtm.

401(K) PLANS

... as of August 2008, the average retired worker in this country was receiving a monthly Social Security check of just $1,086.10. This works out to $13,033.20 a year: U.S. Social Security Administration, www. ssa.gov/policy/docs/quickfacts/stat_snapshot/.

... these big financial services companies are able to siphon more than $150 billion a year out of our 401(k) accounts. That's more than 3% of all the money we've got invested in them—meaning that 401(k) participants' plans have to earn more than 3% a year just to break even!: February 1, 2008, radio interview on *Marketplace Money* with Matthew Hutcheson, marketplace.publicradio. org/display/web/2008/02/01/avoiding_ hidden_401k_fees/.

As of March 2008, some 55 million American workers had more than $4.3 trillion invested in defined contribution plans like the 401(k) and its cousins. By 2015, experts predict we'll have nearly twice that much invested: "The U.S. Retirement Market, First Quarter 2008," Investment Company Institute, www.ici.org/stats/latest/retmrkt_ update.pdf; Dave Carpenter, "Study: Defined contribution plans quickly changing," *USA Today,* June 26, 2008, www.usatoday.com/money/ economy/2008-06-26-2592203825_x.htm.

Most people who sign up for 401k plans contribute around 4% of their income: http://finance.yahoo. com/expert/article/millionaire/46383.

As of 2009, the IRS allows you put up to $16,500 a year into a 401k plan. If you are over age 50, you can contribute up to $22,500 a year. In 2010 and beyond, the ceilings will be adjusted annually to keep up with inflation: Internal Revenue Service, 401(k) Resource Guide, www.irs.gov/retirement/ participant/article/0,,id=151786,00.html.

This is great, since the participation rate at companies that have automatic enrollment is roughly double that of companies that don't: Andrew Balls, "The Path of Least Resistance in 401(k) Plans," National Bureau of Economic Research, www. nber.org/digest/apr02/w8651.html.

More than 80% of all 401k plans offer them as an option, and as of the middle of 2008, they held more than $204 billion in assets—nearly 100% more than they did in 2006: Emily Brandon, "Questions to Ask About Your Target Date Fund," *U.S. News & World Report,* September 8, 2008, www.usnews.com/articles/business/ retirement/2008/09/08/questions-to-ask-about-your- target-date-fund.html; Lauren Young, "Target Date Funds Hit Their Stride," *BusinessWeek,* July 3, 2008, www.businessweek.com/magazine/ content/08_28/b4092054950813.htm.

... that some experts believe that by 2013 they will account for 75% of all 401(k) assets, New York Times, April 6, 2008, www.nytimes.com/2008/ 04/06/business/mutfund/06target.html?scp=1&sq= target+date+fund&st=nyt.

As of the summer of 2008, there were roughly 40 companies offering more than 250 individual target-date funds to choose from, with new ones coming onto the market just about every other day: Daren Fonda, "Target Date Funds that Hit the Mark," *Smart Money,* January 17, 2008, www. smartmoney.com/investing/mutual-funds/Target- Date-Funds-That-Hit-the-Mark-22420/.

According to a calculation that Vanguard did for the New York Times, a 35-year-old with $20,000 in his 401k who takes out and repays two loans over the next 15 years will end up at age 65 with about $38,000 less than someone who never borrowed: Ron Lieber, "When Credit Gets Tight, a 401(k) Loan Becomes Tempting, "*New York Times,* April 5, 2008, www.nytimes.com/2008/ 07/05/business/yourmoney/05money.html?_ r=1&scp=1&sq=401(k)%20borrowing%20 Vanguard&st=cse&oref=slogin.

one government regulator told Bloomberg News, "This is close to a predatory lending practice": Ron Lieber, "When Credit Gets Tight, a 401(k) Loan Becomes Tempting," *New York Times,* April 5, 2008, www.nytimes.com/2008/07/05/business/ yourmoney/05money.html?partner=rssnyt&emc=rss.

According to experts, when you figure in these fees and other hidden charges, the average 401k plan actually costs its participants somewhere between 3% and 3½% of what they've got invested each year. And in some cases the cost is as high as 5%: 2/1/08 radio interview on Marketplace Money with Matthew Hutcheson, http://marketplace. publicradio.org/display/web/2008/02/01/avoiding_ hidden_401k_fees/.

In 2006 and 2008, workers at a number of giant corporations (including Wal-Mart, Boeing, Deere, and General Dynamics) sued their employers for saddling them with unnecessarily expensive investment choices. What the companies did was to give 401k participants a choice of only "retail" mutual funds, which charge relatively high management fees, instead of the lower-priced institutional funds that are available to large clients: Corey Himrod, "401(k) Update: Wal-mart Strikes Back Against 401(k) Lawsuit," WalmartWatch.com, July 23, 2008, http://walmartwatch.com/blog/archives/401k_ update_wal_mart_strikes_back_against_401k_ lawsuit/.

The suit against Wal-Mart says the company's practices cost its employees $60 million over six years: Corey Himrod, "401(k) Update: Wal-mart Strikes Back Against 401(k) Lawsuit," Walmart- Watch.com, July 23, 2008, http://walmartwatch. com/blog/archives/401k_update_wal_mart_strikes_ back_against_401k_lawsuit/.

Although the number of companies offering automatic enrollment is increasing, nearly 60% of employers still require workers to join on their own: Emily Brandon, "A 401(k) Automatic Enrollment Snapshot," *U.S. News & World Report* blog, July 29, 2008, www.usnews.com/blogs/planning-to-retire/2008/7/29/a-401k-automatic-enrollment-snapshot.html.

When the company was flying high in the late 1990s, most of them had loaded up their 401k accounts with Enron stock. Then, in 2001, Enron collapsed, costing them their jobs—and nearly 60% of their retirement assets: Patrick J. Purcell, "The Enron Bankruptcy and Employer Stock in Retirement Plans," CRS Report for Congress, 1/22/02, www.appwp.org/documents/rs_21115.pdf.

Some 7,000 employees of the fallen Wall Street giant Bear Stearns suffered the same fate in 2008, losing both their jobs and a big chunk of their life savings as the value of their company stock plunged from nearly $170 a share to less than $10: Bear Stearns, Wikipedia, http://en.wikipedia.org/wiki/Bear_Stearns.

And look what happened to Lehman Brothers, whose stock went from $82 a share in the summer of 2007 to zero a year later: Lehman Bros, Wikipedia, http://en.wikipedia.org/wiki/Lehman_Bros.

IRAS

. . . for most of us, the equivalent of roughly $13,000 a year: U.S. Social Security Administration, www.ssa.gov/policy/docs/quickfacts/stat_snapshot/.

As long as your joint adjusted gross income is less than $159,000, your contribution is fully deductible: Publication 590 (2007), Individual Retirement Arrangements, Internal Revenue Service, www.irs.gov/publications/p590/index.html.

The income ceiling is $110,000 if you're single or $160,000 if you're married and file a joint return: Publication 590 (2007), Individual Retirement Arrangements, Internal Revenue Service, www.irs.gov/publications/p590/index.html.

In 2009, the maximum is $5,000 a year plus an extra $1,000 "catch-up contribution" for people 50 or older. In 2010 and beyond, the limits rise with inflation in $500 increments: Publication 590 (2007), Individual Retirement Arrangements, Internal Revenue Service, www.irs.gov/publications/p590/index.html.

Surveys show that slightly more than half of all baby boomers—that giant generation that's currently reaching retirement age—do not plan to quit their jobs when they hit 65. In fact, three out of four current retirees still do some sort of work: Stephen Ohlemacher, "Many Baby Boomers Plan to Retire Late," CBS News, June 12, 2007, www.cbsnews.com/stories/2007/06/12/national/main2917476.shtml.

IRA penalty exceptions: Publication 590 (2007), Individual Retirement Arrangements, Internal Revenue Service, www.irs.gov/publications/p590/index.html.

PENSION PLANS

four out of five government workers are still covered by them . . . one out of five private-sector workers is entitled to a pension: National Compensation Survey, released by U.S. Department of Labor, August 2007.

44 million American workers are covered by some 30,000 defined benefit plans backed by a total of more than $6 trillion in assets: U.S. Dept. of Labor, http://www.dol.gov/_sec/media/reports/annual2007/SG4.pdf; "The U.S. Retirement Market, First Quarter 2008," Investment Company Institute, www.ici.org/stats/latest/retmrkt_update.pdf.

Four out of five state pension plans are currently underfunded, with one in five having less than 70% of the assets it will need: "2007 Wilshire Report on State Retirement Systems: Funding Levels and Asset Allocation," Wilshire Associates, March 5, 2007, www.wilshire.com/BusinessUnits/Consulting/Investment/2007_State_Retirement_Funding_Report.pdf.

69% of married women go for the single life payment, while 72% of married men choose the joint payment option: Urban Institute study, "Single Life vs Joint and Survivor Pension Payout Options: How Do Married Retirees Choose," September 1, 2003, www.urban.org/publications/410877.html.

Starting in 2009, all private plans were required to send participants an annual funding notice that lists their assets and liabilities, funded status over the past three years, and how their assets are invested: Pension Rights Center, www.pensionrights.com/policy/legislation/ppa_2006/pension_funding_notices.html.

airline pilots saw their benefits reduced by as much as 75% when Delta, United, U.S. Airways, and Aloha Airlines all ended their pension plans: Kelly Yamanouchi, "Grounded Life Wasn't for Pilot," *Denver Post,* June 5, 2007, http://www.denverpost.com/obituaries/ci_6061482?source=bb; Dale Russakoff, "Human Toll of a Pension Default," *Washington Post,* June 13, 2005, www.washingtonpost.com/wp-dyn/content/article/2005/06/12/AR2005061201367.html.

The maximum PBGC benefit for plans that ended in 2008 was $51,750 for those retiring at 65 and $23,288 for those retiring at 55: "PBGC Announces Maximum Insurance Benefit for 2008," Pension Benefit Guaranty Corporation press release, 10/30/07, www.pbgc.gov/media/news-archive/news-releases/2007/pr08-07.html.

as of 2007, the PBGC's long-term obligations exceeded its assets by some $14 billion: Amy Schatz, "Pension Benefit Guaranty to Diversify Portfolio," *Wall Street Journal*, February 18, 2008, http://online.wsj.com/article/SB120338429118775777.html.

SOCIAL SECURITY

In 2008, it paid out $608 billion in benefits— nearly 21% of the entire federal budget and more than 4% of the nation's gross domestic product. While the average benefit is only slightly more than $13,000 a year, that's enough to keep an estimated 40% of all Americans age 65 or older, who would otherwise be struggling, out of poverty: Wikipedia, en.wikipedia.org/wiki/Social_Security_(United_States)#cite_note-4.

by 2017 Social Security will be paying out more in retirement benefits than it collects in payroll taxes. By 2041, the experts say, those reserves will be gone and, unless new revenue sources are found, the system will have only enough money to pay retirees about three-quarters of what it pays them now: Social Security Administration, "Status of the Social Security and Medicare Program: A Summary of the 2008 Annual Reports," www.ssa.gov/OACT/TRSUM/index.html.

most people who apply for Social Security disability benefits these days are rejected initially: Barbara Basler, "Backlog of Claims Leaves Social Security Recipients Waiting," *AARP Bulletin Today,* November 2007, http://bulletin.aarp.org/yourmoney/socialsecurity/articles/sick_of_waiting.html.

disability claims have doubled since 2001 and the Social Security Administration is swamped with a backlog of cases. As a result, most initial disability applications are routinely denied: Barbara Basler, "Backlog of Claims Leaves Social Security Recipients Waiting," *AARP Bulletin Today,* November 2007, http://bulletin.aarp.org/yourmoney/social security/articles/sick_of_waiting.html.

ANNUITIES

According to a survey by AARP Financial . . . : "When it comes to financial jargon, Americans are Befuddled," AARP Financial Inc., April 17, 2008, www.aarp.org/aarp/presscenter/pressrelease/articles/when_it_comes_to_financial_jargon_americans_are_befuddled.html.

insurance companies do pay agents up-front commissions as high as 15% of the amount of every annuity they sell: Pat Curry, "Why Annuity Sales Have Skyrocketed," Bankrate.com, www.bankrate.com/brm/news/investing/20010807a.asp.

ONLINE SHOPPING AND AUCTIONS

Internet sales scams—particularly those involving online auctions—are among the fastest growing

category of consumer complaints: Consumer Federation of America press release, "Survey Identifies America's Top Consumer Complaints," July 30, 2008, www.consumerfed.org/pdfs/07_complaint_release.pdf.

About half of all the complaints about online shopping involve problems related to Internet auctions: Internet Crime Complaint Center press release, "Reported Dollar Loss From Internet Crime Reaches All Time High," April 3, 2008, www.ic3.gov/media/2008/080403.aspx.

Know your rights. Federal regulations can be found at: Federal Trade Commission, "Selling on the Internet: Prompt Delivery Rules," www.ftc.gov/bcp/edu/pubs/business/alerts/alt051.shtm.

In June 2008, a French court ordered eBay to pay a $63-million judgment for allowing counterfeit Louis Vuitton bags, Christian Dior clothing, and Guerlain, Kenzo, and Givenchy perfume to be sold on its site. Luxury brands like Hermès and Rolex won similar cases against eBay in previous years: "Court fines eBay over fake goods," BBC News, June 30, 2008, http://news.bbc.co.uk/2/hi/business/7481241.stm.

APPLIANCE PROTECTION PLANS/ EXTENDED WARRANTIES

Americans buy upwards of 100 million appliance protection plans and extended warranties each year, spending a total of more than $9 billion annually: Leslie Pepper, "Should You Buy An Extended Warranty?" *Parade*, February 10, 2008, www.parade.com/articles/editions/2008/edition_02-10-2008/Extended_Warranty.

A retailer typically keeps at least half—and often more—of the purchase price of every extended warranty he or she sells: "Why you don't need an extended warranty," *Consumer Reports,* November 2007, www.consumerreports.org/cro/money/news/november-2006/why-you-dont-need-an-extended-warranty-11-06/overview/extended-warranty-11-06.htm.

Experts estimate that for every 100 warranties sold on electronics and appliances, only 15 people ever file a claim: Leslie Pepper, "Should You Buy An Extended Warranty?" *Parade*, February 10, 2008, www.parade.com/articles/editions/2008/edition_02-10-2008/Extended_Warranty.

According to the Los Angeles Times, Amazon.com's extended warranty lists 35 cases in which protection doesn't apply, including "plasma TVs used in altitude levels above 6,000 feet above sea level": Michelle Quinn, "Extended warranty firm touts quick fix," *Los Angeles Times*, December 17, 2007,www.latimes.com/business/la-fi-warranties-17dec17,1,7648303.story?coll=la-headlines-business.

In 2007, an Ohio-based company called Ultimate Warranty went bankrupt, leaving nearly 140,000 customers who had paid upwards of $45 million for extended warranties holding contracts not worth the paper they were printed on: Alina Tugend, "For Extended Car Warranties, Resist the Showroom Pitch," *New York Times*, August 2, 2008, www.nytimes.com/2008/08/02/business/yourmoney/02shortcuts.html?pagewanted=print.

Apple offers first-rate tech support for its Macs, but it's free only for the first 90 days. After that, the company charges $49 for every phone call—unless you buy its three-year AppleCare warranty, in which case you can make as many tech-support calls as you want for no extra charge: Apple Inc., www.apple.com/support/programs/.

GIFT CARDS

In 2007, nearly 200 million Americans spent roughly $97 billion on gift cards. But the recipients of those cards used them to make only about $89 billion worth of purchases: "Why let unused gift cards go to waste?" Associated Press, December 20, 2007, www.msnbc.msn.com/id/22348233/.

29 states have passed laws imposing restrictions on gift cards: National Conference of State Legislators, www.ncsl.org/programs/banking/GiftCardsandCerts.htm.

Starbucks gift cards are not good at many Starbucks outlets in airports, supermarkets, and bookstores: "Watch for these gotchas," *Consumer Reports*, December 2007, http://www.consumerreports.org/cro/money/shopping/shopping-tips/gift-card-pitfalls-12-07/watch-for-these-gotchas/gift-card-pitfalls-watch-for-these-gotchas.htm.

... if you buy a Visa-branded US Bank gift card online, you'll be charged $6.95 for delivery ... but after that it's 50 cents a call—$1, if you insist on talking to a human being ... After six months, if you haven't used the card, what's called a dormancy fee kicks in: "2007 Gift Card Study comparison chart," Bankrate.com, http://www.bankrate.com/brm/news/cc/20071112_gift_card_results_a1.asp?caret=2.

When Sharper Image declared bankruptcy in 2008, it stopped accepting its gift cards—leaving consumers stuck with an estimated $25 million of suddenly worthless plastic: Marty Orgel, "Not worth the plastic they're printed on," *MarketWatch*, March 3, 2008, http://www.marketwatch.com/news/story/bankruptcies-often-leave-consumers-holding/story.aspx?guid=DCBBEB36-F293-4EDF-B2DC-1F515E91A746.

Crate & Barrel and Starbucks won't replace a lost or stolen card unless it's been registered: "Watch for these gotchas," *Consumer Reports*, December 2007, http://www.consumerreports.org/cro/money/shopping/shopping-tips/gift-card-pitfalls-12-07/watch-for-these-gotchas/gift-card-pitfalls-watch-for-these-gotchas.htm.

REBATE OFFERS

As New York Senator Charles Schumer put it in a letter to the Federal Trade Commission a few Christmases ago: "[R]ebates unfailingly bring in billions in excess profits for companies that offer them, but when it comes to saving the shopper a dime, as rebates claim to do, they fail the consumer more often than not": Schumer press release, January 2, 2006, http://www.senate.gov/~schumer/SchumerWebsite/pressroom/press_releases/2006/PR01.Rebate.010205.html.

According to experts, an attractive-sounding rebate can goose the sales of a product by as much as 500%. So every year companies offer some 400 million of them worth roughly $8 billion on products ranging from cars to cell phones to computer software to food: Kimberly Palmer, "Why Shoppers Love to Hate Rebates," *U.S. News & World Report*, January 18, 2008, www.usnews.com/articles/business/your-money/2008/01/18/why-shoppers-love-to-hate-rebates.html; "States make grab for unclaimed rebates," *Minneapolis Star-Tribune*, May 31, 2008, www.startribune.com/business/19379034.html?page=2&c=y.

TAX PREPARATION

we spend upwards of $11 billion on it each year: 2008 Barnes Reports published by the U.S. Tax Preparation Services Industry, http://www.barnes-reports.com/Tax%20Preparation%20Services-Definition.pdf.

Six in ten taxpayers hire someone to help them fill out the forms and calculate what they owe, while millions more rely on computer programs like TurboTax: Janet Paskin, "10 Things Your Tax Preparer Won't Tell You," *Smart Money*, February 19, 2008, www.smartmoney.com/spending/rip-offs/10-things-your-tax-preparer-wont-tell-you-22581/.

only two states, California and Oregon, require tax preparers to be licensed: Janet Paskin, "10 Things Your Tax Preparer Won't Tell You," *Smart Money*, February 19, 2008, www.smartmoney.com/spending/rip-offs/10-things-your-tax-preparer-wont-tell-you-22581/.

In a 2006 investigation, the Government Accountability Office sent staffers to 19 different chain outlets to have an imaginary couple's taxes done. According to its report, "nearly all of the returns prepared for us were incorrect to some degree": Janet Paskin, "10 Things Your Tax Preparer Won't Tell You," *Smart Money*, February 19, 2008, www.smartmoney.com/spending/rip-offs/10-things-your-tax-preparer-wont-tell-you-22581/; Albert B. Crenshaw, "Some Tax Preparers Don't Add Up," *Washington Post*, April 6, 2006, www.washingtonpost.com/wp-dyn/content/article/2006/04/04/AR2006040401863.html.

a total fee of $200 or so for an itemized return at H&R Block: "Should you do your own taxes this year?" *Consumer Reports*, January 2008, www. consumerreports.org/cro/money/news/2006/02/ should-you-do-your-own-taxes-this-year-206/ overview/.

REFUND ANTICIPATION LOANS

That's probably why about 9 million of us sign up for them each year: "Many Taxpayers Who Obtain Refund Anticipation Loans Could Benefit From Free Tax Preparation Services," U.S. Department of the Treasury, August 29, 2008, www. ustreas.gov/tigta/auditreports/2008reports/2008401 70fr.pdf.

They rake in more than $1 billion a year providing these virtually riskless loans: Herb Weisman, "In a hurry to get your refund? Beware," MSNBC, February 7, 2008, www.msnbc.msn.com/ id/23036078/.

APRs as high as 1,200%: Herb Weisman, "In a hurry to get your refund? Beware," MSNBC, February 7, 2008, www.msnbc.msn.com/ id/23036078/.

In addition to charging you 36% annual interest on your RAL, they also tack on a $29.95 activation fee and a $20 check processing fee: H&R Block, www.hrblock.com/taxes/pdf/2008_RAL_pricing_tool. pdf.

CHARITABLE GIVING

According to an investigation by the Los Angeles Times: Doug Smith and Charles Piller, "The Give and Take for Charity," *Los Angeles Times*, July 6, 2008, http://articles.latimes.com/2008/jul/06/local/ me-charity6.

U.S. charities raise more than $300 billion a year in pledges and donations: Tim J. Mueller, "Donating your money do's and don'ts," *USA Today*, October 7, 2008, www.usatoday.com/news/nation/ charity/2008-10-07-donation-dodont_N.htm?loc= interstitialskip.

CABLE AND SATELLITE TV

experts estimate that we consumers fork out as much as $6 billion a year more than we should: Michelle N. Hankins, "The Bundles and Ties that Bind: Debating Cable a la Carte," *Billing World and OSS Magazine*, September 1, 2004, www. billingworld.com/articles/feature/The-Bundles-and-Ties-that-Bind-Debating.html.

cable rates have nearly doubled since Congress deregulated them in the mid-1990s: "FCC Report Recommends More Cable Choices," Consumer Affairs.com, April 30, 2007, www.consumeraffairs. com/news04/2007/04/cable_choice.html.

15 million U.S. households still get their TV the old-fashioned way—with an over-the-air antenna: Doug Lung, "FCC: 14 Percent of Viewers Depend on Off-Air TV Signals," *TV Technology*, November 30, 2007, www.tvtechnology.com/ article/18732.

65 million of the nation's 110 million TV households are wired for cable, while around 30 million homes subscribe to one of the nation's two DBS (for direct satellite broadcast) services, DirecTV and EcoStar's Dish Network: Danny King, "Dish Subscribers Dip as Sales Meet Expectations," *TVWeek*, August 4, 2008, www.tvweek.com/ news/2008/08/dish_subscribers_dip_as_sales.php.

fiber-optic networks being built mainly by Verizon and AT&T—had attracted around a half-million subscribers: Danny King, "Dish Subscribers Dip as Sales Meet Expectations," *TVWeek*, August 4, 2008, www.tvweek.com/news/2008/08/dish_ subscribers_dip_as_sales.php.

More than 98% of all communities wired for cable are served by only one provider: "Business Review Letter Request by The National Cable Television Cooperative, Inc.," U.S. Department of Justice Antitrust Division, October 17, 2003, www.usdoj. gov/atr/public/busreview/201379.htm.

CELL PHONE PLANS

there are now 3.3 billion cell phones: Wikipedia, "Mobile Phones," http://en.wikipedia.org/wiki/ Mobile_phone.

there are more than 262 million wireless subscribers in the U.S.—roughly 86% of the population— yakking away on their cell phones an average of 23 minutes a day: "CTIA – The Wireless Association Releases Latest Wireless Industry Survey Results," www.ctia.org/media/press/body.cfm/prid/1772; CTIA-The Wireless Association, "Mid-Year 2008 Top-Line Survey Results," http://files.ctia.org/pdf/ CTIA_Survey_Mid_Year_2008_Graphics.pdf.

In all, Americans spend nearly $150 billion a year on wireless phone services. The average bill runs $48.54 a month: CTIA-The Wireless Association, "CTIA—The Wireless Association Releases Latest Wireless Industry Survey Results," www.ctia. org/media/press/body.cfm/prid/1772.

experts estimate that the average cell phone user lets 40% of his plan minutes go to waste: TracPoint Wireless, http://tracpointwireless.com/Minuteguard. html.

the cell phone population exploded by nearly 700% between 1995 and 2007: CTIA-The Wireless Association, "Mid-Year 2008 Top-Line Survey Results," http://files.ctia.org/pdf/CTIA_Survey_Mid_ Year_2008_Graphics.pdf.

For example, while T-Mobile's basic national plan gives you 1,000 minutes for $49.95 a month, its regional plan gives you 3,000 minutes for the same price—though calls made from outside the region or to a number outside the region will cost you 49 cents a minute. Similarly, for $39.99 you can get a national plan from Alltel that includes 500 minutes or a regional one that gives you 700 minutes: T-Mobile, www.t-mobile.com; Alltel, www.alltel. com.

as a result of a series of class-action lawsuits filed against a number of the major carriers, all of them have begun prorating their fees—meaning that the further along you are in your contract, the lower the fee: "Cell Phone Plans," Consumer Search, www.consumersearch.com/www/electronics/cell-phone-plans/review.html.

TV report on lost and stolen cell phones: CBS 5 ConsumerWatch report by Jeanette Pavini, http://cbs5.com/.

RESIDENTIAL PHONE SERVICE

Numbers for landline phone subscribers in the U.S.: Laura M. Holson, "Phone Giants Fight to Keep Subscribers," New York Times, July 23, 2008, www.nytimes.com/2008/07/23/technology/23phone. html.

four out of five residential phone customers stick with the established local company: Kim Leonard, "Customer loyalty on the line for local phone companies," Pittsburgh Tribune, February 6, 2005, www.pittsburghlive.com/x/pittsburghtrib/s_300303.html.

Companies like Lingo, Packet8, VoIP.com, and Vonage offer unlimited local and long-distance calling for around $25 a month: "Residential VoIP Comparison," MyVoipProvider.com, www. myvoipprovider.com/Residential_VoIP_Comparison.

With Skype, you can make unlimited calls to anywhere in the U.S. and Canada for just $2.95 a month. What's more, for $9.95 a month, you can make unlimited calls to 34 other countries, including most of Europe, Australia, New Zealand, Chile, China, Japan, and Korea: Skype, www.skype.com.

Vonage and Packet8 also offer similar service, but they charge as much as $25 a month for it: Vonage, www.vonage.com; Packet8, www.packet8.net.

BUNDLED SERVICE PLANS

by 2010 roughly one out of every three U.S. households will subscribe to at least a triple-play service and a growing number of us will have quadruple-play, which adds cell-phone service to the mix. Americans are expected to be spending nearly $120 billion a year on bundled services by then: "U.S. Bundled Services Revenue to Surge in 2010," Parks Associates, February 2, 2006, http://find articles.com/p/articles/mi_m0EIN/is_2006_Feb_2/ai_n26746675.

Some companies like WOW and Time Warner have been offering price guarantees to customers willing to sign long-term contracts (typically at least 24 months): Marla Matzer Rose, "'Bundled' services not always a deal," Columbus Dispatch, August 3, 2008, www.dispatch.com/live/content/business/stories/2008/08/03/buck_telcom.ART_ART_08-03-08_D1_D1ATE7C.html?sid=101.

AIR TRAVEL

nearly 212 million people traveled on domestic U.S. carriers in the summer of 2008: Dan Caterinicchia, "Summer 2008: Fewer Fliers, but Packed Planes," Associated Press, May 13, 2008, www.aviation. com/travel/080513-ap-summer-2008-traffic.html.

nearly 30% of domestic U.S. flights failed to arrive on time in 2008: "Nearly 1 in 3 domestic flights late in February," Associated Press, April 3, 2008, www.msnbc.msn.com/id/23938695/.

the cost of jet fuel soaring (it nearly doubled between 2007 and 2008): "Jet Fuel Costs Changing Way Airlines Work," CBS News, March 19, 2008, www.cbsnews.com/stories/2008/03/19/eveningnews/main3952729.shtml.

Airfares jumped by 20% in 2008 and are expected to climb another 40% by 2012: "Summer Airfares Up 20%," Farecast, May 28, 2008, http://farecast.live.com/blog/2008/05/summer-airfares-up-20/.

The new baggage fees alone cost travelers close to a billion dollars a year: Micheline Maynard, "The Catch Phrase Is 'à La Carte' as Airlines Push Additional Fees," New York Times, June 19, 2008, www.nytimes.com/2008/06/19/business/19air. html?scp=67&sq=airline+fees&st=nyt.

HOTELS

It earned an impressive pre-tax net of $28 billion on total revenues of $139 billion in 2007: "2007 At-a-Glance Statistical Figures," American Hotel & Lodging Association, www.ahla.com/content. aspx?id=23744.

more than a third of all U.S. hotel rooms sit empty every night: "Weekly U.S. Lodging Performance for the week ending 11 October 2008," Smith Travel Research, www.hotelnewsresource.com/article35163.html.

hotel surcharges picked nearly $1.8 billion out of travelers' pockets in 2008: Andrea Bennett, "How to Avoid Hidden Hotel Charges," Travel + Leisure, June 2008, www.travelandleisure.com/articles/how-to-avoid-hidden-hotel-charges.

some hotels will charge you upwards of $7 just for picking up the phone whether or not you complete a call! Dan Schlossberg, "Consumers Revolt Against Hotel Surcharges: Some Hotels Levy Phone Charges Even If You Don't Make Any Calls," ConsumerAffairs.com October 22, 2006,

www.consumeraffairs.com/news04/2006/10/travel_
hotel_phones.html.

TRAVEL PACKAGES

*Back in 1999, the Federal Trade Commission and
21 federal and state law enforcement authorities
sprung "Operation Trip Trap":* Federal Trade
Commission press release, "FTC Helps Consumers Avoid The 'Trip Trap'," August 3, 1999,
www.ftc.gov/opa/1999/08/triptrap.shtm.

*Of the 3,900 industries for which the U.S. Better
Business Bureaus fields complaints, the travel industry consistently ranks in or near the top 25:*
"BBB Warns Vacationers: Travel-Related Fraud
is on the Rise," Better Business Bureau, May 15,
2007, http://us.bbb.org/WWWRoot/SitePage.
aspx?site=113&id=1869d6a9-82aa-49a1-8419-
40a8251fa916&art=709.

ACKNOWLEDGMENTS

First and foremost, I want to thank you, the reader of this book and my past books. When I first began writing back in 1997, I never imagined the journey it would take me on—helping to answer your questions and address your need for more financial education. I thank you from the bottom of my heart for your trust in me, for your letters and emails of encouragement and thanks—and for the gift of purpose you have all given me.

All of my books—and so far there have been 10 in the FinishRich series, with more than 7 million copies in print—have been projects of love. My mission has always been to promote financial literacy—and in many ways, this book is the pinnacle of a decade of work. There is no way I could have done this alone, and I am grateful for the hundreds of people who over the years have helped me do what we do.

FIGHT FOR YOUR MONEY involved the biggest team of dedicated individuals we have ever assembled to put the best of what we know into a book that can help you. As a result, there are many, many people to thank.

I want to begin by once again acknowledging my grandmother, Rose Bach. She inspired me to write the first book in the FinishRich series, *Smart Women Finish Rich,* and now a decade later, as I put the final touches on this book, I just want to say to my grandma again how much I miss you and love you and know you are watching and cheering me on from heaven. You were the true inspiration behind FIGHT FOR YOUR MONEY—having grown up in the Depression era, you were the one who taught me that "cash is king, savings are golden, and there is no such thing as a fixed price."

To Allan Mayer, after a decade of working together, this was truly our most challenging book to date. Thank you for your trust and insight and commitment to this project. You are a consummate professional, and I am honored to have worked with you for so many years. Ours has been a fabulous partnership, one I truly feel grateful for.

To Liz Dougherty, this is now the eighth book since 2002 we have worked on together. I simply cannot thank you enough for your commitment on this one. You not only kept it all together and on time—but most important, you also made this book the best it could be with your guidance and love. You are simply the best, and I thank the angels every day for bringing you into my life.

To the team of researchers we leaned on for insight and expertise, thank you! In particular, I'd like to single out Dan Carney (for all things automotive, including car buying, car selling, car leasing, car renting, and car repairs), Diana Dawson (air travel, health insurance, home-based businesses, hotels, hospital bills, and travel packages), Phuong Cat Le (bank accounts, credit cards, credit scores, debit cards, identity theft, online shopping, pay-day loans, and refund anticipation loans), Marilyn Lewis (home buying and selling, home building and remodeling, and home mortgages), Kara McGuire (charitable giving, college saving, divorce, gift cards, gym membership, life insurance, rebates, and tax-preparation services and software), and Helen Huntley (401(k) plans, annuities, estate planning, IRAs, pension plans, and Social Security).

To my team at Doubleday Broadway Publishing Group—this book has had your excitement and attention since the first day we presented it. Thank you for always believing in me, my missions, and my dreams. I feel so lucky to have been with one publishing company my entire career—and I am so excited to cap off a decade of success with you by launching *Fight for Your Money*. To Kris Puopolo—your wonderful editing hands were all over this manuscript from the beginning to the end, and this book would not be what it is without your brilliant insight. David Drake, every day I wake up feeling lucky and blessed to have had you promoting my books and missions for a decade. You are simply as good as it gets—with your feedback, creative ideas, and passion, you make me better with every book. To Stephen Rubin and Michael Palgon, as always I thank you for your unwavering support and commitment. And to the entire Broadway Team—Catherine Pollock, Rebecca Holland, Stephanie Bowen, and Chris Fortunato—thank you so much for your hard work and dedication to this project. Thanks, too, to Jean Traina for the jacket design and Ralph Fowler for the interior design.

To my literary agents, Suzanne Gluck and Jay Mandel at the William Morris Agency, you have championed this project from the first day I envisioned it. Thank you for getting this book off the ground so successfully and for guiding its development.

To Stephen Breimer, my attorney and confidante, you are always there for me and I am always truly grateful. In many ways, you have been like a father to me throughout my writing career, and it has been a pleasure and a delight to work with you.

To Elisa Garafano, thank you for managing me on a daily basis in what has been a really exciting and busy year. I am truly grateful to you for always being so committed to me and all I do. Your insight on this book was invaluable, and your constant enthusiasm has kept me going on the tough days. Thank you!

To my son, Jack Bach, you light up my life and make every day special and meaningful. Telling you I love you doesn't do justice to how much I love you, but I want you to know that you are the most important thing that ever happened to me in my life and I simply love you more than the "the whole world." To Michelle, I will always love you and I'm beyond thankful for the son you brought into our life.

Finally, to my family: my mom Bobbi and my dad Marty—thank you both for your constant love and support. I wouldn't be here doing what I do without your love and encouragement. And to my sister Emily, I am so proud of you—thank you for everything you do as my little "sis."

—David Bach
New York, October 2008

INDEX

ABOUT THE AUTHOR

David Bach has helped millions of people around the world take action to live and finish rich. He is the author of eight consecutive national bestsellers, including two consecutive #1 *New York Times* bestsellers, *Start Late, Finish Rich* and *The Automatic Millionaire*, as well as the national and international bestsellers *Go Green, Live Rich, The Automatic Millionaire Homeowner, Smart Women Finish Rich, Smart Couples Finish Rich, The Finish Rich Workbook,* and *The Automatic Millionaire Workbook.* Bach carries the unique distinction  of having had four of his books appear simultaneously on the *Wall Street Journal, BusinessWeek,* and *USA Today* bestseller lists. In addition, four of Bach's books were named to *USA Today*'s Best Sellers of the Year list for 2004. In all, his FinishRich Books have been published in more than 15 languages, with more than seven million copies in print *worldwide.*

Bach's breakout book *The Automatic Millionaire* was the #1 Business book of 2004, according to *BusinessWeek.* It spent fourteen weeks on the *New York Times* bestseller list and was simultaneously number one on the bestseller lists of the *New York Times, BusinessWeek, USA Today,* and *The Wall Street Journal.* With over a million copies in print, this simple but powerful book has been translated into 12 languages and has inspired thousands around the world to save money automatically.

Bach is regularly featured in the media. He has appeared six times on *The Oprah Winfrey Show* to share his strategies for living and finishing rich, along with numerous appearances on CNN's *Larry King Live,* ABC's *Live with Regis and Kelly, The View,* NBC's *Today* and *Weekend Today* shows, CBS's *Early Show,* Fox News, and CNBC. He has been profiled in many major publications, including *The New York Times, BusinessWeek, USA Today, People, Reader's Digest, Time, Financial Times, Washington Post, Wall Street Journal, Los Angeles Times, San Francisco Chronicle, Working Woman, Glamour,* and *Family Circle.* He is also a featured contributor and columnist with *Redbook* magazine.

David Bach is the creator of the FinishRich® Seminar series, which highlights his quick and easy-to-follow financial strategies. In just the last few years, more than half a million people have learned how to take financial action to live a life in line with their values by attending his Smart Women Finish Rich®, Smart Couples Finish Rich®, and Find The Money Seminars, which have been taught in more than 2,000 cities throughout North America by thousands of financial advisors.

A renowned motivational and financial speaker, Bach regularly presents seminars for and delivers keynote addresses to the world's leading financial service firms, Fortune 500 companies, universities, and national conferences. He is the founder and Chairman of FinishRich Media, a company dedicated to revolutionizing the way people learn about money. Prior to founding FinishRich Media, he was a senior vice president of Morgan Stanley and a partner of The Bach Group, which during his tenure (1993 to 2001) managed more than half a billion dollars for individual investors.

As part of his mission, David Bach is involved with many worthwhile causes, including serving on the board for Habitat for Humanity New York and co-founding Makers of Memories, a charity organization dedicated to helping women and children who are victims of domestic violence.

David Bach lives in New York. Please visit his web site at www.finishrich. com.

NEW!

Now Is the Time To
FIGHT FOR YOUR MONEY AND FINISH RICH!

Start Today with a FREE...

FINISH**RICH**coaching
Consultation

Call now to schedule your FREE consultation and learn to fight for your money!

- Determine your debt-free date!
- Be prepared to handle any financial emergency!
- Know when you can retire comfortably!
- Learn how to reduce the amount you pay in taxes!
- Discover the best way to manage your income, assets and debts!

"I've designed this program to help you save a fortune...and Finish Rich!"

— *#1 New York Times Bestseller*
David Bach

Dramatically change your financial future with 1-on-1 financial coaching. Call or visit us online and register for a **free 30 minute consultation**.

VISIT
www.finishrich.com/ffymcoaching

 OR

CALL
1-866-528-6312

EXCLUSIVE BOOK SPECIAL

It's time to take the battle to the next level...

FIGHT FOR YOUR MONEY AND RETIRE A MILLIONAIRE

FIGHT FOR YOUR MONEY POWER PACK

➡ **7 DAY TEST DRIVE** ⬅

A 13 step battle plan for living a debt-free lifestyle!

- How to get a quick start on the road to financial freedom!

- A proven roadmap to a lifetime of wealth and financial freedom!

- The ultimate weapon to radically improve your financial future!

GO TO

www.finishrich.com/ffymdownload

TO GET STARTED!

INSTANT BESTSELLER

NEW YORK TIMES
WALL STREET
JOURNAL
USA TODAY

"*Go Green, Live Rich* gives great tips, useful to everyone, about how to save money and the planet at once."

—ROBERT F. KENNEDY JR.

Let David Bach show you a whole new way to prosper—by Going Green.

50 Simple Ways to Save the Earth (and Get Rich Trying)

Go Green, Live Rich

AUTHOR OF **5** *New York Times* BESTSELLERS

DAVID BACH with Hillary Rosner

Most people think that "going green" means sacrificing their bottom line for a healthier planet. But David Bach proves you can have it both ways—if you put the great ideas in his acclaimed book to work for you...

- Bring your lunch to work. Save $2,250 a year and together we'll reduce our landfills by 1.8 million pounds of trash.

- Pay your bills online. You'll save $400 a year and together we'll spare 18.5 million trees.

- Turn your savings into millions by catching the "green wave" of investing.

IN STORES NOW

The Bestselling Series by
David Bach

with over 5 MILLION books in print!

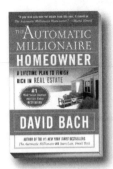

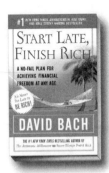

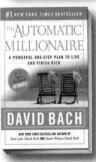

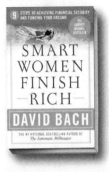

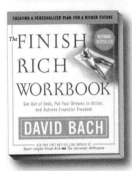

No matter where you start, David Bach can help you Finish Rich!

THE FINISHRICH™ BOOK SERIES

Broadway Books

www.FinishRich.com